MW00652315

# Black Man Green Beret

*Muhammad Bilal (Brother Shadow)*

TO BROTHER JAMES,
HOPE YOU ENJOY THIS STORY. IT
WILL BE A MOVIE ONE DAY.

FRATERNITE 2018
SHADOW

I

# Black Man Green Beret
## The Semi Autobiography of Brother Shadow
*Muhammad Bilal (Brother Shadow)*

**VR902 PUBLISHING**
Post Office Box 252
Fayetteville, NC 28302

Copyright ©2017 **VR902 PUBLISHING**
*Library of Congress Copyright*

All rights reserved.
Printed in the United States of America by VR902 Publishing.
No part of this book may be reproduced, stored in a retrieval system, or transmitted, in any form or by any means, electronic, mechanical, photocopying, recording or otherwise.

Literary Advisor: *Angel Love*
Editor: *Adrienne Washington*
Editor: *Patricia Blue-Bilal*
Cover photo: *Jerry Towns*
Biography photo: *Sam Kilpatrick*
Photo editing: *proimageediting.com*

# Contents

# Dedication

*This book is dedicated to both my maternal and paternal grandmothers:*
**Velma Cooper-Brevard (Henderson)** *and* **Richardean Jamison-Mitchell (Moody).** *They are my direct ancestors who showed me the most love during their short period of time on this earth. They are the standard that many people judge all the love they receive throughout their lifetimes on – the love of a grandmother and her grandchild.*

✳ ✳ ✳

*To everyone who supported* **Humanitarian Operation Protection Elephants (H.O.P.E.)** *the nonprofit 501c3 on my behalf, with a financial donation whether small or large. Thank you all for believing that we as humans should try to do something to stop the endangered African Elephants from being hunted and slaughtered into extinction.*
*Thank You for supporting my efforts to travel back to the African continent and do what I can to help. I just can't say thank you enough. If you have NOT had the opportunity to donate please follow the following link, via your web browser:*
*https://www.generosity.com/animal-pet-fundraising/support-hope-anti-poaching--4/x/10443776.*

*The link is for the 2017 campaign and once that campaign is complete, look for Brother Shadow on other H.O.P.E. campaigns on generosity.com or visit www.saveivory.org for more ways to support Muhammad Bilal (Brother Shadow) in the good fight to help preserve African wildlife. Contact* **Steve Brignoli,** CEO *of* **Beyond SOF** *and* Chairman *of* **Humanitarian Operations Protecting Elephants (H.O.P.E.)** *if you have any questions about this awesome non-profit organization.*

**From the first 10,000 copies of this book Black Man Green Beret (BMGB), I hereby pledge to donate one dollar ($1) from the proceeds of the profit of each copy of this book (sold at retail price) towards the 2017 H.O.P.E. campaign.** *For a maximum grand total of ten thousand dollars ($10,000) towards saving African Elephants and other wildlife from extinction by poachers and illegal hunters.*

*Thank you for your HOPE contributions:* **Angel Love, Elijah Shaw, Patricia Bilal, Timothy Garnes, Paul Rossi, Maliik Jefferson, Edward Epps, Troy Hilderbrand, Ausean Fields, Gene Harrison, Corey Sweetenburg, Jerry Towns, Adrian Horton, Steven Turner, Sean McCaffrey, Zaira Pirzada, Chad Light, Barbara Tracy-Santos, Laura Downs, Rahsaan Cooper, Patrick Jackson, Alquan McCormick, Dana Dennis, Jennifer Lewis, Everett Long, Nicholas Niday, Edward Cooper, Tamyra Butler, Antonio Ervin, Gilda Harris, Padmapani Muzquiz, Keith Allen, Amanda Fry, Matthew Drewe, Sidney Johnson, Walter Scott, Angela Harry, Curtis Gissendaner** *and to those donors who gave anonymously or whose financial contributions could not be made public.*

*Thank you all, I will not let you down.*

# Dear Reader

This book is my testimony about some of my life and times on this planet. At over 50 years of age, I am already older than most of my grandparents ever lived to see.

*Born in the ghettos of the South Bronx and raised on the mean streets of Harlem in New York City. There is no way I could completely describe the journey I've taken, all the things I've seen, or this life I've lived. At first, I thought that I would have to write a comic book to tell my life story, otherwise no one would believe me. As I re-tell my own story, it's hard for me to even believe parts of it myself.*

*From pulling relatives out of the Crack House to walking inside the White House. Crawled around in the mud of South Korea as an Infantryman at Camp Greaves, up on the DMZ and I've crawled down through the access tunnel of the Great Pyramid of King (Pharaoh) Khufu in the city of Cairo, Egypt in Africa.*

*I've stood still as bullets from enemy AK-47's flew past my face during a firefight in the Sadr City section of Baghdad, Iraq in support of Operation IRAQI FREEDOM 2, and I've stood on the exact same spot in Jerusalem, Israel on Mount Olives that many Christians believe Joshua Ben Yosef (Jesus Christ) ascended into heaven from.*

*With millions of people all crowded together down on 42nd Street in Time Square watching the New Year's Eve ball drop, and I've stood alone looking at the actual Burning Bush at Saint Catherine's Monastery at the base of Moses Mountain in the Sinai Desert.*

*I've donned a "Red Beret" as a Tenderfoot Scout in the Boy Scouts of America, Troop 007 in (the former) Muhammad's Temple of Islam in Harlem, New York and I've donned a "Green Beret" after graduating the U.S. Army's Special Forces Qualification Course at Camp Mackall/Fort Bragg, North Carolina.*

If you have the time, I have a story to tell.
*Wanna hear it?*
Well here it go.

In Accordance With (IAW) various military publications Special Operations Forces (SOF) are those specifically organized, disciplined, trained, and equipped to conduct and support special operations. SOF, in its simplest term of explanation means, those military forces that are "special" from the main body, main group or the bulk of military forces.

Every branch of the military has their own version of SOF to include the U.S. Army, from which I am retired.

All U.S. Army SOF personnel are under the operational command structure of the U.S. Army Special Operations Command. This includes Military Information Support Groups (formerly called Psychological Operations Groups or PSYOP's), Civil Affairs Units, the U.S. Army Special Operations Sustainment Brigade, the Special Operations Aviation Command, the U.S. Army JFK Special Warfare Center and School, the U.S. Army Ranger Regiment (with its subordinate Ranger Battalions) and the Special Forces Regiment (with its subordinate Special Forces Groups).

Although SOF is the broader term for all types of Special "Operations" Forces units, the only SF or "Special Forces" unit, especially within the U.S. Army is the 1st Special Forces Regiment. *I'm not talking about those units above that, that officially don't exist.*
**The Special Forces "qualified" members of each of the numerical Special Forces Groups within the SF Regiment are easily identified in certain environments by their distinctive unit headgear of a "Green Beret."**

It is common to consider or call members who graduate the required training to earn their distinctive headgear by that name, you know like the way many people make the following claim: *"My Uncle was a, Green Beret - in Vietnam."*

Well, mine was.

However, the U.S. Army has made changes to ensure that not all members who are "assigned" to these units wear the distinctive headgear. Only those members who have completed at least these levels of training earn that right.

1.  The first is the Special Forces Assessment & Selection (SFAS) course, which is basically the Special Forces try-outs to see if you really want to go through the actual SF training and to see if you're the type of soldiers that is compatible for the Special Forces way of life (living the dream). Successful completion of SFAS does not guarantee you will be selected for SF training either, and it sure doesn't make you a "Green Beret".

    SFAS was created in the late 1980's early 1990's so earlier generations of SF qualified soldiers may have even left service before this "try-out" course was created.

2.  The second is the actual Special Forces Qualification Course (SFQC) commonly referred to as the "Q-course". It is a collection of other schools (called phases), that culminate in a final training exercise. Many men have died in Special Forces training attempting to complete the courses and become Special Forces (SF) qualified, and earn the right to wear the coveted "Green Beret".

3.  Lastly is the language course. Every single U.S. Special Forces soldier is bi-lingual in at least one other language besides English, period. We must all pass a Foreign Language Proficiency Exam to ascertain our level of proficiency in that foreign language. Your Foreign Language Proficiency Bonus (FLPB) or "Flip-Pay" is determined by what level you score on your foreign language exam.

There is a much more to the SF way of life (the quiet professionals) than the three steps I'm describing; [1] SFAS, [2] SFQC & [3] Foreign Language Training.

However, I am explaining especially in this book the MINIMUM training and schooling required for anyone to identify if someone else was really SF "qualified" or not.

First question to combat a suspected poser individual is, *"What foreign languages do you speak?"*? That normally stops the embellishment and/or the bullshit right there, and there is no need to go any further.

> *Each chapter of this book is constructed in such a manner where first I will attempt to illustrate how my training in Special Forces has helped prepare me for an event later in life. Or how my life prepared me for the SF training. That initial portion of each chapter will be written in bold and italicized print.*

Secondly, I will try to show how that Special Forces training or way of life differs from the regular "big" U.S. Army. I have certain friends and even family members who only know the version of what Hollywood has told them about the U.S. Army in general, and the SF community specifically. They don't really know the difference between a Corporal and a Colonel, or an M-4 or a P-38, or the CID from a CIB. I will attempt to explain and clarify these terms in their simplest version. Or as they say, I will put it down where the goats can get it.

Finally, each chapter will have a significant event or life lesson *(or more)* that I feel will be significant to the overall story.

Although this book is not written in chronological order, I highly encourage you to read each chapter in sequential order, a particular term or phrase may be crucial to the chapter you are reading or the overall effect of the book.

Society has become so impatient, that even Hollywood had to re-do the way they make movies now. The hero now dies in the beginning of the film, and as he/she is having a flashback the movie tells their story.

Television shows are no longer watched in weekly sequential order, people wait until the entire season is over and binge watch them all together. *Then they wonder why the good show was cancelled?* **Because, you didn't watch the show when it was on, so the network didn't get the credit for the ratings, that's why!**

1.  I hope my ancestors are pleased with the telling of our story. All of the people in my historical lineage who made me who I am today., I hope you are all looking down (or up) at me and are happy with who you produced.

2.  I hope and pray that this book serves as some type of leadership manual. Whereas the military defines leadership as providing **purpose**, **direction** and **motivation**, I hope and pray that this book enhances the life of the reader in some way and provides one of those three elements of leadership.

3.  I hope, pray and dream of helping prevent the youth of today from making the same or similar mistakes that I have made in the past. Not trying to tell anyone how to live their life, but to highlight the fact that some mistakes that we made have much more dangerous consequences now than when we made them.

# All praises and glory belong to the man upstairs only the mistakes have been mine.

# 1

# FOR WHAT OF A NAME

*There are 335,597,550 people living in the United States of America.*

*There are a total of 2,247,995 personnel in the U.S. military.*

*335 million people, protected by 2 million service members. For every 335 people, only 2 of them are serving in any branch of the U.S. military, let that sink in. 2 out of every 335.*

*Currently the United States Congress limits the total number of service members in all branches of the military to around two million. Of the 2,247,995 service members in the U.S. military, in all of the combined branches, approximately one million service members are in the various components of the U.S. Army (exactly 1,081,291).*

*Regardless of the size of the entire U.S. Army (or the Big Army), all the U.S. Army's Special Operations Forces (SOF) are just a small part of it, and the*

*U.S. Army Special Forces (Airborne) is a just a small part of the U.S. Army's SOF component.*

*Of the approximately one million soldiers in the United States Army:*
- *541,291 of them are on active duty*
    *(438,670 enlisted/98,126 officers)*
- *342,000 soldiers are in the Army National Guard*
- *198,000 soldiers are in the Army Reserves*

*So, if the total number of officers & enlisted personnel on active duty in the U.S. Army is about 540,000 soldiers; then about 10% of that number or about 54,000 soldiers are members of the U.S. Army's SOF units, and an even smaller number of them are in the "Special Forces Groups".*

*Many soldiers (like me) operated in the regular Big Army; active, guard or reserve component before we attended SOF training.*

*This is a small example of the SOF training mindset. I will NOT explain anything that is not already open source, or common knowledge through a quick on-line search of various topics.*

*I wouldn't want to dilute the training experience of any future warriors about to undergo the rigors of SOF training in general, and SF training specifically. I want them to get it the way I got it; the hard way.*

*Secondly, since this book is now a part of that open source media, I am not giving any information to our country's adversaries or enemies, who may wish to put American lives in danger. I still have several close friends who are serving on active duty or are in harm's way, and I will not compromise their safety for monetary profit in this book.*

*Lastly, and most importantly, many years ago I signed a Nondisclosure Agreement (NDA) like most service members, with the U.S. Army when I enlisted. Although I am now retired from active duty, I am still legally obligated to honor that commitment, just as I have honored my oath of enlistment when I swore to defend the constitution, and protect this country from all enemies, foreign and domestic.*

*If you desire to attend, you will go to Special Forces Assessment & Selection (SFAS) on a Temporary Duty (TDY) basis, and then return to your unit (or proceed to another unit) upon completion.*

*If you both successfully complete SFAS commonly referred to as "Sore Feet And Shoulders" AND you are selected, you will return back to your parent unit, with an invitation to return back for more fun. You will "then" begin to START your Special Forces training in the Special Forces Qualification Course (SFQC) commonly referred to as the Q-course.*

*If you do NOT complete SFAS (or if you "do" complete it, but do NOT get selected in the end) you will return to your parent unit and NOT be invited to return for SFQC and you will continue with your regular military career, providing you did not sustain a career ending medical injury.*

*Students have died just attempting to complete SFAS. During the summer of 1990, students died during training because the heat-index was so hot. Since SFAS training classes were suspended during those summer months, I attended in the first Fall class. It was about 3 times its normal size – and the attrition rate was astronomical starting with the first day!*

*When you started training you did not have your rank or name sewn on your uniform like normal U.S. Army soldiers. You were issued a roster number and that number was sewn on to your pant leg, the front of your uniform top and on your headgear.*

*You are being assessed and evaluated for selection at ALL TIMES. Instructors can see you from a distance and write whatever their assessments of you was at any time and you will never know. You can be eating chow in the D-FAC (mess hall), using the latrine, sleeping, running, walking, reading, talking. It doesn't matter what you do, you are being assessed for selection at all times, and the only way you're addressed is as candidate and roster number you've been assigned.*

*That's it.*

*As important as it is to have military customs and courtesies in the Big "regular" Army, especially the way your rank and name permeates EVERYTHING in the Big Army. Your name (and your rank) mean almost NOTHING during Special Forces training. In SFAS, you are all students (candidates) and are all equal. The instructors are assessing you and they are not intimidated by your rank or the name you may have made for yourself back in the Big Army.*

*That really stuck with me as almost everyone has a name, or should I say a "nick-name" they were called as a child but as they grow and evolve, they no longer wish to be identified by that moniker.*

✳✳✳

The U.S. Army places all persons in categories, and there are specific rules and norms for addressing each and every person depending upon what category they are in. All civilian employees of the U.S. Army and any civilian dealing with members of the U.S. Army are addressed by the title "Sir" or "Ma'am" – no exceptions.

That is the default title to address them by, showing respect to the military chain of command that all soldiers understand from day one: that civilians run the military, not soldiers.

The Commander-in-Chief of the military is the President of the United States, a civilian. The next in order of succession of command is the Secretary of Defense, another civilian, responsible for all branches of the U.S. Military. Next is the Secretary of the Army, also a civilian. Then we finally get down to the Chief of Staff of the Army (who is the highest ranking General Officer).

All civilians, be they members of Congress, addressed as Honorable Mr. John Doe, Congressional Representative from the 999th District or the average Taxi Cab Driver, Mr. James Doe, they are all addressed to as Sir or Ma'am, without question.

All U.S. Army soldiers are broken down into two categories: officers and enlisted. Then there are sub-categories within each. All commissioned officers are called Sir or Ma'am and all enlisted soldiers are called private or sergeant, there are a few exceptions to this rule.

Technically, there are three types of officers in the U.S. Army; <u>commissioned</u> officers, <u>warrant</u> officers and <u>noncommissioned</u> officers (NCO). However, the word "*officer*" almost exclusively implies and is used for the category of commissioned officers.

Of the three categories of soldiers, whether active duty, national guard, reserve or retired service members. The first is commissioned officers, they are simply called officers. There are three sub-groups of officers within that category known as; company grade officers, field grade officers and general officers.

Company grade officers are found at the company level and normally comprise the ranks of Second Lieutenant (O-1), First Lieutenant (O-2) and Captain (O-3).

Field grade officers, they normally command and staff units of battalion or brigade size, are the ranks of Major (O-4), Lieutenant Colonel (O-5) and Colonel (O-6).

General Officers are; Brigadier General (O-7), Major General (O-8), Lieutenant General (O-9) and General (O-10).

The term "Be My Little General" (B.M.L.G.) is normally taught to most U.S. Army Privates so they can learn the order of succession for the ranks of General Officers. B.M.L.G. as in; "B" for Brigadier General – one star, "M" for Major General – two stars, "L" for Lieutenant General – three stars, and "G" for a full General – four stars.

Almost all company and field grade officers are referred to as "Sir" and all general officers are normally referred to as "General" and the name of the officer is rarely used by enlisted personnel when addressing them. General officers are almost always referred to as a superior class of commissioned officers, distinct, separate and above all other commissioned officers.

Warrant Officers in the U.S. Army are considered and classified as officers, and are above all enlisted personnel in the pay grade and rank structure. All the Warrant Officers from Warrant Officer One (WO1) through Chief Warrant Officer Five (CW5) are addressed to as Mister or Mrs./Ms. Depending upon gender. However, it is a very common practice, although not encouraged by Army regulations, to address all Warrant Officers above the grade of WO1 as Chief (as in "Chief" Warrant Officer).

All Warrant Officers in the pay grades of W-1 through W-5 are rendered all the rights and privileges of commissioned officers.

For example, there is a Dining Facility (D-FAC) historically referred to as a Mess Hall and then there is a separate Officers' Mess facility. Warrant Officers can eat in the officers' mess, NCO's cannot. Warrant Officers can join the Officers Club, NCO's cannot.

In fact, there is a separate club at most military installations for enlisted personnel, specifically called the enlisted club. Some bases used to have two enlisted clubs, one for the NCO's and another one for the lower enlisted soldiers (so they do not fraternize)

*Every lower enlisted club I've ever visited was referred to as the "stab & jab club" or some other derogatory name because of the controlled inevitable violence (fighting/stabbing) that occurs there.*

Warrant Officers are also billeted in the officers' quarters – NCO's are not.

| Rank | Pay Grade | Title | Sub-Group | Informal |
|------|-----------|-------|-----------|----------|
| **OFFICERS** | | | | |
| **Commissioned Officers** | | | | |
| GEN | O-10 | General | *General* | *General* |
| LG | O-9 | Lieutenant General | *Officers* | *General* |
| MG | O-8 | Major General | | *General* |
| BG | O-7 | Brigadier General | | *General* |
| COL | O-6 | Colonel | *Field Grade* | *Colonel* |
| LTC | O-5 | Lieutenant Colonel | *Officers* | *Colonel* |
| MAJ | O-4 | Major | | *Major* |
| CPT | O-3 | Captain | *Company Grade* | *Captain* |
| 1LT | O-2 | First Lieutenant | *Officers* | *Lieutenant* |
| 2LT | O-1 | Second Lieutenant | | *Lieutenant* |
| **Warrant Officers** | | | | |
| CW5 | W-5 | Chief Warrant Officer 5 | *Chief Warrant* | *Mister (Mrs./Miss/Ms.)* |
| CW4 | W-4 | Chief Warrant Officer 4 | *Officers* | *Mister (Mrs./Miss/Ms.)* |
| CW3 | W-3 | Chief Warrant Officer 3 | | *Mister (Mrs./Miss/Ms.)* |
| CW2 | W-2 | Chief Warrant Officer 2 | | *Mister (Mrs./Miss/Ms.)* |
| WO1 | W-1 | Warrant Officer | *Warrant Officers* | *Mister (Mrs./Miss/Ms.)* |
| **ENLISTED** | | | | |
| **Noncommissioned Officers (NCO's)** | | | | |
| **Senior Enlisted Soldiers** | | | | |
| SMA | E-9 | Sergeant Major of the Army | *Senior NCO's* | *Sergeant Major of the Army* |
| CSM | | Command Sergeant Major | | *Command Sergeant Major* |
| SGM | | Sergeant Major | | *Sergeant Major* |
| 1SG | E-8 | First Sergeant | | *First Sergeant* |
| MSG | | Master Sergeant | | *Master Sergeant* |
| SFC | E-7 | Sergeant First Class | | *Sergeant* |
| SSG | E-6 | Staff Sergeant | *Junior NCO's* | *Sergeant* |
| SGT | E-5 | Sergeant | | *Sergeant* |
| CPL | E-4 | Corporal | | *Corporal* |
| **Junior Enlisted Soldiers** | | | | |
| SPC | E-4 | Specialist | *Soldiers* | *Specialist* |
| PFC | E-3 | Private First Class | | *Private* |
| PVT | E-2 | Private | | *Private* |
| PVT | E-1 | Private / Recruit | | *Private* |

Noncommissioned Officers (NCO) in the U.S. Army, are enlisted soldiers in the ranks & pay grades of E-5 through E-9.

A soldier in the pay grade of E-4 could have the rank of a Corporal, or the rank of a Specialist. If a soldier in the pay grade of E-4 has achieved rank of Corporal, they are considered a Junior NCO. However, if they are in the pay grade of E-4 but have the rank of Specialist, they are lower enlisted soldiers and are not considered Junior NCO's.

There are several soldiers in the rank and pay grade of Specialist/E-4 who are very professional, motivated and well disciplined.

However, it is common for a Sergeant of any rank to order a group of lower enlisted soldiers to perform a task by saying, *"You Privates go do this or that."* That leaves the Specialist/E-4 in a precarious situation, whereas he or she is not a Private but also, not a Sergeant.

There are more soldiers in with the rank of Specialist (E-4) in the U.S. Army than any other rank and pay grade.

So, it is common knowledge that if you want something done, delegate the task to the Specialist's "infamously known as the E-4 Mafia."

Conversely, if they do NOT want to do something their rank insignia of an eagle on a shield can be referred to as a "sham shield" for their use (abuse) of the system against itself for shamming or malingering. Example: A Specialist saying, *"Sergeant I would love to join you and the rest of the squad for that 10-mile road march with 65-pound ruck sack tomorrow morning, however I have a dental appointment at that time. If you make me march and I don't make it back to my dental appointment, I'll be considered category-4 "non-deployable" and the Company First Sergeant already said we all have to be prepared for this next deployment".* So, the Sergeant and the Privates go on a long hard road march in the morning, while the Specialist plays video games in his barracks room, until he goes to the military dental clinic.

Since 1959 the U.S. Army has had soldiers in the ranks & pay grade of Specialist who "traditionally" did not lead soldiers directly and may have had extremely technical jobs and skill sets.

> Specialist Nine (SP9/E-9)
> Specialist Eight (SP8/E-8)
> Specialist Seven (SP7/E-7)
> Specialist Six (SP6/E-6)
> Specialist Five (SP5/E-5)
> Specialist Four (SP4/E-4)

Specialist Eight (E-8) & Specialist Nine (E-9) ranks were abolished in 1968 when the U.S. Army added the rank of Command Sergeant Major, long before I ever enlisted.

Specialist Seven (E-7) was discontinued in 1978 so other than historically or in the movies, I have never seen a person wearing that rank.

However, I was on active duty in 1984, and had been for a few years already, when the U.S. Army had a mass formation of each unit and every Specialist Six and Five was laterally-promoted to the corresponding NCO rank.

> Specialist's Six (SP6/E-6) became Staff Sergeant's (SSG/E-6)
> Specialist's Five (SP5/E-5) became Sergeant's (SGT/E-5)

**The only Specialist rank which still exist in the U.S. Army today is that of Specialist Four (SPC/E-4).** It used to have the three-character abbreviation of SP4 and was changed to SPC.

Because of the visual similarity between the characters "P" and "F" (SPC/E-4 and SFC/E-7) many people still refer to the Specialist as Specialist Four, as in Spec-Four Bilal (pronounced Speck). As I stated previously, the Specialist rank and pay grade of E-4 is the most common rank in the U.S. Army. As of July 2016, out of the 473,844 soldiers in the U.S. Army, 115,033 of them were Specialist (E-4).

Soldiers in the pay grade of E-1 through E-3 are called Privates, regardless of rank.

A Private (E-1) could be the equivalent of a basic recruit and there is no insignia of rank.

A Private (E-2) is called the same as a Private (E-1), but that rank of an E-2 is represented by one chevron which soldiers informally refer to as mosquito wings. *Many people say the Vietnam Veterans Memorial Wall in Washington, DC is shaped like this rank, if you view it from above. I was too young to serve in Vietnam, so you'll have to find one of those veterans to ask them their opinion. If you do, please thank them for their service to our country, since we as a nation did NOT give them the proper respect they deserved upon their return from that conflict back then.*

A Private First Class (E-3) is sometimes called a PFC and the ranks insignia of one chevron has one rocker stripe attached underneath.

Regardless of rank or pay grade, all Privates in the U.S. Army are referred to as simply "Privates". Example; *Private (no name) go over there and do such and such, or Private Bilal who told you to do that? Private Bilal I am assigning you to an area beautification detail, so go outside and police up the liter from the area – conduct a good police-call and make the place look real nice. If it doesn't grow, pick it up – then put it in the trash can. Gum wrappers, cigarette butts, whatever is on the ground around this building go pick it up Private and properly dispose of it.*

So, you see how important your name and rank are in the big U.S. Army, verses how much is does NOT mean during a person's Special Forces training?

Now let me tell you a little about my civilian or government name, nicknames and the creation of my call-sign, Shadow.

All of my grandparents both maternal and paternal are ascended with the ancestors now. None of my biological grandparents lived to become over 65 years of age. All of them died from preventable diseases attributed to people in poor financial situations because of generational poverty, such as: heart-attack, hypertension & high blood pressure – exacerbated by alcoholism, or were murdered.

| Relationship (age at death) | Birth & Ascension Dates |
|---|---|
| Maternal Grandfather (**32**) | *Mom's Father (August 1927 – July 1958)* |
| Maternal Grandmother (**42**) | *Mom's Mother (June 1931 – October 1973)* |
| *Maternal Granddad (70)* | *Mom's Dad (October 1919 – July 1989)* |
| Paternal Grandfather (**64**) | *Dad's Father (March 1925 – July 1989)* |
| Paternal Grandmother (**59**) | *Dad's Mother (June 1931 – July 1990)* |
| *Paternal Granddad (70)* | *Dad's Dad (June 1916 – August 1993)* |

My maternal grandmother **Richardeen Moody** (1931-1973) was born in Bamberg, South Carolina. She married my grandfather **Willie Jamison** (1927-1958) who was from Denmark, South Carolina.

Going a little further back in my maternal grandmothers' ancestral lineage, I can trace both sides of her family. Her maternal grandmother (my great-great-grandmother) was named **Louise** and she married an Irishman named **Eddie Dowling** who was born in 1878. They had a total of seven children and one of them, was a girl named **Almeda (Meta) Dowling** who was born in 1902 (my great-grandmother).

The oldest relative I physically have a photo of is **Simon Moody**, who was born in 1860 in South Carolina (my great-great-grandfather). He married a woman named **Momma Hightower** who was of Native American ancestry.

Between my great-great-grandfather Simon Moody and his first and second wives, he had a total of thirteen children; [1] **William**, [2] **Sylvia**, [3] **John**, [4] **Daniel**, [5] **James H**, [6] **Anna**, [7] **Lexie**, [8] **Charlie L.**, [9] **Jacob**, [10] **Mary**, [11] **Motley**, [12] **Robert** & [13] **Clara Ann**.

Their eighth child was a son named Charlie L. Moody, born in 1895 (my great-grandfather) in Bamberg, South Carolina.

Together both of my great-grandparents Almeda Dowling and Charlie Moody had fifteen children. **One of them was my grandmother Richardeen Moody**.

So, my grandmother Richardeen had fourteen siblings (seven brothers and seven sisters) whom all originate out of Bamberg, South Carolina. Whether they were all born there I cannot say.

All of their children are my mother's first cousins.

So, by default they are also, my cousins. Although using the proper terminology they are all considered my "First Cousins Once Removed". However, I am willing to bet that nine out of ten people couldn't properly identify the once, twice or thrice removed titles.

So, the way I grew up was, if ANY relative was older than you; if they were female they were called your Aunt, and if they were male they were called your Uncle, period.

Now when you get down to my actual maternal grandmother Richardeen Moody's descendants, she had a total of nine children (five boys and four girls), of which my mother is the oldest.

My mother (grandma Richardeen's first and oldest child) married my dad Eddie Akbar and together they had three children ([1] **me**, [2] my sister **Angel** and [3] my brother **Rahsaan**). In later years my mother became the matron of our families' oral history and custodian of almost all documents and photos.

Then in succession is my Uncle **Earl** (grandma Richardeen's second child), whom I use to just call Uncle Earl. He had 4 children with his wife, my Aunt **Needa** whom is now deceased. My sister and I use to play with our younger cousins [1] **Sandra**, [2] **Earl**, [3] **Tutti** & [4] **Amanda** all the time when they lived in the South Bronx on Prospect Avenue. I know my Uncle Earl was a Vietnam Veteran and a former Drill Sergeant in the United States Army. I tried to locate him using the U.S. Veterans Administration and through my contacts as a licensed Private Investigator. However, I have been informed that his information and whereabouts are only available to his immediate next-of-kin. So, I passed what information I had gathered about him on to my cousin Sandra some years ago.

Then there is my Uncle **Stanley** (grandma Richardeen's third child), who use to remined me of the actor Ron O'Neal's character "Youngblood Priest" in the movie Super Fly (1972). Besides my father, I thought my Uncle Stanley was the toughest man alive. He had 6 children that I know of, named; [1] **Ebony**,

[2] **Rahsaan**, [3] **Richardeen**, [4] **Stanley Jr.**, [5] **Shamika** and *another* [6] whose name and their whereabouts are unknown to me. I remember they used to live on Bronx Park South right across the street from the Bronx Zoo, near where I grew up at, but I believe they moved to the Hamilton Heights area of Harlem some years ago.

Then my Uncle **Willie James Jr.** (grandma Richardeen's fourth child), whom we all use to call Uncle Junior. Man was he smart! Even as a child I recall him being the smartest person that I ever knew. He could read music and play several different musical instruments. He had traced our family ancestry through diligent paperwork and research (years before the age of computers) all the way back to the Indigenous American tribes on one side of our family (maternal grandmothers), and all the way back to the West Coast of Africa on the other side of our family (maternal grandfathers). He was talking Cameroon, Nigeria, Benin, Togo, and Ghana almost 40 years before I would confirm his research through DNA analysis. I remember he had a wife named **Carolyn** and they had a daughter named [1] **Naomi**. If she is still alive, my cousin Naomi would be about 40 years old now. Well after my maternal grandmother was murdered in the South Bronx, over $5 dollars' worth of Food Stamps – my family was never the same after that. My Uncle Junior took it the hardest, and for years he stopped talking, period. I heard that my Aunt Carolyn left the United States, and took their daughter back to the South American country of Brazil. I would sometimes see my Uncle Junior wandering the streets of New York City once or twice a year. The last time I believe I saw him, he was running for a west-bound MTA bus on 125th Street, in Harlem. He had a distinct walk and I could pick him out of a dimly lit crowd. I believe I may have even scared him when I approached, and his whereabout to me are again, unknown.

Then there is my Uncle **Bruce** (grandma Richardeen's fifth child), whom I never knew growing up. For whatever reason, he was raised with foster parents out on the West Coast in California. Almost 50 years later, I heard from my mother that he resurfaced and was looking to reconnect with his biological family. He supposedly has *two children* [1 & 2], and I understand that my Uncle Bruce now resides on the East Coast, and his grown children live out west.

Then there was my Uncle **Richard** (grandma Richardeen's sixth child and youngest son), whom everybody used to call Uncle Rickey – Pretty Rickey is what they used to call him! Although he is also now deceased, Uncle Rickey was my favorite Uncle. Maybe because he was so young, and closer in age to me than the others that I could look up to him as the "big brother" that I never had. I do remember as a child in New York City I ran away from home (more than once), because I wanted to find the real "Sesame Street" and I went to my Uncle Ricky's house, when I couldn't find it. Another time I ran away from home, and the police found this little lost kid named "Timmy" in the Bronx. I was too scared to have them take me back home to my mom & dad, so you guessed it – I had them take me to my Uncle Ricky's house. I know from oral history that I have about 6 first cousins connected to me through my Uncle Ricky, through **Gail**, my Aunt **Lovey** or my Aunt **Cynthia**, (*or through their re-marriages after his passing*). They are [1] **Lamont**, [2] **Tangie**, [3] **Cahsaan**, [4] **Monique**, [5] **Nicky** & [6] **Assata**. My Uncle Rickey passed away in Yonkers, NY in 1986. His favorite NFL football team was the NY Jets and because of him I was a fan of the team since I was a little kid in 1969 when he gave me a NY Jets shirt (*in 1992 I became a NFL Carolina Panthers fan, but that's another chapter*).

Then there was my Aunt **Debbie** (grandma Richardeen's seventh child), who was more like a big sister to me. She lived upstate New York in a town called Liberty, NY and had two children; my cousins [1] **Ausean** & [2] **Travis**. For several years Ausean actual was raised as my other younger brother. He and my brother Rahsaan have a history they cemented when I departed for the military when they were both 8 & 9 years old. My Aunt Debbie passed away in New York in 1996.

Then there is my Aunt **Rosalyn** (grandma Richardeen's eighth and last child), who everyone calls Aunt Roddy. She has my grandmothers spirit and is one of the funniest people you will ever meet. The three of them, Uncle Ricky, Aunt Debbie and Aunt Roddy use to spend the most time with me as a child growing up. As I look at old family photos, maybe it was because they were my mother's youngest brother and sisters, so they were closer in age to me. More like big brother and sisters, than Uncle and Aunts'. Anyway, Aunt Rody lived upstate New York in a town called Monticello, NY and has four children; [1] **Taisha**, [2] **Andrew**, [3] **Jermaine** and [4] **Emma**.

When I would leave New York City during my summers as a young teenager, I would go up to the Ten Mile River Boy Scout Camps in Narrowsburg, NY which is about 30 minutes away from Liberty and Monticello, NY. I remember visiting them both (Aunt Debbie & Aunt Rody) on my way up to summer

14

camp, and again at the end of the summer before the three-hour bus ride back down to New York City.

*My grandmother had another daughter (grandma Richardeen's ninth child) who did not survive childbirth. So, I do not know the sequential order of her birth.*

When my mother and father had my younger brother Rahsaan in 1974, my father was heavy into jazz music – and he still is. At that time, one of his favorite jazz artist was Rahsaan Roland Kirk who was so good, he could play several different instruments "simultaneously". By my mother being the oldest sibling and naming my younger brother Rahsaan, she influenced a slew of my Aunts & Uncles to name their sons with the etymology of Rah-Saan. So, I have cousins named Ahsaan (spelled Ausean), another named Cushaan (Cusean), and two others named Rahsaan.

> **I consider all of my Aunts and Uncles children "my Cousins".**
>
> **I do NOT, and will NOT differentiate, distinguish nor favor between the many branches of my family tree.**
>
> **So, whether by marriage, biological, adopted, foster, in-law or whatever means they are related to me, my maternal grandmother Richardeen had 9 children (my mother and her siblings) and she has 26 grandchildren (of which I am the oldest) that I know of.**

Numerically speaking, if I have 25 first cousins who are all in their 30's, 40's and 50's, it would be safe to guess that my grandmother has well over 100 descendants, and I'm not even counting "their" children. I know several of my cousins (and my younger brother) are grandparents already, and one of my cousins is a "great-grandparent".

However, I bet if I were to hit the billion dollar *"Lottery Jackpot"* I would have no problem locating them all – because many of them would find me, talmbout *"Hey Cuz"*!?!

My grandmothers first husband, my maternal grandfather was a military veteran. He was in the U.S. Army during WWII and served in the European Theatre when the US military was still segregated by race, just like the rest of society. I can only imagine the horrors & discrimination he faced back then, in addition to watching captured enemy "white" officers being offered customs and courtesies that he was denied because he was a black-man in the segregated south.

Example: *Captured enemy POW's who were officers could eat in certain mess-halls while my grandfather (and other black troops) could not, unless they were entering through the back door to clean or cook or some other menial type of KP duty.*

Discrimination and wanton violence led him and my grandmother to eventually leave South Carolina and migrate to New York, where my mother was born. My mother Alwillie Jamison was born in Harlem, Hospital in New York City and was raised in both the Lower East Side of Manhattan and in Brooklyn.

I can also trace my maternal grandfather, **Willie Jamison's** ancestral lineage, and I can document both sides of his family also. They originate from Denmark, South Carolina which is just 10 miles away from Bamberg, South Carolina and the very next town over from my maternal grandmothers' family. I have traced my family history to a common church between both towns called Capernaum, which I've heard all my life erroneously pronounced as "Cape-Onion" Baptist Church.

My maternal great-great-great-grandmother (his-grandmothers-mother) was named **Killingsworth** and she married a man named **George Anderson** my great-great-great-grandfather (his-grandmothers-father). Together they had a daughter named **Jane Anderson**.

My other maternal great-great-great-grandmother (his-grandfather-mother) was named **Jane Dicks** and she married a man named **John Aaron** who was my great-great-great-grandfather (his-grandfathers-mother). They had a son named **Lawrence Green**.

My great-great-grandmother Jane Anderson married my great-great-grandfather Lawrence Green. They both had a daughter, named **Elizabeth Green** (1876 - 1955) my great-grandmother (my grandfather's mother) and she was born in Barnwell, South Carolina.

The oldest relative I can trace on my mother's fathers side of the family, was an enslaved African woman from what is now called the country of Nigeria. That is the lineage through which my grandfather **Wilbur Jamison** hails from.

Together, Wilbur Jamison and Elizabeth Green had nine children in Denmark, South Carolina. **One of them was my maternal grandfather Willie Jamison who had eight siblings (5 brothers and 3 sisters).**

When my biological grandfather Willie Jamison died my grandmother married her second husband – my granddad **Bobby Mitchell** (1919-1989) who help raise my mom.

My mother always tells me of the time she left New York City when she was a little over 11 years of age to visit her grandparents, the Moody's down in South Carolina, and she stayed down there for a few years returning up to New York City when she was around 14 years old.

She always refers to that time as two and a half years a slave!

She explains the blatant overt discrimination she faced down there in the segregated south of the 1950's and how it contrasted with the covert systematic discrimination in the North. She told me about working in a segregated restaurant in Bamberg, South Carolina near highway 301 as a dishwasher & helper of her grandmother who was a cook, and the horrors of "going to town". How she always fell asleep in class because she worked every night in the restaurant with her grandmother. How she and the rest of the field "negroes" didn't stay in school year around once the season changed to planting or harvest time. How her hands bled from picking cotton and how her grandfather interacted with the property owner "Mr. Carlie" who rode around the plantation, I mean farm, on a white horse.

My paternal grandmother **Velma Henderson** (1931-1990) was born in Birmingham, Alabama. She married my paternal grandfather **Robert "Bob" Cooper** (1925-1989) who was from Verbena, Alabama.

Going into my paternal grandmothers' ancestral lineage will take me to Birmingham, Alabama. Her father (my paternal great-grandfather) was name **Ed Henderson**, and he was born in 1896. He married **Eliza Owens** (my paternal great-grandmother) who was born in 1897 in Talladega, Alabama.

Together they had four children; [1] **Windman**, [2] **Christine**, [3] **Ed** and [4] **Velma**.

> ## To me, my grandmother Velma Henderson
> ## was the greatest woman who ever lived, period.

Her first husband was named Bob Cooper (my paternal grandfather) and her second husband was named Sam Brevard (my paternal granddad).

My granddad **Sam Brevard** loved my grandmother more than I have ever witnessed any man, love any woman, in my entire life. He purchased her burial plot "before they both passed" and she is buried with him in the same plot as you read these words.

*I consider the biological man who created you to be your father, and the man who raised you to be your dad. Some people have them both in the same person, meaning their father is their dad. So, I call my dad's biological father my grandfather, and the man who showed me what a grandparent could be my granddad.*

You can just imagine my surprise when I stumbled across an old family photograph showing both my grandfather & granddad were in the same blue "lodge" together.

I understand that many grandparents do not have the same responsibility to raise a child as the parents. But every now and then a grandparent may have to correct a child, even if it's for the child's own safety. I can close my eyes and think back over my entire life, and I do NOT have one bad memory of my grandmother. I do know that even though we lived in the South Bronx off Prospect Avenue & 163rd Street, I can't ever remember her front door being locked. There was always someone going in or out of her apartment on the first floor, and music and partying was the "daily standard". My paternal grandmother lived on the first floor of a six-story tenement building, and my maternal grandmother lived on the sixth floor.

In fact, history has it that that is how my mother and father met before I was born. Both of my grandmothers were drinking & partying buddies, along with old man Snipes who also lived on the first floor, who has a famous relative: yeah, somebody knows something - New Jack City (1991) .

18

Many people will think I am crazy, but I have a vivid memory from before I was even one year old. I remember leaving my dad's mom (maternal grandmother) apartment on the first floor and crawling up six flights of stairs to see my mom's mother (paternal grandmother). I remember crawling on the cold marble floor and the image of what the little square tiles looked like. I remember going up each landing and using the metal railing to pull myself up with. I remember which floors had barking dogs, and which floors were extremely quiet. I remember in my mind it took "forever" to get up those stairs, but I knew that I was leaving a place that I was loved, protected and felt safe at. In search of my other family where there was always more love, attention and affection.

You see, my father was an only child and my mother was the oldest. So, my dad's side of the family was full of partying and good times, and my mom's side of the family was full of people, family, friends and more good times. We lived there a couple of years, until my sister was born. Then we moved into a bigger apartment building on the corner of 178th Street and Vyse Avenue (also in the Bronx).

Well, my paternal grandmother used to tell me as a child that; her family was from Birmingham, Alabama but my [paternal] grandfather's side of the family was from Ba-Bena, Alabama. I used to look at and study road maps as a kid, but never could locate Ba-Bena, Alabama. Even in later years, when I enlisted in the US military and was training at Fort McClellan, Alabama (near Anniston).

Well I eventually found them!

They may all reside in and around Birmingham, Alabama now; but they originally hail from Verbena, Alabama in Chilton County.

My great-great-grandfather was named **Jack Postell** from Autauga, Alabama. Autauga County is about 25 miles south of Verbena, Alabama just north of Montgomery. My grandfathers-grandfather **Jack** married a woman named **Kit** who was a Seminole Indian (Native American).

Jack & Kit had a daughter named **Ida Postell** in Marion, Alabama in 1903. That beautiful woman, my great-grandmother Ida Mae Postell (1903-1986) married a man named **Whitstone**, and then later in life married my great-grandfather **Willis Cooper**.

19

Willis Cooper was born in 1909 in Jefferson County, Alabama, but his family originally hailed from Tennessee. So, Ida Mae Whitestone (Postell) and Willis Cooper had five children. <u>One of them was my paternal grandfather Robert (Bob) Cooper who was born in 1925.</u>

**Bob Cooper** had four siblings (3 brothers and 1 sister); [1] **James J.W.**, [2] **Pearl**, [3] **Benjamin**, and [4] **James (Bo)**. Between my grandfather's and his siblings, they had a total of 15 children (all about my father's age), those fifteen children in turn had 41 children who are about my age. They make up a very, very large branch of my family tree. Just imagine those forty-one cousins of mine who are about my age (and I'm 50, and have been the same 50 years old for a few years now). You can just imagine how many Second Cousins Once Removed I have from just that one side of the family.

I was told that my paternal grandfather's oldest brother's actual name is the letters "J.W." However, when he joined the military back then, they said you must have a name, so they "assigned" him the name James William for his initials J.W. *(Today's military just gives anyone without a middle name, the name NMI, which stands for No Middle Initial).* That may briefly explain how my paternal great-grandmother has two of her sons named "James".

Anyway, my grandfather's oldest brother J.W. and his wife **Adlay** had two children named; [1] **James Jr.** and [2] **Carolyn**. My grandfather's oldest sister **Pearl** did not have any children that I know of. My grandfather's brother **Benjamin** (my dad's Uncle Ben) had three children that I know of; [1] **Curtis**, [2] **Pat**, and [3] **Peanut**. His son Curtis is one of my dad's several first cousins, so that would make him my First Cousin Once Removed (but remember if ANY male relative was older than me, I just refer to them as my Uncle). My grandfather's youngest brother **James** (my dad's Uncle Bo) had nine children that I know of; [1] **James Jr. (Huk or Hulk)**, [2] **Charles**, [3] **Roy Lee (Peanut)**, [4] **Willie Mae**, [5] **Shirley**, [6] **Simone**, [7] **Wykeenia**, [8] **Cynthia (Biddy)** and [9] **Vanessa**.

Although he had a big family, and his brothers and sisters went on to have even bigger families, my paternal grandparents only had one child - my dad. If you ever had the pleasure of meeting my father, you will know that they literally broke the mold after he was made. Because he is that special.

My grandfather Robert Cooper, was in the U.S. Army during WWII. He served in the European Theatre, also when the U.S. military was segregated by race just like the rest of society –like my other grandfather. The horrors & discrimination he faced in the deep south as a military veteran caused two significant events to happen that directly affected me.

First, he suffered from what would have been diagnosed as "extreme" Post Traumatic Stress Disorder (PTSD), but since they didn't call it that back then, and because the treatment of some veterans was bad back then, so imagine a black veteran being considered a second-class citizen. He never got diagnosed nor treated and because he self-medicated himself, I never got to establish the bond a grandson should have with his grandfather.

Eventually my paternal grandmother married her second husband – my granddad Sam Brevard (1919-1993) and he raised my dad as his own son. He is the man I aspired to grow-up and become like, and he was a super positive role model for his community until the day he died. My granddad was a bad motor scooter.

The second event that occurred on my paternal side of the family that had a direct impact on my life, was my dad. My dad Edward Cooper was born in Birmingham, Alabama in the 1940's and the racism was so bad and so evil, that; he had to be sent up North to live, for fear of him being lynched.

So, my parents, both with family roots in the south and deep south met in the South Bronx of New York City, got married and had me.

In 1839 a group of prominent philanthropists founded a hospital for old retired slaves.

It was originally called "the Home for the Colored Aged" by those philanthropists who were known as the "Society for the Relief of Worthy Aged Indigent Colored Persons". It was located on 141st Street and Southern Boulevard in the South Bronx and in 1899 its name was changed to Lincoln Hospital in honor of the former 16th President of the United States of America.

I was born there in the 1960's as Edward Timothy Cooper.

My first or given name was Edward, just like my dad.

My paternal grandmother Velma had a brother named Edward or Ed, so I can only assume that she named her first-born son and only child (my dad) after

21

her brother. Since I was my dad's first-born son and oldest child I can only assume that I was to be a "Jr." to my dad. That probably would have made me Edward the 3rd or Edward III, but it didn't happen like that. Although my mother had nine brothers and sisters, my father was/is an only child. Since he grew up with no siblings, I was told that he convinced my mother to have another child, so I would have a brother or sister, and not grow up an only child the way he did. So, a couple of years later my parents had their second child, a daughter – and I gained a little sister. Almost ten years later that, my parents had another child, another son – and I gained a little brother.

It's safe to assume that every generation wants their children to grow up to be better than the previous one generation.

My middle name is and always has been Timothy.

My mother said she got that name from the 1st and 2nd books of Timothy in the bible. Whereas her father (my grandfather Willie Jamison) and her grandfather (my great-grandfather Charlie Moody) were both Southern Baptist Ministers in South Carolina, I can see that origin.

### But why Timothy?

I've asked her, because there were other names of other people in the bible, she could have chosen. So why did she choose Timothy? I've asked her why not James, or Peter, or John, or Matthew, or Mark, or Luke?

She told me that she knew someone with each of those names, but she didn't know anyone with the name Timothy.

Besides I don't know if she knew it over 50 years ago, but the book of Timothy has a very special meaning to me, especially the 2nd Book of Timothy, Second Chapter, Eighth Sentence or Verse (2 Timothy 2:8); *Remember that Jesus Christ of the seed of David was raised from the dead, according to "my" gospel (KJV)*. I'm not a biblical scholar nor do I profess to know all things biblical, but I do know how to read and the answer that what many people are seeking about the truth; is right there in that sentence, hidden in plain sight!

Paul is listed as one of the 12 apostles, and according to biblical history he wrote 3 letters (or books) in the bible. The two letters to Timothy called; 1 Timothy and 2 Timothy in the bible, and the book of Titus.

From as early as I can remember I have always been known by my middle name of Timothy or a variation of it. As a child, any of my aunts or uncles would ask my mother if they could take "Timmy" outside to play. My aunts used to take me across the street from our apartment building on Union Avenue in the South Bronx to the handball courts behind Jane Adams High School. My uncles used to take me up to Prospect Avenue to use me to help them pick-up girls. Because I was such a skinny little kid, I was the proverbial – Little Timmy.

When my sister was born a few years later, we were affectionally known as Timmy & Angel or "Raggedy Ann & Andy" (because we were poor and wore patches in our clothes). I'm well into my fifties now, I stopped counting the years when I first reached 50 a few years ago. However, people in my old neighborhood in the South Bronx still refer to me as Timmy.

As I grew older I remember going by the shortened version of "Tim".

*Although at 6'3" and 270 pounds I'm not really that guy "Little Timmy" any more.*

Every person has:
- 2 biological parents,
- 4 grandparents,
- 8 great-grandparents,
- 16 great-great-grandparents
  (*grandparents of grandparents*),
- 32 great-great-great-grandparents
  (*parents of grandparents of grandparents*),
- 64 great-great-great-great-grandparents
  (*grandparents of grandparents of grandparents*), and so on, and so on.

So, if any person traces back 8 generations there would be 128 separate people who had to come together at various times to eventually create - you.

I believe for simplicity sake that each person can trace their ancestral heritage through three ways.

- First: There is the direct paternal lineage which is your fathers, fathers, fathers, father and so on, and so on.

- Second: There is the direct maternal lineage which is your mothers, mothers, mothers, mothers and so on, and so on.

- Third: Then there are all the other various combinations of your ancestral heritage that you can trace your lineage through. Like your mother's, father's, mother's, mother's, father's father. That person would still be your maternal grandfathers-grandmothers-grandfather, and you would be a decedent of that person, but not a direct-line decedent of the paternal or maternal lineage.

So, let's talk about the two direct lineages.

**First is my mother's maternal lineage.**

Mitochondrial DNA (mtDNA) has been passed down from mother to daughter, consistently over the last 500 – 2,000 years. Every female child receives mtDNA from their mothers, who received it from their mothers, who received if from their mothers, and so on.

Since every person has a belly button and you came from some woman, you can trace your individual mtDNA with ease. I did mine, through DNA analysis and came up with a 100% sequence match with the Akan people, in what today is called Ghana.

This means whoever she was, whenever she arrived on the North American continent, through mass migration, ancient travel or enslavement – she was a member of the Akan people. She passed her mtDNA down to her children, and her daughter(s) passed down that same mtDNA to their daughters, and so on and so on. This pattern continued unchanged down to my maternal great-great-grandmother. She passed that mtDNA sequence down to her children (one of whom was my great-grandmother). My maternal great-grandmother, Almeda was biracial and because of the segregation practices in the deep south, she is buried in the "white" cemetery with her paternal side of the family to this very day. Racism was prevalent in every part of society, from before birth until after death.

My Great Grandmother Almeda, she passed down that mtDNA down to all 18 of her children, one of whom was my grandmother. My maternal grandmother Richardean passed down that same mtDNA to all 9 of her children. Since its passed down from mother to daughter, both my aunts and my mother passed down the exact same mtDNA maternal sequence. My mother passed it down to my siblings and me. While my brother and I will not be able to pass our mtDNA to our children, my sister has passed it down to her children. While her sons' children (my nephews), will inherit the mtDNA from their mothers, her daughter (my niece) can continue the sequence.

**The other direct ancestral lineage is the father (paternal).**

That is the direct lineage passed down from father to son since like forever. Since every person born has a biological father, who had a father and so on and so on.

My paternal grandfather did not know his last name. I will repeat that my paternal grandfather did not know his family's last name. He only knew the name that was passed down to him. This means my father also did not know his last name. He knows the last name that was handed down to him – but that is not my family's last name.

No matter how far back in my ancestral lineage you go, you will find that I am just like the majority of black people who live and were born in the United States today are. Because of that ugly period of history, that we call chattel slavery, many of us are unable to recall what our family name was. Whether that male ancestor was born free in America, an enslaved African person, an indigenous person or native-born person – the last name that we carry says a lot about our heritage.

Many last names or surnames that people carry originate from one of four major sources from their ancestors. [1] Patronymic or Matronymic Surnames, [2] Occupational Surnames, [3] Descriptive Surnames or [4] Geographical Surnames.

Patronymic or Matronymic surnames can originate from the actual given name of your parents. If your fathers first name was John you may be called

Daughter of John, or Son of John, or John's Son. If there were many children, you would all be called John's Sons or Johnson. That family name would be passed down to each generation, regardless of the first or given name of a person. So today we may have many people named Bob Johnson or Willie Johnson who don't know the origin was the first person with that name was called John and every decedent of him carried the last name John's Sons – or John's Son – or Johnson.

Occupational Surnames were names based upon the occupation of your ancestor. Like the baker, the barber and the candlestick maker. Normally if your grandfather worked in a mill, and your father worked in a mill, you can pretty much determine that you were also going to grow up - and work in a mill. Your family name could eventually become Miller since you were a family of mill workers. Or Miner if your family worked in the mines, or Baker if your family was traditionally the town bakers, or Cooper if your family made barrels or coffins out of wood.

Descriptive Surnames are based upon a physical feature or quality of an individual that was passed down from family to family. Imagine if your last name was Green, and you did the research and found out that your father's fathers', father (go back 20 generations) and it was based upon his having green eyes.

Then you have Geographical Surnames which originate from the geographical location that family originated from, like Woods, Underbrook, Overhill, Crosscreek, Jordan, etc,

For those who do not know American History, humans who were enslaved in this country were considered property and not even classified as humans in many instances. If a slave owner had a lot of property it would all have his name and in many cases; his physical branding. If a person named Palmer owned a very large slave plantation, everything on the land would legally belong to Mr. Palmer. Example; Mr. Palmer's land, Mr. Palmer's house, Mr. Palmer's trees, Mr. Palmer's horses, Mr. Palmer's slaves and so on. No matter what the first or given name of a slave, if he belonged to Mr. Palmer he carried Palmer's last name. If he or she was sold to another plantation, say for example; a Mr. Charlie - then he or she became Mr. Charlie's property and would then possess that owners last name.

Cooper is just the last name of a family that was the last person to hold my paternal ancestor in bondage or human slavery until after the American Civil War and the United States Constitutional Amendments; specifically, the 13th constitutional amendment (1865) that ended slavery and the 14th constitutional amendment (1868) that gave black people citizenship.

That name was passed down to my grandfather's grandfather, who passed it down to my grandfather's father, who passed it down to my grandfather who passed it down to my father, who passed it down to me.

However, my father did another great thing besides creating me – he and my mother acknowledged that, that was not his true family name and decided to do something about it. Remember I told you my father left the deep south of racially segregated Alabama in the 1940's and 50's when black people were still being lynched – just for being black.

In the early 1970's when I was still a child both of my parents became very active in the Nation of Islam under the leadership of the Most Honorable Elijah Muhammad. In order to combat the institutional racism that existed in our country against melinated people of color in general, and black folks who were born in the United States of America specifically, he was very radical. Just being black in America was already tantamount to committing a crime back in the day. Our very existence was viewed as a threat to the American way of life, because that's the way it had been for over 400 years.

Chattel slavery existed in our country for almost 375 years, from around 1492, until the end of the American Civil War in 1865.

Then for another 100 years, from 1865-1964, physical slavery was replaced with racial segregation as the law of the land. Many members of the dominant population in society wish to maintain the status quota, so there were many who fought to keep black people in an inferior and subservient unnatural position of inferiority. The criminal insurgency and rise of the ku klux klan, white supremacist and paramilitary groups. Many southern states passed new state constitutions and laws to specifically disenfranchise all black and many poor white people. Housing, employment, voting, every single way of life was affected. Black people where physically prevented from voting with the threat of lynching, death or worse (yes, there are things worse than death).

Many innocent family members were murdered because a blood thirsty mob could not find their intended target, so they killed innocent women, children and babies. It took the civil rights movement and an act of the United States Congress for black folks to get the right to vote in 1965, fair housing in 1966 and a host of other civil right in 1968.

Not "Equal Rights" to be taken from another person just to level the playing field, but simply "Civil Rights" right to be treated as a human being.

So, with the momentum of the civil rights era of the 1960's, and the climate of our country and the awakening of people to finally be proud of who you were, just the way our creator created each of us – many people started to research the truth.

Realizing that Cooper (or whatever) was not the family name, it was not the original name of our ancestors, and keeping that name was actually perpetuating the subconscious mentality of being someone's slave or property (like when you go to sleep in your Master's Bedroom at night), the Nation of Islam had a policy at that time. You could keep your first name that was given to you by your parents, but you would no longer use that last name that belong to the actual family that enslaved your ancestors. You would adopt the letter "X" to signify that you did not know what it was, and you would keep that letter X as your last name until research was done to determine what your true family last name was – or you adopted or were given a new one.

Like when Malcom Little became Malcolm X.

The place of worship was called a temple not a church back then. We attended temple number 7 on 116th Street & Lenox Avenue. That was the same exact same temple that El-Hajj Malik El-Shabazz (Malcom X) used to lead until shortly before his assassination in 1964. That temple was then led by the Honorable Louis Farrakhan. At the time of the Most Honorable Elijah Muhammad's death in 1975 there were well over 75 individual numbered temples across the United States with an untold number of Black-Muslim members.

If a black person name John Smith joined the nation back in those days, he would drop the surname "Smith" and adopt the name "X", becoming John X until his true family surname could be found.

Later if there was another black person that became a member of that same temple, he may have had the name of John Jackson prior to becoming a member. So, since there was already a John X (the man formerly known as John Smith), John Jackson would become John 2X, because there was already a John X in that temple.

Now if another man with the first name John joined, for example John Jones. He would become John 3X and so on, and so on.

When my parents join the nation in 1970 my father became Edward 84X and I became Edward 85X. Although we are talking almost 50 years ago, I remember this part vividly as if it was yesterday. Because I was in kindergarten and the first grade at the time and I had to write my name Edward 85X on all my assignments.

If you think kids are mean today, and there is a problem with ostracizing or bullying kids in school – just imagine my situation.

I was already being called Little Timmy because of my size and now I have the daily harassment from other kids like, *"why you got numbers in your name"*? I couldn't articulate an answer yet, I was in the first grade, but it didn't stop there.

Lessons in the temple did not stop at the topic of religion. What I later found in life to be the truth was taught in the temples about science, history, mathematics, etc. So, when I would attend public school I would clash with the curriculum and teachers about what was being taught in public school.

Public school taught that Abraham Lincoln freed the slaves.

The temple taught me that was not completely true.

They taught the correct history that when Abraham Lincoln issued the Emancipation Proclamation in 1863, it stated that all slaves, "in *states that rebelled against the Union*", were now free.

He did not free ANY of the slaves who remained in bondage in states that remained loyal to the Union.

All the states the succeeded from the Union and formed their own country, called the Confederate States of America (CSA). They even had their own President (Jefferson Davis). So, Lincoln's proclamation didn't free anybody in those states either, because they didn't even recognize themselves as being part of the United States anymore.

So, the day after the emancipation proclamation was done, the status of not one person who was enslaved had changed.

So, he didn't free anyone like history teaches us. The actual changes or amendments to the United States Constitution abolished slavery in 1865 – and technically when they put the word "*except*" in the 13th amendment, they didn't completely abolish slavery either.

In New York City, students were grouped in order of intelligence (at least back then they were), and I have a decent memory coupled with the fact that my mother keeps copies of everything.

I attended Pre-K and Kindergarten at Public School (P.S.) 67 on Mohegan Avenue in the South Bronx, of New York City. The school building was between Honeywell Avenue & Southern Boulevard right off of 178th Street.

For Elementary School, I attended first grade through fifth grade at Public School (P.S.) 6 on Tremont Avenue, between Vyse and Bryant Avenues.

For whatever reason, I can't recall my first-grade teacher, at PS 6. I sustained a head injury that year that "may" have affected my memory. However, I do remember the rest of my elementary school teachers.

**Ms. Malitz 2nd grade**
**Mrs. Delany 3rd grade**
**Mrs. Saton 4th grade**
**Mr. Gellis 5th grade**

By the time I graduated elementary school, after the 5th grade, I was already reading at a junior high school (middle school) **8.1 grade** reading level, and my mathematics were at a high school **9.5 grade** level, thanks to the external teachings I received at Muhammad's Temple Number 7 on 116th Street and Lenox Avenue, in the Harlem section of Manhattan in New York City.

In New York City, middle school is referred to and called junior high school. So, I attended Loraine Hansberry Intermediate (Junior High or Middle) School I.S.167 located in the West Farms area of the South Bronx community where I grew up. Physically located at the intersection of West Farms Road and Boston Road. Directly beneath the number 2 and 5 trains stop at the East Tremont Avenue station.

I was assigned in the 6th grade to class 6-1 (Mr. Freiman was my teacher) which is where your "A" average grade students were assigned.

Class 6-2 was where students who averaged a "B" were assigned, 6-3 were your "C" average grade students, 6-4 was were your "D" average grade students, and so on.

The 1970's were a very turbulent time for my family. In fact, I would say that was a very turbulent time for many impoverished families in the South Bronx. Whatever I was dealing with in life at that period of time caused me to go from a straight "A" student to straight "F's".

I was held-over in the 6th grade or what many people called - left back.

I remember my parents, the guidance counselors and my teachers trying to determine what was wrong with me. They determined whatever was effecting my school work was not because of my intelligence, so this is what they did.

I had to retake the sixth grade to make up all the work I failed AND do the work with my peers in the seventh grade: *at the same time!*

In class 6-5 (Mr. Arroyo was my teacher) and 7-2 (Mr. Zavleck was my teacher) that same year. I was advanced back up with my peers, and attended the eighth grade on time in class 8-2 (Mr. Meyers) with classmates I'm still friends with to this very day.

I kept the last name 85X until my true family was discovered, the name "Bilal".

At the same time, my parents gave me the first name of Muhammad after the Greatest Boxer ever: Muhammad Ali.

So, the evolution of my name was as follows.

| 1960's | *Edward Timothy Cooper* | |
|---|---|---|
| 1969 - 71 | *Edward 85X* | *2 years* |
| 1972 - Present | *Muhammad Timothy Bilal* | *45 years* |

| 1982 - 2006 | *Sergeant Bilal (U.S. Military) DoD* | *23 years* |
|---|---|---|
| 2006 - 2017 | *Mr. Bilal (Business Owner)* | *11 years* |
| 2007 - 2017 | *Shadow (PMC WPPS/WPS) DoS* | *10 years* |

My parents legally changed my name from (Cooper) 85X to Bilal, just like a married woman would change from her former last "maiden" name, to the last name of her husband after they get married. It occurred when I was still in Elementary School, way before I attended Junior High School at I.S. 167 Loraine Hansberry.

Although my full name is Muhammad Timothy Bilal, by the time I went to high school everyone was referred to by only their first name, and mine is Muhammad. Only old friends who knew me from around the neighborhood where I grew up would still call me by my middle name - Timmy.

I attended Theodore Roosevelt High School in the Bronx of New York City. It was located on Fordham Road directly across the street from Fordham University. Assigned to the Honors Academy I stayed out of trouble and academically we competed with the other kids in the College Bound Discovery Program.

Theodore Roosevelt was one of the zone high schools in the New York City public school system. In New York, middle school students, "apply" and take an exam in order to attend various high schools all across the city. Examples are: the high school for music and arts, or the high school for science, or the high school for mathematics, engineering, or the high school for dance and theatre, etc.

If a student does not get accepted to a specialty high school or their school of choice they are assigned to their "zone" school depending on their address. When I was assigned to Theodore Roosevelt I wasn't scared, but I was in shock because in the late 1970's Theodore Roosevelt High School (TRHS) in the Bronx was considered the worse high school in several categories.

With an enrollment of thousands of students, it had the highest dropout rate of any school in the New York City Public School System at the time, by the time they shut down my previous high school it had a graduation rate of just 3%.

That means 97% of the freshmen who started at that school would not graduate on time in 4 years, if they graduated or lived at all. Super-seniors at 18 & 19 were the norm, and Ultra-seniors at 20 & 21 were not uncommon. It is at age 21 where you actually age out of public school eligibility.

Of the 75 police precincts in New York City, Theodore Roosevelt High School was in the territory of the 46th adjacent to the 48th and was the most criminal and homicidal of all its precincts. I remember working a part-time job in school when Paul Newman filmed the movie Fort Apache the Bronx.

So, I was called Muhammad by my classmates and Timmy by my neighbors, until I enlisted in the U.S. Army. at 17 years of age, with my parents' permission in SEP 1982.

Regardless of what your first (given) name was, or your middle name was, or your "nickname" was; the U.S. Army only uses your last name, and your last four numbers of your social security number (*no, I'm not telling you my social security number*). Then they add your rank, and that's the only name you will hear for your entire 20-year career, unless you get promoted. So, I was called, Private Bilal.

My family wasn't the only black Americans at the time to experience an awaking, and drop that former "slave-name" and adopt a new one. Here are a few examples of some great people who did the same.

Ferdinand Lewis Alcindor Jr., born 1947, is a great American retired Professional Basketball Player who played 20 seasons in the National Basketball Association (NBA) for the Milwaukee Bucks and the Los Angeles Lakers. Six times he was selected as the NBA's Most Valuable Player (MVP), 19-time NBA All-Star and selected NBA All-Defensive Team member 11-times. He won 6 NBA championships as a player and 2 as an assistant coach. He was voted the NBA Finals MVP – twice. He was honored as one of the 50 Greatest Players in NBA History in 1996. While in high school in New York City he led his team to 3 straight New York City Catholic championships, a 71-consecutive basketball game winning streak and scored 2,067 total points –

a New York City high school record. His team won the national high school boys basketball championship when he was in the 11th grade. After high school, he attended UCLA. He played on three consecutive national championship basketball teams and was a record three-time MVP of the NCAA tournament. He was so successful during his high school and college years that after the 1967 season the "dunk" was banned in college basketball (until the 1976-1977) season primarily because of him, so he developed a "sky hook" shot. At the time of his retirement in 1989, he was the NBA's all-time leader in points scored (38,387), games played (1,560), minutes played (57,446), field goals made (15,837), blocked shots (3,189) and defensive rebounds (9,394). He remains the all-time leading scorer in the NBA. In 2007, ESPN voted him the greatest center of all time, in 2008, they named him the "greatest player in college basketball history". He is a basketball coach, bestselling author and was a martial arts student of the late Bruce Lee. In 2012, he was selected by the Secretary of State to be a U.S. global cultural ambassador. In 2016, he received the Presidential Medal of freedom from the President of the United States. You may not know him by the name Lew Alcindor, but you may know him as Kareen Abdul-Jabbar.

Yvette Marie Steven, born 1953, is a great American Recording Artist whose career has spanned over 50 years. Over the past five decades she has won 10 Grammy Awards and sold an estimated 70 million records worldwide. She is ranked at number 17 on the VH1's original list of the 100 Greatest Women of Rock & Roll. She was nominated in 2015 for induction into the Rock and Roll Hall of Fame as a solo artist; she previously was nominated in 2011 as a member of her group. She has four gold singles, four gold albums and two platinum albums. Billboard magazine has ranked her as the 65th most successful dance artist of all time in December 2016. You may not know her as Yvette Marie Steven but you may know her as Chaka Khan.

Cassius Marcellus Clay Jr (1942-2016) was an activist and the Greatest Professional Boxer that ever lived, in my opinion. He is widely regarded as the most significant and celebrated sports figure of the 20th century. He won the Olympic Gold Medal at 18 at the 1960 Summer Olympics in Rome. At age 22, he won the WBA, WBC and lineal heavyweight boxing titles and was a prominent leader in the 1960's Civil Rights Movement and my personal hero. He was an ordained minister and as such, a conscientious objector. He refused to be drafted into the US military because of these reasons and was stripped of his heavyweight boxing titles, his boxing license and millions of dollars in endorsements. He fought his legal battles all the way up to the United States Supreme Court in 1971, and won. That legal action forced him to lose four years of his peak and prime fighting years, and he was still able to come back and eventually regain the heavyweight boxing title. He later lost the title in his later years - and won it again. Becoming the only man in history to win the heavyweight boxing title three times and he is the only three-time lineal heavyweight boxing champion. He is the only boxer of any weight class to be named "The Ring" magazine fighter of the year 6 times. He is ranked as the greatest athlete of the century by "Sport Illustrated". He was such an outspoken and provocative spokesman that he recorded 2 spoken word albums, a R&B song and received two Grammy Award nominations. He performed in several films as an actor and a Broadway musical. You may not know him as Cassius Clay but everyone knows him as Muhammad Ali.

That was the evolution of my name until I retired from the U.S. military in 2006. As a civilian, I went from being called Sergeant Bilal in the military to being called Mr. Bilal.

In some civilian communities, especially in business people refer to each other by their first name. So, when people call me Muhammad or refer to me by that first name, it feels funny. Because I have not used anything but my last name in the military for well over 20 years. The mister part always sounded funny to me, but protocol being what it is, I understand its use.

When asked to spell my name, I always say Muhammad – just like the boxer.

With the post 9-11 society we live in now, you would think just saying my name "Muhammad" would be tantamount to yelling stick 'em up, or worse! I still get hate mail and hate messages to this day, from people who don't even know me – just based upon their bias, bigotry and ignorance of my name. Only the man upstairs knows how many employment opportunities I did not get because of someone else's preconceived prejudices.

But a very influential man once told me that for every person that refuses to do business with me because of my name, there is another person who will specifically seek me out for employment – just because of my name. He said, *"Don't be ashamed of who you are"*.

I never forgot that.

*Your name, could you spell it for me please?*

I always say, **"M-U-H-A-M-M-A-D"** just like the boxer.

Normally when it's spell with an "O" as in Mohammad, that denotes an origin or spelling from a location other than in North America.

Many people from West Asia, North Africa and the Middle East spell their name that way. When it's spelled with an "E" at the end, as in Mohammed; normally that tends to denote a very radical version of the name, culture and religion. This is not written down anywhere in any book that I have read, it's just from my perspective over the last almost 50 years on this planet – that's the way it's spelled.

Many people are incarcerated or imprisoned and become religious in an attempt at rehabilitation, and changing their lives around from a life of crime (that landed them in prison) to becoming a better more productive member of society. They become born-again Christians, Buddhist, Muslims or members of other religious faiths.

Just as there are several types of Christians; such as Baptist, Methodist, Catholic, Protestant, Jehovah Witness and several other denominations. There are also several types of Muslims; such as Sunni, Orthodox, Shia and the version most associated with some black people in America – called "Black-Muslims".

You can normally tell what type of muslim that person is (or was) based upon the way the spelling of their name is – especially if their name is, Muhammad.

Mohamed with one "M" instead of two "MM" and a "O" and an "E" is probably Egyptian.

Mohammad with two "MM" and an "O" is probably from Iran, Afghanistan or Pakistan

Muhammod with two "MM" and an "O" is probably from the region called the Far East like Bangladesh.

Muhamed with one "M" and a "E" is probably Bosnia and Herzegovinian.

It is believed to be the most common name in the world, and an estimated 150 million people on this earth that have the name Muhammad in some variation of its spelling. To put that into perspective, that's the equivalent of every male in the United States having the name – Muhammad". That's how populous that name is on this earth.

Which brings me to the name Shadow.

*** 

I first went to Iraq in 2004 is support of Operation IRAQI FREEDOM (OIF2), while still on active duty in the U.S. Army. I retired from active duty a few years later in early 2006.

After I retired from the military, I started working in Iraq in late 2007 during Operation IRAQI FREEDOM, for a Private Military Company (PMC) in support of the United States Department of State (DoS). I worked on the WPPS/WPS contract as a DoS Security Contractor, performing Diplomatic Security duties as a – Personal Security Specialist (PSS).

We were all issued nick-names or call-signs and I was given the name Shadow. I used that name while in Iraq and other countries in the area known as the middle-east in 2007, 2008, 2009, 2010, 2011, 2012 and 2013. There were men I worked with daily for several years whom I do NOT know their full government name. If I receive a "friends request" from them on social media, I would not immediately recognize their legal name and must search through photos to determine who they are.

My teams over the years were full of men & women with unique call-signs such as; *Mac*, because he drove a Mack Truck back in the regular "real" world during his regular job. *Dorothy*, because he was from Kentucky or Nebraska or Kansas or some Wizard of Oz type of place. *Chowhall*, because he was a big guy and he was always eating – in the chow hall. *Coach*, because he talked about sports constantly, and he knew what he was talking about too. *Dirty*, because he resembled that character "Dirty Pig Pen" from the Charlie Brown cartoons. *Stretch*, because he was extremely tall. *Whitey*, because his name was Blanco (so they didn't have to reach far to think of a call-sign for that one). *Doc*, because he was the team medic. In fact, I think every team I've ever been on or with the medic or corpsman was named "Doc". Narc, because he used

37

to be an undercover narcotics police officer back in the world. Rainman, because he could not sit or stand still like he had Tourette's Syndrome or was extremely autistic. But he was the smartest guy on the team, and he was actually the team leader. Manilla because he lived, you guessed it – in Manilla in the Philippines. In fact, there were several former and current PMC's who choose to live in the Philippines, Costa Rica or Thailand.

All American civilians who work overseas are called expatiates or "expats" for short. Many of the service members are affectionally called "Troops", as in "Please Support Our Deployed Troops" with this yellow ribbon

> **U.S. Army** personnel are called – **Soldiers.**
> **U.S. Air Force** personnel are called – **Airmen.**
> **U.S. Navy** personnel are called – **Sailors.**
> **United States Marine Corps** personnel are called - **Marines.**

But I say again, all the American "civilians" who work overseas are called expats, even if they do not work in a combat zone.

The country that is being operated in, is considered the "host-nation". So, all people who are citizens of that country are call Host Country Nationals (HCN) citizens or personnel. So, in Afghanistan the HCN's are Afghan's, and in Iraq the HCN are Iraqi's.

Then there are people who were not Americans and they were not HCN's either. So, since they originate from a third country – they are called TCN's which stands for: Third Country Nationals.

There were TCN's from dozens of other countries working in Iraq when I was there, working for the U.S. and other coalition forces. There were Kenyans, Sri Lankans, Bosnians, Peruvians and most notably Ugandans.

As I worked with some of the Ugandans and other expats I noticed the way several of the expats (and some service members) treated the Ugandan TCN's. We as Americans tend to treat everyone from everywhere else who speaks different or has an accent other than our version of English, we treat them in a condescending manner. In grade school, if there was a substitute teacher and he/she spoke with an accent, we would sometimes act a fool, not knowing that person may possess a PhD in whatever the subject matter is. So, I can understand the conduct of the "Big Ugly American" even if I don't condone it.

But when I heard one expat call another Ugandan TCN "boy" it stunned me at first.

Come here Boy!

That Ugandan went running over to the expat, happily, and I was literally in shock. Later I would find that same Ugandan TCN (who was much smarter than many of the others) in my charge. As he now worked for me I went about ascertaining the reason for his acceptance of them calling him boy.

He told me that back in Uganda when the PMC was inprocessing them, he was in charge of making the tea. Since Uganda is a former colony of England, just like the United States of America once was; I understood the importance of tea to their culture. He told me that since he was in charge of making the tea, they in turn reverted to calling him the Tea-Boy and many times they just called him "boy" and the call-sign stuck.

I explained to him how that was such a derogatory name for a man. I explained to him that even though he didn't think they meant any harm by it, that I knew, that they knew, exactly what they were doing. So, I told him that day I was NOT going to call him boy or tea boy for that matter. I explained to him that using the military phonetic alphabet of "T" as in Tea and "B" as in Boy was the words "Tango" for the letter "T" and "Bravo" for the letter "B". So, I started calling him Tango-Bravo and the call-sign stuck. In fact, I eventually had to create call-signs for all my TCN's because they had their entire lives to learn their names and I had just met them. So whenever there where hundreds of them together and say, four or five of us expats had to go get our prospective individual groups or platoons, I wanted to know my men immediately. The first one had a beard, and every time we linked up with them after chow I could identify the TCN in my group with the crumbs in his beard. So, I called him "Crumbs" and the name stuck.

Every head count I was always short or missing one TCN. When I double-checked that same man was always running for formation, late - from the latrine. So, the other TCN's reverted to calling him "Doo-doo Man". I didn't micromanage the duty roster, but out of maybe 30 TCN's I need 26 or 27 every day for duty. So, there was always a few that didn't have to report for duty that day, or were on sick-call or something like that. Anyway, there was one that would intimidate the others into pulling his duty for him. I explained that they all got paid the same amount and asked why would they all tolerate his bullying behavior. One of them told me, that TCN was the cousin of the president back in their home country. So, his call-sign was VIP. He overheard the informant talking to me and said, "just wait 'til we get back to Uganda".

Another had been up in the guard tower directly overlooking the Nisour Square incident when it occurred the previous month in September 2007. He was interviewed by federal authorities several times, so his call sign was FBI.

There were several of the Ugandans who had call-signs and nicknames and wore them as a badge of honor. But I will never forget the way some of the expats tried to use their authority to promote their racist agenda, by calling Tango-Bravo, a Boy.

The second incident really stuck out in my mind.

There was another American expat, not a TCN who worked for the same PMC on the same project that I did. There were two main groups of expats that operated in Iraq in support of Operation IRAQI FREEDOM and Operation NEW DAWN when I was there; those expats that remained inside the wire on the FOB's, compounds and camps, and those of us that went outside almost every day for whatever reason.

Everyone faced danger, and I mean extreme danger just being over there. There are people who were killed in their sleep by rockets, mortars or whatever their cause of death was. So, I am not classifying one job over another. But there is a very big distinction between those who worked outside the wire, and those who did not. Almost all the men and women who worked inside the wire were working for a PMC that worked for the United States Department of Defense (DoD). There were very specific rules that they operated under regarding the prohibition of fraternizing, alcohol consumption and the use of weapons, ammunition & explosives. They were expressly prohibited from touching, handling, using or firing weapons. I think that had something to do with their legal status, or the rules of war, or whatever, I was not in that category - so I don't know.

But the second category almost down to every man and woman I operated with over there, did not work for the DoD.

40

They (we) all worked for the United States Department of State (DoS), the DoJ, the DoE or some other federal cabinet level position or entity. It was almost guaranteed that weapons, ammunition and explosives were required – and issued to us in order to perform our jobs. At one time I was issued a handgun, a M-4 carbine, a M-249 SAW, a M-240B machinegun and all the flares, grenades and ammunition that a basic infantryman in combat would have.

The expat I am talking about belong to the former group as a type of "supply sergeant", not the latter group. When I met him, and he told me his call-sign was "Shine" again I was baffled.

*You are a big black man and you let people call you "Shine?"*
*Yeah, because I have a shiny bald head.*

*Brother, are you serious?*

*Don't you know that in the early 1900's black people were regulated to menial labor and derogatory jobs in life regardless of their educational abilities. We as a people were required to scrub toilets, and wash other people's clothes and shine their shoes. To add insult to injury after you were down on your knees shining another man's shoes, they would rub your head and say that's a good shine there boy, in a condescending manner. As if to say that's a good dog. But they thought that the black people back then didn't know they were being slick. If you were smart enough to catch on they would consider you an "uppity-negro" and you were subject to being lynched and killed.*

I never knew what happened to that expat, but I would hope that he had adopted another call sign - I just never happened to have crossed paths with him again.

So, when the call sign "Shadow" was bestowed upon me – there is a small part of me that felt that it may have had some racial undertones, because I was the only black guy on the team. During my military career, I learned from a lot of great military leaders who underwent horrors and discrimination that I probably couldn't even imagine. Enlisting in the 1980's many of my immediate leaders, NCO's and officers were veterans from the Vietnam era. Every now and then I would run into an older veteran from the Korean War era who still worked on the base or in the community in a civilian support capacity of some sort. One of them told me a long time ago a bit of advice I'll never forget.

He said, *"Sergeant just being here [volunteering for specialized military training] means that you're special, and not like the other brothers [most brothers I knew would NOT volunteer again for additional "special" training]. As you advance in the military and progress to more and more elite units, like airborne, pathfinder, ranger or special forces; you will find many times that there may be only one other brother in the unit with you. But you will rarely find, three of you or more in the same elite squad, platoon, team, etc. But if you do, and you should happen to take a team or unit photo, do not stand on the end.*

*Or they will crop your black-ass out the picture!"*
**Thank you, Ranger Malone!**

I never forgot that.

After I retired from the U.S. military, when I graduated the DoS WPPS training in a small town located in West Virginia, I never thought about my race, because I am who I am, and I've been who I've been my whole life. (Just like most people don't think about walking, or breathing, they just do it). But over 90% of the town's population were members of the dominant society, the demographics of that small town of 1,026 people was as follows: 90.6% White, 8% Black, 3 Native Indians and 1 Asian person. The WPPS class that I graduated from did not have a more diverse ethnic composition in its student body, in fact, I possessed the most melinated skin tone in the class.

When it was graduation day, I remember the WPPS instructor saying, *"Get your stuff together and let's take this group class photo. Now let's get this right one time, because I ain't going to be taking pictures all damn day!"*

I remembered what I was told by that old Army NCO years ago, about being on the end of a group photo. So, at 6'3" I'm pretty tall, standing in the back-row middle is no big deal – in fact as one of my old airborne brigade command sergeants major used to say, it's too easy. Right before the instructor is about to snap the photo, one of the other students says out loud; *"Hey let's all stand on our tippy-toes and block Bilal out of the photo!"* Most of them do it on que and I'm standing there thinking to myself, WTF?!? So now I'm standing on my tippy-toes also trying to appear taller, than the other students who are trying to appear taller than me, just so they can block my face out the group/team photo.

But no, I don't think it was about race, I just was different than the rest and didn't develop the norms and relationships required in most small group dynamics. Most importantly, I didn't have any disposable income at all. I'm talking all I had was a loaf of bread and some turkey meat to get you through the training weeks. (When the WPPS training transitioned to WPS and moved from West Virginia to Louisiana, the students stayed on a control compound with a dining facility type mess hall). So, I couldn't afford to go out and drink beer after duty hours with most of the other class members. But, there were a few individuals who I did develop a pretty close friendship with, and some of them I still speak with on social media sites up until this present day.

The classmates that treated me the most fairly and never showed a racist attitude towards me were; Coach, Soup and Nomad.

I'm not saying that everyone else was bad, what I am saying is that, these guys stuck out as the most who gave me a fair shot. Most of the instructors didn't care what race or color you were, they were so professional that they just wanted the best men (and women) to meet the standard, or go home. I would eventually work with Coach on an operational team down range, and just like I thought – he was a stand-up guy. I wish him nothing but success and hope that he excels in whatever his endeavors are.

I remember Soup literally giving me the shirt off his back. Most people who know me know that I sweat something profusely. After a training iteration one morning as the sweat was drying on my back, I started sneezing. Soup gave me a dry 5.11 type of shirt and said, *"here put this on."* Good dude. I also remember on one rotation out of the "middle east" when he was on the same aircraft as I was. After we departed from Iraq, the PMC we worked for would purchase us "economy" tickets from Kuwait, Jordan, Dubai or wherever back to the continental United States for our R&R leave rotations home. Several expats would pay additional money or our own to upgrade to "economy plus" or something. I remember boarding the plane behind Soup at the front and after the flight attendant looked at his ticket stub, he went to the left. In my brain, I'm thinking he's going to talk to the pilot or something.

I turn to the right and walk past all the people sitting in the First-Class section, then past the Business section, then past the Economy Plus section with the extra leg room, all the way back to the PMC company purchased seats in the Economy section with the rest of the team members. We land, and I find out Soup was sleeping in seat number 1 or 2, way up front in a bed. How did you do that brother? He explains to me that you can get an airline company credit card, and pay ALL your bills with that card. Mortgage, cars, everything, because each purchase racks up equivalent frequent flier mile points – which he used for an upgrade. Man, I was always learning from him.

The other guy, Nomad, well he earned his call-sign right there on graduation day.

As we were filling out paperwork, the HR personnel from the PMC told us that we would receive our training bonus of a certain number of dollars per, for every day of training. Since we graduated, we would receive that bonus and those who didn't complete the training would not. Additionally, we were required to remain committed to that PMC for a period of a few weeks after graduation. They would pay us a daily stipend just to remain at home a few days, until a position opening occurred down range in theatre. If after a certain period of time, whatever it was, if we had not been deployed by then: then we would be released from our contractual obligations with them and were free to work with another PMC. Most of us had a new Home of Record (HOR) or a temporary address until deployment, except him. After going back and forth with the HR administrator about his home address, he was asked, "If you get killed down range, where will we ship your body?" "Where will you go and wait, exactly at what location, until we call you with an assignment down-range"?

His answer was funny, even until this day.

He replied, *"I'm going back to my room (the hotel rooms they leased for us), until you deploy me or until y'all put me out on the street!"*

He literally had no address, and was given the call-sign Nomad that day!

Funny guy.

I was called Bilal (Sergeant Bilal for almost 20 years & then Mr. Bilal for years) until I arrived in Baghdad, Iraq on the U.S. DoS WPPS program in NOV 2007.

That's when I was bestowed the call-sign Shadow.

But even if someone had negative intentions when they bestowed that call-sign upon me, that could have all been in my mind, because almost everything in this world is based upon your perception. Maybe it had nothing to do with me being black at all. Maybe I am just a big guy who blocks out the sun when you're standing before me by casting some shade or a shadow on you. Although, I just have always been trying to bring you light.

Someone once told me, *"Shadow you're the only shadow that I know that gives light."*

So regardless of whatever situations related to the evolution of my current name or moniker, no matter what someone calls me: *I Know Who I Am!*

As I have said before, each person has two parents, four grandparents, eight great-grandparents, 16 great-great-grandparents and 32 great-great-great-grandparents, and so on, and so on.

There are about 32 great-great-great-grandparents for each person if you go back tracing just five generations from yourself.

**I proclaim myself to be an "American" period.**

An aboriginal original American by my Birth Right. I am one of the descendants of the original copper-colored people, the european explorers found when they first got here to this New World.

My people were born right here in what is called North & South America, and are "original" to this land. My people have been on this land for a very long time.

Don't believe me, go argue with them giant Olmec head statues of black people that have been discovered right here in North America, from an Olmec society that developed in what is now called Mexico, at least 1500 B.C. (that's about 3,517 years ago).

As a very famous man once said, *"We Didn't Land On Plymouth Rock, Plymouth Rock Landed On Us!"*

Another famous man whose birthday we celebrate every year on the third Monday in January said, during his famous "I Have A Dream" speech; *"One Hundred Years Later [after the Emancipation Proclamation] The Negro [currently erroneously referred to as African-Americans] Is Still Languished In The Corners Of American Society And Finds Himself In Exile – In His Own Land!"*

I really like the mentality of some people who proclaim that, *"we want our country back"* and *"Make America Great Again!"* Because this is my country. I can trace my lineage back to several of my ancestors, some to the 1700's. Some people ignorantly tell black folks to go back to Africa, when they themselves are children of parents who were born in other countries. Some are grandchildren or children of recent european immigrants, who have no historical authority to tell someone who was already living here, who is a real American and who isn't.

I can say that I am the descendant of an *Indigenous American* because I am Muhammad Bilal (also known as Brother Shadow), son of Alwillie Jamison (my mother), daughter of Richardean Moody (my grandmother), daughter of Charlie Moody (my maternal great-grandfather), son of Momma Hightower (my great-great-grandmother) who was an Original American.

I can say that I am the descendant of a *Native American* because I am Muhammad Bilal (also known as Brother Shadow), son of Eddie Akbar (my father), son of Robert "Bob" Cooper (my paternal grandfather), son of Ida Mae Postell (my paternal great-grandmother), daughter of Kit (my great-great-grandmother) who was a Seminole Indian.

Some ignorant people still say, well Shadow, since you claim to be a "black man" (instead of an unhyphenated-American) why don't you just go back to your country - Africa.

To those ignorant people I say, *"why don't you give me a ride there, while you're on your way back to whatever country you came from! Beside Africa is NOT even a country, it is an entire continent with 55 individual countries on it, you big dummy."*

Additionally, I have already gone back to Africa; several times.

I just explained that my ancestral claims are to this land right here, in the United States of America, especially since some of my ancestors were enslaved here and built this country "for free". However, please don't think that I am disavowing my lineage from the African continent. If fact, if historians and anthropologist are correct, we ALL originate "out of Africa". That means all human life on this plane of existence, came from the African continent and I can trace exactly which areas my ancestors originate from.

*Nigeria* by way of my unnamed maternal great-great-grandmother (my grandfather's grandmother) of Nigerian Ancestry who was the mother of my great-grandfather Wilbur Jamison (my grandfather's father) who was the father of my maternal grandfather Willie Jamison, who was the father of Alwillie Jamison, who is my mother.

*Ghana* by way of my maternal great-great-grandmother (my grandmother's grandmother) Louise who was the mother of my great-grandmother (my grandmother's mother) Almeda Dowling who was the mother of my maternal grandmother Richardeen Moody, who was the mother of Alwillie Jamison, who is my mother.

**Of my 16 great-great-grandparents, 15 of them were melinated people of color. Either Native American, Indigenous American, Black-American or an African. One of them was of european ancestry and was an Irishman.**

I also acknowledge the *Irish* ancestry I have by way of my maternal great-great-great-grandfather Harry Dowling who was the father of my great-great-grandfather Eddie Dowling, who was the father of my great-grandmother Almeda Dowling who was the mother of my maternal grandmother Richardeen Moody, who was the mother of Alwillie Jamison, who is my mother. But that would confuse many of you who don't know that back in the day there was no unified "white nationalist identity" here in the United States.

The English fought the Irish, the Germans fought the French, and just about every person of european decent claimed their ancestral lineage from their specific country of origin, and not the entire "continent of europe".

Members of the dominate society here in America used to refer to each other as Germans, or Frenchmen, or Italians, or whatever their national country of origin was. Racism as we know it in the United States, didn't really start until after Bacon's Rebellion in 1676 when members of all classes of society (black & white people together) revolted up against the ruling elite class in our country. The powers that be needed to divide and distract the mass of people (both black & white) so that they would never unite again, and rise up against the power structure.

You see the ruling elite knew that if the common people ever stopped fighting each other, and realized that they were all being oppressed by the same people; it would be game over for the elite.

So only about 5% of the population know the truth about, how the 10% of the ruling class, control the 85% of the masses of people.

If they can pit people against each other, and the most basic and easiest method is to pit white against black, they could continue to rule and oppress the masses.

A very ancient African proverb is "Man - Know Thyself"! If you do NOT know where you came from, how will you know where you are going? Start by researching your name and its origin, you may learn something about yourself that you never knew.

But it all starts with – a name.

**2**

CHAPTER TWO
# NEGATIVITY IS CONTAGIOUS

*U.S. Army Special Forces training is extremely voluntary; I did not say voluntary - I said extremely voluntary. Over 40-years ago, with the ending of the United States of America's involvement in the Vietnam conflict, the US military began ending the conscript induction (or military draft) service, and on 01 JUL 1973 the US military became an all-volunteer force. It remains an all-volunteer force today for all branches of the military. If a person voluntarily enlists in the U.S. Army, they would still have to volunteer again to receive additional "special training" because special forces training is not mandatory and not available to everyone.*

*First of all, you have to be already in the military and have achieved the rank of Corporal or Specialist and the pay grade of (E-4).*

*Yes, there are exceptions to every rule.*

*Yes, there is a such thing as people enlisting "right off the street" with a guaranteed contract to go (try-out) for Special Forces. Yes, I have seen Privates of various ranks within SF training; PVT's, PV2's or PFC's – but all of those are the exception not the norm for two very important reasons.*

*First when you add the administrative process, the hold times, all the training and phases involved, plus language school training – you will realize that Special Forces is not just a school. In fact, it is a specific Military Occupational Specialty (MOS) or job within the Army. You can go to*

49

Airborne School and still be whatever your individual MOS is. You can go to Ranger School and still be whatever your individual MOS is. You can go to defensive/offensive anti-terrorism tactical driving training and still be whatever your individual MOS is. However, even if you are a first time go in every phase of U.S. Army Special Forces training to include language school you will probably be in SF training for longer than 52 weeks, so we're talking "years" of training to learn something. Upon successful completion, you will then be re-classified into a Special Forces operational MOS in the 18-numerical series (18B, 18C, 18D or 18E). No way to do all that if you didn't want to volunteer, plus it would be a colossal waste of money and resources.

Second there is an unwritten and unspoken norm within the SF community, that is not only what the SF community can do for you, but what are you bringing to the community. Back then you had to already serve a certain number of months/years in the regular "big" army before you "went SF." Then, when and if you made it, not only would you have the additional "special" training; you would be bringing into the SF community; skill sets that are valuable and immeasurable like; bandmember, air-condition repairer, motor vehicle mechanic, etc., etc.

Either way you also had to be the right age.

You could enlist in the US military at 17 years of age with your parents' permission, like I did, but you could not go try out for SF until you were at least 20 years old; unless you got a waiver. You also couldn't go SF if you were too old, or over the age of 30 either.

Regardless of your age, you had to score a certain number of points on the U.S. Army's Physical Fitness Test (APFT) which is broken down by event and age group. You had to score the required minimum number of points in each event, in the 17 to 21-year old age category regardless of what your individual age was.

Must have 20/20 vision (or corrected) and meet medical fitness standards as outlined in a SF Physical Army Regulation (AR). Many soldiers who meet and exceed the military and the Army's physical fitness standards do not meet the minimum physical standards to even apply for SF training.

There is another critical physical fitness performance event that must be completed and that is the SF swim test, wearing complete duty uniform to include boots, normally conducted directly after the APFT.

Then you had to be smart, and you still do. If you were not a high school graduate you may have gotten a waiver to enlist in the military, but you had to be a high school graduate, score extremely high on the Armed Services Vocational Aptitude Battery (ASVAB) and it is preferred that you have at least one-year of college completed. Special Forces training is so advanced that Special Forces Qualification Course (SFQC) graduates can bring their military training Joint Service Transcript (JST) to their local community college and according to the American Council on Education (ACE) they will already have the necessary transfer credits for an Associate Degree (A.S.) in General Studies upon completion.

You must be a U.S. citizen. There are some soldiers in the U.S. Army who are legal residents of the United States but are not US citizens. You can enlist in the US military depending on your immigration status, but In-Accordance-With (IAW) federal law you cannot become a warrant or commissioned officer if you are not a US citizen.

Additionally, you cannot become U.S. Army Special Forces qualified if you are not a US citizen.

When in the Big Army I remember a time as a Squad Leader when one of my junior NCO's told me he was getting out of the army. I encouraged him to re-enlist (re-up) like all soldiers who believe in the military encourage others to do. He told me he wanted to, but because he wasn't a US citizen he had to get out: he had reached his service limit which was five years back then I believe. Confused I thought, what do you mean you're not a US citizen. He said, "Sergeant I'm a Jamaican citizen because I was born on that Caribbean island, not in the US". I told him, but you're a Sergeant in the U.S. Army. Regardless, rules are rules and Army regulations are regs that cannot be broken; without a waiver.

You had to complete a series of prerequisites at your individual military unit before you showed up to attempt the SF training. You will culminate by running about 3 miles a day at 6 to 7-minute per mile pace, 500-meter swim using any stroke except your back, ruck marching with a minimum of a 50 pack on your back for at least 18 miles and a host of other events. Even if you do all the events you still had only a 78% chance of completing the SFAS course – before you get selected to attend SFQC.

You must be Airborne qualified or volunteer for Airborne training, no exceptions.

There are service members that attend the U.S. Army Ranger training school who are not airborne qualified. The norm is to become an airborne ranger in one of the operational battalions of the Ranger Regiment. There are several military leaders who attend Ranger training and many of them do not attend airborne school before they go back (or on) to their parent military unit. They are considered non-airborne Rangers or referred to with the derogatory term "Leg" as in a Leg Ranger.

But there is no such thing as leg in Special Forces, period.

If there is an exception to this, I have never heard of it during 20 years of active duty, 10 years since I've retired, and I still live in the Fort Bragg / Fayetteville, NC community to this day.

Plus, you must have or be eligible for a "Secret" level security clearance, which is not required of all soldiers, but is required of all Special Forces soldiers.

I explain all these perquisites to highlight how difficult it is for someone to attend SF training, now completing all the training "and" getting selected at the end is a whole different story.

The U.S. Army will send a soldier to training on a Temporary Duty (TDY) basis, meaning they will attend field sanitation training, air assault school, ranger school or whatever school/training and then return them to their parent unit. But if that soldier was married with children, his/her family members would remain at his parent duty station until their return.

If a school is over 179 days long, the U.S. Army will normally move, called a - Permanent Change of Station (PCS), that soldier to the next duty station because it is the most cost-effective way.

So, if a soldier is stationed at Fort Drum, NY and has been there for several years, he may come down on PCS orders to go to his new duty station in Alaska at Fort Richardson near the city of Anchorage. If that soldier was an

*Infantryman in the 10ᵗʰ Mountain Division at Fort Drum, NY and was going to Fort Benning, GA to attend Airborne School. That solider would attend Airborne School (jump school) in a TDY basis for 3 to 4 weeks enroute and then proceed to their new unit at Fort Richardson, AK.*

*But here is a situation the military was faced with.*

*Many people have heard that in 1966 a Vietnam Veteran and Green Beret named Barry Sadler wrote a song with Robin Moore called the "Ballad of the Green Berets". It remained at Number One on the Billboard Hot 100 for five weeks, was the #1 Single of the Year for 1966 and was a crossover smash hit in easy listening & country.*

*The lyrics were written in honor of U.S. Army Specialist 5 James Gabriel, Jr. (Green Beret) the first native Hawaiian to die in Vietnam, who was killed by Viet Cong gunfire while on a training mission 08 APR 1962.*

*One verse of the song mentioned Gabriel by name, but it wasn't included in the recorded version.*

*Since song lyrics can NOT be quoted in a book without the proper clearance from the writer, owner, publisher, etc. I will only allude to a prominent verse.*

*Where 100 men wearing Airborne wings try to earn the coveted "Green Beret" but only 3 complete the task.*

*I love that song, particularly because I graduated the U.S. Army's Special Forces training courses, and earned my "Green Beret".*

*But the U.S. Army is just one component of the U.S. military at the Department of Defense (DoD) and the DoD is just one part of the entire U.S. government's apparatus. At the end of the day, the bean counters (accountants, auditors & politicians) understand that even though we cannot drop the standards of the most elite training units in the military if we want to maintain their lethality. There is no way the attrition rate is 97%, so somebody must do something about it.*

*Here is an example of what I witnessed serving in the military during the early 1980's, before SFAS was created. For example; say a "Sergeant Smith" is stationed at Fort Riley, Kansas and has a unique MOS. After years in Kansas* the U.S. Army decides it's time to PCS Sergeant Smith to Grafenwoehr, Germany. So, they move SGT Smith his wife, kids, the dog, the truck and all his household belonging to his new duty station. As soon as he arrives there, SGT Smith volunteers for SF training (I've been to Grafenwoehr and I know soldiers who would volunteer to go to the stockade or combat rather than stay there). Anyway, when SGT Smith volunteers for SF training which is at Fort Bragg, NC; the U.S. Army now must PCS SGT Smith his wife, kids, the dog, the truck and all his household belonging now to his new-new duty station in North Carolina.

Why because as I stated earlier that SF training is longer than 180 days, and normally nobody is going to get paid TDY funds for that long of a duration – it's just cheaper to PCS them.

Now say during his SF training, SGT Smith doesn't make it to the end, or is dropped from training for some reason, he now is sent to another parent unit on Fort Bragg to serve out the remainder of his enlistment. The problem is SGT Smith's MOS is so unique, that no unit on Fort Bragg has it, so he must be PCS'ed again to a unit that requires him. So, if that unit is at, say Fort Bliss, TX for example; then the U.S. Army now must PCS the good SGT Smith, his wife, kids, the dog, the truck and all his household belonging to his new duty station in Texas.

The U.S. Army is a big machine and soldiers can get lost in the clogs of that machinery, but some bean counter somewhere said, "Wait a minute". Something is extremely wrong with this here and requires investigation. Only 3 out of every 100 men will win the Green Beret, but what happens to the other 97 of them.

Well upon investigation it was determined that many of the 97% that fail, do not fail academically. They don't fail because of a medical injury or a medical disqualification. They don't fail the physical events, no matter how hard they may be. Many of them just quit when the training got hard - and it got hard, on day one. Many of them quit or "Voluntary Withdrew" (VW) from training because they never wanted to be there in the first place.

Or because they were disillusioned about what it takes to be the best of the best.

So, the U.S. Army said, lets fix this extremely high attrition rate during the first phase of training or the first 30 days. Let's create a program BEFORE service members attend SFQC and let's call it Sore Feet And Shoulders (SFAS). Let's make the training TDY and let's smoke their bags to see if they really want to be here in the first place. Let's physically torment them, make them carry tanks and run forever and never sleep and see if they really want to be here. Of course, you all know I am being sarcastic as too the origin of SFAS's creation, because I really don't know. But I do know it's called Special Forces Assessment & Selection course and it's held at a satellite base of Fort Bragg. I say service members because many candidates are not regular army soldiers, some are members of the sister armed services (Marines, Air Force, Navy). Some are members of allied forces (but there are things they will not see in training because they are not US citizens). I'm not going to tell you what happens there as I explained in the forward. But what I will tell you is that if you don't want to be in SFAS, you will have ample time to VW, in fact you are encouraged to VW and quit before you waste valuable training resources, time and possible injure or kill yourself.

Negativity is contagious.

So, in SFAS when you are tired, sleepy, hungry, in pain and woefully out of your depth; the ever present SFAS Cadre will make you an offer you can't refuse. They do it all the time, so when you decide to take the cadre's offer to quit or Voluntary Withdraw (VW) from training, you can go to the shack of shame for a hot shower, coffee, donuts and you are immediately removed from training.

I mean immediately.

I remember talking to other candidates and turning around and the ones that were standing behind me were gone. An instructor may say something like, prepare for the 50-mile road march in 30 minutes, and people would quit. I'm not saying there was such an event, I'm saying that once one person got the defeatist attitude and the spirit of negativity in him – it was contagious. He would cause other people to doubt themselves and they would quit too.

Once you VW'ed you were immediately transferred to another barracks. The entire training compound was under revitalization and new barracks, buildings and a Dining Facility (DFAC) or mess hall was built in the late

*1980's early 1990's. The building that held the people who quit, or the VW's was called the "Shack of Shame".*

*The look on the faces of many of those who were inside that shack was shameful. As we would see them peer from the windows or stand outside it was pitiful. I know most of them hated being in there. I know many of them wanted to be shipped back to the main post of Fort Bragg to outprocess as soon as possible, so they wouldn't have to see the looks they received from cadre and other candidates still in training. That look was the saddest look you ever wanted to receive. Even the civilians that served you food in the DFAC served you with shame and pity.*

*I know, because before I graduated the SFAS and SFQC – I failed SFAS the first time I tried and was in the, "the Shack of Shame."*

***

In the late 1980's I was an Infantryman MOS 11B stationed at Fort Richardson, Alaska with the then 6th Infantry Division (Artic Light).

I enlisted in the military while still in high school during my junior year under the U.S. Army's Delayed Entry Program (DEP) in 1982, from the US military Recruiting Station on Fordham Road in the Bronx, New York. So, 11 months later after I graduated from Theodore Roosevelt High School (now defunct), across the street from Fordham University, I served on active duty for 4 years, from 1983-1987.

After I ETS'ed from active duty I, like almost all soldiers, still had a military commitment obligation within the original enlistment contract to serve in the Individual Ready Reserve (IRR). In lieu of serving in the inactive IRR, I chose to serve in the Simultaneous Membership Program (SMP). Where I would be a MOS 09S performing two functions simultaneously: first I would be a member of the U.S. Army Reserve / National Guard, and second I would be a full-time college student at a local university.

In JAN 1989 after that break from active duty, I re-enlisted in the U.S. Army as 11B. Being prior service I only had to attend the Advance Individual Training (AIT) portion for a new MOS since I was reclassifying from my prior service MOS of 35K Avionic Mechanic and had already attended basic training.

My new MOS of 11B Infantry is only taught at Fort Benning, Georgia for active duty U.S. Army soldiers, and since it is also a basic training location, all infantrymen attend both Basic (BCT) & Advanced Individual Training (AIT) together at that location.

Fort Benning, Georgia is considered the Home of the Infantry, and both the BCT & AIT is combined into a continuous 16-week program called One Station Unit Training (OSUT). So as a SP4/E-4, I re-enlisted and attended the wonderful training evolution of those service members who wear an Infantry Blue Cord decoration over and under the right shoulder & epaulette of our dress uniform top, and infantry blue disc behind our Individual Branch and US Insignia on our dress uniforms.

Echo Company, 1st Battalion/19th Infantry at Sandhill (old Infantryman called it Sand Hilton) was where I became an 11B Infantryman, before PCS'ing to Fort Richardson, Alaska.

While serving as an 11B in Alaska, I distinctly remember volunteering for SF training. I was a very motivated young soldier and my 2-mile run time was 10:15 at its best. There was so much support when I left Fort Richardson, TDY, for Fort Bragg to attend SFAS. Everyone I knew in my unit encouraged me to go. Everyone had tips and pointers on how to successfully complete that training. Strangers that I encountered on base as I prepared to depart to the lower-48 states were full of stories about their brother or uncle or somebody who was a U.S. Army Green Beret. I cannot recall one person who discouraged me. Since I was one of the fastest runners in my unit, I thought I was the best.

There is a phrase in SF that I had to learn the hard way.

| **NEVER FIRST, NEVER LAST, NEVER LATE, NEVER LIGHT** |
|:---:|
| **NEVER** |

I didn't completely understand that phrase until I learned it, the hard way.

If you are always first, and the fastest, and the best; you are probably not a very good team player and will have a very difficult time succeeding in an environment where individualism could get you killed.

So, I was told something that sounded like this. *"Thanks for trying out for SFAS, but you're not what we're looking for at this time. However, when you return to your parent unit to train some more, in about six-months you are welcome to re-apply and return here to try to complete SFAS again".*

I was told that I should be honored, because many people are told they didn't make it – and they are **forbidden** from returning to try again.

It seemed like every person I ran into upon my return back up to Alaska was now negative towards me.

> *"I knew you weren't going to make it!"*
> *"You thought you were better than us, well well look at you now?!?"*
> *"It was harder than you thought, huh?"*

I could probably write a book about all the negativity that I received and how contagious it was. Once one person made a negative comment towards me, it seemed like every person in the vicinity would chime in – with negativity.

What hurt me most, was the people that I thought believed and supported me and my vision who turned negative on me. Jealousy is just a part of interacting with other humans, the grass always seems greener on the other side. But when people that I looked up to turned on me it really hurt.

The U.S. Army is built on negative reinforcement.

> *"Half-Right Face"*!

That is the command all soldiers standing in a formation will hear before the mass punishment begins. The next command is, "Front Lean and Rest Position Move"! The front lean and rest position is the starting position for the push-up exercise, and corrective push-ups are the start for almost all corrective training for junior enlisted soldiers in the U.S. Army.

Didn't do something correctly, *"Drop and give me 50 push-ups!"*

Late to formation, *"Drop and give me 50 push-ups while I write your counseling statement!"*

Forgot to shave this morning, *"Drop and do push-ups!"*

You didn't have your head on a swivel and see that [commissioned] officer walk past you, or you were day dreaming, so you didn't or forgot salute him. He chewed me out for that, so now I'm going to PT you, so you won't ever forget again.

*"Get in the front lean and rest position!"*
*"Mountain climb!"*
*"Bear Crawl!"*

Years later my introduction to another famous unit went something like this. Sergeant Bilal, *"Welcome to the unit, you see that piece of shit Private in the hallway? You take him outside and smoke his sorry ass, and when he come back inside he better be sweating, if not: I going to smoke you."*

But the worst type of negative reinforcement is when the entire unit gets smoked for something someone else did or did not do.

120 men outside at 05:30 hours (5:30am) getting ready for a 5-mile run together and the temperature is only 12 degrees outside. If one person "forgot" to bring their gloves, so we don't look uniform together, now we all must remove our gloves.

120 men in an Infantry Company standing in the rain and one person forgot his wet-weather gear, so now everyone must remove his poncho or whatever, and get wet.

But my favorite is when one-person messes up off-duty; DWI, speeding ticket, shoplifting, whatever. So now everyone except that person is going to receive negative reinforcement training so they don't want to make the same mistake.

*"Half-Right Face!"*
*"Front Lean and Rest Position, Move!"*

I don't know when it happened to me, but I had been seeing it all my military career. People who could take a negative situation and turn it into an extremely positive one. "Oh, were surrounded, good, now we can attack and fire in all directions".

In 1984, I attended and graduated the U.S. Army's Airborne School at Fort Benning, GA. During the first week or phase of training at airborne school where remedial PT and punishment is the standard for everything, in an attempt to toughen you up for the parachute landing falls (PLF's); I, like most other soldiers, was in awe of the airborne school instructors who wore the Black baseball caps with their uniforms. The instructors were called, "Sergeant Airborne" and because of their headgear they were referred to as "Black Hats". The training unit I was in was called the 42nd Company at the time and was the second building from the street. We were lined up for the first formation of the first day when the Blackhats were instilling respect for their authority and absolute obedience to their commands, so you don't accidently get yourself killed doing the dangerous activity of jumping out of an airplane in flight.

Well I remember there were some Sailors from the US Navy in our training class, and when we were given the command to "Stand at Attention" and don't move – I vividly remember a Sailor from the last rank throwing a (red or purple) Smoke Grenade from the back rank over the entire platoon towards the front where the Airborne Instructors were at.

*WTF?!?*

*"You can't smoke us, we brought our own smoke,"* is what they yelled!

> *"Half-Right Face!"*
> *"Front Lean and Rest Position, Move!"*
> *"In cadence, exercise!"*
> One-Two-Three, **ONE!**
> One-Two-Three, **TWO!**
> One-Two-Three, **THREE!**
> One-Two-Three, **FOUR!**
> One-Two-Three, **FIVE!**
> One-Two-Three, **SIX!**

Man, did those Blackhats smoke our bags (or so I thought at the time). That was one of the first times in the military that I realized that negativity is contagious – so you must change it into positivity or remove from your life, period. I witnessed those sailors, I don't know if they were U.S. Navy Seals yet. But those sailors would shout out ZERO every time the cadence was called for us to do the four-count exercise of push-up.

*"One-Two-Three, **ZERO!**"*
*"One-Two-Three, **ZERO!**"*
*"One-Two-Three, **ZERO!**"*
*"One-Two-Three, **ZERO!**"*

They were teaching me a lesson that I would later use in my life to succeed during moments of adversity. Life gives me pain; embrace the pain, really like the pain, enjoy the pain, in fact ask for more pain, and once life determines that you really like the pain – it stops becoming pain.

I took all that negativity that I was receiving in Alaska and turned it into the positive leadership that I needed. Leadership according to the U.S. Army is to provide the proper Purpose, Direction and Motivation necessary to accomplish a given task.

I knew six-months later when I returned to Fort Bragg for SFAS, SFQC and some other training that I would complete the courses. Because I had resolved to the fact that I was going to graduate the entire training evolution, whatever it was, earn my Special Forces Tab and Green beret, or I was going to die trying, either way I was not coming back to the big army as a failure because that just wasn't an option to me.

Graduate and continue my career or die in training and get awarded those accolades and honors posthumously, but either way I was going to graduate.

Years later I would read a book that expressed this frequency I was now operating on. It was an expression of absolute positivity and belief that something was going to materialize. If I could imagine something that was the first step. But if I could envision myself actually doing it, then I don't know how, I don't really care, I just know that it will be done.

If there was a task I wanted to accomplish like, say I want to be able to bench press 225 pounds on my own. Since that's only two 45-pound weight plates on the end of a 45-pound bar it could be done because I've seen it done before.

Images create your reality.

Next, I had to see myself benching that weight. I couldn't do it before, but I could actually visualize in my mind's eye, me doing that.

Well guess what, there is a lot of hard word that goes into doing it: but it will be done because I can envision myself doing it. Then I envisioned 315 pounds, then 405 pounds, then 495.

I never benched over 500 pounds before for one reason and one reason only.

It wasn't because of lack of training, or diet, or age, or anything else; it was only because since I never could envision myself doing it, I didn't believe it.

Since I didn't believe it, I could not achieve it.

The world record for bench press is like 730 pounds raw. Then there is a record of a bench press of over 1,000 pounds with equipment like gloves, a shirt, or wrist wraps. Bottom line is that it is possible, but only to those who believe it is possible and work to achieve that goal.

Imagine what the election of Barrack Obama did for the psyche (conscious and unconscious) of many people. I'm not talking about his politics; Republican, Democrat, Independent, Conservative or Liberal, that's your business. I'm talking about his physical presence as the 44th President of the United States. Many people where taught like me, that you can grow up to become anything you want to be in this country, in this world for that matter. But if you never saw something before, it's hard to imagine yourself in that position if you've never visualized it before. Just imagine 43 consecutive caucasian men as President of the United States and you're trying to tell a young kid who is not of predominantly european descent that he can grow up to become president. That's next to impossible because it's hard to accomplish something if you cannot visualize it.

I once told a fellow soldier who was caucasian to imagine if he lived in a country that was in Central Africa for example. Imagine that all 40 something Presidents of that country were black men for the last 200 years. Imagine that the images on all of the currency was of black men, imagine that all the country's heroes, all the images on all the stamps, all the statues of great men were of black men. Then to imagine me (or anyone else) telling him that he could grow up to become anything he wanted, even the first "white" president of that country.

It was at that moment that he understood the significance and the importance of images and I try to explain that to people every chance that I get.

Take a look at the following movies: *Night of the Living Dead (1968), Rosemary's Baby (1968), The Exorcist (1973) The Texas Chainsaw Massacre (1974), The Omen (1976), The Shining (1980), A Nightmare on Elm Street (1984), The Blair Witch Project (1999), Paranormal Activity (2009)* they all have one thing in common.

I have never seen any of them, and if I have my way: I don't intend on seeing any of them.

I have never watch a movie from the horror genre in my life. That don't make me worse or better than the next person, I'm just different. I just deliberately choose to not allow movies from that genre into my conscious or subconscious mind.

I love Action movies, and Thriller movies with a good plot, and Comedies – I mean who doesn't love a good Comedy Movie. But to combat the negativity that is so prevalent in this world I really love animated movies. I could watch the following animated movies on almost any given day: *The Lion King (1994), Toy Story (1995), A Bug's Life (1998), Shrek (2001), Finding Nemo (2003), The Incredibles (2004), Kung Fu Panda (2008), Up (2009), How to Train your Dragon (2010) and Zootopia (2016).*

What I don't get is how the movie industry does not stick to genres, it really bothers me when they attempt to cross market their movies during the previews. For example: *If I go to see an action movie in the movie theatre; why would they show previews to some horror movies?*

I'm not going to watch those and the few moments that you put your unsolicited horror movie previews up on the big screen, I'll be meditating, praying and thinking good thoughts and vibrations.

I do not do negativity, especially when it concerns the spirit world or that which does not agree with my soul. Many times, when it's difficult for a person to go or stay asleep, they are wrestling with the negative images and thoughts they put into their mind earlier that day.

Imagine watching a horror movie then going to sleep, waking up talking about you had a nightmare. Ninja please!

I have developed a business technique that I now use in my personal life. The business at **Shadow Protective Services, LLC** had grown at a rapid rate at one point (back when we were conducting the low-end static security jobs). If there was a contract that had, lest say 15 separate job sites, stores, apartment buildings or whatever locations need coverage, that would require a lot of manpower. Just 10 hours of coverage per day, per site is manpower extensive (10 hrs. day x 7 days x 15 sites = 1,050 hrs. week). Whereas even a full-time employee is only 40 hours per week, it would take 2 employees per site just to cover everything. So, you're already looking at 30 employees. Now add in the floater personnel and additional reserve persons needed for sick days and weekends (because this ain't the military).

In the military, you can work 7 days a week, with about 4 hours of sleep per night, and you're still going to get the exact same paycheck. There ain't no overtime. Plus, if you are as we say in the military "on the tip of the spear" and you're engaging enemy forces in combat, you may not even get that 4 hours of sleep. What you going to do, charge the enemy for overtime?!?

But in the civilian world, anything over 40 hours is overtime (time and one half) in most cases, and employees don't care about your overhead, they want to get paid.

Now imagine running the same project with part-time seasonal employees. So, you could easily have almost 50 employees and supervisors calling you, to ensure the project runs smoothly.

Then you have to add in the human factor of communication or should I say miscommunication. Well Shadow, *"I thought you said, be there at 9 pm instead of 8 pm."*

No, I said, **"20:00 hours, which is 8 pm in civilian time. But since you don't understand the 24-hour clock, there is no one at the site to relieve the guard that is still on duty."** He's not complaining because he's getting overtime pay, which the client is not paying me for.

So, I started "refusing to accept phone calls" and text only.

That way I had a written record of what was said. Plus, it was so much easier, limiting the nonessential communication to just text messages.

I normally tell every new employee to call me, once. Then to hang up and text me a professional photo for my phone contact roster with their full name and call-sign (nickname). That way "if" they ever needed to contact me in the event of an emergency, I knew exactly who was calling me.

But if they call me for any nonessential communications, we have a problem.

Everybody that knows me knows I don't do problems.

Only situations that need decisions, but I don't do problems.

*"If you have a problem that can be solved by money, then you don't have a problem"* You just have a temporary situation.

So now I keep 2 phones, a personal phone number and a business phone number. That business number is answered 24-hours a day, by an answering service and they filter all my incoming calls, business, professional, solicitations or whatever.

Then I have my personal number. If anyone calls my personal number that I did NOT give the number too, I'll ask them how did they get my number. If they said a certain person gave it to them, I'll block them and the person that gave the number to them. It's not personal, it's just business, because I need my sanity. I'm very approachable about a lot of things. But I'm very guarded about who I let into my personal space.

Because some people will bring you negativity, if you let them, and some people will betray you. The worst thing about betrayal is that the people who you know are your enemies will never betray you.

They can't, because you already don't trust them.

**Betrayal can only come from someone you trust.**

I once had a person that I thought was my good friend, whom I confided in a whole lot. I thought we were working together towards a common goal, when all along he was sabotaging my name, reputation and slandering me, every chance he got.

What hurt me more than anything, is that he would smile in my face while he was doing it, and I didn't know because I thought he was my friend.

I had never said a negative word against him, ever.

But out of the blue someone told me he was gossiping about me pretty bad. I didn't believe that person, at first because that just seems so out of character from the person that I knew. Then another person told me. Then another.

The fourth person really hurt. That person told me that the negative guy really wanted to "hire" him away from me, but whatever he did, *"don't tell Shadow."* I couldn't believe it, so I confronted the guy. *"What the heck is this I'm hearing about you hiring my people behind my back?!? After I get them all trained up, fingerprints ran, background checks, paid for them to get their registration cards, carrying them on my company liability and workmen's comp insurance, then you go and hire them: pay them under the table, behind my back? Then you tell them "not to tell me", what's up with that?!?"*

He doesn't even deny it, he actually says to me, *"I was just testing their loyalty for you brother!"*

That's like someone trying to talk to your woman behind your back, and you confront them about it, and they say, *"I was just testing her loyalty for ya brother!"*

So, my interactions with him became further and further apart.

I was part of an Executive Protection detail for a client, and months later I had to depart the detail. I received nothing from the Executive Protection (EP) agent I was relieving, when I first got on the detail. The person I was relieving (an off-duty LEO) actually said, *"Oh you're the new guy? Good-bye!"* as his tires left skid marks in the street because he departed so fast.

No proper hand-off, no right seat ride, no area orientation, nothing. I'm in a new city, with a new client, new principle (with a direct threat against their life), from known felons and this is what I get.

Well months later that same negative backstabbing person is going to be my relief, I'll call him "Negatron" since he is so negative and to keep it simple.

Remember, at this time I still didn't know the depths of his treachery. Months later he (Negatron) came on the EP detail right after me and guess what? At the time I didn't know he was backstabbing me, so I set him up for success. When Negatron arrives in this particular city to relieve me, I give him the proper hand-off. I did a personal dossier of the principle to ensure that he, as the new "Executive Protection Specialist" would be able to not only keep the principle alive. But he would be able to do it with the upmost efficiency, and the most accurate information available. The principals' allergies, favorite radio stations, the preferred temperature in the limo, everything he needed to be successful.

Guess what Negatron did?

*HE GOT HIMSELF FREAKING FIRED FOR FALLING ASLEEP ON THE JOB!!!*

*How in the hell can you do that?*

*Your job is to keep a person "ALIVE" who has a death threat against their life, and you fucking fall asleep?!?*

I was back in Fayetteville/Fort Bragg, North Carolina area when I got that sad information and I couldn't believe it. But it was true. The guy who was secretly competing with me (*and I didn't even know it*), had just gotten fired for committing one of the most egregious acts a protector could possible commit.

Sleeping on the job.

*But wait, there's more!*

He gets back to the Fayetteville/Fort Bragg, North Carolina area and tells people that *"he had to go take my place because "I" fell asleep on the job."*

*WTF?!?*

*You don't want to do the hard work that I do, you take credit for the good that I do, and now you're trying to place the blame for the mistakes that YOU made as if "I" committed them.*

So yeah, I stay as far away from negative people as possible. They can be real "tricky", but once a person shows you who they really are, believe them. The first time.

✳✳✳

I had a guy text me once and the text said, *"Call me"*.
*"No, you can text me, what do ya need?"*

*"Can I borrow $10,000 dollars?"*

Yes, he actually asked to borrow ten grand. *Well, first of all I don't have ten grand to loan you. Even if I did, what makes you think I would "loan" it to you?*

**So, my new rule about money is, anybody can borrow, any amount of money they want from me, at any time, for any reason. They just have to follow two simple rules:**

> <u>First rule:</u> You have to pay me back, no matter what!

> <u>Second rule:</u> You can only "borrow" from me, up to half the amount that you have ever loaned to me in your entire life.

*Example; if over the course of our lifetimes, you have loaned me a sum total of $500 dollars. Well you can now borrow $250 at any time, for any reason, but you still have to pay me back (see rule number one).*

But for many people rule number two makes it real simple, because they have never loaned me "anything" in their entire lives, zero, nadda, nothing.

So, half of nothing is nothing, simple.

If I get a text message from someone that says, *"call me"*.

Just know that I'm not going to call you.

Whatever you want to talk to me about, you can text me. Because from experience if you can't text it, and you don't have my personal number, it's probably something negative. And as I have explained in detail during this past chapter, I don't do negativity – because negativity is contagious.

**3**

# NUMBERS DON'T LIE

*As I have stated earlier in this book, I attended SFAS the first time in 1990, and did not pass.*

*I returned to SFAS in early 1991 and was eventually selected for Special Forces training and attendance at SFQC.*

*When I attended SFAS I distinctly remember the Commanding General (CG) of the United States Army John Fitzgerald Kennedy Special Warfare Center & School (USAJFKSWC) talking to all of us candidates in a large auditorium together. I remember the CG because years before that time, he was the Commanding Officer of the 1st Special Forces Group (Airborne) and the Group Commander as a full bird Colonel; when I was assigned to the 1st SFG(A) in a support capacity. Now he was the CG, I didn't expect any special treatment, in fact he probably didn't even know who I was, (remember I was initially a member of the Support or Service Company and not a Special Forces "Operator", there is a big difference).*

*Additionally, back in the Infantry unit I came from up in Fort Richardson, Alaska I was one of the best soldiers in my unit according to the U.S. Army's standards.*

*Infantry soldiers have two special awards that we covet in addition to all the other special skill set qualification badges and tabs. That's the Combat Infantryman Badge (CIB) and the Expert Infantryman Badge (EIB).*

Not to dilute or tarnish the CIB, because almost everyone in the U.S. Army wants one. They want one so much so that the non-infantry (everyone else in the U.S. Army, like 90%) have created a similar award: called the Combat Action Badge (CAB), since the CIB is only awarded to Infantry & SF personnel in combat.

But what is well known throughout the Infantry community is that "every Infantryman or Special Forces soldier" who serves in combat will get awarded the CIB.

Although it is an individual award and not a unit award, once the unit deploys to a combat zone, almost every infantryman assigned to that unit, in theatre, will eventually get awarded a CIB.

There are many Infantrymen who fought with extreme hardships and gave their blood, sweat and tears, many of them have died.

Some Infantrymen are assigned to the most desolate and remote outposts, conducting combat patrols daily. Many infantrymen have had their Forward Operating Base (FOB) camps and Combat Operating Post (COP) sites under constant, if not daily, attack by enemy mortars and rockets.

Then there are those Infantrymen who never even leave the FOB for whatever reason; be it medical limitations, personal, or luck of the draw.

Someone has to stay back at the FOB and guard the remaining weapons in a weapons room at all times, someone has to guard the base while the rest of us are out on patrol. So, although the CIB is coveted by all Infantryman, and envied by many in a support capacity who cannot earn it (because they are not Infantryman). The CIB must still be backed up verbally by reputation, location and time of service. Otherwise how would anyone know you were not a FOBBIT who never deployed outside the wire or engaged the enemy forces in direct combat.

That is not the case with the Expert Infantryman Badge (EIB) because the EIB is only awarded after a soldier completes a course of testing that demonstrates he has proficiency in Infantry skills: on the Expert Level.

The EIB test is conducted by various infantry battalions throughout the U.S. Army and is normally administered by other infantry personnel from another *unit, who are holders or were awarded the EIB. If an infantry battalion has 400-500 soldiers assigned, normally only about 50 or 60 will earn the EIB during the testing period, that's about 10 infantrymen per company.*

*The test consists of about 37 separate individual tasks that must be performed expertly (step by step) in a very specific sequential order.*

*Some of the tasks include an Army Physical Fitness Test (APFT), Day and Night Land Navigation, 12-mile Forced Road March and over 30 other individual tests; on First Aid procedures, Chemical Biological Radiological Nuclear (CBRN) procedures, Call for Indirect Fire, Techniques for Movement under Fire (by the book), Camouflage, Hand and Arm Signaling, Range and Distance Estimation, Communications procedures with a Field Radio, Map Reading, Terrain Identification, Military GPS, Weapons proficiency like; load, unload, perform functions check, clear, correct malfunctions on various infantry weapons (pistols, rifles, grenade launchers, rocket launchers, anti-armor weapons, hand grenade & mines (both anti-personnel & anti-armor), M249(5.56mm) SAW light machinegun, M240(7.62mm) medium machine gun and the M2(.50 caliber) heavy machine gun.*

*If any infantryman fails a task with a NO-GO rating, he must "retake" that specific test, on that tasks, and receive a GO rating.*

*Strike One!*

*If he fails "another" second task with a NO-GO rating, he must retest on that particular task also to receive a GO.*

*Strike Two!*

*If he fails a third task with a NO-GO, he is NOT ELIGIBLE to retake it, and is considered a NO-GO for the entire EIB testing period, and will NOT receive the EIB award.*

*Strike Three, you're OUT!*

*Additionally, if any infantryman fails the re-test on any one task (a double NO-GO) he is also considered a NO-GO for the entire EIB testing period and will not receive the EIB award that year.*

*Pop-up flyball is caught, you're OUT!*

> *A double NO-GO on any one task and you're out of the running.*
> *More than 2 NO-GO's total, and you're out the running.*

*If an infantryman gets all first time GO's at all 37 stations, he (or she now) is considered "True Blue" EIB.*

*The EIB test is administered only once per year by a unit, so if you're a NO-GO you're told, "better luck next time, see you next year". There are many senior military leaders in the infantry community who have earned the CIB, but have failed to earn the EIB so many times; that they just stop trying to get it. It's common to hear from some Infantrymen who do not have both awards say, "I don't need a EIB because I have a CIB".*

*Well anyway, during my Infantry Battalions EIB testing term, I was the "only soldier" in my company to earn it.*

*The only one.*

*The Army has a test to determine the physical fitness level of its soldiers, called the Army Physical Fitness Test (APFT). Soldiers are graded on three separate events; push-ups, sit-ups and a 2-mile run.*

- *A soldier has 2 minutes to complete as many correct push-ups as they can perform, correctly.*

- *Then they have 2-minutes to complete as many sit-ups as they can perform, correctly.*

- *Then they must run on a measured 2-mile course as fast as they can, within an allotted time.*

*The maximum score is 100 points in each event, broken down by age group and gender, for a total of 300 possible points.*

*The minimum passing score is 60 points in each event, for a total minimum passing score of 180 (60+60+60) out of 300 (100+100+100) total possible points.*

*Example; if a male soldier can complete 70 push-ups within the 2-minute allotted time frame, he would earn the following points:*

> *99 points (17-21 years old)*
> *94 points (22-26 years old)*
> *93 points (27-31 years old)*
> *95 points (32-36 years old)*
> *97 points (37-41 years old)*

*If a soldier was over 41 years of age, and did the exact same 70 push-ups within 2-minutes on their APFT they would mathematically "max out" at 100 points.*

*So, they "could" continue to be scored on an extended scale of over 100 points earning one additional point, per additional push-up performed. So this would be their score for the same 70 push-ups.*

> *104 points (42-46 years old)*
> *111 points (47-51 years old)*
> *114 points (52-56 years old)*

*Utilizing the U.S. Army standard of 60% in each event is a passing score (below that score of 60 the soldier is assigned to a remedial PT program for scoring less than that) 60 points in each event is only, 180 points total.*

*I remember "believing" that the average soldier in the U.S. Army had a 225 average or 75% in each event but I do not know of any historical data to correlate that with.*

*What I do know and what is common knowledge is that a soldier must score at least 229 points on the APFT with no less than 60 points on any event, using the 17-21 years old age group to qualify to attend the Special Forces Assessment and Selection course (SFAS): Special Forces try-outs.*

*If a person can only score the minimum 180 points (which is well below the average), why would they even try to go someplace where the word "Special" is in the name of the course and implies that which is above the average, like Special Forces?*

*Anyway, I was constantly scoring on the extended scale, above 300 points when I was an Airborne Infantry soldier in the "regular" Big U.S. Army, because I scored over 100 points in each event.*

*The passing 2-mile run time for the 17-21 years old age group is 15:54 for 60 points or 60%.*

*Meaning that a male soldier must be able to run a distance of 2-miles in under 15 minutes and 55 seconds in order to just pass. That's almost an 8-minute per mile average. He would have to run 2-miles in 13:00, or less, in order to "max out" with 100 points for that event.*

*The fastest 2-mile run time I've ever recorded on an APFT in the Big Army before going to SFAS was 10:15.*

*Needless to say, I was pretty good in almost every category I could think of, and was the best soldier in the U.S. Army.*

*Or so I thought - man was I wrong.*

*In 1990 when that Commanding General (CG) started to speak, he began with the common initial motivational speech that almost all commanders, leaders, coaches and authorities give to groups of men who are about to be tested.*

*Look at the man on your left, look at the man on your right, look around you. You are the best soldiers that the military has to offer, and all of you will not make it thru this assessment.*

*I looked around and began my personal assessment of my fellow SFAS classmates.*

*I said to myself.*

*"I think I'm faster than that guy".*

*"I bet I'm stronger than that guy, he looks weak".*

*"How did that guy get here, he doesn't even look like he belongs here"?*

*Over and over, we all did self-assessments and self-evaluations, and comparisons amongst each other. I was pretty confident that I was going to pass this SFAS thing, with ease.*

*Man, was I wrong.*

*Then the CG said, "If you've ever played a sport and were physically active stand up"!*

*Every man in the auditorium stood up.*

*Then he said, "If you've ever played a sport on a team, remain standing"!*

*I could swear I saw movement in the auditorium, but I was so busy basking in my own self grandiose internal chest thumping feeling good about myself moment that I didn't even notice.*

*Then he said something that shocked me.*

*He said, "If you've ever played a sport on a team, or any sport, that performed at the State level remain standing"!*

*Well, I was a pretty good soldier physically, and was a decent athlete in high school, but I didn't win no State Championship or nothing like that. So, I sat down, along with a couple hundred others.*

*But there were still about 250 men still standing up!*

*Then the CG said, "If you've ever played or performed any sport on the collegiate level remain standing"!*

*A few more men sat down, but many more were still standing up.*

*Then the CG said, "If you've ever played or performed any sport on the national level remain standing"!*

*A few more men sat down, but by now for the first time I was actually doubting myself.*

*Thoughts went thru my mind like,*

*"What have I gotten myself into"?!?*

*"Are you freaking serious"?!?*

*and*

*"What the fuck"?!?*

*Then the CG said, "If you've ever played or performed any sport on the international level remain standing"!*

*A few more men sat down, but many more were still standing!*

*Then the CG said, "If you've ever played or performed any sport on the Olympic level, or above - remain standing"!*

*There were about 50 men still standing!*

*Some of them men still standing, were some of the same men that I underestimated and thought I was better than, just by their physical appearance. Man, was I wrong.*

*Then the CG went around the auditorium and said to the men standing, "Tell us your story"!*

*I was already feeling woefully out of my comfort zone by this time, but the men all said stories like this.*

*"I was on the U.S.A. Olympic boxing team, but I broke my arm, so I joined the military".*

*"I was on the U.S.A. National Taekwondo Team and won a Bronze medal in the Olympics".*

*"I was the fastest person in the world to do this".*

*"I hold the Olympic World Record for that".*

*"I am the second fastest person in the nation to do so and so, I earned a silver medal at the nationals".*

*"I was on the Olympic team for this, or that, or this"...*

*I had already learned my lesson in humility, and not to judge a book by its cover. Not to judge any man by the color of his skin or his physically appearance, but by the content of his character. But that day was a whole different type of humble pie I was eating.*

*We started that SFAS class with about 500 candidates. I am deliberately not using the term students, because I'll reserve the term "student" for SFQC "the Q-course" where a person will actually be taught Special Operations: Doctrine, Tactics, Techniques and Procedures.*

*However, this was SFAS, or more appropriately should be called the Special Forces "try-outs" to see what you got and if you really want to be there.*

*Of the 500 candidates that were there (we had an abnormally large class), only 101 of us made it to the end. Everyone else was medically injured or dropped, physically could not complete the training/testing, academically did not meet the standard, flat out quit or did not make it until the end for some other reason (men died in the SFAS class before me, which stopped the U.S. Army from running SFAS for a month or two, which resulted in my class being so large).*

*None of my classmates died in training, however it must feel like dying to them; to make it all the way to the end, and NOT get selected for Special Forces training.*

*That's right, just because you made it to the end, doesn't mean you will be selected for SFQC.*

*Of the 101 of us that made it, they only selected 65 of us.*

*We were given completion/graduation certificates and directed to return TDY back to our parent units. Sometime later we would be given military PCS orders to return to Fort Bragg, North Carolina and begin our actual Special Forces training in the SFQC.*

\*\*\*

Many people, especially those in the U.S. military may have heard the phrase that we don't fight unless we have a 3 to 1 advantage over our enemy. Well that is not entirely accurate.

It all starts at the small unit level and it is all about numbers, or numerically superior forces whom can mass at the appropriate time.

At the elementary level, many of us have seen the old cowboy movies where two cowboys where shooting at each other. They have revolvers and take turns standing, aiming and taking shots at each other. Then they must duck behind cover while they re-cock their pistols and their opponent is taking a shot at them. Then they continue this until one of them is hit by a bullet.

Some of the scenarios show a cowboy rapidly firing his pistol, by pulling the trigger, and cocking the pistol with his non-firing hand. But he must then eventually duck down behind some barrels or some other type of temporary cover while he reloads, before he can stand up and shoot again.

But if it was possible for one of the cowboy's friend to keep shooting at the enemy, the friend would at least keep the enemy's head pinned down (a type of suppressive fire) while the cowboy could maneuver around and flank the enemy from one of the sides, depending on the terrain.

In the military if that same scenario occurred, one soldier could keep the enemy pinned down, while the other soldier could maneuver around to the enemy's flank and get close enough to use a hand grenade on the enemy.

A basic U.S. Army Infantry Rifle Squad consists of about 9 men, divided into 2 Infantry Fire Teams.

An Infantry Fire Team consists of a Fire Team Leader, an Automatic Rifleman, a Grenadier and a Rifleman.

The U.S. Army Infantry Rifle squad is led by a Staff Sergeant/E-6 and he is equipped with an M-4 Carbine Rifle. He normally controls the movement of his 2 Fire teams by designating A or Alpha Team to travel in the front of him, and B or Bravo Team to travel in the rear of him.

The Alpha Team is normally lead by a Team Leader (TL) in the rank of Sergeant/E-5 and he is equipped with an M-4 Carbine Rifle.

He would have an Automatic Rifleman (AR) in his team normally in the rank of Specialist/E-4 and he would be equipped with an M-249 SAW (Squad Automatic Weapon).

He also would have a Grenadier in his team normally in the rank of Private First Class/E-3 who would be equipped with an M-203 Rifle/Grenade Launcher.

Finally, there would be a Rifleman in the team in the rank of Private/E-2 equipped with a M-4 Carbine Rifle to complete the 4-member Fire Team.

The team members are paired in buddy team units, the (TL) and the (AR) would be battle buddies, and the (G) and the (R) would be battle buddies.

The squad leader could use the technique where one fire team moves ahead a particular distance to locate the enemy forces. The goal would be for the Fire Team to locate, close with and destroy any enemy forces they encounter with speed and violence of action.

If the Fire Team encounters an enemy soldier or a 2-man enemy out post (OP) or lookout post (LP), they should be able to defeat the enemy in that engagement based upon numerical superiority.

However, if the Fire Team met stiff enemy resistance that prevented them from moving forward towards their objective (say they lost the element of surprise), or encountered an enemy force slightly larger than they can handle. Then hopefully the Squad Leader did not commit the entire Rifle Squad, and there is enough room or terrain for his other Fire Team (Bravo Team), which has the same identical make-up and composition as the Alpha Team to maneuver around the enemy on the flanks and defeat them.

There are three Movement techniques that small units can use depending upon several different factors. Each technique has its own characteristics with advantages and disadvantages.

Traveling, Traveling Overwatch and Bounding Overwatch.

**Traveling** movement technique is normally used when enemy contact is not likely. The lead Fire Team in the Squad must still travel a distance ahead of the squad leader and the other fire team, so that "if" contact is made with the enemy, the entire squad is not caught in the opening engagement. There should still be some room for the other Fire Team to maneuver and for the Squad Leader to develop the combat situation at hand.

**Traveling Overwatch** is normally used when enemy contact is possible. The lead Fire Team in the Squad travels at a greatly increased distance from the rest of the squad, depending upon the terrain, the environment and other factors.

**Bounding Overwatch** is used when enemy contact is expected and imminent. When you are actually conducting a battle drill called, "Movement to Contact", or you may be actually close to your objective, but the battle or engagement has not commenced yet. Individual Fire Teams actually leap and bound over each other, supporting each other from covered and concealed positions if possible.

Now back to the actual fighting where the lead Fire Team is engaging the enemy.

If during the maneuver to flank the enemy force it is determined that the other Fire Team cannot do it, there is a simple battle drill for that. They (the other Fire Team) would basically get on-line with the Fire Team already in contact with the enemy, and the "entire Rifle Squad" would now become a base of fire for the next higher element to join the engagement and battle the enemy.

According to the Chain of Command and the NCO support channel which supports the Chain of Command, one Squad Leader would not contact another Squad Leader.

A Rifle Squad Leader would contact his next higher element, which is the Infantry Rifle Platoon.

The entire Rifle Platoon would repeat the same basic battle drill. One Squad already in contact and the Platoon Leader would send another Rifle Squad to maneuver around and flank the enemy forces. The Platoon leader normally would travel with the maneuver element, and the Platoon Sergeant would be with the remaining third Rifle Squad to reinforce the base Squad in contact, reinforce the maneuver Squad, establish a Causality Collect Point (CCP), establish an Enemy POW collection point, or a host of other duties and responsibilities that must be performed under combat situations, simultaneously.

If for whatever reason the entire Platoon could not defeat the enemy force, they would not contact another Platoon.

According to the Chain of Command, they would contact the next higher element which is the Infantry Rifle Company, which has several other Platoons in it.

They would repeat this battle drill over and over until the battle is won or until decision are made on the battlefield that are way above my pay grade and level of experience.

Now here are the numbers. Understanding that the composition of a Marine Rifle Squad has 3 Fire Teams in it, a U.S. Army Rifle squad has 2 Fire Teams in it (Alpha and Bravo).

There are normally 3 Rifle Squads in an Infantry Platoon, and depending on the composition of the Infantry unit (Air Assault Infantry, Airborne Infantry, Mechanized Infantry, Ranger Infantry, Light Infantry, etc.) there may be an organic or additional 4th squad called a Weapons Squad. The Infantry Platoon is led by a Platoon Leader normally in the rank of Second Lieutenant (2LT/O-1) assisted by a Platoon Sergeant (PSG) normally in the rank of Sergeant First Class (E-7) commonly referred to as a Platoon Daddy. *Second Lieutenants are sometimes unofficially referred to as "butter bars" because their gold rank insignia is bronze/brown/yellow in color when worn subdued on their utility uniforms. Thus, resembling a stick of butter. This is unofficial and "can" be view a highly disrespectful, so don't do it.*

**There are three Infantry Platoons in a normal Infantry Rifle Company.**
Depending on the composition of the Infantry unit there may be an organic or additional 4th Platoon and or a Headquarters Platoon with heavier weapons organic to it, like 60mm mortar systems.

**There are three Infantry Rifle Companies in a normal Infantry Battalion.**
They are labeled A, B and C using the traditional military phonetic alphabet called Alpha, Bravo and Charlie companies. Sometimes there is a 4th Company probably called a Heavy Weapons Company or "D" for Delta Company with bigger weapons systems, like the 81mm mortar (or they could be assigned to

the Headquarters Company). There are additional assets and anti-tank crew served weapons. There are a lot more people, weapons systems and things to discuss, but I'm focusing on the 3 parts to each higher element.

**There are three Infantry Battalions within a normal Infantry Brigade.**

**There are three Infantry Brigades (or Regiments) within an Infantry Division.** Some Brigades or Regiments are stand-alone units that are not subordinate to any higher division.

There are Regular U.S. Army Divisions and there are U.S. Army Reserve & National Guard Divisions:

Types of regular U.S. Army Divisions: 1st Armored Division, 1st Cavalry Division, 1st Infantry Division, 2nd Infantry Division, 3rd Infantry Division, 4th Infantry Division, 7th Infantry Division, 10th Mountain Division, 25th Infantry Division, the 82nd Airborne Division and the 101st Airborne Division.

Types of U.S. Army Reserve & National Guard Divisions: 26th Infantry Division, 28th Infantry Division, 29th Infantry Division, 34th Infantry Division, 35th Infantry Division, 38th Infantry Division, 40th Infantry Division and the 42nd Infantry Division

**There are historically three Divisions within an Army Corps, example:**
XVIII Airborne Corps at Fort Bragg, North Carolina; 82nd Airborne Division, 101st Airborne Division (Air Assault), 10th Mountain Division and the 3rd Infantry Division (Mechanized)

III Corps at Fort Hood, Texas; 1st Infantry Division, 4th Infantry Division, 1st Calvary Division and the 1st Armored Division

I Corps at Fort Lewis, Washington; 7th Infantry Division

**There are three Corps (or there where three) within an Army or Army Group.**
First United States Army, U.S. Army Forces Command
Second United States Army, U.S. Army Cyber Command
Third United States Army, U.S. Army Central Command
Fifth United States Army, U.S. Army North
Sixth United States Army, U.S. Army South

Seventh United States Army, U.S. Army Europe (USAREUR)
Eighth United States Army, U.S. Army Korea
Ninth United States Army, U.S. Army Africa

Now please understand that there has been a major reorganization to the U.S. Army command structure and operational organization or composition since my retirement from active duty well over 10 years ago.

**The focus is now on individual Brigade Combat Teams, instead of whole fighting Divisions.**

However, the basics for fighting remain the same, numerically.

3 Fire Teams in a Squad, 3 Squads in a Platoon, 3 Platoons in a Company, 3 Companies in a Battalion, 3 Battalions in a Brigade, 3 Brigades in a Division, 3 Divisions in a Corps, 3 Corps in an Army Group.

Example: If an element like an infantry rifle squad cannot fight though and destroy an enemy element, or they get pinned down, they will become a base of fire so that the next higher unit can enter the fight. The next higher element for a squad in contact is not another sister squad, but the entire platoon that the squad in contact belongs too. The squad in contact or the one pinned down will establish a base of fire, while another infantry rifle squad will maneuver around the enemy in an attempt to flank them. The third squad not in contact, and not maneuvering, may be employed as the leader (Second Lieutenant/Platoon Leader) deems necessary.

Many times, units will have Standard Operating Procedures (SOP) on what to do whenever anything happens, especially because the leader normally goes with the maneuver element (lead from the front) and the PSG will normally help establish the Casualty Collect Point (CCP) – or whatever task is necessary to insure the platoon wins the fight.

All of this is practiced in training, in a Battle Drill called: Movement to Contact. The basic Infantry Battle Drill of Movement to Contact has been rehearsed and used for Infantry forces for hundreds of years.

While I was in Iraq on active duty during Operation IRAQI FREEDOM 2 there was a slight variation of that battle drill. The word movement was (unofficially) taken out, because there was no "movement" part to the contact.

83

You just go outside your base, your FOB or your Combat Outpost (COP) and then enemy will come to you, period.

I have been in the United States Army for most my adult life. Placed on the U.S. Army Retired rolls in 2007 after 20 years of active duty.

| 1982-1983 | Delayed Entry Program (*Inactive Duty*) | 1 year |
| --- | --- | --- |
| **1983-1987** | **U.S. Army (Active Duty)** | **4 years** |
| 1987-1989 | New York National Guard/U.S. Army Reserves | 2 years |
| **1989-2007** | **U.S. Army (Active Duty)** | **17 Years** |

Immediately after retiring from active duty I started working as a Security Contractor.

First it was as a contractor stateside (CONUS) with various companies, then eventually overseas "Outside the Continental United States" (OCONUS).

I have been doing bodyguard work for a very long time.

Shortly after working overseas in the middle east as an armed security contractor, I realized that was my calling in life.

**To be some kind of teacher and/or a protector or bodyguard.**

So, since I was a North Carolina resident ever since I retired from the U.S. Army after 20 years of active duty, I changed my residence from the State of New York, to the State of North Carolina and made the Fort Bragg/Fayetteville, North Carolina area my home.

In fact, upon my demise, I wish to be interned on Fort Bragg at the Sandhills Veterans Cemetery adjacent to Spring Lake, North Carolina with all the other paratroopers and veterans.

**\*\*\***

The state of North Carolina uses a governing body or board for Bodyguards, Armed Security Officers and others called the Private Protective Services Board (NCPPSB). The PPSB doesn't have a separate license for Executive Protection Specialist (Bodyguards) and Private Investigators.

*In Accordance With (IAW) North Carolina General Assembly General Statues 74 Chapter C-3 Private Protective Services Profession defines, Subchapter (a)(8) **Private Detective** or **Private Investigator** – Any person who engages in the profession of or accepts employment to furnish, agrees to make, or makes inquiries or investigations concerning any of the following on a contractual basis:*

a) *Crimes or wrong done or threatened against the United States or any state or territory of the United States.*

b) *The identity, habits, conduct, business, occupation, honesty, integrity, credibility, knowledge, trustworthiness, efficiency, loyalty, activity, movement, whereabouts, affiliations, associations, transactions, acts, reputation, or character or any person.*

c) *The location, disposition, or recovery of lost or stolen property.*

d) *The cause or responsibility for, libels, losses, accidents, damages, or injuries to persons or to properties.*

e) *Securing evidence to be used before any court, board, officer, or investigative committee.*

f) *Protection of individuals from serious bodily harm or death.*

The last sentence, subchapter (f) *Protection of individuals from serious bodily harm or death,* is what gives Private Investigators the authority to operate for hire as protectors of human life. Commonly defined as Bodyguards, or Executive Protection (EP) Specialist, or Executive Protection Officers, or Close Protection Officers (CPO), or Close in Protection Specialist, or whatever name you want to call members of that profession.

*Additionally, the North Carolina Administrative Codes, Title 12 – Justice, Chapter 7 Private Protective Services list the associated fees, bonds, licensing and registration requirements for Private Investigators.*

Several other states have a separate licensing or registration section for Bodyguards (Executive Protection) and another one for Private Investigators like the northern neighboring State of Virginia.

The southern neighboring State of South Carolina does not.

But in North Carolina IAW the NCPPSB you must be a Private Investigator to do Bodyguard (Executive Protection) work.

So, I became a Private Investigator, and then an Armed Private Investigator.

Since we both have the same licensing and registration cards; <u>Private Investigators</u> and <u>Executive Protection Specialist</u> share the same work load.

But many of the former retired law enforcement personnel who specialize in investigations and surveillance, and professional work in that area do not want to do executive protection.

Conversely many of us Private Investigators who come from a traditional body guard lifestyle (military, security contractors, etc) do not want to do traditional private investigation work.

It is fairly easy to determine which is which.

Just go to the website of any Private Investigation company and read the biography, background and training of the Private Investigator you wish to hire and determine for yourself.

My biography is located on my company's website (<u>www.sps500.com</u>) "S.P.S.500" which stands for Shadow Protective Services 500, because well over 10 years ago when I started doing bodyguard, safety, security and protection type of work in this industry, my compensation was $500 a day.

Anyway, the most common inquiry I receive as a Private Investigator is one question two ways; A woman will ask me, what could she do because she thinks her man (husband, boyfriend, fiancé) is cheating on her with another woman. Or a man will ask me, what could he do because he thinks his woman (wife, girlfriend, fiancé) is cheating on him with another man.

First, I am not going to give anyone any legal information, so please check with a local attorney familiar with (and licensed) practicing law in your state, county, city, town or local jurisdiction.

Second, get you a free consultation from a good divorce lawyer if you need one, because a Private Investigator can only attempt to confirm or deny the information that is already out there. You should be prepared to decide what you're going to do with that information once you receive it.

A simple trick I teach is based upon math, after a basic consultation with someone. For example, let's say someone engaged to be married and suspicions that their fiancé is cheating on them. Based upon our conversation they believe that that person is cheating on them every Thursday or every payday or whatever the frequency is. Because everyone leaves a trail or pattern, you have to look for it.

If its determined that the other person has a fake business trip or baby shower or meeting on a particular day, I suggest that they confirm the odometer reading of the other person's car, before they leave. Upon their return casually retrieve the mileage from that vehicle.

Now your basic math will determine that they normally drive say 20 miles per day; 9.5 miles to work and 10.5 miles home because they take the scenic route. But on this particular day that you suspect them of infidelity, you record that they have driven over 250 miles. Now you do the subtraction from the vehicles departing miles (let's use and example of 82,250 miles) from its current mileage (82,500). Mathematically that vehicle has gone a maximum of 125 miles somewhere and 125 miles back, for a total of 250 miles.

Next you get a road map from your local store, gas station or big box store for your geographical location. Let's use Raleigh, North Carolina for this example. You draw a line exactly 125 miles on a map (according to the maps scale) from your location, for example completely around Raleigh, NC in all directions. You now have determined the exact limit of where that car could have traveled that day.

Florence, Columbia and Spartanburg, South Carolina are all physically outside of your zone of search. I'm not saying they didn't go to those places, I'm saying its mathematically impossible for "that car" to have driven to those cities that day. Norfolk, Charlottesville and Fredericksburg, Virginia are also all physically outside of your zone of search possibilities. Now again, I'm not saying they did not go there, I am saying it is physically impossible for that car to travel to those areas on that particular day, because all those cities are outside of the 125 miles each way radius.

Many times, the answer is right along the boundary lines they just drew. It just so happens that a place called South Hill, Virginia is exactly 96 miles north of Raleigh, North Carolina. Even if they took the scenic route back, that is right at the limits of a less than 250-mile round trip.

Now the person tells me that they think the fiancé is seeing a woman who lives in Fredericksburg, Virginia because she has been "liking" all of his photos on all his social media sites recently. Her inquisitiveness has led her to do a quick search of this woman's social media pages and it is determined that "that" woman lives in Fredericksburg, Virginia.

Just so happens that South Hill, Virginia is the exact halfway point between both of those cities and would make a perfect rendezvous location for both suspected cheaters (him traveling north from Raleigh, North Carolina and her traveling south from Fredericksburg, Virginia). Check the local hotels in the area and you'll probably find your answer. Now this was a completely fictions example I just made up to illustrate my point.

So of course, it is way more work to private investigations than that.

But I just used a small illustration of how mathematics could help solve a case for a Private Investigator.

*Why?*

Because:

## Men lie,

## Women lie,

## Numbers don't lie.

# 4

# ALL AROUND THE WORLD

*If I gave you an exam, where a passing score would be 70% out of a possible maximum 100% you would probably agree that; that would be the standard across most fields in academia, correct?*

*Yeah, I know some use a 65% standard, but let's just go with 70% for the point I'm about to illustrate.*

*What if I told you that I would give you an exam where there were 197 possible answers, and each answer was worth 1 point? So, there was now a possibility that you could score a maximum of 197 points, but you still had to score above a minimum of 70% to pass the exam.*

*You would probably say that your chances are now significantly above what they were in the first example, correct?*

*Now what if I told you that I would give you one dollar for every correct answer, but you had to get at least 70 answers correct, of the 197 questions, would you still be interested in taking the exam?*

*For most people, the answer was already yes, but now with the momentary incentive, the answer is definitely yes!*

*Now remember, if you score 69% or less you will fail, and you get nothing.*

*So here is the exam, take out a blank piece of paper and a writing utensil.*

*The U.S. military preferers to use blue or black ink (although other SM's with look at you like you're crazy if you choose the blue ink, so only use black ink for military documents), academia prefers a lead number 2 pencil (which is not as dark as a number 1 pencil). The number 1 pencil is much darker and can be used to write on the back of something that doesn't require a hard impression like the back of a picture, but it smudges too easily. The higher number 3 or 4 pencils leave a much lighter impression and are much harder to read. So, the number 2 pencil is the default standard in the United States. The legal community prefers blue ink (so they can distinguish an original signature from the black & white copy).*

*I don't care what you choose to write with for this test, just put the electronic tablets, cellphones and computers away. No books to reference at all, just the knowledge in your head.*

*Now here are the instructions for the exam.*

*Using only the paper and writing utensil in front of you, with no additional or outside assistance or interference, write down the names of as many of the 197 independent nations and countries that there are in this world, that you can.*

*This is a timed event, do the best you can do.*

*I did not do this exercise ever, in any of my Special Forces training.*

*But this is the best exercise I could create in my mind, that I could share with you, to replicate the level of intelligence and world awareness the average U.S. Army Special Forces soldier possesses.*

*How many of you would pass this exam by naming over 70 of the 197 independent countries or nations that there are in this world?*

*How much money would you have if I gave you a dollar for each correct answer?*

*Too difficult?*

*OK, here is an easy one. This one contains about 50 correct answers, maybe a little more, so each correct answer is worth two points.*

*Of the 50 independent nations and countries on the continent of Africa, how many can you name?*

*Yes, South Africa is one of the countries at the bottom of that continent, and Egypt is one the countries at the top of that continent, but at last count there were 52 other independent nations or countries on that continent. How many of them can you name?*

*OK, enough about "Africa" Shadow*

*There you go with that "black stuff" again.*

*So, how about I talk about something closer to home. Let's try North America.*

*Not including the South American continent (but the southern portion of the North American continent referred to as "Latin America" is included in this example), using just the continent of North America only, can you name just 5 of the other 20 independent countries or nations on the continent of North American that are NOT; Canada, Mexico or the United States of America?*

*There are 23 of them, and I just named the obvious 3.*

- *That leaves 20 other countries in North America, can you name just 5 of the other 20?*

*I'll wait.*

*These are just some of the examples I am using to illustrate the global situational awareness of many soldiers who are considered "Special" and above average. Many of you are special civilians because you're aware of your surroundings, and not just standing around with your head stuck in the ground waiting for something to happen. You are a person who probably goes out into the world, and makes things happen.*

*3 basic types of people in this world; (1) those that go out and make things happen, (2) those that sit and watch things as they happen, and (3) those who have no idea what just happened.*

*Let's get personal with the questions, instead of talking about Outside the Continental United States (OCONUS) or overseas, let's talk about travel inside the Continental United States (CONUS).*

- *Who is the Governor of your individual State?*

*I'll wait.*

- *OK, who is the Mayor of your City or Town?*

*Each person who is a resident of the United States has about three people who represent them in the United States Congress (there are 2 U.S. Senators from each State in the Union, giving us 100 U.S. Senators in the Senate or the Upper Chamber of the U.S. Congress).*

- *Who are your two U.S. State Senators?*

*Each person who is a resident of the United States has one person who represents them in the United States Congress (there is 1 US Representative from each Congressional District in each State of the Union, giving us about 435 Representatives in the US Congress or the Lower Chamber of the US Congress).*

- *Who is your US Representative (Congressmen or Congresswoman, or Congressperson, or whatever title you want to call that "honorable" person), who represents you in the United States Congress?*

*If you ask the average soldier who wears a "Green Beret", I am willing to bet that he can tell you a little bit about not just being a good citizen, but about life in a foreign country also, because he has probably just returned from one.*

✱✱✱

As a Security Professional, an Executive Protection Specialist, and the founder of Shadow Protective Services, LLC: I get a lot of aspiring individuals who want to become Security Guards, Armed Security Officers or Private Investigators (Executive Protection).

For those that want to become "bodyguards" I normally tell them that it's not all about muscle brawn and guns.

In fact, it's way more important to use your mind and "prevent" a fight, than win a fight, whereas the motto of the company is, *"A problem avoided is better than a problem solved."*

I normally give those aspiring individuals a simple test, on a very personal level.

*Now I'm gonna give that same test to you.*

Take out a piece of paper and with a pencil write the numerals one through ten down the side of the paper, so you can write out the ten answers for this test.

*Or if you've already purchased this book, just write your answers below.*

1.

2.

3.

4.

5.

6.

7.

8.

9.

10.

Now **without** looking at your cell phone, write down the telephone numbers of 10 people that you know. This is a timed event, do the best you can do!

How many of you passed with a score of 70% at least?

Many people don't even have the mental capacity to remember a bunch of phone numbers, because they have it stored in their "smartphone".

Like my dad always says, *"smartphones and dumb people."*

If you get into some type of trouble, and lose your phone or it is stolen, or the battery dies, or you land in a OCONUS country that operates on a different cellphone frequency than the one you are accustomed to and your cellphone don't work – what if you need help? What if someone offers to help you and says, "here use my phone and call whoever you need too!" If you have all of your information stored on your "smart phone" and don't know any telephone numbers to call, what are you gonna do?

*What do you call people who speak at least two languages?*
Bi-lingual.

*What do you call a person that speaks three languages?*
I don't know, maybe Tri-lingual?!?

*What do you call a person that can speak only one language?*
American.

✳✳✳

Grace and Mercy. A very wise man once taught me that "Grace" is when you get something good that you weren't even supposed to get. "Mercy" is when you don't get the punishment that you were supposed to get, as reciprocity for whatever it is you did.

So, I thank my Ankh-cestors, the Great Architect of the Universe, and the man upstairs for bestowing upon me the grace and mercy to travel to many other foreign countries and continents on this earth.

As I write my information down in this book, I realize that documenting most of my travels to all the cities, states and countries I have traveled to wouldn't fit into this book. I am currently on my fourth passport booklet.

After the first one expired, I received my second passport. When that one got full of stamps from foreign travel, I had the U.S. Embassy where I was at, add additional pages. When that one got full I received my third passport. I am now on my fourth US passport booklet, and hope to fill that one with travels from at least 10 new countries before the end of 2020.

I have realized that it would add another couple of hundred pages to this book, to properly document everything. That would raise the page count of this book from over 400 now, to well over 500 or 600 pages. Economically that is not going to be possible. The cost to produce that physical book; hardback and paperback versions, production cost, shipping and handling – it's just not economically viable.

So just starting this chapter I've already determined that I will have to write another book after this one.

Probably called; *"The Worldwide Adventures of Brother Shadow"*, or something like that.

The U.S. military has taught me that travel is broken down into two major categories; CONUS and OCONUS.

**CONUS stands for travel *within* the Continental United States.**
Specifically, the connected 48 states between the countries of Mexico and Canada. Yes, Alaska and Hawaii are 2 of the 50 states that also make up our country. However, they are physically separated from the other 48 states. You can NOT drive to the state of Alaska, unless you drive through the country of Canada first. You can NOT drive to the state of Hawaii, unless you have a submarine or a big ass boat. So, for the purpose of military travel they are NOT considered CONUS. Of the 48 connected or contiguous states, I have personally traveled to 38 of them. *On my bucket list before I leave this earth, is the physical travel to all 50 states and United States territories before this thing is all over.*

**OCONUS stands for travels *outside* the Continental United States.**
Of the 197 other countries and nations outside the United States of America I have travelled to over 30 other countries that I can discuss, via military service (DoD), duties with the U.S. State Department (DoS) as a Security Contractor, or on vacation in an unofficial capacity.

If I fly OVER a country, I do NOT include that country on my list. However, if I do have an international layover of a flight, and can de-plane, and leave the airport and conduct a Class 2 download (a number 2), then not only have I been to that country, but I have physically left evidence "behind".

*Notice the pun and play on words right there - behind?*

My international travels have taken me to: Schofield Barracks (U.S. Army) and Hickam (USAF) Base in the U.S. State of *Hawaii*, and to Elmendorf (USAF) Base, Fort Richardson - Anchorage, and Fort Wainwright - Fairbanks (U.S. Army) in the U.S. State of *Alaska*.

I've also traveled to, but not limited too: *Algeria, Austria, the Bahamas, Belgium, Bosnia and Herzegovina, the Cayman Islands, the Czech Republic, Egypt, France, Germany, Hungary, Iceland, Iraq, Israel, Italy, Jamaica, Japan, Jordan, Kosovo, Korea, Kuwait, Mexico, Morocco, Panama, the Philippines, St Martin* (French), *St Maarten* (Dutch), *Tunisia, the U.S. Virgin Islands*, and the city of *Dubai* in the *United Arab Emirates* (UAE).

/I have had some really great visits and tours overseas (OCONUS), but some of the more memorable were:

✳✳✳

*Panama*
I deployed to Fort Sherman, Panama while assigned to the 82nd Airborne Division's, 4th Battalion, 325th Airborne Infantry Regiment which is part of its 2nd Brigade Combat Team. That was an awesome deployment and for obvious reasons (because I'm not stupid) I can't talk about that deployment in its entirety, at least not in this freaking book! But at Fort Sherman I remember staying in the massive open bay barracks, maybe entire companies of soldiers could fit in there. The big industrial fans and the warm jungle air, it was awesome. I miss that type of camaraderie.

Similar to the way today's soldiers are anxious and looking forward to desert or mountain operations and deployments, because of the ongoing combat operations in Afghanistan, Iraq and the surrounding countries. Well, in the 1980's and 1990's my generation of soldiers were raised on Vietnam veterans, movies and culture.

The jungles of Panama were the closest we were gonna get.

The Jungle Operations Training Center (JOTC) had an obstacle course called *"Green Hell"* and I remember it being some of the most fun I've ever had. Physically exhausting, but an adrenalin rush if you ever wanted one. Swimming across the warm waters of the lagoon, making survival rafts and learning to operate in a jungle environment.

There was an unwritten rule that we weren't supposed to operate or move at night in the dense jungle.

The black sticky palm trees and the numerous hazardous obstacles that were everywhere. I remember we were ordered to move at night, and you could only see the glowing "Cat Eyes" on the back of the patrol cap of the soldier in front of you. I remember when we would take the cap off of our head and drop it to the ground, causing the man behind you to stop in horror thinking that you fell into a hole.

Until somebody in my unit really did. He fell maybe thirty feet straight down, and we were ordered to go to "white lights" immediately. Meaning stop training and turn on your white lens of your flashlight to find this soldier. He was really messed up, but since he was in another unit, I don't know what happened to him.

I remember once soldier fell asleep in the jungle and a bat landed on his head. It sucked the blood out of his forehead, and the next morning he had a big white patch on the front of his forehead from where the bat was sucking blood from him all night. Apparently, the vampire bats in Panama have some type of local anesthetic in their spit, that can put that portion of your body to sleep and you wouldn't even know they were there.

One more reason, I don't sleep!

Safety briefing before we get a pass for a few hours, and I just remember hearing *"Do NOT go to the city of Colon,"* it is off-limits for all soldiers. So, you know what all the paratroopers did right?

I remember flying back to Fort Bragg (then Pope AFB) on the 463L pallet completely exhausted. That was an awesome deployment, and I encourage every soldier to get some "Jungle Training" if the opportunity affords itself. Because, every conflict will not be fought in the desert.

## Portugal

I have also been to the Azores islands in the Atlantic Ocean. The Azores are a part of the country of Portugal, just like the island of Puerto Rico is a part of the United States. The Azores are about 850 miles west of the country of Portugal on the european continent, and 1,000 miles away from the continent of Africa. I do not remember spending days on those islands awaiting a military refueling stop or visiting with the local population. However, I do know that I conducted a Class 2 download there, so yup I was there.

## Republic of South Korea (ROK) and North Korea

I was once stationed in South Korea (1995-96) up on the Demilitarized Zone (DMZ) at Camp Greaves with the U.S. Army. That location is (was, because it is no longer there) the only U.S. Army base that was up north of the Imjin River that separates the two countries of North Korea and South Korea in several areas. That was the hardest year of my life, and because of the phase during which it occurred, and I frequently compare it to a prison sentence.

Anyway, while up at Camp Greaves, I took a USO tour of Camp Bonafis, which is physically "inside" the Demilitarized Zone (DMZ) Panmunjom and actually on the North Korean side of the border. It's officially called the Democratic People's Republic of Korea (DPPK), but what I saw was very different from a democracy or a democratic way of life.

While we were there, we went inside the Joint Security Area (JSA) which is the high-tension area where North Korea and South Korea forces meet, and delegations between the two countries take place. *Before you go into the DMZ you are warned that you are entering a hostile area and possible severe injury, or death may result because of hostile enemy action.*

Inside the JSA there are a bunch of building, and one particular building is long and rectangular shaped. It is North Korea on one side of the building and

South Korea on the other. There is a negation table in the middle of the building, and there is a line across the table, whereas that side of the table is North Korea and this side of the table is South Korea.

There must be some type of agreement whereas the guards from either side lock the door from the inside, and allow maintenance, visitation, tours or whatever to occur from each side. I distinctly remember during the USO tour, while we were inside that building, that persons were allowed to go tour on the North Korean side, and several visitors refused to even venture deeper into the room.

There was a fear that the North Korean guards would bust into the room and grab you, and if you were on that side of the table, you were actually in North Korea. I recently heard on the news that a defector tried to run from North Korea to the South Korean side and there was an exchange of gunfire. The actual name of the Camp, "Camp Bonafis" is named after a U.S. Army officer who along with others was attacked and killed by North Korean guards in 1976 at that location. Research "Korean Axe Murder Incident" for the details.

I wanted to conduct a Class 2 download on that side of the room, but that did NOT happen. So yeah, I was on the North Korean side of the room, and so therefore technically I've been to North Korea. Now my time in the country of South Korea was a little bit more eventful. I was actually deployed to South Korea on two separate occasion, both about 10 years apart during my military career. Both times were completely polar opposites.

1985, I'm going to assume the date because that was over 35 years ago. We deployed to the Republic of South Korea on a Temporary Duty (TDY) basis. I do not know if the information during that deployment has been declassified yet? So, I will NOT be disclosing what I did, because I'm NOT trying to go to jail for divulging classified information (Confidential, Secret or Top Secret), but I can tell you that we deployed in the vicinity of Camp Humphreys, South Korea. Which was a large U.S. Army Garrison and had one of the largest U.S. military airfields in Asia at the time.

It is located near the city of Pyeongtaek where a South Korean Naval base is located. Directly outside of its gates is the village (community) of Anjeong-ri. Pronounced An-John-Ree, which rhymes with the word Jealousy.

I know that because, although I was active duty military, because of my "special" status I was NOT restricted to the military installation over there at that time.

So, whenever I was off-duty I would go outside the gate pass the soldiers who had to be back on the base, as I was singing the then hit song "*Jealousy*" by the group Club Nouveau. But I would replace the word Jealousy with Anjeong-ri.

*"Anjeong-ri, I don't want no damn legs around me!!!"*

I remember Nikes cost only $5 a pair, and I brought back with me maybe 20 pairs of sneakers, in every color back to the United States.

I remember we conducted a foreign parachute jump exchange with the South Korean military, and I was awarded the South Korean Parachutist badge. Although I have earned several foreign jump wings over the course of my military career, the "Korean Parachutist badge" is the one foreign military award that I wear the most frequent.

I was very impressed with the South Korean (ROK) Rangers and Marines. They were very professional and the ones I saw were real squared away. I remember life being one big party back then!

We were there approximately 45 days before we returned to CONUS. Other than the bad news I received upon my return to the continental United States, I don't have a bad memory of my first tour in South Korean.

I mean it was cold, but since I stayed TDY off-base someplace: even the floor had heated tiles. This influenced my decision years later when I was in the infantry, and the U.S. Army wanted to reassign me to South Korea for a 1-year tour.

Sure, sign me up, how bad could it be?

1995, I arrive in South Korea with memories of how great a time I had last time I was in that country. Although that was a TDY deployment, and this was a Permanent Change of Station (PCS) move. I remember landing in Seoul and linking up with a military liaison. The first question I was asked after they secured my military documents was; *what is your MOS and how tall are you?*

We were then transported to the U.S. Army Garrison Headquarters. I had been in the military for some years by this time, so I had known soldiers who were assigned to all types of great units over there. There was the U.S. Army Det-K (the Special Forces unit), the Pathfinder Detachment, the military Honor Guard and there is even a program for U.S. Army soldiers to work "outside" of their designated MOS called "Special Duty". I mean somebody has to hand out the towels at the gym on base.

Within hours of our arrival, we are all gathered into a big auditorium for processing. A NCO arrives on stage and I immediately notice the unit patch on his left shoulder sleeve.

All U.S. Army soldiers wear the patch of the unit they are assigned to on their left shoulder sleeve.

On their right shoulder sleeve is worn the identification patch of the unit a soldier has severed in combat with. If they do not have a unit patch on their right should, (normally) they have not served in combat.

Additionally, on the left side above the unit patch that all soldiers in the same unit wear, are the special skill-set identifying "Tabs" worn above the unit patch.

Example the entire 25th Infantry Division is made up of subordinate brigades, battalions and companies with various functions and purposes. If they have a detachment, or platoon, or company of Airborne Scout in that division; and they are on jump status – they, those members will wear an "AIRBORNE" Tab above the 25th Infantry Division unit patch on their left shoulder sleeve.

If individuals within that element (platoon, company, etc) are Ranger qualified graduates of the U.S. Army's Ranger school – those members and those members only will wear a "RANGER" Tab,
above the "AIRBORNE" Tab,
above the 25th Infantry Division unit patch.

*This method applies to all soldiers in the U.S. Army in every unit. So back in the day if you saw a soldier wearing three tabs, like; SPECIAL FORCES, RANGER and AIRBORNE he was considered Triple Tabbed, or wearing a "Triple Canopy" above his unit patch on the left sleeve.*

Anyway, we are inprocessing into Korea and the NCO that is on stage is wearing a "cookie patch."

I (like many soldiers) can easily identify the major units of the U.S. Army (division size and above) by the very distinctive shoulder sleeve insignia unit patch; *1st Infantry Division (Big Red One), 2nd Infantry Division (Indianhead), 3rd Infantry Division (Marne Division), 6th Infantry Division (Red Star or Artic Light), 7th Infantry Division (Hourglass Division or Bayonet Division), 8th Infantry Division (Golden Arrow Division), 9th Infantry Division (Old Reliables), 23rd Infantry Division (Americal Division), 25th Infantry Division (Tropic Lightning), 42nd Infantry Division (Rainbow Division), 92nd Infantry Division (Colored), 10th Mountain Division (Light Infantry), 82nd Airborne Division (All Americans), 101st Airborne Division (Screaming Eagles), 1st Cavalry Division (First Team), 1st Armored Division (Old Ironsides), 2nd Armored Division (Hell on Wheels), 3rd Armored Division (Spearhead), I Corps (1st Corps or America's Corps), III Corps (3rd Corps, Phantom Corps or America's Hammer), XVIII Airborne Corps (Sky Dragons)*

There are some other units in the U.S. Army that are smaller in size that also have shoulder sleeve insignia.

But for a separate brigade, regiment or other size unit, they have to be really special for their unit patch to standout immediately from the norm. Some examples are: *1st Special Forces Regiment (with the subordinate Special Forces Groups), Ranger Regiment (with the subordinate Ranger Battalions), the 173rd Airborne Brigade, the 555th Parachute Infantry Battalion (Triple Nickel) and some of the U.S. Army's Armored Cavalry Regiments (ACR's).*

Now this doesn't mean anything negative against any other unit in the United States Army. I am just highlighting and illustrating for you, the reader, so you can ascertain my mind set at the time.

So many of the soldiers in the U.S. Army who are not able to easily identify the unit patch of an individual, if they are not one of the ones I listed above (if I omitted or failed to list any current or historically distinguished units please charge it to my memory and not my heart), they are unofficially referred to by many soldiers as a "cookie patch". Because they normally are in the shape and size of a cookie, not large shoulder sleeve patches like the ones listed above.

So, I'm in South Korea day one, and this NCO with an unrecognizable cookie patch gets on stage and calls out a bunch of soldier's names. I will try my best

NOT to stereotype anyone, because many times people get it wrong when they stereotype me.

But all of the soldiers that he called out, looked "smarter than me", like they possessed some highly technical MOS and skillsets.

Then another NCO gets on stage, and he's wearing a cookie patch and does the same thing. Calls out names and the soldiers all look smart. So now I'm guessing that these are all the soldiers that have the MOS and jobs that keep the military and the U.S. Army running smoothly. Then another NCO gets on stage and calls the last list of names, these soldiers don't look as smart as the first batch, but they definitely don't have that "Infantry hard as nails look."

So I can now safely assume that everyone with a Combat Service Support (CSS) MOS has been called and has left the room; *Microwave Systems Maintainer (25P), Satellite Communications System Operator (25S), Financial Management Technician (36B), Musician (42R), Career Counselor (79S), Public Affairs Broadcast Specialist (46R), Religious Affairs Specialist (56M), Dental Specialist (68F), Animal Care Specialist (68T), Shower/Launder and Clothing Repair Specialist (92S), or the Water Treatment Specialist (92W).*

All the remaining soldiers in the room get a very long noticeable wait for the final NCO. We call this gap in time - the pregnant pause.

The last NCO walked to the front of the auditorium and he don't have a clipboard or a list in his hand. But, he does have the big 2nd Infantry Division patch on his left shoulder sleeve. His words to us: *"None of you have been drafted by the good units down south, get your shit and get on the buses outside, you're all going up north to the Second Infantry Division. HOO-AHH?!?"*

Hoo-aah… is what we replied with in unison. No enthusiasm and laced with sarcasm. Hoo-aah can mean whatever you want it to mean, it's just how you say it. We head up north to Camp Casey/Hovey to the inprocessing location called "the Turtle Farm." Why do they call it the Turtle Farm you ask?

Well, the in-processing and out-processing happens at this location, and at this one particular building. You in process through one door and it normally takes one whole entire long ass year, before you walk through the other door to outprocess. Slow just like a turtle.

I run into one of my old paratrooper buddies from Fort Bragg. He's cadre at the turtle farm, so I just know he's gonna get me into a good unit near his location. Heck, maybe even cadre status like him.

He comes back out with this sad look. *You know how you can tell the one kid who was bad in school, because he's walking from the bus stop real slow, with his head down, kicking rocks?*

Well that's the look my paratrooper buddy gave me.

*Man, they sending you up to Camp Greaves, is what he tells me.*

**Where's that at bro?!?**

*Way up on the DMZ, I'm sorry brother my hands are tied on this one.*

A few days later we out process and all load a bus that will take us to our new units of assignments. It literally took "all damn day" to get to every camp before the bus arrived its final destination; at Camp Greaves.

It's dark November/December and there is an eerie mist of ice and fog that that permeates through the bus. Turns out that we are at the checkpoint on the south side of the Imjin River, and the Camp is on the north side.

Almost every camp we just visited and dropped soldiers off at, had a village or town outside it's gates, and a civilian population to augment it.

Not at Camp Greaves, there is no village near there and civilians are NOT allowed beyond this point.

We get boarded and checked by U.S. Army MP's, the South Korean ROK soldiers with the bomb sniffing dogs. The bus then proceeds to cross this "one lane bridge" that is wired with explosives, to be blown in the event of an emergency.

We can actually see all the wires, and I realize that I will be on the wrong freaking side of this bridge when and if they blow it.

When we get to the northern side, I can see a vehicle waiting for its turn to traverse back to the southern side of the river. We are stopped and boarded again, but by U.S. Army Infantry soldiers from nearby Camp Greaves and the South Korean ROK soldiers.

When they finish, they salute the bus and sound off with the unit motto of the 1st Battalion, 506th Infantry (Air Assault): STANDS ALONE!!!

The unit being Air Assault wears an oval backing behind the Air Assault wings, if you've earn them – and NOT the Airborne wings. Yeah, things were a little different over there.

I am immediately assigned to Bravo Company, 1/506 Infantry as a Rifle Squad Leader (SL). But the SL that I am replacing has not departed yet, so I am assigned a M-249SAW and designated the assistant squad leader.

**What the heck is that?!?**

*I ain't never heard of no such position. I've heard of the backup quarterback in football, but I aint never heard of no assistant quarterback position.*

But wait, there's more.

I am assigned to a room in the barracks with 3 other Staff Sergeants.

**Oh, hell no! This ain't happening!**

I'm gonna go to see the unit First Sergeant and get this taken care of. When I get there, the First Sergeant opens his room door and I notice he has a roommate too! So much for complaining.

That tour of duty, just got worse and worser. I know that not a word, but it best describes how I was feeling. Bad-er and bad-er. Up until the day I left it was not a good tour for me.

I joined a fraternity while I was over there. It got so bad the fraternity lost their charter to operate. The hazing was so physically bad, that when I arrived back CONUS from that tour of duty, my clothes were stuck to my body from where the blood had dried and got stuck to my clothes, during that long flight back.

## Japan

It had to be late 1985 when I was stationed at Fort Lewis adjacent to McChord, AFB (now called Joint Base Lewis-McChord) when we did a training mission near Japan. I'm quite sure it was involving the 1st Battalion of the 1st Special Forces Group (Airborne) of which I was assigned to at that time.

Back then the 1st Battalion was stationed in Japan (and they still are), and the 2nd and 3rd Battalions of the 1st SFG(A) were stationed on North Post on Fort Lewis. When I left fort Lewis in 1987 they were beginning construction a new complex on main post for the 1st SFG(A). I believe they may have even added a 4th Operational Battalion to the SF Group.

But I don't know, because like I said: *I left there over 30 years ago.*

My training mission in or around Japan, was very uneventful and for whatever reason it left me with the impression that I never wanted to return to that location. The food was excellent over there, and next to Italian cuisine I prefer Japanese food any day of the week. I really enjoyed all my time traveling with the military, and there were several locations in that part of Asia that I would love to return back too, if I could (*I mean if things were the same*). But Kadena AFB in Japan just didn't do it for me. Relationships between the military (U.S. Army, Navy, Air Force & USMC) and the local civilian communities are always in the news.

Kadena, AFB is the largest and most active U.S. Air Force base in the region. It is near the city of Okinawa on the Okinawa Island part of Japan.

✳✳✳

## the Republic of the Philippines

In direct contrast to the Japan deployment, almost like night and day (or cold and hot), was my time deployed to the Philippines.

I can say without a doubt, that was one of the BEST deployments that there ever was. Remember this was just 10 years after Vietnam was over, and over 15 years before the events of 9-11.

I distinctly remember flying into the mountains of the Philippines in the 1980's because there was a severe problem from the communist guerrilla fighters of the New People's Army (NPA) in the countryside.

I remember they use to impose revolutionary taxes upon the local population by hacking peoples arms off with a machete, to steal their watches to fund their illegal activities.

I remember when our unit left the Philippines after that deployment was over, the NPA guerrillas were NOT a problem in that area anymore.

We deployed to Clark, AFB when it was still a U.S. military air base. Control of the base was transferred back to the Philippine government in the late 1980's and early 1990's. Then a volcano called Mount Pinatubo erupted and almost destroyed what was left after the US personnel departed.

I remember staying, again off-base. We lived in Angeles City with the local population and I can remember having the time of my life. I remember having a beer at a local bar and it cost 1 Philippine Peso. The currency exchange rate at the time was like 20 PHP to 1 American Dollar. So, in my young Buck Sergeant mind, that meant the beer cost One Nickel, and I could get 20 beers for every dollar I had. I remember I had a local Philippine "girlfriend" and life was good as far as I was concerned. I had another girlfriend who was an Airman in the U.S. Air Force on Clark AFB, and another girlfriend who was a Sailor in the U.S. Navy stationed at Subic Bay, Naval Base.

I remember eating a local dish that I thought was hot beef and cold rice. But really was some type of Yak or mountain Goat or something. Not only did it make me sick, but it put me in the hospital over there. But I was still happy.

One of the soldiers in our unit went AWOL, and when we found him, he had acquired *"the time and companionship"* with all the girls from this one bar. When we went to his room, he had like 20 women in there with him, and we had to physically fight to bring him back. Man, that was funny! He was screaming, *"I aint never going back! I aint never going back!"*

The whole time we were taking him back.

*the Arab Republic of Egypt*
*the State of Israel*
*the State of Palestine*

The three countries I am now discussing, did not have the same borders they have now, when I visited them years ago. Specifically, the State of country of Palestine did not exist in its present form until 2012.

The areas of the Sinai desert where my unit deployed was captured by Israel during a war with Egypt. But the area was returned when MFO troops stared to patrol the area.

From the end of 1994 until the summer of 1995, I was stationed in the middle-east desert on the Sinai Peninsular of Egypt, for six-months with a Multi-National Peacekeeping Force of Observers (MFO).

In 1979, a Peace Accord was reach at Camp David by *the 39th President of the* **United States** *Jimmy Carter*, between **Israeli** *President Menachem Begin* and **Egyptian** *President Anwar Sadat*. Basically, it called for Israel to withdraw its troops back into its previous (Egypt/Israel) border and for a Multi-National Peacekeeping Force of Observers (MFO) to station it's troops *"between"* the two countries in the Sinai Desert of Egypt, as a buffer zone.

The MFO is headquartered in Rome, Italy with two regional offices; one in Tel-Aviv, Israel and the other in Cairo, Egypt. There are several units with various specialties that make up the composition of the MFO; most notably three separate Infantry Battalions a U.S., a Fijian and a Columbian Battalion.

The following 12 other countries also participate in the MFO in some capacity; *Australia, Canada, Columbia, Czech Republic, Fiji, France, Hungary, Italy, New Zealand, Norway, Uruguay* and *United Kingdom*.

Most of the U.S. soldiers who are PCS or permanently stationed in Egypt are a part of the North Camp near El Gorah and El Arish, Egypt (halfway between Cario, Egypt and Jerusalem, Israel. While the U.S. Infantry unit is stationed in various outposts and camps all throughout the Sinai, but based out of South Camp near Sharm El Sheikh and Naama Bay, Egypt.

At the time I was assigned to the 4th Battalion, 325th Airborne Infantry Regiment as part of the 82nd Airborne Division, from Fort Bragg, North

Carolina, and we were selected to be the U.S. Infantry battalion for the MFO, for that rotation.

We were replacing an Infantry Battalion from the 101st Airborne Division out of Fort Campbell, Kentucky. I was part of the Advance Party that arrived before the main body of soldiers and I was selected to be in the Color Guard during the Change of Responsibilities/Command between the two units (from the 101st to the 82nd Airborne).

I was in the Scout Platoon and I am approximately 6'2" or 6'3" tall, depending on who is measuring me. Almost every honor guard or color guard unit I've seen has been composed of the four tallest members of the unit. *That's part of the reason I got stationed up north when I was in Korea, but that's another story.*

Anyway, rumor has it that a very short NCO in the 101st Airborne that we were relieving was overheard bragging about how he will never have to stand in a color guard because of his diminutive height. I do not know if that rumor is true. But I do know what I'm about to say to be fact, because I was there.

Apparently, that units Command Sergeant Major (CSM) got the three smallest soldiers in his battalion, to stand with that short NCO and form a color guard.

From a distance they all look uniform and equal. Just like the U.S. Army likes to have things. But they were standing next to us, the four tallest and biggest members of our unit from the 82nd Airborne.

It looked like the Pygmies of Botswana, were being replaced by the Masai of Kenya, or the Watusi of Ruanda. I remember looking out my peripheral vision and looking almost straight down at their color guard standing next to me.

The main body of the battalion arrived and continued to uphold the traditions of the 82nd Airborne Division. There was some type of military/athletic competition in the Sinai between the various military units there, and historically everyone competed for Second Place. Because the Fijians would win the competition, every year.

Except that year.

The Americans won, led by the members of the Scout platoon from Headquarters Company 4/325 AIR, 82nd Airborne Division.

I turned every set back that was set upon me, into a set-up for greatness.

After duty-hours I studied and took several college courses in History and English, with the University of Maryland, and Central Texas College.

We didn't have cell phones back then, so I wrote a letters home.

Every.

Single.

Day.

I wrote almost 200 letters during that deployment, I know because I numbered each and every single one of them on the back. I worked out almost every moment I was off-duty and the desert environment was extremely conducive to outdoor workouts. It looked like Venice Beach at the out-door gym sometimes. I swam every day. Let me repeat that, I swam miles and miles every single day.

Somehow, I got to be responsible for of all the military lifeguards down at the beach.

There was an old legend there named **Herb Brav**. He was a *"Green Beret"* retired Command Sergeant Major in the U.S. Army, who served in both the Korean conflict and the Vietnam War. After 30 years of honorable service to our country, he served another 27 years for the MFO. When he died, his death was announced on the floor of the United States Congress while it was in session. He had photos all over his gymnasium of all the world class athletes that he had trained, to include a young Mike Tyson.

I heard he was friends with Jack Lalane and the former *35th President of the United States, John F. Kennedy.*

I could write a book with all the information I learned from working with the legendary Herb for six-months, and maybe I will. This is some of what Herb did to me.

Every morning, he made all the lifeguards enter the water at Herbs beach, and swim out the inlet to the edge of the reef (maybe 500 feet). Then we would

110

turn left and swim to the boundary edge of the reef, turn around and swim to the other edge, turn around swim to the other edge, turn around and swim back to the mouth of the inlet, and then swim back to shore. He figured if you couldn't do the three-five mile, swim you weren't in shape to work that day.

So, every morning I executed this swim. It's January and the water is a little cold, but more importantly its dark. I could swim before I met Herb, but after him I felt like I was a shark.

Until one morning after doing this swim for several months, the BMNT (dawn but not sunrise) now provides enough light, where I can see deep down into the water.

It's shallow as you swim out of the reef, but once you get to the edge of the shallow water, the Red Sea drops off and it's pretty deep. In fact, its 1,600 feet deep (that's 160 stories down) and at its maximum depth its 7,250 feet deep (725 stories). So, when I make my turn to start my swim, my mind starts to play tricks on me. As I look down below me I "think" I see Sharks. But I know that I am just imagining things, so I keep on swimming.

But every time I look down I see what I think are Sharks. So maybe I am seeing Manta Ray fins, or Dolphin fins, or somethings else.

I get back to shore and I ask herb for the first time,
*"Excuse me Herb, but are there sharks down there?"*

*"Yeah there's sharks down there"*, he replies without missing a beat. *"There have always been sharks down there. You just didn't know it, so you weren't afraid, so there was no danger. But now that you know, they can smell and sense your fear, so be careful... and take off that digital watch."*

I say to Herb, *"Are you freaking crazy, you had me swimming with freaking sharks?!?"*

*"Yeah, yeah, he says. You'll be alright. If one of 'em comes up to you, just say HOO-AHH (while under water) and punch 'em in the nose, they'll leave you alone."*

*The next morning, I conduct my swim and swim right into a black garbage trash bag. You should have seen the fight I had with the water that day. Between me yelling*

111

*HOO-AHH and drinking sea water, and punching this trash bag in the dark, I know I must have been a sight to see from the beach!*

I heard Herb once conducted a free swim from Alcatraz Island to San Francisco.

Don't know if that true, but I do know that he did swim from our base in South Camp out to Tiran Island and that's near Saudi Arabia!

*WTH?!?!*

He swam across the Red Sea, regularly, with over 40 different species of Sharks. Sand Tiger Sharks, Hammerhead Sharks, Spot Tail Sharks, Grey Reef Sharks, White Tip Sharks, Black Tip Sharks!

*I mean what in da world?!?*

The U.S. Army eventually forbid other soldiers from swimming with him, out to the islands, when it got too dangerous.

I think the Star War character of Yoda the Jedi was based off of the real-life Herb Brav. But Herb was a real deal Djedi Master.

I would watch him every day ride down to the beach for his swim, on his bicycle. One day he falls off his bike, he gets up and starts kicking his bike, and screaming at it. *"You're not a team player! You're not at team player!"* is what he says to his bike.

Working with Herb, I got in the best shape of my life. 35 pull-ups easy. Run another 2 miles, after just swimming 5 miles, too easy.

Free dive without air tanks, just a mask and flipper fins, too easy.

Some of his mantras, that I live by to this day were:
**"When the will is strong, everything is easy!"**

**Pain is just weakness leaving the body.**

**When the Man with the Skill meets the Man with the Will, the Man with the Skill gonna die...**

I have heard another version of that:

**Hard Work Beats Talent,**
**When Talent Doesn't Work Hard.**

I may have been NCOIC of the military lifeguards, but Herb was the HMFIC of the beach. In fact, it's called Herb's Beach to this very day. Look it up!

The man was a legend.

Last story about Herb Brav.

He once told me, *"You're not supposed to die."*

So of course, me being the eager young Buck Sergeant that I was, asks Herb, ***"What do you mean you're not supposed to die?"***

He says, *"We've all been conditioned to die. But if you get shot you're not supposed to die."* He said, *"If you cut a chicken's head off, it will still run around without its head, because it is too stupid to know it's supposed to die. If you cut an animals abdomen open, it will run around with its intestines hanging out, yes it will die eventually, but initially it doesn't know it's supposed to die."*

He says, *"We have been conditioned by the media on television and movies to think that when we get shot we're supposed to die. If you get shot in the head, you don't die until you give up the will to keep living."*

He says, *"If you ever notice when very old people pass away. They normally pass away after a significant event. Like a great-grand baby being born, or grandpa dies after grandma, or a college graduation."* He says, *"That people hold on up until that significant event and then they die, when they give up the will."*

Years later, I would find his words to be some of the truest words ever spoken.

Legend has it, that Herb was a POW during the Vietnam War. That he planned his escape from the moment he was captured. That when he was captured and blindfolded, he counted his footsteps to pace the distance to the POW compound where he would be held captive. That during the long trek to his place of captivity, they came upon a river, and put him in a boat. *How did he count his footsteps to measure distance while he was sitting in a boat?* He didn't.

113

Legend has it that he counted his heartbeats.

Legend has it that he was an unruly and uncooperative prisoner. That he was taken from the camp and executed in a field outside the camp, by getting shot in the head: bullet coming out the other side of his skull. That the enemy prison guards left his body, to go back to the POW camp and get some prisoners to bury his body. But when they got back, he was gone.

Supposedly, he had crawled away in the jungle to the river, and swam back to safety. That when he was shot in the head, the bullet penetrated his head, but took the path of least resistance and travelled around the circumference of his skull, missing his brain entirely, and exiting out the other side of his head.

Legend has it that he never gave up the will to live, and that's what he must have meant, when he told me you're not supposed to die; even if you get shot in the head. Unless you give up the will to live!

He said to me over and over and over again, he said to everyone who ever met him, *"When the Will Is Strong, Everything Is Easy!"*

Herb taught me some real Djedi secrets in the deserts back then. But his legend will live on. We can't talk to him anymore to distinguish fact from legend, because he passed from this plane of existence on this earth in 2012.

So as to NOT get an OPSEC violation, I won't talk about the duties of the soldiers during the MFO. Their strengths, deployment dispositions or individual unit composition. You'll have to talk with a current member of the MFO for that.

There is an old military phrase called *"Loose Lip Sink Ships."* It means to NOT discuss the operational details of a unit's mission or movement. That would constitute a violation of Operational Security (OPSEC).

In late 1985, another unit of soldiers from the 101st Airborne had just completed their six-month rotation as members of the MFO in the Sinai desert in Egypt. *They were on their way back to their home base at Fort Campbell, Kentucky; when they were all killed. Their aircraft crashed in Gander, Newfoundland in Canada killing all 248 passengers and 8 crew members on board.* The public report says the plane crashed was an accident. But whatever the cause was, it highlights the fact that you don't discuss troop movements!

**\*\*\***

Whenever I wasn't doing my job or training over there; I took advantage of the various tours that were offered. You would be amazed at how many soldiers do NOT venture outside their military bases to experience the culture, cuisine and lifestyle of the local population.

If my memory serves me correctly, the tours were organized by the USO, but I could be mistaken. I do know that one of the tours was from the base at South Camp to Mount Sinai (Moses Mountain).

I gladly went on that tour, and remember that there were several slots available for other soldiers to participate, but only a few of us took advantage of that opportunity. We had maybe a two-day pass to North Camp. We traveled by bus for three-hours to Mount Sinai, enroute to North Camp.

Mount Sinai is commonly referred to as Moses Mountain and is mentioned many times in the Bible and the Quran. According to many people in the Jewish, Christian and Islamic faiths, it is the site where Moses received the Ten Commandments from God and gave Gods laws to the Israelites.

We were offered an opportunity to climb up the 7,500 feet to its summit either one of two ways. One, ride by mule or donkey halfway up to the top, and then climb the stairs to the summit. Two, climb the stairs all the way up to the top.

From what I remembered most of the older soldiers and commissioned officers rode halfway up, and all the grunts and younger infantryman (like I was back then) started the climb. This was the real stairway to heaven, because it was like climbing up hundreds and hundreds of flights of stairs. Whenever you "think" you're approaching the top, you are just reaching a false summit, that you can't see beyond. Because there are more stone steps to climb.

Somewhere near the top, we came across a beautiful body of water. But most of us Infantrymen just stuck to using our trusty two-quart canteens that we brought with us to drink out of.

I remember finally getting to the top and expecting to experience a spiritual event of some type. Only to be met by a small Bedouin kid whom we saw at the bottom of the mountain, selling Coca-Colas to us at the top.

I was thoroughly surprised.

But more importantly I was tired.

I remember sitting down at the top and looking over almost all of the Sinai desert in either direction. The view was perfect from there and I really did some self-reflecting time while up there.

I know that biblical history teaches us that Moses returned down from the top of Mount Sinai with the ten commandments.

That these commandments would be awesome guidelines or rules for anyone, of any religion to follow. Whether they be Jew, Christian, Muslim, Hindu, Buddhist or whatever. Many different religious groups follow different tradition for numbering these 10 commandments in order, when they do follow them.

1. *God is God*
2. *You shall have no other false gods before God*
3. *Do not take the name of God in vain*
4. *Remember the Sabbath day and keep it Holy*
5. *Honor your Mother and Father*
6. *You shall not kill/murder*
7. *You shall not commit adultery*
8. *You shall not steal*
9. *You shall not bear false witness against your neighbor*
10. *You shall not covet your neighbor's wife, or anything that belongs to your neighbor.*

If we as people all across the world would just follow these statements, whether they be the word of God, inspired by God or just religious dogma: I believe we would all live a much better life.

I also know that according to the very same biblical scholars and scriptures; that Moses was supposedly educated in all the ways of the Egyptians according to the Holy Book of Acts, in the Seventh Chapter, and specifically the Twenty-Second sentence (or verse). Normally written as Acts 7:22.

**According to the Ancient Egyptians, there were 42 laws of Ma'at that were in existence thousands of years BEFORE the 10 commandments.**

These 42 laws were in place since at least 2900BC *(that's at least 4,917 years ago)*. You can research them for yourself, or go to the countries in North Africa (the middle east) and see them for yourself, because they are still there, written in stone.

If even the bible says that he (Moses) was learned in ALL the ways of the Ancient Egyptians, let's look at the 42 Laws of Ma'at and see some of what Moses learned in Egypt.

The 42 Laws of Ma'at are sometimes referred to as the 42 Negative Confessions. To prove that your spirit or your heart was as light as a feather. You know the heart that is supposed to be weighed by the scales of justice on judgment day.

1. *I have not committed sin.*
2. *I have not committed robbery with violence.*
3. *I have not stolen.*
4. *I have not slain men or women.*
5. *I have not stolen grain.*
6. *I have not purloined offerings.*
7. *I have not stolen the property of God.*
8. *I have not uttered lies.*
9. *I have not carried away food.*
10. *I have not uttered curses.*
11. *I have not committed adultery.*
12. *I have made none to weep.*
13. *I have not eaten the heart [grieved uselessly, or felt remorse].*
14. *I have not attacked any man.*
15. *I am not a man of deceit.*
16. *I have not stolen cultivated land.*
17. *I have not been an eavesdropper.*
18. *I have slandered no one.*
19. *I have not been angry without just cause.*
20. *I have not debauched the wife of any man.*
21. *I have not debauched the wife of man (repeats the previous affirmation but addressed to a different deity).*
22. *I have not polluted myself (drugs & alcohol).*
23. *I have terrorized none.*
24. *I have not transgressed against the Law.*
25. *I have not been wroth (highly incensed, angered).*

26. *I have not shut my ears to the words of truth.*
27. *I have not blasphemed.*
28. *I am not a man of violence.*
29. *I am not a stirrer up of strife or a disturber of the peace.*
30. *I have not acted or judged with undue haste.*
31. *I have not pried into matters.*
32. *I have not multiplied my words in speaking.*
33. *I have wronged none, I have done no evil.*
34. *I have not worked witchcraft or blasphemy against the King.*
35. *I have never stopped the flow of water.*
36. *I have never raised my voice arrogantly, or in anger.*
37. *I have not cursed or blasphemed God.*
38. *I have not acted with evil rage.*
39. *I have not stolen the bread of the God.*
40. *I have not carried away the cakes from the spirits of the dead.*
41. *I have not snatched away the bread of the child, nor treated with contempt the god of my city.*
42. *I have not slain the cattle belonging to God.*

Whether Moses received the ten commandments from God on the top of the mountain or whether the biblical allegory is confused with actual history, you have to judge for yourself. I will NOT lead, nor mislead any person when it comes to matters of faith. Because if I was to tell you some of the things I have seen, many of you would not believe me anyway.

I can only speak the truth as I know it, and relay what I have researched.

For example, I am glad that many people have renamed Mount Sinai as Moses Mountain. It makes it so much easier to locate in the Sinai desert of Egypt. But many people also believe that the actual African King Thutmose I, is the actual Moses. Especially, since his reign as King of Egypt (what we call Pharaoh) coincides with the actual biblical historical time.

*Many people who had some hidden addenda and practiced RWS did not want the masses of the world to equate the great Kings of African countries, with the Kings of european countries. So, the melinated African Kings (especially those from Sudan, Egypt and/or Kush) were called Pharaohs. As if to mean a royal title "other" than or less than a King.*

Anyway, when we get to the bottom of the mountain we go visit Saint Catherine's Monastery. It was built about 1,500 years ago (between 548 and 565) and it is one of the oldest monasteries in the world. It is one of the oldest continually operating libraries in the world, and the home of the monks who laid all them steps up Moses Mountain.

To lay all them stone steps from the bottom of that mountain to the top, took several years. I'm talking probably a few hundred years from what I witnessed.

There is also a Chapel and a Mosque there, and its grounds are considered sacred by many Christians, Jews and Muslims.

The monastery was built around the Burning Bush. The one that Moses heard the voice of God speak to him from.

No, it is NOT still burning!

But it is still there. Yes, I believe it to be the actual bush, and yes I believe it is thousands of years old. *Whether anyone believes God actually spoke to Moses from that bush, or if Moses existed or was an ancient allegory: I will not answer here. That is a question or re-affirmation for them to make about their own faith.*

I am addressing whether I believe *"that bush called the burning bush"* that I saw could be thousands of years old. I believe so, because there is ancient vegetation all around us, still vibrant and alive to this very day.

- There is a 1,600 year old Cypress Tree on Vancouver Island in Canada.

- There is an 1,800 year old Sugi Tree on Yakushima Island in Japan.

- There is a 2,300 year old Sacred Fig Tree in Anuradhapura, Sri Lanka.

- There is a 3,600 year old Patagonian Cypress Tree in Los Rios, Chile

- Right here in the United States of America in Inyo County, California there is a very old Great Basin Bristlecone Pine Tree that is still living. It is reported to be 4,849 years old; and its name is Methuselah.

So yeah, I can believe that there is a bush in Africa, in the north-eastern country of Egypt that is about 2,000 years old. But like I said, when I saw it, it wasn't burning, and I didn't hear no voices coming from it.

***

I actually took three separate trips up to Cairo, Egypt from South Camp (our base down at the southern tip of the Sinai Peninsular) during that rotation, just to see the historical sights.

When we arrived in the region, my first trip was in late January 1994. It was very cold, and you can tell by the clothes that I was wearing (in the photos in this book, or the photos on the website at **www.BrotherShadow.com**). I'm wearing a black watch cap, and my hands in my pockets. You can see the type of clothes the locals were wearing.

My second trip to Cairo was in the Spring of '94, and that was primarily to see all the sights in the Ancient Egyptian Museum and to do some shopping with the vendors.

My final trip to Cairo, was in early Summer '94 before I departed. My attire was commensurate with the hot humid weather.

Every trip, in addition to seeing the other historical sites; whether they were through the ancient City of the Dead, to the Museum, the Sphinx, or shopping with the vendors, I always insured that I visited the great pyramids.

Because of the encroachment of the city of Cairo, you could almost never tell the ancient Egyptian Pyramids we almost adjacent to the city. I mean one minutes you're in the city, then you turn a corner and blam! You are now looking at the Great Ancient African Egyptian Pyramids.

The three main Pyramids that sit on the Giza location are known at *the Great Pyramid of Khufu, the Pyramid of Khafre* and *the Pyramid of Menkaure.* The common Greek names for these three pyramids are *Cheops, Kephren* and *Mykerinus*. There are several other smaller pyramids at the complex site, and the Great Sphinx is at the current entrance to the complex site.

As big, and large, and massive as they are, they all use to be bigger when they were covered with a smooth limestone casing, from top to bottom. Only the Pyramid of Khafre still has some of its original limestone casing near the top of it.

There used to be Seven Great Wonders of the Ancient World.

1. The Greek **Lighthouse of Alexandria** (280 BC)
2. The Greek **Colossus of Rhodes** (290 BC)
3. The Persian **Mausoleum of Halicarnassus** (350 BC)
4. The Greek **Statue of Zeus at Olympia** (460 BC)
5. The Greek **Temple of Artemis at Ephesus** (550 BC)
6. The Babylonian **Hanging Gardens of Babylon** (600 BC)
7. The African Egyptian **Great Pyramid of Giza** (2580 BC)

The Great Pyramid at Giza is the only one that still remains largely intact today. Since it was built by Black Africans over 2,580 years before Joshua Ben Yosef (Jesus Christ) was here, that makes that structure approximately 4,597 years old. I highlight the fact that the Ancient Egyptian were Black Africans, because they made statues of themselves, in their own image, that you can see today.

*Just look at the image of Black African Queen Tiye. She looks like just about anybody's grandmother from any major urban metropolitan center in America today; Detroit, New York, Chicago, Houston, Atlanta, Los Angeles.*

- *She was the **wife** of the **18th Dynasty King (Pharaoh) Amenhotep III** (who ruled Egypt from 1386 to 1349 BC).*
- *She was the **mother** of the **18th Dynasty King (Pharaoh) Akhenaten** (who ruled Egypt from 1352-1336 BC). He was recorded to be the first man on earth to profess a belief in the concept of "one God".*
- *She was the **grandmother** of the 18th Dynasty King (Pharaoh) Tutankhamun (who ruled Egypt from 1332-1324 BC). Many people erroneously refer to his as King Tut.*

*His father believed that the one true Gods name was Amun, so his sons name was Tut-Ankh-Amun (Tutankhamun), but was later changed to Tut-Ankn-Amun (Tutanknamun). Many people disagree with me, but they still say the God Amun or Amen upon the conclusion of their prayers, to this very day.*

But based upon the currently population of Arabs who live in Egypt today, you could subconsciously think that the population back then was Arab also, not true! If you get most of your historical information from popular television and movies, you could also think that the great ancient leaders of that country were european, also not true!

I also keep repeating the phrase, "Ancient African Egyptian" because many people refuse to even look at a map, and see that the country of Egypt is physically on the continent of Africa. Along with approximately 55 other independent countries. Many people don't believe that Egypt is in Africa, they believe it is in some mythical made up place called the middle-east.

*Well if that is true, where is the middle-west?*

*Or the middle-north?*

The truth of the matter, is that there are only seven known continents inside this planet; (1) Africa, (2) Asia, (3) Australia, (4) north America, (4) south America, (6) Antarctica and (7) europe.

Some people who practiced RWS considered europe to be the center of the world, and the country of England to be the headquarters. *Just look at where Greenwich mean time, or Zulu time starts at?*

- All of the countries that were on the european mainland geographically east of England, were considered **"the Near East"**.

- All of the countries that were located in South West Asia and North Africa were considered **"the Middle East"** of England.

- All of the predominantly Asian countries in the Orient region were considered **"the Far East"** of England. *But to travel to any of them from the United States, you would have to travel west, WTH?!? I have to travel West to go to the Far East, that doesn't pass the smell test, and sure don't make sense to me.* **Like having a lift kit on a luxury sedan, or dropping a pick-up truck putting curb feelers on it. What?!?**

Anyway, when I visited the Great Pyramid complex, I remember going "inside" the Great Pyramid of the African King (Pharaoh) Khufu. Supposedly, an entrance was created by actual tomb raiders, and its entrance is actually called "the Robbers Tunnel".

There was a wooden ramp leading up to the entrance and it was real dark once we got inside. We proceed up, down and up a series of interior ramps.

As I maneuvered inside the interior of the Great Pyramid through the corridor I remember thinking two distinct thoughts.

- First, I believed that if anyone was claustrophobic it was gonna be extremely difficult for them to gets as down far inside as we have proceeded.

- Second, I found it very difficult to comprehend that I was actually inside the Great Pyramid. This great structure literally stood the test of time. Around the time of Joshua Ben Yousef (Jesus Christ), this structure was already, well over 2,500 years old – and that time (the biblical times of Jesus) was 2,000 years ago.

Once we got deep inside the pyramid the most vivid memory I had was entering the "King's Chamber" where a giant stone sarcophagus was located. It was solid granite and was bigger than the actual entrance to the chamber. I didn't climb inside of it, because like many people who know me know; I don't play with the spirit world. I know it's power. It is so quiet inside the Kings Chamber, that a person can really reflect on their inner self. Much like when I was up on Moses Mountain and the peace and solitude was similar to when a paratrooper exits and aircraft while in flight. *You know the awesome quietness, where you can actually hear your parachute opening and deploying?* Well, that's the kind of peace and quiet I felt inside the Kings Chamber.

I toured the Ancient City of the Dead that is adjacent to the massive pyramid complex on the Giza plateau. I vividly remember standing under the great Sphinx statue. The location where many fraternities, and sororities, and other "secret" societies metaphorically pledge their oaths at, across the burning sands. Well I metaphorically, symbolically and physically rode "Cylde" through the burning sands of the desert, and stood beneath the real Lions Paw, where I received "the word".

The Egyptian Museum of Antiquities in Cairo was one of my favorite museums in the world to visit. After the Smithsonian African-American History Museum in Washington, DC and the American Museum of Natural History in New York City.

The Egyptian Museum in Cairo has over 120,000 items inside and many of them are hidden in plain sight: especially if you don't know what you're looking for.

But there is a great spiritual awakening in this world and people are starting to, as they say, ***"come out of the matrix."*** So, whenever you have to resort to burning books and destroying knowledge because it doesn't reinforce your belief system, or religion, or dogma: ***you have just validated your own weaknesses and deficiencies.*** Many artifacts and mummies from the Egyptian Museum were destroyed during the Egyptian Revolution of 2011, especially the statues and items depicting the Ancient African Nubian or Egyptian, Kings and royalty.

***But just like many rioters and looters in Urban America who appear to destroy, tear up, and burn down their own neighborhood. It's easy, when you don't own anything, and you know the stuff that you're destroying in not yours.***

So, the "bad" Egyptians that were destroying the artifacts are just validating the fact that; they are NOT the descendants of the original people who built all those great wonders, and left the statues of themselves and historical artifacts.

The Nile River in Egypt reminded me of the Tigress and Euphrates Rivers in Iraq, for their historical importance in human development. But, the Nile River in Africa really reminded me of the Mississippi River here in the United States. Whereas what the Nile River was to the melinated Africans over there, the Mississippi River was to the melinated inhabitants here in America. Whether they were red, black, brown or yellow; there is no debate that there were already "*people living*" in our country years before the european explorers "*discovered*" this new world.

***

I also took several trips ad USO tours into the country of Israel while I was stationed with the MFO. Similar to how people I know in my hometown of New York City have never been to the Statue of Liberty, never been on the Staten Island Ferry, never been on a horse carriage ride through Central Park, never been to the Chrysler Building or the Empire State building. Mainly because they live there and take those things for granted. However, a visitor or tourist will tour New York City and see more in a 96-hour (four day) trip, than many New Yorkers will see there in their lifetimes.

I was the same way in North Africa, I mean the "middle-east".

If I wasn't working, I was training. If I wasn't training, I was learning. If I wasn't learning, I was visiting the once in a lifetime sites and locations.

The country of Palestine didn't exist as it does today, but the lands that it encompasses I did visit. We traveled to the cities of *Eliat, Beersheba, Bethlehem* and *Jerusalem*. I distinctly remember visiting Jerusalem. It was very memorable because it is known as the center of the religious world for Christians who practice **Christianity**, Jews who practice **Judaism**, and Muslims who practice **Islam**.

There is a Wailing Wall or Western Wall that remains from the Second Jewish Temple (516 BC – 70 AD). According to tradition, the Second Jewish Temple replaced Solomon's Temple (the First Jewish Temple) when it was destroyed by the Babylonians. The Wailing Wall is one of the holiest sites in **Judaism**. I saw many people praying at the wall, and leaving message and notes inscribed on paper and inserted into the cracks in the wall.

It is also the site where many Muslims believe that the Prophet Muhammad tied his steed on his night journey to Jerusalem, before he ascended into heaven. An **Islamic** shrine has been erected there with a gold roof called, the Dome of the Rock (691 AD). It can be seen from all over the city of Jerusalem, especially the hilltops, and it is also at the Temple Mount complex.

Less than a 30-minute walk away, maybe one mile in distance is the Mount Olives. The mount has been used as a Jewish cemetery for over 3,000 years and has approximately 150,000 graves. Many people want to be buried there based upon the tradition that states that when the Messiah comes, the resurrection of the dead will begin there. This site is central and extremely holy to many who practice **Christianity** because it is believed to be the site where; once crucified Joshua Ben Yosef (Jesus Christ) actually ascended into heaven from.

I know the distance because; we walked it.

Many of us off-duty soldiers from different faiths, races, creeds, and religions, walked the historical route that Joshua Ben Yosef (Jesus Christ) walked enroute to his crucifixion.

That route is called the Via Dolorosa, the Way of Sorrow or *"Stations of the Cross"*. It traces the path, and there are Roman Numeral Markers at various locations along the way. I took some photos back then, and hope to post some of them on my website (www.BrotherShadow.com).

The various Roman Numerals would state a significant event that occurred at that location, on the Station of the Cross. The tour guide would say something that sounded like this:

- "Here at Station Three ( **III** ), this is the spot where he fell.

- "Here at Station Five ( **V** ), he couldn't carry this cross any longer so the Romans compelled a man named Simon Peter *(the father of Alexander and Rufus)* to help carry the cross.

- "Here at Station Ten ( **X** ), he was stripped of his garments."

I remember we took a small tour bus up to the top of the hill, to the location historically referred to at his crucifixion site. I remember looking back at the massive number of graves around that location, and many of them had flat stones on top of the gravestone markers. I remember looking out over the ancient city of Jerusalem, and seeing the historical center of three of the worlds major religions; *Christianity*, *Judaism* and *Islam*.

I remember thinking to myself, all of these people have been fighting each other for a very long time, and all three religions have the same enemy. Whether you call him (or it) the devil, or satan, or shaitan, or diabolos, or negative influences, or negative energy, or bad vibes, or the darkside, or dark forces or whatever it is that is inherently against the good order or nature.

There is so much more I want to talk about during my middle-eastern adventures, that I will now "have to" write another book. Especilly, when I talk about being inside the tomb, and seeing the granite slab that they supposedly laid his body out on.

I remember we went to Tel Aviv, on the West Bank, and to the Gaza strip. I remember a Liberty pass from MFO North Camp and enjoying the beautiful beaches of the West Bank of the Gaza strip. There were hundreds of other obviously soldiers with close cropped military hairstyles there. Several of us were in individual groups, and all were from different countries.

***

*the Republic of Iraq*
I spent a total of seven years in Iraq (2004, 2007, 2008, 2009, 2010, 2011, 2012 & 2013) in support of Operation IRAQI FREEDOM and Operation NEW DAWN; with both the U.S. Military (DoD) and the U.S. State Department (DoS).

My first time into Iraq was in 2004, while I was still on active duty with the U.S. Army during Operation IRAQI FREEDOM 2 (OIF-2). I am not embellishing when I say it's classified and I can't talk about it. *Because my deployment to Iraq is still classified and I can't talk about it.* While on active duty, I went to Iraq "in a TDY status" with other Department of the Defense personnel, some of them civilians. I was the only NCO in a detachment of commissioned officers and civilians. My additional charge when I left CONUS, was to bring them back alive.

If the project I was assigned to has been de-classified, or will become so in the near future – I will then gladly discuss the specifics of my missions at that time.

But NOT before.

Just know that I rotated to several active combat units within the 1st Cavalry Division and participated in both dismounted and mounted, Infantry/Calvary Combat Operations. Some from Camp Cuervo (formerly Camp Muleskinner) which became Camp Rustamiyah. Some from Camp Headhunter (became Camp Independence) then Camp Al-Istiqlal. Some from FOB Union III (became FOB Al-Tawheed). I spent many days hunkered in various "duck and cover bunkers" on the massive headquarters that were located at Victory Base Complex called (VBC). That was near the Baghdad International Airport (BIAP).

But the months I spent attached to TASK FORCE LANCER based around the 2nd Battalion, 5th Cavalry Regiment (2/5 Cav) of the 1st Cavalry Division is what I am most proud of.

127

The sacrifices those soldiers made before I got there, while I was there and after I left were so heroic; that we (all Americans) owe them a debt we can never repay. The stories I heard upon my arrival were unbelievable. Just imagine, you're the last man left out of everyone in your original squad that deployed. Or imagine your platoon sustaining 17 casualties during one rotation. Or imagine the FOB on pace to becoming the most mortared base in U.S. Army history. *I don't know if that true, but FOB War Eagle was mortared and rocketed, almost every day.*

Every.

Single.

Day.

If you don't believe me, go get the New York Times best-selling book about the unit; *"The Long Road Home: A Story of War and Family"* by Martha Raddatz.

If you need to see it on television, watch the National Geographic miniseries on from your local service provider or check your DVR for listings.

Upon my return CONUS from Iraq in support of Operation IRAQI FREEDOM I had fulfilled my 20 years of active duty of honorable service, and was placed on the Retired Rolls of the U.S. Army.

Part of the reason for my retirement was based upon what I saw over there during that deployment. I was determined that nothing on earth could get me to go back to that location, I was done with Iraq.

I worked various jobs as a civilian instructor and as a civilian security contractor in the United States. I worked for *Olive Group* and *MPRI*. The best job that I ever had was during this time, when I was employed as a Civilian Observer-Controller (OC) for a subsidiary of Northrup Grumman. We were OC's for the Special Forces Qualification Course (SFQC) "Q-course." We were instructors for phase II of the SFQC, which at the time was Small Unit Tactics and Weapons.

So, I was teaching the next generation of our countries "Green Berets."

Every night I would come home from training covered in mud, saw dust or whatever. Sometimes I wouldn't be home for days. It was awesome!

Then the contract ended and everyone who wasn't "pick-up" by the new company that won the government contract over *Northrup Grumman* became unemployed. This wasn't job security like I had in the active military.

So, with the mortgage and other bills starting to pile up, I received an offer from a PMC to work in Iraq, on a DoS program. I would be protecting American diplomats, I would have all the weapons and tools that I had while on active duty, plus none of the restrictions of "the Big Army".

So, I convinced myself that, had I stayed in the U.S. Army I would be back over there anyway, on another deployment as somebody First Sergeant/E-8. So, go over there and make a few dollars for a few months. Well, I didn't know they were gonna offer me "a gazillion dollars" to do what I liked doing anyway. I wind up staying in Iraq for six more YEARS!!!

I deployed to Iraq so much, I had an Iraqi Visa in my passport. I deployed with that PMC to *Bashara* and *Tallil* in Southern Iraq. Then spent some time in *Baghdad* at the flag pole.

Man, do I miss those days!

✱✱✱

*the Italian Republic (Italy)*
I have decided that I will DEFINETLY write another book. There is just too much information I want to include in this book, and it is already past the publishers recommended guideline of 380 pages. I'm at 425 already. I'll have to make the font size a two, and people will have to read this book with a magnifying glass if I try to squeeze any more words into it.

Just know that my deployment to Italy with the U.S. Army's 173rd Airborne Brigade, was the most pleasurable experience for my family. However, I was deployed from Italy almost nine months out of every year, for the three years I was there.

For arriving there with the SETAF Infantry Brigade, to the reflagging of the unit into the 173rd Airborne Brigade.

I was the narrator for the units' re-activation ceremony since Vietnam. I was also the narrator for "the XVIII Airborne Corps and Fort Bragg NCO Academy" on base while I was assigned there. Yes, I'm the voice that you would hear when you attended the parades and graduations ceremonies on post.

I would say, "LADIES AND GENTLEMEN, PASSING THE REVIEWING STAND NOW IS SO AND SO, FROM SO AND SO. PLEASE RISE AND REMAIN STANDING FOR THE PASSING OF THE NATIONAL COLORS!"

Yep, that was me!

So it wasn't a surprise to me when I was chose to become the narrator for the 173rd Airborne Brigade.

***

I showed up to the unit in Italy, and I'm sterile. I choose to not wear any patches and additional skill set badges on my duty uniform (so I'm wearing a sterile uniform), so people would treat me like a noncommissioned officer.

No better or worse.

The Brigade Command Sergeant Major assigns me to a particular subordinate Battalion and a specific Company. I report to the company and the units First Sergeant takes one quick look at my uniform. He doesn't see any Jumpmaster Wings (because I'm not wearing them). He doesn't see a Ranger Tab, or no other additional skill identifying badges either. I don't even have on Air Assault Wings. He tells me to go back to Brigade because he doesn't have a job for me. I make the mistake of trying to tell him that the Brigade CSM sent me here, because I thought he was finish talking to me, and it was my turn to speak. *"Get the fuck outta here"* or words to that effect is what he says to me.

So, I report back to the Brigade CSM and he tell me to go find a desk in the S-3 shop and go to work. I start out as the Brigade S-3 (Schools) NCO and quietly do my job: sterile. One day the Brigade CSM tells me to take his Driver under my wing and get him straight, to get promoted one day. I create a flawless "Counseling Packet" because I had just come from the NCO Academy where it was my job to train junior enlisted soldiers to become NCO's.

He's apparently impressed because he then tells me to take control of all the Command Drivers. Them Privates and Specialist were running while, and on auto pilot. Because, anyone who ask them to do something: they would state that they had to drive for the Commander, or Deputy Commander, or the Executive Officer or something else.

So, I tell them all, we are going to do P.T. in the morning, and they start with the bullshit. One says, "I have to get the vehicle ready for the Colonel early in the morning." Another one says, "I have to pick up, whatever in the morning."

I tell all of them, I don't give a damn what you gotta do. If we gotta have P.T. at 03:30 instead of 06:30 in the morning, so you can have time to do your jobs then that's what it's gonna be. I don't care, you all will get the required four hours of sleep, but that's all I have to do…

…and them hours don't have to be consecutive!

So, the next day when the Command Staff Group arrives, they hear

>    **One, Two Three**, ONE!!!
>    **One, Two, Three**, TWO!!!
>    **One, Two, Three**, THREE!!!
>    **One, Two, Three**, FOUR!!!
>    **One, Two, Three**, FIVE!!!

We are already doing morning P.T., and we will keep doing it unless we're dead. We are training as long as we are alive. The Brigade CSM tells me, great job and that he wants me to go for the NCO of the Month Board, or the Sergeant Morales Board, or something. He says for me to bring him my personnel (201) file. Then he says, *"Never mind I'll get it from S-1 myself."*

Later that day, he has my file and he's screaming up and down the halls of the Brigade Headquarters.

> *Sergeant Bilal!!!*
> *Sergeant Bilal!!!*
> *Where are all your damn badges and patches at?!?*
> *Jumpmaster?!?*
> *Special Forces?!?*
> *WTF?!?*

Everyone in the Brigade S-3 shop is looking at me like *"Who is he talking about, because he couldn't possibly be talking about me."*

I reply to the Brigade CSM with, **"Well Sergeant Major, you know that Army Regulation (AR) 670-1 states that I only HAVE TO wear all my badges and tabs on my dress uniform."**

> *"I don't wanna hear that crap. You put them badges and patches on."*

**"Well Sergeant Major, I feel that people treat me..."**

> *"I don't give a damn what you feel. In fact, why are you not doing push-ups while I'm talking to you. PUSH! PUSH Sergeant, and every time I see you without them patches, badges and tabs you're gonna push."*

**"But Sergeant Major..."**

> *"Butt my ass, them badges are NOT for you. They are to inspire the confidence in your subordinate soldiers as a testimony of your training and awards."*

Long story short, I eventually wear my BDU beautification devises.

This S-3 Officer comes up to me weeks later, and apologizes to me. I said, **"For what Sir?"** He says that all these weeks he has been looking at the Special Forces Tab on my uniform, but his mind made him think that it said, "President Hundred" the marksmanship tab.

He says to me, that he couldn't believe that I was, you know Special Forces – Special Forces. As if there is some other type?!?

I have to give a big shout out to all of my brothers in *Zillah Military Lodge number 167*, to the *Pride of the Mediterranean Consistory number 350*, and to my brothers in *Dulkaada Temple number 226* Ancient Egyptian Arabic Order of the Nobles Mystic Shrine.

Thanks for showing me what real fellowship and brotherhood is all about. The except opposite of what I saw in Korea years earlier. Thanks for making me a better man, and I better stop writing now, before I say something that violate my fraternal obligations.

There is a difference between a "Free MASON" and a "REAL Ma-Son" and since I happen to be both, some of us can talk, and some of us can talk-talk.

\*\*\*

The United States of America is a Constitutional Federal Republic composed of 50 separate States, a Federal District and five major self-governing Territories.

The 50 states include 48 connected or contiguous states. *Two others; (1) Alaska and (2) Hawaii (which are not connected).*

The federal district is Washitaw, I mean Washington, District of Columbia (DC) which is the country's capital, but not a part of "any" one individual state.

The five major permanently inhabited self-governing territories are:

1.  Puerto Rico
2.  the U.S. Virgin Islands
3.  Guam
4.  the Northern Mariana Islands
5.  the American Samoa Islands

All residents of all the U.S. states and those territories are all U.S. Citizens and recent news articles have highlighted to me the fact that many American citizens do not know that Puerto Rico is a part of the United States.

Their ignorance or RSW won't allow them to distinguish.

Remember when I said that CONUS for the military meant the connected 48 states between the countries of Mexico and Canada?

Yes, Alaska and Hawaii are 2 of the 50 states that also make up our country. However, for the purpose of military travel they are NOT considered CONUS. They are considered OCONUS.

*Hawaii*

Since 1959 the Hawaiian Islands have been a part of the United States. Like many people I only knew about Hawaii from what I saw on television and in the movies. *Gilligan's Island* (1964-67), *Hawaii Five-O* (1968-80), *The Don Ho Show* (1976-77), *Magnum P.I.* (1980-88) and *Fantasy Island* (1977-84) were popular television shows that shaped my views about Hawaii.

Several movies all led me to believe that Hawaii was on big happy paradise because that's I all ever saw, and images shape our reality.

I did not know that the State of Hawaii was actually a group of 8 large islands and several smaller ones. I did not know that the majority of Hawaii's population (953,207 people about 72% of the state's population) live on the Island of Oahu, which also has the city of Honolulu – the state capital on it. I did not know that the main resort area of Waikiki Beach with its tall hotels and office building was there, or that the Pearl Harbor Naval base was on that Island.

I erroneously thought that the entire state of Hawaii was one large island, and everyone lived in a virtual paradise.

My first visit to the island of Hawaii, or should I say the Hawaii Island(s) was during my military service when we traveled to Hickam, Air Force Base for a training exercise. My unit at the time (early 1980's) was one of the first in the U.S. military to transfer the older Vietnam era UH-1 Huey helicopters in for the new UH-60 Blackhawks. So, we folded the main roto blades and put them on a big USAF C-5 Galaxy Aircraft and flew to Hickam, AFB. As a U.S. Army helicopter (avionics) mechanic, one of my first jobs was to reassemble the helicopters In Accordance With (IAW) the applicable military technical manuals and regulations. We had the required tools to accomplish our job, but for whatever reason I needed a particular item, that I did not have in my individual tool box.

I asked the members of our sister service, the U.S. Air Force for assistance and in no time, a truck was driving on the flight line to bring me the required tool. Here comes another dose of reality, when the guy driving the truck that I thought was bringing me the tool, stops and opens up the side of the truck like he was driving your local neighborhood ice cream truck.

*What do you need he says?*

I'm standing there in shock, because in the U.S. Army, I had an extremely large oversized tricycle with a carriage in the back to transport my tools, documents, manuals and repair parts from the hangar to the aircraft on the flight line.

But this Air Force guy is driving a truck, that's not really a truck. The whole truck "is" the tool box, and according to him, that's his MOS. His job is to bring the right tool to the right person, so they can do the right job, WTH?!?

We leave the Air Force base, and stayed on the U.S. Army base called Schofield Barracks. It was just like every other army base that I have ever been too, you've seen one you've seen them all. But we stayed on the base in a section called, "Area X" in GP medium tents. Not a bad deployment and the training was extremely realistic.

We still had Specialist 5 (SP5/E-5) and Specialist 6 (SP6/E-6) in the U.S. Army back then. So, NCO's did Sergeants stuff and Specialist did technical stuff with equipment.

There is an Aircraft Crew chief assigned to each aircraft in the U.S. Army. The bigger aircraft (planes or helicopters) may have multiple crew chief's. All aircraft may also have other crewmembers, but there is only one "main" crew chief per aircraft. So, since the Blackhawk helicopter has a Crew chief who maintains and services "his or her" aircraft, they also perform functions as a door gunner when the aircraft is operational. But the other side of the aircraft may have a door gunner, who is also a crew "member" from the various aviation maintenance crewmembers on the ground; armament, avionics, electricians or aircraft maintenance supervisors. Several times members (like me) would have to be on "flight status" to identify a complaint or validate a repair you just made. A helicopter is not like a car, where if the mechanic made a mistake, you can just pull over to the side of the road. Plus, there were times, that a pilot would tell me an avionic devise did not work in flight. I would repair or replace the item; radio, navigation equipment, light fixture, whatever it was. Later the same pilot would tell me he experienced the same problem, and I would explain everything I did to fix the problem.

Well one particular time I was on a test flight to replicate a problem and it happened. The stress that was place on the airframe in flight caused an issue that could not be replicated on the ground. I then understood the necessity of having some members of the ground crew on flight status.

I remember flying along the civilian population, very fast and low about 50-100 feet above the water at Waikiki Beach in a Blackhawk helicopter and looking straight down into the clear blue water. I had never seen water that blue, that clear in my life. That operation in Hawaii was one of the best experiences I have had. *The exotic paradise that is parleyed to the general public is all true, and if you ever get a chance to travel to Hawaii I highly suggest that you do so, at least one in your life.*

However, I cannot conclude this paragraph/chapter without telling you about one eye opening experience that I had. I traveled to the beaches on that Hawaiian island and had a great time one day when I wasn't scheduled to work, but when it was time to travel back to the base, specifically to "Area X" I mistakenly got on the wrong bus. As the bus left the beach area, I noticed that the buildings started to look a little less affluent. The further we traveled inland (this particular direction) the more dilapidated the buildings looked. Then I saw an upside-down shopping cart.

Almost everyone knows that an upside-down shopping cart is the "unofficial" boundary marker for the hood or the ghetto. People who don't have a car, take public transportation (bus or trains). Many times, the bus stops "in the hood" do not have adequate overhead shelter for the elements, nor benches to sit on. So, people will push their groceries from the market to the bus stop in the shopping cart from the store they just shopped at, and flip it upside down, to sit on until the bus arrives. Now when they leave as the bus depart, the carts just remain there and get weathered as time passes and they become unofficial boundary markers.

Well not only did I see upside down shopping carts, but I could have sworn I saw liquor stores and the down trotted members of society.

My grandmother used to say, *"Even heaven got a ghetto. Who do you think is gonna wash and clean all them white robes?"*

I remember going to Hickam, AFB for lunch one day, and standing in awe and amazement at the way the U.S. Air Force puts money and time into the Airman's quality of life. The DFAC (Dining Facility) or Mess Hall line was extremely long. I saw all the crabs or lobsters in the fish tanks along the walls and just assumed that the decorative fish tanks where there for aesthetic purposes. Nope. The service members (Airman, Sailors & Soldiers) were picking out which seafood item they wanted the cooks to prepare for them.

Since I have never eaten lobster or crab, that thought had never entered my mind. Whatever I got to eat, I was amazed at the efficiency that the U.S. Air Force used to charge each person for each meal.

After you got all your food, the headcount person at the cash register charged you for each individual item. I had some type of military meal card, so I don't remember paying cash money. But I thought about how different that was from the U.S. Army way of doing things. In the Army, you pay for your food first when you enter the DFAC (with meal card or cash) and whether you eat one biscuit or the cooks hook you up with extra portions it didn't matter.

The U.S. Air Force was "a la carte" and the U.S. Army was "buffet price".

✶✶✶

*Alaska*
My deployment to Alaska focused on the U.S. Army based of Fort Richardson (Anchorage) and Fort Wainwright (Fairbanks).

Alaska is the largest state of the 50 United States by land area (bigger than the states of Texas, California and Montana combined), it is bigger than the combined land areas of the 22 smallest U.S. States.

It became a U.S. State in 1959, and with the Trans-Alaska Pipeline (completed in 1977) bringing in so much oil revenue, the state repealed its state income tax in 1980. That's right there is currently **no state personal income tax**. In fact, there is a general Permanent Fund Dividend that the State of Alaska grants to all "residents".

**In 2016 that amount was $1,022.**

So that means if a husband and wife were living in Alaska, and they had 3 children living with them, theoretically they would not "pay" a state income tax on 15 APR (since there is no state income tax). But the State would pay them a refund total amount of $5,110 (5 checks) one for each of the family's residents.

The payments fluctuate each year; the lowest was $331.29 (1984) and the highest was $2,072 (2015). I know because during my tenure stationed in Alaska at Fort Richardson near Anchorage, Alaska I was a resident.

However, I changed my residence years later and you can't just change it back. You have to actually live there. There were several factors involved in me making the statement that I'm about to make, but here it is:

**Fort Richardson, Alaska was the best duty station I was ever assigned to, period.**

The last U.S. census in 2010 estimated the population of the entire state to be about 741,894 people. Back in the day when I was stationed there the population was 550,000 residents. That means that the State of Alaska has 2 Senators, just like every other state in the Union (regardless of population size), but only enough people to have 1 Congressional Representative (for the entire state).

For example:
2 Senators & 53 Congressmen: California
2 Senators & 36 Congressmen: Texas
2 Senators & 27 Congressmen: Florida
2 Senators & 27 Congressmen: New York
2 Senators & 13 Congressmen: North Carolina
2 Senators & 1 Congressman: Delaware
2 Senators & 1 Congressmen: Alaska

The State of Alaska does not have subordinate counties inside of it like the majority of the other U.S. States, it is divided into 16 "boroughs".

1. **Anchorage** is the largest city (291,826 people)
2. **Fairbanks** (31,535 people) is the second largest
3. **Juneau** (31,275) the State Capital is the third largest

Fort Richardson was right outside of the city of Anchorage, which is located in the South-Central area of the state. Anchorage being the most populous city in the state, contains more than 40% of Alaska's population.

It is also the third least populous state.

I've have traveled to the following 36 States out of all 50 U.S. States to include our nation's capital in *Washington D.C.; Hawaii, Alaska, Alabama, California, Delaware, Florida, Georgia, Idaho, Illinois, Indiana, Iowa, Kentucky, Louisiana, Maine, Maryland, Minnesota, Mississippi, Montana, New Jersey, New York, North Carolina, North Dakota, Ohio, Oklahoma, Oregon, Pennsylvania, South Carolina, South Dakota, Tennessee, Texas, Utah, Virginia, Washington, West Virginia, Wisconsin,* and *Wyoming*

For whatever reason I can't think of the other two U.S. States that I have traveled too. But I know I have been to 38 of the 50 US States.

I have a goal to visit as many of these remaining states that I have not seen, before the end of next year; *Arizona, Arkansas, Colorado, Connecticut,* **Kansas, Massachusetts, Michigan,** *Missouri, Nebraska, Nevada, New Hampshire, New Mexico, Rhode Island* and/or *Vermont*

# 5

## CHAPTER FIVE
# THEY SHOOTIN!

*I have already stated several times in this book that I was not going to divulge nor discuss any information of a classified or sensitive nature. I will only explain that which is already common knowledge and available on-line when discussing the training in the Q-Course or Special Forces Qualification Course (SFQC); specifically, the Special Forces Weapons Sergeants (18B) portion of which I was a graduate.*

*To my brethren in the Special Operations Community who feel that I should remain, "A Quite Professional", and not talk about what we do or what we have done at all – respectfully, many of y'all do not know my journey nor my story. You may put the "Sponge Bob Square Black Face" on all of your photos - over the faces of fellow operators.*

*But let's keep it real, or as the common vernacular today says – let's keep it 100%.*

*Every mission that was "that" sensitive, we were too busy doing our jobs to take photos anyway. The United States Army Special Operations Command Recruiting Battalion maintains a social media presence "on-line" to include photos on Twitter, LinkedIn, YouTube, Flicker and their own website.*

*Even the United States Secret Service has a social media presence, to include a Facebook page.*

With that said, let's take down the holier than thou, moral attitude you may have towards me, unless it's about race, religion and/or your perception of my nationality. But I'll address the racism and bigotry I've experienced in another chapter.

But for now, I'm talking about many of the times someone used the expression "They Shootin"!

Everyone in the Special Operations Community (from the operators to the administrative personnel, from the supply sergeant to the cooks), everyone, has something special in their training curriculum that members of the regular Big Army do not have, one of the reasons they're called special operations forces.

In the Special Forces community, it is even more so.

Within the U.S. Army Special Forces none are more organically trained to deal with a variety of weapons and ammunition than the 18B, the Special Forces Weapons Sergeant.

In the Special Forces community, there used to be both; a Light Weapons Sergeant and a Heavy Weapons Sergeant, however when I completed the training and graduated in the early 1990's they had been combined into just one MOS (consisting of both light & heavy).

The standard description of the Special Forces Weapons Sergeants duties includes (but are not limited to): Employing highly demanding conventional and high-risk unconventional warfare tactics and techniques in the employment of individual domestic and foreign small arms, light and heavy crew served weapons, anti-aircraft and anti-armor weapons. Supervises and performs construction of hasty fortifications and controls execution of tactical conventional and unconventional operational employment and functioning of all types of U.S. light weapons (up to and including .50 caliber Machinegun), US heavy weapons (up to and including the 4.2inch mortar, the 120mm mortar and the 106mm Recoilless Rocket), man-portable air defense weapons and US anti-armor weapons (including anti-tank missile systems), to perform tactical operations. Maintains proficiency with the employment and functions of all foreign high-density light and heavy weapons, man-portable air-defense and anti-armor weapons. Evaluates terrain, selects weapons emplacements, sites, and assigns targets and areas of fire.

All Military Occupational Specialties (MOS) in the U.S. Army are grouped into career management fields. Those beginning with the numerical numbers 18 are reserved for Special Forces personnel. Just like all the MOS's beginning with the numeral designation 11 are reserved for Infantry personnel (11A, 11B, 11C, etc).

| | |
|---|---|
| 18A | Special Forces Officer |
| *180A | Special Forces Warrant Officer |
| 18B | Special Forces Weapons Sergeant |
| 18C | Special Forces Engineer Sergeant |
| 18D | Special Forces Medical Sergeant |
| 18E | Special Forces Communications Sergeant |
| *18F | Special Forces Assistant Operations and Intelligence Sergeant |
| *18Z | Special Forces Senior Sergeant |
| 18X | Special Forces Enlistment Option (Basic SF Recruit) |

MOS's marked with an (*) asterisk are not available during SFQC training. They are only available to well qualified specially selected SF personnel already within the Special Forces community.

Except for talking to the 18X, I wouldn't advise anyone who is not extremely proficient in whatever field they are occupied in – to question, test or challenge a person who possess one of these 18 series MOS's.

When the topic is weapons, the Subject Matter Expert (SME) in this field is the 18B. In one of the above paragraphs you read the 18B general job description. But let me tell you what else the 18B does in school while training during the "Q-course".

He learns every weapon that has a trigger, period.

First there was the classified portion of training, where we learned things you wouldn't believe in your wildest dreams exist. I don't know if it was designed that way, or if the foreign allied students were doing something else at the time and the cadre instructors decided to utilize the training opportunity available.

*But it started with a phrase that when something like this, "Now that we can talk amongst ourselves, this is how you kill a lot of people".*

*Sometime later we moved on to pistols.*

*All of them.*

*Every caliber, every type, revolver, semi-automatic and automatic. Name, nomenclature, makes, models, disassembly, assembly, operation & maintenance.*

*Then we went into every type of rifle there was, from ancient firearms to modern, bolt action, level action, magazine fed, whatever. We learned it all.*

Shotguns?
*Yes. Single barrel, double barreled, semi-automatic, homemade and futuristic.*

Submachine Guns?
*Yes.*

Light machineguns?
*You mean like the 5.56mm M-249 Squad Automatic Weapon (SAW)?*

*Yes, and every other type of light machinegun they make.*

Medium machineguns?
*Yes.*

*Like the 7.62mm M-240 machineguns, (they replaced the old M-60's) and several others medium sized machineguns in existence. The machine gun has killed more people in modern warfare than all the atomic bombs used in warfare - combined. I used to teach a class called machinegun theory later in my career as an Infantry Doctrine Writer at the U.S. Army Infantry Center and School, but that's another chapter.*

*Maybe even another book.*

Heavy Machineguns?
*Yes.*

*Not just the M-2 .50 caliber. We learned machineguns so large that you have to get inside a harness to use them. Looks like something out of a turret in a Star Wars movie.*

*Anti-armor weapons. Any weapon that is specifically designed to defeat armor whether stationary or moving, small vehicles like cars and trucks or large vehicles up to and including armored tanks.*

*Mortars of all shapes and sizes; small medium & large like the 60mm, 81mm and the 120mm 4.2inch mortar systems. Forward Observer procedures for the indirect fire and the Fire Direction Controller (FDC) procedures for all of them high angle fire, death from above machines.*

*Anti-aircraft weapons. Every type that the US has ever made, to include those of our NATO allied countries armies. Can you just imagine the level of security clearance you need to have in order to learn how to shoot down airplanes?*

*Then when you are done learning all these weapons systems, all day every day, guess what you do?*

*You go learn the foreign former WARSAW pact countries version of the exact same thing. Not in a book, but hands on you learn everything there is to know about weapons both foreign and domestic. When you finally learn everything, then you have to prove it like you do everything else in the U.S. Army by completing exams on the material you learned. There were written exams, oral exams and hands-on testing.*

*When you finally complete all of that, if you're still a student in training and haven't flunked out yet, you will go to a range at an undisclosed location someplace and shoot everything you just learned how to operate.*

*You will probably shoot something every day, all day, from sun up to sun down. No, no, don't go nowhere, we gotta do this all at night too.*

*You know night firing.*

*I remember one week before we went to a range in the "Q-course", I had developed carpal tunnel syndrome in my hands from loading so much small arms ammunition into magazines, preparing and prepping mortar rounds, opening crates of ammunition that seemed like it was arriving by the truck load.*

*I was already an Infantryman (11B) and a Paratrooper in the regular Army when I arrived for training.*

*Additionally, the regular U.S. Army has (had) separate MOS's for some of the individual weapons systems we learned and used. MOS 11C is a Indirect Fire Infantryman, MOS 11H used to be Heavy Anti-Armor Infantryman, and the entire MOS 14 series branch in the U.S. Army is dedicated to Air Defense.*

*But as an 18B Special Forces Weapons Sergeant you will learn parts of all of them.*

# 6

**CHAPTER SIX**

# RUNNING AND GUNNING

Every military base I've been too has had some type of training range to fire weapons.

Some of them are specifically designed for large sized units to train their soldiers with their weapons on, before they embark on a major deployment or operation. Some of the major unit training at locations are; the Joint Readiness Training Center (JRTC) in Louisiana, the National Training Center (NTC) at Fort Irwin in California, the Jungle Operations Training Center (JOTC) at Fort Sherman in Panama and the 7th Army Joint Multinational Training Command (JMTC) at the Grafenwohr Training Area in Germany and the Hohenfels Training Area near the Czech Republic boarder.

Out of all the regular military bases I have been too (especially stateside other than the mega base in Fort Hood, Texas), the military range complex at Fort Bragg, North Carolina is the best to me.

Fort Hood, Texas is the largest U.S. military installation (by land mass).

Fort Bragg, North Carolina is the largest U.S. military installation (by population).

Fort Bragg, NC has more than 52,280 Active Duty soldiers, and 12,624 Reserve Component and Temporary Duty (TDY) students there. With over 50,000 active duty military personnel and a range and training area that encompass 178,000 acres over six counties in the State of North Carolina; you could expect it to have a continuous 24 hours a day, 7 days a week, 365 days a year Range Control Operation Center, like it does. There are 87 live-fire ranges (containing over 2,000 automated targets) and more than 100 other training facilities that cater to soldiers on Fort Bragg and personnel from other locations. There were over 70,000 aircraft movements on the base last year, which included helicopters, Unmanned aircraft systems (UAV) and US Air Forces Cargo and Troop Carrier Aircraft.

One of the most memorable ranges on the base, is located along Manchester Road called OP-13.

Remember earlier in this book when I told you that there was a military battle drill called Movement to Contact?

You can find it in the U.S. Army Field Manual (FM) 3-21.8, which superseded the old FM 7-8? Or you can ask ANY Infantryman what it is.

When conducting the Movement to Contact battle drill on OP-13, military units can safely conduct this battle drill up to Company and Battalion size elements.

I distinctly remember during my time with the 82nd Airborne Division's, 2nd Brigade - while assigned as an Airborne Infantry Rifle Squad Leader. I was assigned to Bravo Company (Blackhawks), 4th Battalion, 325th Airborne Infantry Regiment (Gold Falcons) and we were training, conducting a live fire operation on a fixed "enemy" location at that range. We conducted this Movement to Contact battle drill over and over and over. Each iteration of the drill was at least 1-hour in duration. We trained and did it until we got it right, then we did it again.

We did this battle drill using another unit's personnel as the Opposing Force (OPFOR) or "enemy" and we used blank-ammunition. Everything was exactly the way we were to do it during later iterations when we finally transitioned over to using live ammunition: without the OPFOR personnel.

When we transitioned to live ammunition, and there were no soldiers playing the role OPFOR on the "Objective" (OBJ) it went something like this.

Our Airborne Infantry Battalion was to conduct an airborne parachute assault on a nearby Drop Zone (DZ), then move out on foot and conduct an operation on an enemy stronghold. One of our sister infantry companies (like Delta Company) would go ahead and set up a strong security presence in the vicinity of the OBJ area. They would prevent any enemy personnel from escaping off of the OBJ, once the shooting commenced. They would prevent any enemy reinforcements from arriving onto the OBJ to help them. They would also engage the enemy on the OBJ from a position that had a higher vantage point of the OBJ with indirect and direct fire weapon systems. The mortar section (in the Headquarters & Headquarters Company) would engage the enemy with indirect fire weapons systems like the 81mm mortars and attempt to destroy the enemy on the OBJ as we approach them.

This isn't no classified tactic, it's in every war movie you have ever seen.

The Artillery (King of Battle) and the Mortars blow up the enemy, as the Infantry (Queen of Battle) approaches.

Well synchronized units that train together can virtually walk the friendly indirect fire in front of the Infantry right up until the Infantry is directly upon the enemy forces, then shift their fire off of the OBJ. Then the Infantry can close with and destroy the enemy in close combat and capture the terrain.

Too Easy.

The artillery or air bombardment stops the ground attack is coming.

How many times have you heard the term, "Cover me while I move"?!? Simply means on a smaller scale to shoot at the enemy. He probably can't shoot back at us while your shooting at him, that gives me time to move to a better location. We were just doing this on a much larger scale.

As the Headquarters & Headquarters Company (HHC) & Delta Companies are in position we can move towards the enemy. The company I was in at the time (Bravo Company) was the designated lead company that would gain the toe hold, for company that was designated the main effort (Alpha Company), they would charge through the toe or foot hole that we gained and complete the mission. The Battalion commander might hold the Charlie Company in reserve until they are needed.

I don't know what he would do because I wasn't no Battalion Commander, I can only tell you what I saw from my perspective and two levels up. Every soldier is taught that he/she may have to lead other soldiers from a position of authority two levels up, because people get killed in combat and you never know what could happen.

So now it's B Company (with our 3 Infantry Platoons), of which my platoon (2nd Platoon) is designated to go up to the OBJ obstacles with the Combat Engineers - who are attached to us. They have an explosive charge called a, "Bangalore Torpedo" which is really a lot of explosive charges placed inside a bunch of connected tubes. The intelligence on the OBJ (Scouts from the HHC) state that the OBJ is surrounded by rows of concertina wire, chicken wire and other anti-personnel obstacles. The Combat Engineers are going to slide the bangalore torpedo under the obstacles of wire and then fall back a little bit and blow a big hole through the obstacles.

Then they will re-approach the obstacle and proof it, to insure they created a gap in the wire and that the obstacle is now breached. Then the main effort platoon can run through that hole, that breach, and gain a foothold in the first building, or first trench or whatever is on the OBJ where the enemy is at. Then once our company has a toe-hold, the main effort company A Company, can get inside and capture, kill or destroy the remaining enemy.

The problem is that the enemy is not gonna just let the Combat Engineers get close enough to their location. Everybody who has common sense knows that when the explosions from the artillery and mortars stop raining down, the ground attack is coming.

During personal combatives, the jab always sets up the opponent for the knockout punch.

So, our job was to provide the closer-in, close in support of the Combat Engineers and ensure they don't get killed on the OBJ trying to breach the obstacle.

So, the entire battalion conducts this massive airborne operation on one of Fort Bragg's DZ's. We march towards our objective, the entire battalion, with range safety personnel officers and some other VIP's. As we approach the OBJ and personnel are breaking off to go to their assigned positions we become the only platoon facing the enemy as planned. We get closer and the other squads break off do their jobs and it's just my squad and the engineers. So, we fight up to the OBJ using individual movement techniques; three to five second rushes, high crawling and eventually low crawling. As we get to the point where the engineers are going to breach the obstacle, I have my squad break off into two Fire Teams.

My Bravo Team Leader, led by a buck sergeant (SGT/E-5) takes his Fire Team of men to the right of the OBJ breach point. I designated it that way, because he was the senior of my two Fire Team Leaders. I move towards the left side of the OBJ with the other more junior Alpha Team Leader. Remaining just a little behind them both, so that I can control the men of my squad and react to whatever may happen, I see the engineers connect these tubes together. They slide it under the wire (in a horizontal position slightly canted) while there is still simulated direct fire coming at us, because we are attempting to breach the enemy's obstacle around their OBJ.

We all pull back a minimum safe distance, and I can tell you now, even with all those range control & safety observers with us, we all did not run back no 200 meters in defilade to safety like the books says.

CLACK BOOM!!!

The explosion goes off, and there is a big cloud of smoke and dirt. This is also the signal for that other sister platoon of ours to come from behind us and charge through the breach (the hole) we just created. Which is also the signal for the other companies to do whatever it is they are going to do.

We rush back up to proof the wire with the engineers and guess what?

There is a large gap in what would have been a wall of concertina wire - but it is not completely breached. There were still some strands of wire attached, which would have amounted to tangle foot for anyone attempting to run through it to get to the trench line on the other side. If we had time we could correct this, but main effort company, led by the remaining platoons or our company were now running towards us.

Running towards a complete breach (a break in the wire) that is supposed to be there, that is NOT there!

We can fix this because every Infantryman knows that an Infantry Squad carries everything but the kitchen sink on their backs from the barracks with them. The engineers and my some of my Bravo Fire Team on the right are pulling the wire in an attempt to create a bigger breach from the right side. The engineers and my some of my Alpha Fire Team on the left are pulling the wire in an attempt to create a bigger breach from the left side. Since the rest of my soldiers are laying down in the prone fighting position engaging the simulated enemy I reach for one of my soldiers buttpacks that's attached to his Load Bearing Equipment (LBE) harness to retrieve the squads baby bolt cutters. But I can't find it, it's not where it's supposed to be at.

So, I said, *"Private where are the bolt cutters?!?"*

He replies that he doesn't have them.

*"What do you mean you don't have them"?*

*"I left them in the barracks Sergeant!"*

**"WHAT THE FUCK YOU FUCKER"**, or words to that effect is what I scream at him!

I know you had the bolt cutters, because we had a layout and inspection before we left. I called out every item on the company packing list and I personally saw you pack the bolt cutters", I replied to him. Yes, Sergeant, but after your layout and the inspection - I put them back in my barracks room.

At that moment, it looked like I physically grabbed that Private by the back of his LBE and attempted to beat the living hell out of him. It could have looked like I was gonna drag his ass all across that OBJ. It looked like I grabbed his battle buddy too, with my other hand and violently yanked them both to their feet and was about to run towards the enemy location. It looked like I was gonna drag them both inside the enemy location and find a nice place to perform wall-to-wall counseling, but I tripped on the tangle foot and all three of us laid on top of the few remaining connected strands of concertina & chicken wire.

What we were actually doing was performing a body breach and the rest of the company, ran across our backs and jumped into the trench line, as we laid in the dirt and mud with the concertina wire, and completed the breach with our bodies.

152

Remember when I said we conducted this MTC battle drill over and over, and that each iteration was at least 1-hour in duration. Well we conducted that drill all day for almost three days straight. We did a blank fire, another blank fire, and then another blank fire. Then we did a blank night fire, then another blank night fire, then another. Then we did a live fire, then another live fire. We did that drill until the entire unit (the whole Infantry Battalion) ran out of all the ammunition we brought with us for training (both blank and live).

Then we did it again, with no ammo!

We did it over and over, and over. When the Infantry Battalion Commander was finally satisfied, we were rewarded with road marching all the way back to the barracks area. Oh, do I have some stories to tell you.

# 7

CHAPTER SEVEN

# MISSION, MEN, MARRIAGE, ME

During the early 1990's the U.S. military was having a large Reduction-In-Force (RIF) of its personnel because the Persian Gulf War had just completed. There were about 750,000 soldiers on active duty and their goal was to reduce that number to 450,000 active duty soldiers.

So, someone got the bright idea to have an early retirement option.

If you had over 15 years of active duty, you could retire from active duty with like 35-40% of your base pay.

Rather than wait to serve 20 years and retire with 50%.

Military retirement pay increases 2.5% for every year you serve over 20, so at 30-years of active duty service you could retire with 75% of your pay.

If you enlisted at 18, you could retire at 38 (with 20-years of service).

However, even though all base pay in the military is essentially the same across all branches of service *(an E-4 in the U.S. Army - Infantry makes the same base pay as an E-4 working in U.S. Air Force - Finance)*, if you did 30 years in a physically demanding MOS you would normally be put out to pasture because of the extremely physical damage you would have done to your body. There is no differential in the military pay scale based upon a servicemembers job (Army MOS), everyone's base pay is based upon rank, period.

In the U.S. Army, if you flunk out of any of the technically demanding Advance Individual Training (AIT) centers after your Basic Training or Boot Camp, you will normally be reassigned/reclassified into the Infantry. It is that physically demanding of a job.

Sleep deprivation, heavy rucksacks (backpacks), walking everywhere, gas chamber, immunizations for stuff they don't even do anymore because it has been deemed dangerous, and then add jumping out of planes, *(if you want to become a paratrooper)* to that list.

Anyway, when the U.S. Army first offered the early out program to all Army MOS's; it was **rumored** that almost every SFC/E-7 in the Infantry jumped at the chance and retired.

I don't know how true that is, but I do know that for a short period of time I was a Platoon Sergeant (PSG) in a line Infantry Company, in the 82nd Airborne Division as a Sergeant/E-5.

Our Platoon Sergeant (PSG) was a Sergeant First Class who had just been transferred to the 82nd Airborne Division's, Advance Airborne School.

I became the acting Platoon Sergeant because I was the senior ranking Squad Leader (with time in service). This was in 2nd Platoon, Bravo Company, 4th Battalion/325th Airborne Infantry Regiment (AIR) in the 2nd Brigade Combat Team of the famous 82nd Airborne Division.

The 82nd Airborne Division is considered "America's Division", so almost everything in the Division is color-coded Red, White and/or Blue. Including the names of the subordinate units.

Their used to be three Infantry Brigades of about 5,000 men each within the Division, plus an additional Brigade for support.

In the 1990's the three Infantry Brigade Combat Teams of the 82nd Airborne Division were as follows:

- 1st Brigade, 504th Parachute Infantry Regiment (PIR)
- 2nd Brigade, 325th Airborne Infantry Regiment (AIR)
- 3rd Brigade, 505th Parachute Infantry Regiment (PIR)

The **1st Brigade of the 82nd Airborne Division was based around the famed 504th Parachute Infantry Regiment.** During World War II, an enemy officer who was killed had written in his diary about the American Parachutists; "Those devils in baggy pants, who pop-up out of nowhere". The nickname stuck with the unit up until this very day, the Devils in Baggy Pants.

It's 3 subordinate battalions were:

> 1st Battalion, 504th PIR (Red Devils)
> 2nd Battalion, 504th PIR (White Devils)
> 3rd Battalion, 504th PIR (Blue Devils)

**The 2nd Brigade of the 82nd Airborne Division was based around the 325th Airborne Infantry Regiment (AIR), called the Falcon Brigade.**

Its 3 subordinate battalions were:

> 1st Battalion, 325th AIR (Red Falcons)
> 2nd Battalion, 325th AIR (White Falcons)
> 3rd Battalion, 325th AIR (Blue Falcons)
> 4th Battalion, 325th AIR (Gold Falcons)

Sometime before my arrival in the unit, the 3rd Battalion/325th AIR was transferred to Italy with all of its lineage and honors, and the 4th Battalion/325th AIR was assigned to the 82nd Airborne Division at Fort Bragg, North Carolina. Since there was already a Red, White & Blue color designation system, and the Blue went to Italy with the 3rd Battalion/325th AIR, the 4th Battalion was designated the "Gold Falcons".

---

On another note:

*The U.S. Army Special Operations Forces (SOF), 75th Ranger Regiment has three operational Ranger Infantry Battalions <u>I was never a part of either of them</u>, this is the common folklore on Fort Bragg in the 1990's.*

*1st Ranger Battalion, 75th Ranger Regiment (Hunter Army Airfield, Georgia)*

*2nd Ranger Battalion, 75th Ranger Regiment (Fort Lewis, Washington)*

*3rd Ranger Battalion, 75th Ranger Regiment (Fort Benning, Georgia) with the Ranger Regimental Headquarters, additional support units and the U.S. Army Ranger School.*

---

The previously listed are the actual U.S. Army Ranger Units; whose unit insignia (patch) resembles a Scroll.

Graduates of the U.S. Army's Ranger "school" are awarded a Ranger "tab" to wear above whatever their actual unit of assignment patch is on their left shoulder.

So, when someone says they are a U.S. Army Ranger the mantra is that the "Ranger tab" is a school, but the "Ranger scroll" is the Ranger way of life. Almost all the leadership in the Ranger Regiment wear a ranger tab on top of their ranger scroll because they have graduated the school as well. Many members of the other units in the U.S. Army affectionally call members who have served in either "battalion" of the Ranger Regiment; "Bat Boys". It has always been an honor to have a "former" Bat Boy assigned to your unit, without a doubt you knew you were getting the best light infantry soldier in the world.

Anyway, other than the Ranger Units, many military leaders (both commissioned officers and NCO's) attend the U.S. Army Ranger school at Fort Benning, Georgia: before leading other combat units. It is virtually impossible to find a leader in "any" infantry unit in the U.S. Army who hasn't gone to and graduated from Ranger school. It was rumored back then, that the 4th Battalion/325th AIR (Gold Falcons) had more Ranger "tabbed" soldiers than any other infantry unit - other than the actual 75th Ranger Regiment. *So, the 4th Battalion/325th AIR (Gold Falcons) had another nickname; as the unofficial "4th Ranger Battalion" back in the early 1990's.*

Besides the 3rd Battalion, 325th AIR had the unit moniker of "Blue Falcon" as is the military culture code for "B.F." or Bravo-Foxtrot or Buddy-Fucker, and who wants to be affiliated with a unit full of buddy-fuckers?

Example:

Sergeant to his Squad, *"Where is Private Jones?"*
Everyone in unison, *"We don't know Sergeant, we think Private Jones may be at sick-call!"*
The Blue-Falcon: *"No, Sergeant - Private Jones when out on the town partying last night even though he was supposed to be restricted to the barracks, he got drunk last night and was still throwing-up in the latrine, the last time I saw him, that's why he's missing from formation".*

Anyway, back to the color codes of the 82nd Airborne Division.

**The 3rd Brigade of the 82nd Airborne Division was based around the 505th Parachute Infantry Regiment (PIR), called the Panther Brigade.** The 3rd Battalion/505th PIR is the unit that carriers the lineage of the 555th Triple Nickle unit, when the U.S. military was no longer segregated by races and that famous unit of our nation's first black paratroopers got absorbed into the infamous 82nd Airborne Division. Its three Battalions were:

> 1st Battalion, 505th PIR (One Panther)
> 2nd Battalion, 505th PIR (Two Panther)
> 3rd Battalion, 505th PIR (Three Panther)

Back to my story as a Gold Falcon.

We return from a field exercise and immediately we must clean our weapons and do a weapons and equipment accountability. It doesn't matter if you return from the field at 01:00 hours (1am), you will immediately clean all the weapons before storing them inside the company weapons room. Then in the next few days all the weapons will get a very extensive cleaning in phases.

So anyway, the Company First Sergeant (1SG/E-8) says to us Platoon Sergeant (normally a E-7 billet, but I was a Sergeant E-5 at the time), let me know when all the equipment is accounted for, and all weapons are cleaned and turned into the company arms room. I like the other PSG's got my men to wipe the mud off their weapons and turn them in to the arms room, so they could go home to their wives, girlfriends or whatever. When all the PSG's report back to the 1SG, he tells us to release our men if we're satisfied until 09:00 hours and we all report back to him.

So, we release our individual platoons (around 40 men each) and report back to him. We wait in his office for a little while, and then he takes us downstairs to the company arms room.

He picks up a weapon and although the mud is wiped from the exterior, it is filthy inside. Then he picks up another weapon. Then another weapon. Then another. He tells us, that if we got alerted for combat right now, our company is not ready.

So, we had to get all those weapons cleaned before we left to go home for the day. Some of us proceed to retrieve some of our men who lived in the barracks, and others want to recall our men who were released already.

*"No, no, no"*, says the 1SG!

You released your men, you clean your platoons' weapons before you go home.

*WTF?!?*

When my men returned to work the next day at 09:00, they had a lesson in weapons maintenance from me that they would never forget. But I also learned a valuable lesson about leadership and taking care of my men, that I would never forget. The mission comes first.

Mission, Men, Marriage, Me in that order.

## CHAPTER EIGHT

# CLACK BOOM!

About 15 years ago the initial invasion into Iraq occurred in the spring of 2003, it was called Operation IRAQI FREEDOM.

After about one year, the units and soldiers who participated in the initial invasion push into Iraq started to rotate back CONUS (the Continental United States) and the next wave of units and soldiers were, as they say – now in the fight.

The second yearly rotation of soldiers was called Operation IRAQI FREEDOM 2 (OIF2), and the next after that was called OIF3. This numerical sequence continued until the rotations stopped being one year in duration. Sometimes units rotated into country for 4 to 6 months, sometimes they rotated for 15 months or longer. This war lasted for over 15 years, before it became known as Operation NEW DAWN in 2012, and US servicemembers are still dying in Iraq to this very day.

There was a time when I was assigned to a mechanized infantry billet operating out of Forward Operating Base (FOB) War Eagle in the North-Eastern portion of the capital city of Baghdad, in one of the nine administrative districts (boroughs) in an area called Sadr City.

Just think, there is a war in Iraq, Baghdad is the capital city, and the Sadr City section is "the hood" of all that (like the South Side of Chicago, South Central LA or the South Bronx) imagine 2.5 million people living in a slum with no running water, no electricity nor sewage collection. People just dumping their trash and waste (including human excrement) in the street.

Go do a quick online research of Sadr City, Baghdad, Iraq (circa 2004) for yourself; and just look at the images.

During a four-year period, from 2004-2008 in the Sadr City section of Baghdad, several thousand Iraqi civilians were killed in street clashes, by roadside bombs called IED's (Improvised Explosive Devises), snipers, suicide bombers, during military raids and in constant air strikes. Some also died due to the lack of food, water and a rising threat from the lack of sanitation services.

Over 1,000 Mahdi Army fighters were killed along with at least 500 members of the Iraqi security forces and several hundred U.S. service members.

Over 32,000 US service members were Wounded-In-Action (WIA) in the country of Iraq.

When I say WIA, I mean their injuries were so severe that they may have lost a limb like an arm or a leg, or their eye sight.

A total of 4,493 of my brother & sister service members were Killed in Action (KIA) in all of Iraq - and almost 300 of those KIA, were in Sadr City.

The giant T-walls of FOB War Eagle were adjacent to Sadr City.

The U.S. Army especially the Infantry community, has a "battle drill" called Movement-To-Contact (MTC), essentially a specific series of movements and formations that are performed enroute to enemy contact - which are contingent upon the mission, enemy, friendly troops available, terrain, weather and several other factors.

When I arrived at FOB War Eagle, I was informed that the Eagle had been "shot off" of that name (it's just FOB War now, or War) and that the MTC battle drill name was now shortened to just "Contact". There was no movement required, just open the gates and roll out in the Bradley's and park, and wait - the enemy fighters are coming to you, guaranteed.

Plus, the FOB will be mortared & rocketed (people will be injured and killed) almost every night because the enemy is shooting at us from a densely populated civilian area (which at the time returning fire would guarantee civilian casualties).

I called my wife back CONUS one night and told her goodbye (forever).

She told me don't talk like that, to speak words of positivity and that I was covered in the spirit by things I wouldn't understand. I told her, that I wasn't no rookie, I wasn't scared. That I was a seasoned Noncommissioned Officer with combat experience already with all the advanced training the military had to offer. But I firmly believed that I would not survive that tour of duty, especially after what I had experienced earlier that day.

I had served in the Light Infantry, Airborne Infantry and Air Assault Infantry. I had been to all types of specialized and advanced training up to and including the kind that's done at Camp Mackall that I cannot talk about for at least 75 years.

But that day, I had seen an M-1 Abrams main battle tank with the turret on one side of the road and the chassis on the other. An M-1 tank cost about 7 million dollars and weights over 60 tons (120,000 pounds), that's like the weight of two 18-wheeler trucks at home.

Do you know what kind of explosion, what kind of force it would take to disable, destroy or flip an Abrams tank?

I had reviewed a After Action Report (AAR) with the photos of a soldier who was at the Camp Victory Base Complex (VBC) where one of the enemy rockets that attacked the base, went astray and into a Container Housing Unit (CHU) or single wide housing trailer, and exited out the other side, entered another CHU just above the reinforced sandbags & Hesco barriers and exit that trailer thru the door, entered another third CHU and the fins from the rocket "scrapped" across a soldiers belly while he lay in his bunk, and the rocket landed in his wall locker, in his body armor - and did not detonate!

I told her I had seen some stuff that was just too damn random, and even with all my training I didn't believe that I would survive that tour.

Here's one of my reasons why.

That morning we were on a mission and we left FOB War, in a multi vehicle formation that included the Bradley Infantry Fighting Vehicle (IFV) I was riding in.

Although it is designed to carry 6 combat ready troops, we had at least 8 plus all the vehicles crewmembers. When you get inside, as the ramp door raises up and closes shut you feel helplessly trapped. You're done if you're claustrophobic, and there is very little movement because the interior is crammed with men, weapons, ammunition & equipment.

The young Private First Class (PFC) sitting across from me lifts his dirty boots up and places them on my lap.

*"What the fuck are you doing soldier!?!"*

Or words to that effect, is what I say to him, but I'm also thinking in my mind is this some "newbie" joke? I'm new to this unit, but I am not new to the army.

*"Sarge" you wanna take your feet up off the floor too!*

*When we hit an IED you're gonna loose both your legs from the knee down.*

He didn't say "if", he said "when" we hit an IED.

*What In The Hell?!?*

*Why am I just learning this, from a Private?*

*Why don't I know this already?*

Because just like when a professional football player in the NFL goes to a different team, he must learn their new scheme: the same goes on in the Infantry and the different doctrinal types of U.S. Army Infantry Units.

You may be a Master Rated Parachutist and your Battalion's Senior Jumpmaster in the Airborne Infantry. But if the U.S. Army sends you to an Air Assault Infantry Unit for your next duty assignment, you must learn their way, their S.O.P. (Standard Operating Procedures) for doing things.

You may be a Rappel Master and the best Army Pathfinder in your Air Assault Infantry Battalion. But if the U.S. Army sends you to your next duty assignment to a Mechanized Infantry Unit you must learn their S.O.P. next.

You may be a Master Gunner (Mike Golf) and the best Truck Commander (TC) in your Mechanized Infantry Battalion. But if the U.S. Army sends you to your next duty assignment in a Light Infantry Unit you must learn their S.O.P., their way.

So here I was, knowing everything the military could teach me about weapons and special operations, already had served in combat and been in every type of infantry unit the U.S. Army had; except Mechanized Infantry. Now the first time I get to actually be in a Mechanized Infantry Unit there is no learning curve. I'm in combat, on a mission, and learning from a Private.

Did I tell you it's dark inside an Infantry Fighting Vehicle?

I mean imagine riding into battle in a coffin, because that's what I was feeling like. Like I was riding to my death, and the day didn't get no better as it progressed.

Although we are adjacent to Sadr City, we cannot go directly to our objective.

We have to parallel south, travel west towards the Sadr City District Advisory Committee (DAC) building, and then proceed north to our OBJ.

As we are traveling enroute to the OBJ, I notice a young Specialist (SPC) and that same PFC arguing.

*No, it's your turn!*

*No, I went last time, it's your freaking turn!*

*Naw mother fucker, I did the last two, so it's your turn.*

One of my street survival methods – is to shut up and observe, everything. Learn as fast as you can, this will all make sense later and the day will get better.

*(Little did I know - it wouldn't get better).*

165

When we finally get near the OBJ, the ramp door drops and I'm done.

First, I'm hit with sensory deprivation from overload. It was pitch black riding inside that Bradley Fighting Vechicle, now we step outside into the blinding hot Iraqi sun.

*I can't see a damn thing, What The Fuck?!?*

It's so bright it feels like I'm staring directly into the sun.

Then the heat hits me, I'm hot inside the vehicle - but the hot darkness is cooler than the hot desert sun. 100 degrees in the shade is much cooler than 120 degrees in the sun.

Full kit, or as the soldiers say, wearing full battle-rattle I start sweating profusely. If anybody know me personally, they know how I can sweat. So, imagine 120-degree Iraqi sun, all that body armor (must have on an extra 150 pounds of stuff today), situational awareness – sweat & stench.

*My nose, what in the hell am I smelling?!?*

The funk was so strong it felt like it physically punched me in the face.

Imagine this portion of the city, 2 million residents with no running water, no sanitation services, and no sewer system.

Just filth everywhere, piles and piles, miles and miles of it. Dead animals everywhere, rotting flesh, flies and feces and urine and flies and trash and more flies and the strongest funky stench you ever smelt in your life. We are literally standing in a running stream of human shit.

Then I hear the speaker system. They must have the loudest propaganda system this side of the North Korean border I've ever heard in my life. It is freaking loud!

Plus, the sounds of the city, just mass confusion of your senses all at the same time.

Conduct SLLS my ass.

SLLS pronounced "seals" is the military acronym that stands for Stop, Look, Listen and Smell the battlefield. So, you can become acclimated to the environment you're about to fight in. Like when Russell Crowe does in the movie "Gladiator", when he grabs a handful of the dirt before he fights, to become one with the terrain, smell the ground the dirt, listen and see the battle before it starts. Well, that was a just movie and here I am in Iraq with all my senses completely overloaded.

Temporarily blinded by the sun, the funk of the city destroying my nostrils, my ears went from hearing the deafening silence of the armored vehicle, to a million-people screaming "killer horse" and the loud speakers. So, I talk to myself, just like any senior leader participating in small unit dynamics. Just stay out these guys' way and don't become a liability to the mission (or a statistic)!

*Sarge you forgot the CD!*
**What?!?**

*Sarge your hand is not free!*
**What!?!**

*Sarge, you're standing on an IED!*

That moment I felt my spirit physically leave my body.

I was now floating above my body looking straight down at my physical body for what felt like a few seconds.

Everything stopped, everything - and I could actually feel myself leaving my body. I was now hovering above my body watching it move before the IED detonated, because I couldn't believe what he was saying to me. So, in shock I go toward the sidewalk. But not on the actual sidewalk, because last week the sidewalk in Sadr City gave away and someone drowned. Yes, they died, they literally drowned to death in all that raw sewage running underneath the sidewalk.

So, as I move away I see the PFC point to a nearby telephone pole. The SPC cuts a wire and the PFC goes to work. He starts digging into the concrete with his knife for the IED.

No - we are not waiting for Explosive Ordnance Personnel (EOD) personnel to arrive, this U.S. Army Infantry PFC is actually digging into the soft concrete for an IED.

You see the insurgents would burn tires in the street, then the soft melted blacktop asphalt or concrete underneath would be peeled back. Then they would dig up the dirt under that, and implant an IED and run the wires from it to a nearby wooden telephone pole with what looks like hundreds of other wires coming from that pole.

Then when they replace some of the dirt and put the asphalt/concrete back, you can hardly tell where the road was disturbed. The IED is already there and they would connect it to a power source and kill soldiers, Iraqi government officials, members of other tribes, or whatever else was their target of opportunity at that moment.

We marked the spot of the IED and sent the information up the chain of command. The entire process must have taken about 30 minutes. Then we continued north, and repeated the process over and over.

We found, identified and disarmed 17 IED's that day.

Everyone in that neighborhood knew when and where the danger was at. They feared the militia men, so they let them plant them roadside bombs there.

Well after much fighting, that unit I served with earned a battle-hardened reputation.

Unlike the United States Marines Corps, members of the United States Army have patches and badges for almost everything. The local population could tell the different U.S. Army soldiers by their different unit patches worn on their shoulder sleeve.

Well the community learned that if you attacked the soldiers wearing the "killer horse patch", that there would be a whole lot of black memorial flags soon.

You see after the initial invasion the insurgents just took off their uniforms and blended in with the local population. They eventually feared the killer horse soldiers more than the insurgents, so when the insurgents wanted to plant more bombs or conduct ambushes- the people would rise up and fight them (everybody had guns). See they learned to fight for themselves rather than allow someone else to commit these atrocities and they had to pay the price.

That was a long day.

When I called my wife to tell her that day, that I wasn't going to make it home, that was just one day out of many. I tried to call her back but the AT&T phone lines back to CONUS in the phone trailer was off.

The US military would blackout all outgoing communications from Iraq (phone, internet, everything) whenever there was an American fatality in country, so they could alert the next of kin thru the proper channels.

AT&T charged a freaking obscene amount of money for us service members to call home, since they had the only method for service members to use. They were worse than the rates they charge inmates in prison when they call their family members (which is ridiculously high as well), just check the profits that AT&T made off of service members during the war, unfreaking believable.

I left that base one day and went to another FOB to do another mission with another unit, I later found out that, that phone trailer was destroyed by a direct hit from an enemy mortar round launched from Sadr City.

Rest-In-Peace (RIP) to all the men & women who did not make it home alive, and my prayers & positive energy/thoughts go out to all those who did return, some with physical injuries - some with Traumatic Brain Injury (TBI), Post Traumatic Stress Disorder (PTSD) and a host of other non-visible injuries and illnesses.

If you are a veteran, or know of someone who is, please ensure that they get into a network of others for veterans who may be facing readjustment issues. Approximately 18 military veterans commit suicide, every day in our country.

You may be strong, but your battle buddies may need your help and you'd never know it unless you asked them. I'm writing my memories and thoughts down in this book. It's therapeutic for me, and when I write them they're not bottled up inside of me anymore. Maybe you could find a release valve or help someone find theirs, because survivors guilt it real.

# 9

# ALL THE AMMO YOU WANT

In 1994, I was stationed at Fort Bragg, NC with the 82nd Airborne Division. My wife and I were still dating at the time and although I lived on base in the barracks, we spent many days together at her place directly off Murchison Road (the Murc). One day I get up to go to work on the base, and she & I had an argument about something stupid. It was so petty and stupid that we both cannot remember what the disagreement was about, and although we are married now and have been for over 20 years, we remember that day like it was yesterday.

You see, I knew something was afoot upon my arrival on base. Because there was an extremely large presence of Military Police on duty that morning. Upon my arrival, I discover the entire unit was on lock down, and are going to war. Lock-down mean once we arrive at work we can't leave, cell phones weren't as common as they are today, the pay phones in the barracks were turned off, all outgoing calls were restricted and there was no-way for anyone to contact you once you arrived at your unit.

No communications with the outside world, and once the unit is all assembled we grab our gear that is already packed and head to an isolation facility on the other side of Fort Bragg. It was adjacent to Pope Army Airfield (then called Pope Air Force Base) and we (the entire 82nd Airborne Division & other units of the XVIII Airborne Corps) are going to invade Haiti during an operation called Operation UPHOLD DEMOCRACY.

I remember her hearing about the planned invasion on the news, and seeing her amongst all the other wives, girlfriends, children, dependents and television news crews gathered outside the holding area, looking through the surrounding gate. We no longer leave the house on a bad note, because you never know when it may be the last time you see someone.

So, we get a mission brief Operations Order (OPORD) and plan the parachute assault down to the most minute details. It was so detailed, that we knew the name of the person who had the key to a specific door, of a specific building on the airfield we were going to assault: and we had a photograph of him as well.

We rehearse and then we participate in the airborne operations pre-jump training. Each individual aircraft has a Jumpmaster (JM) Team consisting of at least a Primary JM, Assistant JM and a Safety for each door. The JM team is responsible for; Organizing and mustering their "stick" or "chalk" of jumpers on the aircraft, Inspecting all items of equipment prior to loading of the aircraft (to include ALICE or MOLLE pack, M1950 series Weapon Case, and any Special Items of Equipment), Inspecting all jumpers for proper donning, fit, and serviceability of their helmet and parachute, Confirmation of in-flight navigation in accordance with flight diagram and Navigation Officer, Safety inspection of the Paratroop Door, Jump Platform, and Clear to the Rear of the dropping aircraft, Identification of in-flight reference points and proper control of the Paratroop Door during exit.

But most importantly the Primary JM of each aircraft is responsible for training all the paratroopers on his aircraft during the "Pre-Jump" sequence of training, called Sustained Airborne Training. This is where all paratroopers rehearse exactly what they are going to do on the aircraft, how to properly exit and actions during their decent to the ground after exiting a high-performance aircraft in flight are covered. Actions upon landing, to include emergencies landings like trees, wires and water landings. There is a JM checklist and a prejump speech the must be given in sequential order "verbatim" from memory so that noting is missed.

Sustained Airborne Training sounds something like this:

*Great day to be an American paratrooper, I am Sergeant Bilal and I will be your primary jumpmaster for this airborne operation!*

*The first thing we will cover are the 5 points of performance!*

*And the first point of performance is PROPER EXIT, CHECK BODY POSITION, AND COUNT!*

*JUMPERS HIT IT!!!*
*(One-thousand, Two-thousand, Three-thousand, Four-thousand)*

*Upon exiting the aircraft, snap into a good tight body position! Keep your eyes open, chin on your chest, elbows tucked tight into your sides, hands over your reserve parachute with your fingers spread wide! Bend forward at the waist keeping your feet and knees together, knees locked to the rear, and count to four thousand!*

*At the end of your four thousand count, if you do NOT feel an opening shock, immediately pull your reserve for a complete malfunction!*

*You have the rest of your life to do this!*

*However, if you do reach the end of your four thousand count, and you do feel an opening shock, immediately go into your second point of performance which is, CHECK CANOPY AND GAIN CANOPY CONTROL!*

Those 180 words are part of a speech that every U.S. Army Jumpmaster will give while conducting sustained airborne training, and that speech will continue for approximately 2,320 more words.

Verbatim.

I know, because I was a US Army Jumpmaster for several years, in fact later on in my career I was my Brigade's Master-Jumpmaster. But let me continue with this story.

Several individual units conducted this "pre-jump" training simultaneously. We did it on the parade field of where the XVIII Airborne Corps NCO Academy grounds are currently located at now.

During our prejump training before this combat mission to Haiti, our primary jumpmaster at the time said, "They know we are coming! They will be shooting up at the aircraft and some of us will NOT make it out the aircraft door alive. The Drop Zone is the airfield and it will be covered with Conex containers, broken glass, burning tires, concertina wire and all sorts of stuff." "We were told that we were the first wave, and that upon hitting the ground and completing a satisfactory Parachute Landing Fall (PLF), we must release our attached canopy release assemblies and fight in our harness." "Don't worry about the main parachute, just fight on to our objectives and secure the airfield, so the follow-on forces could air-land."

A Private asked the Primary JM, *"What about recovery of the parachute?"*

The JM's reply, *"Do not worry about the 'chute, it's a combat loss. Just get your ass to your assembly areas if you're still alive, so you men can accomplish your mission!"*

Now, this is in direct contradiction to what we as soldiers do every day in the military. But I do understand a combat necessity. However, I do know that we must account for everything that we sign for, period.

During practice jumps, which paratroopers must complete at least once every three months in order to remain on jump status, and more importantly get paid their jump-pay. During initial training in airborne school, each paratrooper is taught a specific way to recover his/her parachute. How to figure-eight roll it. How to secure it inside the issued aviators kit bag. We practice how to secure the kitbag with the reserve parachute, the rest of our gear and double-time run off of the drop zone to our unit assembly areas. Special care must be taken to not damage the parachute by using the zipper on the aviators' kit bag, so we are instructed to use the snap-fasteners only. Sometimes, accountability of paratroopers is done by counting the number of parachutes turned in at the assembly area.

Plus, the Parachute Riggers whose job it is to pack and re-pack the parachutes follow a strict set of rules & protocols, because people's lives are at stake during the extremely hazardous duty of parachuting out of aircraft in flight.

Speaking of accountability, there was a time, in another military unit where we had to physically pick up the expended brass casing from EVERY ROUND from every bullet we fired during training, and had to have them all laid out for inspection on a poncho liner, before we could leave the field.

Anyway, the phrase combat-loss echoes throughout the formation in people minds, although no one said a word verbally.

We were issued grenades and live ammo, and as far as I remember you could take whatever you wanted. They issued us all the ammo we could carry, in addition to whatever our basic load was. We load everything up, and walk thru the adjacent gate between Fort Bragg and Pope Air Force Base, to the awaiting aircraft for this massive parachute assault. There must have been well over 100 aircraft, and being that a C-130 can carry at least 64 combat paratroopers – that was a large armada.

We departed and flew towards our OBJ and many of us fell asleep in flight.

We were awakened to the sound of commotion and organized confusion. We were turning the aircraft around and going back to base. This is passed around the aircraft with the universal no-go symbol of the knifehand across the neck, as if slicing a throat.

There is screaming onboard, What the Fuck!?!?

The invasion is gonna happen without us!

Our aircraft is broken and Returning To Base (RTB), but the remaining aircraft are continuing on to the parachute drop.

There was exhilaration by some on board, several soldiers are happy.

Some of them obviously really didn't want to go to war.

In addition to the designated personnel on this mission, at take-off time back at the airfield soldiers were being bumped off the combat aircraft so high-ranking officers could take their slot.

A JM would say, *"Private So-And-So you're scratched."*

A Corporal would shout out, *"No he's not – he's my freaking AG (Assistant Machine Gunner)"*.

A few moments later, another high-ranking officer would approach the tail ramp of the C-130 telling the JM he must get on this aircraft. I am not privy to the big picture. At that time, I was just an enlisted paratrooper in the 82nd Airborne Division and an Infantryman. But I knew enough to see someone try to pull rank, there was way more higher-ranking brass officers than what we needed on this mission. Major's (O-4), Lieutenant Colonel's (O-5), and even a few full bird (O-6) Colonels' who obviously came from some desk job, like maybe at the Pentagon just to participate on this combat jump and earn the coveted "combat mustard stain" on their airborne jump wings.

After believing that our aircraft was RTB, we find out (via a white chalkboard) that the entire invasion is cancelled. A diplomatic group led by former U.S. President Jimmy Carter, U.S. Senator Sam Nunn and retired Chairman of the Joint Chiefs of Staff General Colin Powell persuaded the leaders of Haiti to step down and allow the elected officials to return to power. So, we were going back home to Bragg.

Prior to the info on the white board, we the individual paratroopers didn't have situational awareness with the other aircraft. I'm sure the leaders and the pilots did, but us individual parachutist didn't know the big picture before that time. We had thought it was only our aircraft that was RTB.

We get back to base and de-rig. The entire division must return all the gear and ammunition we were issued.

Some soldiers were missing 7.62mm ammunition, by the box load.

Some soldiers were missing grenades (high explosive & fragmentation).

Some soldiers were missing: M-18 Claymore Mines.

How in the hell did that happen?!?

We were locked inside a controlled area, surrounded by MP's and escorted directly to the aircraft. We went to war, but were RTB back to the departure airfield, and marched right back to the holding areas to return our gear.

Apparently, several soldiers ditched some of their gear, some of their equipment, and some of their ammunition.

I don't know the mentality of those soldiers, but I can only assume that they didn't want to carry ruck sacks (backpacks) that were extremely heavy, so they ditched whatever they didn't want to carry into combat "before" we left. They must have planned on claiming the missing equipment as a combat loss, once the invasion was underway.

But there is no way that stuff just disappeared.

We were supposed to go back to our units, since the invasion was cancelled. But we were all now on lock-down and were not going anywhere, until we found all that missing ammunition and equipment.

Again, I don't know the big picture nor was I privy to any Top-Secret plans. I can only tell you what I experienced from my perspective. Many people were told, especially the news media personnel outside our gates, that the 10th Mountain was going to go to Haiti. We, elements of the 82nd Airborne Division, would air-land as reinforcements: if they ran into trouble.

I don't know if that was true, but I do know that for all of our remaining rehearsals, all of those high-ranking officers were no longer with us.

So, every day, all day and night we got almost the entire division on-line and walked all over, under and around building, trees, whatever to find that missing stuff. It got to a point where we would line up, take one step and look down. Then take one more step and stop, then look down. Then take one more step then stop, then look down. Imagine rows of hundreds of hundreds of soldiers on a police call looking for these items.

Eventually we found them.

Every single item.

There were claymore mines thrown in the dumpsters.

There were hand grenades hidden in the walls of those old WWII barracks.

There was ammunition buried underground.

We all stayed there for days in that Paratrooper Holding Area, I think it was called a PHA (pronounced Pee-Haw) before we went back to our unit areas on Ardennes near the old Airborne PX.

# 10

# COMBAT PT

I left the 82nd Airborne Division and Fort Bragg, North Carolina in November 1995. I was re-assigned to the 2nd Infantry Division in South Korea until October 1996, specifically, the 1st Battalion, 506th Infantry Regiment (Air Assault) Currahee at Camp Greaves, on the northern side of the Imjin River.

That tour of duty sucked, and it started to suck before I even left Fort Bragg, NC.

Things have changed, but I am telling you the story the way I remembered it.

The entire 82nd Airborne Division is an airborne infantry division of the US Army that specializes in parachute assault operations into denied areas. It is the U.S. Army's most strategically mobile division with elements of the division ready to deploy anywhere in the world within 18 hours of notification. As of this writing the division is fighting in the Global War on Terrorism (GWOT) in both Afghanistan and Iraq. So, I don't know about the immediate reaction time of its deployment ability anymore.

But this is how it used to be:

The 3 infantry brigades of the entire division would take turns being the first to go, in the case of a call out for mobilization. Everybody is going, but someone has to be first. That brigade would be considered the divisions ready brigade and its subordinate battalions on various rotating stages of alertness called DRB/DRF-1 or Division Ready Brigade/Division Ready Force-One.

179

Which in turn made the subordinate battalions of that brigade take turns, on down to the individual companies' rotation time on DRF-1 status all the way down to DRF-9.

If your unit was on DRF-1 status, that means your unit was prepared in its entirety (immunization shots, bags packed, weapons ready and everyone assembled to move in less than 2 hours from the initial alert phone call). So, this means that even if you were off-duty at the movie theatre, if your unit got the call they were going to war in 2 hours, with or without you. Extremely stressful time, because you were always checking your answer machine, or calling the staff duty NCO to see your unit's status.

If your unit was on DRF-2 status, that meant you were ready to move within 4 hours.

I think DRF-3 mean 6 hours.

*I say again, I do not know the alert times of the 82nd Airborne Division anymore. The times I have used were just what I "think" I remembered from when I served there well over 20 years ago.*

There was a period of time in which your unit rotated DRF-1 status with other units, but I don't remember what that was.

I do remember that whenever your brigade was to assume DRB status, there was a lot of preparation to do. Weapons qualification, wills & power of attorney, immunizations, dental exams, everything you would need to do to deploy away for one year, or more.

One of the final acts to show that the entire brigade, with all its subordinate battalions, was ready - was to conduct a DRB assumption run.

This run was normally about four miles long, and the entire brigade would run in formation. Battalion, after battalion, company after company. All singing cadence to keep in step, in unison and develop esprit de corps (loyalty, enthusiasm and devotion) amongst your fellow paratrooper brethren. We would start with a morning formation down inside Towle stadium on Ardennes Road and conduct an about-face & salute the nations colors as they raised the flag up at division headquarters in the morning.

Then we would do another about-face and start the Brigade PT session.

> *Extend to the left MARCH!*
> *Arms downward MOVE!*
> *Left-FACE!*
> *Extend to the left MARCH!*
> *Arms downward MOVE!*
> *Right FACE!*
> *From front to rear, COUNT-OFF!*

Each rank of soldiers counts off in unison. Since there are 4 squads in an infantry platoon it's normally; *ONE, TWO THREE, FOUR!*

When the infantry company is lined up, with all its platoons abreast, it's still 4 ranks of soldiers counting off *ONE, TWO, THREE, FOUR!*

But this is the entire brigade, a few thousand soldiers.

So, the command, from front to rear, COUNT-OFF! Sounds like this:

*ONE, TWO, THREE, FOUR, FIVE, SIX, SEVEN, EIGHT.... NINETEEN, TWENTY, TWENTY ONE, TWENTY-TWO..... FOURTY-ONE, FOURTY TWO!!!*

Then the command, even numbers one step to the left, UNCOVER!

Now we begin, push-ups, sit-ups, mountain climbers, side straddle-hops, flutter kicks, you name it were doing it. A light coat of sweat forms on everyone's back.

So, you can actually see the steam, the smoke, rising off of everyone's body.

Hence the term for corrective action of a subordinate soldier, take him outside and smoke him! When you come back he better be sweating, or I gone smoke you!

Anyway, after the PT session is over, we reform into our unit formations and march up to the road, signing marching cadences along the way to keep in step.

> *Left-Left-Left-Right-Left!*

181

*Double-time march!* (Then we all start running, in step)

*A C-130 rolling down the strip!*
*Sixty paratroopers on a one-way trip!*
*Stand up hook up shuffle to the door!*
*Jump right out and count to four!*

Once we get on the road, we run all the way down Ardennes Road to Long Street then down to Reilly Road and U-turn and run back. The same route that the entire 82nd Airborne Division takes during its annual reunion called "All American Week".

In a platoon-sized formation, the Platoon Leader (PL or LT), the officer in charge leads the unit and the Platoon Sergeant (PSG/E-7) brings up the rear of the formation. He is insuring that everyone is in step and no one falls-out of the run formation.

Normally the Squad Leaders take turns calling cadence from the left side of the unit formation, and the platoon runs in unison. The cadence caller in not just the squad leaders, but any noncommissioned officer in the platoon who can do three things simultaneously.

One they have to be able to sing a cadence that keeps everyone in step, so they have to be able to think on their feet.

Two they must run the same pace as everyone else, so they must be in excellent shape. They are calling cadence, with rhythm and trying to huff and puff breath like everyone else.

Finally, number three they must YELL THE CADENCE LOUD ENOUGH SO THE ENTIRE UNIT CAN HEAR THEM!

The end of almost every famous cadence ever called sounds like this:

*NOW THAT I HAVE DONE MY BEST!!!*

*SERGEANT SMITH WILL DO THE REST!!!*

Or Sergeant whoever it is. If you're good at calling cadence, you will stay out there with no relief: THE ENTIRE RUN.

It was a norm for me to call cadence for well over 50% of the run by myself no matter what unit I was in. My time in the 82nd was no different.

On Friday, 27 October 1995 I was clearing (out-processing) my unit to leave the 82nd Airborne for my new duty station in Korea. That morning for PT, the 2nd Brigade was about to assume the status of the DRB/DRF-1 for the 82nd Airborne Division. So, my unit Bravo Company, 4th Battalion, 325th AIR along with every other unit in the brigade was headed to our morning PT formation. Then march down to Towle Stadium for the Brigades DRB run.

The First Sergeant tells all those soldiers with sick-call and physically limiting profiles to fall out of formation. The rest of the unit is going to join the battalion, which is going to join the brigade.

I fall out and the First Sergeant says, *"Sergeant Bilal where Dafuq do you think you're going?!?"*

I reply, **"that I am clearing post, out processing."**

You know turning in my gear, clearing every location on this out-processing list (post library, transportation, central issue facility, etc) so I can depart for my new unit.

He says to me, *"you're not clearing at no freaking 06:30 in the morning."*

**Come on First Sergeant the other NCO's gonna leave me out to call cadence for like the entire run. I gotta be at "whatever place it was" by 08:00 so I can out process.**

*"Get Dafuq outta here",* he says and the units marches on across the street to Towle stadium.

At that time, the 4th Battalion, 325th AIR battalion Headquarters and the rest of the battalions was physically located at the intersection of Bastogne Drive & Ardennes Road, directly across the street from Towle Stadium.

I go back inside the company and it can't be no more than 10 minutes. When I hear thousands of people running and screaming and shouting!

I step outside in disbelief.

I think to myself, the Brigade Commander must have called Zonk!

Zonk is an unofficial U.S. Army command that is used (very rarely) during Physical Training (PT) formations, during extremely adverse weather conditions.

After the command of Zonk is given, the entire unit runs off screaming and shouting back to their barracks rooms or to their Privately-Owned Vehicles (POV's) cars to leave the base in a hurry.

*Rumor has it that the commanders turn around and yell zonk, and if anyone is still there when he turns back around, he will PT you to death. I don't know if this is true because in my twenty-something years of active duty service, the few times I've heard zonk: I disappeared.*

Anyway, there is this screaming and yelling and I'm trying to make sense of everything and then I see blood.

I see several of the soldiers have blood on their PT uniforms and I start deciphering the rumors.

*Someone is trying to kill the Colonel! They shootin! It's just like Vietnam!*

**Shut up Private, you weren't even born during Vietnam!**

**What the hell just happened?!?**

*Well we thought the shooting was the start of the Brigade DRB run, and then we started seeing people drop after they got hit with gunshots, so we just ran. They said it was a guy from next door in Alpha Company!*

The unit command calls everyone into formation for 100% accountability. Something just happened, and we must account for everyone. I am going to share with you what is common knowledge for those who don't already know, but I will not use the shooter's name. That former soldier doesn't deserve the notoriety for the evil deed that he did, and I think that he deserves to die nameless, buried in an unmarked grave.

*A former U.S. Army soldier was convicted of killing one officer and wounding several other soldiers when he opened fire on our units Physical Training(PT) formation at Fort Bragg, North Carolina.*

*He had enlisted in FEB 1992 and by 1993, he was assigned to the 4/325th AIR of the 82nd Airborne Division, and deployed with us to the Sinai desert between the countries of Egypt and Israel.*

*Early on the morning of 27 OCT 1995, he hid in a tree line (like a coward), adjacent to a housing area, alongside Towle Stadium field, and shot into the brigade formation that was assembled in the stadium, eventually wounding 18 soldiers. Several U.S. Army Special Forces soldiers, were conducting a PT run when they observed gunfire erupt from Towle Stadium. They took cover in the woods between the stadium on Ardennes Road and Bastogne Drive, which placed them behind the shooter.*

*Several unarmed members of 325th Airborne Infantry Regiment Brigade Staff, led by the Regimental XO, hastily assaulted frontally into the position the shooter was firing from and forced him to move several times and retreat deeper into the woods. The Brigade's S-2 Officer and the Brigade's Adjutant Officer were hit by rifle fire as the Brigade Staff assaulted into the woods and pursued the shooter.*

*The Brigade's S-3 Battle Captain and the Brigade's Assistant S-2 Officer closed in from the right side of the Brigade Staff assault line as the shooter fled through the woods. When the shooter turned to fire at them, he was tackled to the ground and apprehended by two of the Special Forces soldiers. The shooter was searched and removed from the woods to a position near Bastogne Road where the Military Police (MP's) secured him.*

*He is now prisoner 76651-95-01 on the U.S. Military's Death Row at the U.S. Disciplinary Barracks Fort Leavenworth, Kansas.*

After the shooting, I can only assume that every unit on Fort Bragg was on lock down, because I know that every unit within the 82nd Airborne Division was on lock down. Like I said, I was there, this was my last few days in the unit before I left to PCS (Permanent Change of Station) to Korea. *Then I returned to Fort Bragg after that miserable one-year tour was complete.*

185

There must have been some initial interrogation of the shooter after he was apprehended.

The authorities had to determine was he alone, or did he have anyone else with him?

Where did he get the weapons and ammunition?

In addition to being a coward and a low-life excuse for a soldier, his trial would recommend reduction in rank to the lowest pay grade, Private/E-1 and a dishonorable discharge, while he's on death row at Fort Leavenworth, Kansas.

He must have told the authorities that he accumulated the ammunition for his attack from all the training and deployments we as a unit had participated in.

It is reported that he said, "Everybody does it, we keep it in the barracks". Like a true Buddy Fucker (a Blue Falcon in the negative sense) all the way to the end.

Don't know if its that's true, but that would explain what happened all day long. In addition to the emergency vehicles and helicopters flying all over base; in a first responder type of way, not a military type of way. Every unit conducted a health & welfare inspection of its barracks, looking for contraband weapons, ammunition and other dangerous items.

We sat outside in formation for what must have been hours.

I remember seeing the Military Police (MP) with the working dogs and several members of our Chain of Command and NCO Support Channel arriving in our unit area. They went into our barracks building (B Company, 4/325 AIR) after leaving the shooters company (A Company, 4/325 AIR). After some time, they would call a soldier's name, and everyone would echo that name. That usually meant that the MP's and the authorities found something illegal, dangerous or something that needed explaining.

It had been very quiet, almost too quiet for a long time when I hear them call my name, SERGEANT BILAL!

*What the fuck?!?*

*I know I don't have nothing in my room, I barely even stay in there.*

My name is echoed throughout the formation and I double-time move into the building, going up to my barracks room. I stayed on the second floor almost directly above the Company Commanders office.

Another NCO unwritten rule is, "Do not go into the junior enlisted barracks on the weekend, especially at night". Whatever it is they are doing will be cleaned up by Monday mornings formation.

*Last time I came up these steps with this much apprehension, it was a weekend at night and I had to get something from my barracks room. Silly me. I remember when I went up the stairs and the lights were off on the second floor. I open the door and a flash of green light flies pass my eyes. Then I hear a glass bottle smash, and break against a wall and several loud drunk paratroopers screaming and laughing.*

*Back then I shouted, "WHAT DAFAQ – AT EASE!!!"*

*Then lights came back on.*

*Do you know what they were doing?*

*There were two groups of soldiers on either end of the hallway. They were all drunk and had taken empty beer bottles and filled them with activated Chem-light glow sticks. Then they were playing dodged ball with each other, by throwing these empty glass beer bottles filled with Chem-light glow sticks, at each other, in the dark.*

*Pieces of broken glass would hit them, they would get cut-up and they would all laugh at each other.*

These were the thoughts that were going through my mind as I was climbing up the stairwell towards the First Sergeant.

I race up the top of the stairs in confusion. The first person I see is my Units First Sergeant and he looks freaking pissed!

I immediately think this is a set-up, somebody must have put something in my room.

When I reach the second-floor landing, everyone including the MP's are down the hall to the left. However, my barracks room is to the right.

I start to turn right (to go to my room), but the First Sergeant directs me to go left with a directional knife hand.

I am relieved that I'm not going to my barracks room, but I am also confused as to why I'm directed to go left. I'm anxious to find out why I'm up here in in the first place and then my training kicks in.

As an Airborne Infantry Rifle Squad Leader, I was responsible for the health, welfare, training and safety of the members of my squad. One of my soldiers stays in the room everyone is in front of, and whatever he has done, I'm responsible for it.

That's the U.S. Army way.

One of your soldiers does something great, everyone in your Chain of Command and the NCO Support Channel will want part of the credit for it. But if one of your soldier's fucks-up, your ass is going to pay for it!

I have known young paratroopers to have birds, snakes, cats & dogs, even an alligator in their room.

I have heard of young teenage girlfriends hiding in their wall lockers, all day long, while the young soldier is out training (and the girls wanted to be in there).

I have seen stacks, and cases of beer that could rival any Class-VI store (civilian equivalent of a liquor store), especially after the military created the Delayed Payment Program (DPP) in the 1990's where soldiers could buy any item with a military Credit Card from the base PX.

*Do you know how much alcohol a group of Privates with thousands of dollars in credit, each, can accumulate for a weekend?*

I have seen them traveling from the airborne PX across Ardennes Road towards the barracks with cases upon cases stacked up on dolly's like you would move furniture with.

I get down the hallway to this young Specialist/E-4 from my squad barracks room, and the authorities and the MP's or whoever, has flipped his mattress up and its resting against the wall. It is now revealing whatever contraband was under the mattress and sitting on top of the bed springs of his bunk.

You're not going to believe what was there.

I don't believe what was there.

I was there, I'm writing this book and it's still hard for me to believe what this young trooper had done.

Sitting under the mattress on this paratrooper's bunk in the barracks was a "live" 81mm mortar round.

A freakin 81mm mortar round weights about 10 lbs. (4.5 kg) and can have an effective kill radius of 35 meters (115 feet).

We call the soldier up and I say to him, *"What the fuck were you thinking airborne?!?"*

His response, *"I was gonna take it home with me, when I go on leave Sergeant."*

As Airborne Infantrymen (11B), once we hit the ground we normal walk everywhere we go. Yeah, there are helicopters, and trucks & tanks. But 90% of the time infantrymen are walking everywhere we go.

Indirect Fire Infantrymen (11C) or Mortarmen use hundreds of mortar rounds that are normally initially carried into the battle by many of the other infantrymen in the company. When we get ready to conduct an attack and the mortar section is going to support us, we walk by where they are set up and graciously give the mortar section their extra ammunition (those mortar rounds).

Of course, they will be re-supplied by other means too, but infantrymen arrive at the battle with everything they need. So, I can understand how that young paratrooper could acquire a mortar round, I just don't understand why he would keep a live one – in the freaking barracks!

So, he was transferred out of our platoon as punishment, in fact, he was transferred out of our company, up to the battalion headquarters.

He became a driver for someone on the Battalion Command Staff.

So, while we walk everywhere, he drives.

There is another infamous unofficial military quote in action right there for you, "Fuck up and move up!"

# 11

# BIG POOKIE AND RAY-RAY

Almost every soldier I knew that served on active duty had a side hustle or another civilian job after duty hours, to help make ends meet. Or to generate extra disposable income.

Most of the time the additional income can be acquired by pulling someone's duty for them. Not extra-duty because that is strictly regulated.

But let's say that there is a requirement to pull a rotating 24-hour guard duty on some equipment that belongs to your unit over the weekend, from Friday after the last 17:00 (5pm) formation, until Monday at 06:30 (6:30am) when the entire unit will start the daily Physical Fitness Training (PT) session in the morning.

If the duty roster had been broken down into 6-hour shifts and my shift was on SAT from 18:00 (6:00pm) until midnight, that time frame would interfere with me going away to party at the beach for the weekend. So, there would always be a soldier living in the barracks who had no social life (we called them barracks-rats) who would volunteer to do my shift for me, providing he & I agree on a price that I would pay him first.

Back in the 1980's and 90's when the U.S. Army had black leather boots for duty that must be brushed shined at a minimum, and black leather jump boots for the dress uniform that must be spit shined for wear – I could get paid to shine other soldier's boots for them.

But I would always charge more money to the other soldiers who were the "customers" than what I paid the other fellow soldiers (mostly barracks rats) who actually did the work for me.

I knew soldiers who drove taxi cabs, delivered pizza, you name it. There are young soldiers near several towns adjacent to many military bases working off-duty doing additional jobs, just to make ends meet.

I distinctly remember a very embarrassing time in the U.S. military where there was a news story about how several soldiers who were married with children, qualified for or where actually getting food stamps, welfare and other government assistance programs.

That was an embarrassing time for the military to admit that there were soldiers on active duty who made so little in their compensation income that they qualified for food stamps.

So, guess what the military did?

They gave everyone a very small pay raise the next year (they do this almost every year), and especially the lower enlisted soldiers who previously qualified for public assistance.

Well, there is a very famous military marching cadence that goes like this:

> You're in the Army now
> You're in the Army now
> You'll never get rich, you son of a bitch
> You're in the army now.

It's a well-known fact that you're not gonna make a lot of money in the military. In fact, if a person worked in a local fast food restaurant and you withheld their entire weekly paycheck until the end of the month, and gave it to them in one monthly installment, they might think they had a lot of money. When they really didn't, it's just an illusion.

If a person got paid minimum wage, currently $7.25 per hour, for a 40-hour work week, they would gross $290 per week.

Now if you paid that person monthly they would receive $1,160 ($290 x 4) and since there was a comma in the pay check – they may think that they're making a lot of money.

Anything below $16,240 annual income, for a family of 2, is considered below the Federal Poverty Level. That's one soldier who is married, with no kids.

($16,240 divided by 52 weeks in a year = $312.30 a week)

So, yeah, many active duty soldiers are living just above the federal poverty level, and need additional jobs to make ends meet (even while serving on active duty). I know, because there was a time that I was one of them and many times my additional after duty hours job was in security.

I worked as a bouncer at a strip club in Fayetteville, NC directly off of Murchison Road, way back in the days. It was located near the infamous Vick's Drive-In restaurant. Neither establishments is there any longer, the buildings don't even exist.

I remember working and I always like working security, at the door.

It provided me the best vantage points to see the people approaching the club, but if you were inside danger came from the fatal funnel of the front door and it was already too late to prevent something from happening, so you were already in the react mode: verses the proactive mode.

I used to search people so thoroughly, especially the men, that it would look like I was JMPI'ing a paratrooper and his equipment before a parachute jump.

Knives, No Sir you can bring this in the club.

Gun, No Sir, go put that back in your car.

Drugs, razors blades, whatever, if it was contraband or a prohibited item, I was gonna find it because my safety and the safety of other depended on it.

I became so notoriously proficient, that when certain patrons and members of the local gangs would see me at the door, out of respect for my professionalism - they would turn around immediately and go put whatever they were gonna bring inside the venue back into their vehicles.

One day a man was thrown out the club for being drunk, disorderly and belligerent towards the strippers. The bouncers didn't just throw him out the club, they physically picked him up and threw him out the club. The bouncers inside would always attempt to see who could throw a person the furthest, when they threw him out the club for whatever reason. I tried to console the man, *"Say brother that was wrong the way they threw you out the club. They didn't have to do it that way. Come back next week and I got you."* Meaning he wouldn't have to stand in the long line, my offer was the least I could do. That is what I usually said to people who got thrown out the strip club. I would try to use some verbal judo, try to diffuse the already volatile situation, and it would normally work.

The other bouncers stayed outside the club laughing and joking about how the guy fell, and didn't pay attention to their surroundings.

That night, that guy came back from around the corner in a car driven by someone else tearing through the parking lot. He stuck his arm out the window, with his pistol and commenced to conduct a drive by shooting.

Blam! Blam! Blam! Blam! Blam!

I see the bullets coming at us, then I notice all his shots were aimed at the other bouncers congregating at the door. The one bouncer who threw the guy was part of the rest of them trying to run back inside the club for cover. He was shot in the buttocks and went to the hospital that night. So, I don't know if that was karma, or if the guy wasn't really that drunk. You could see bullet holes all over the outside of that club from the weekly shootouts.

# 12

# POP THE TRUNK

I'm at the same club, different night. Working the door like I prefer so I can see everything before it happens. Another night, another man is thrown out the strip club.

I later find out that this guy snuck a small .32 caliber semi-automatic pistol inside the club earlier that evening. He removed his work boots and took out the insoles. Then he put the pistol inside the boot, but under the insole and wore the boots laced up very sloppy and lose. The exaggerated walk resembles a slightly tipsy person, but not intoxicate enough where they won't let him in the club: to spend his money.

Anyone who sneaks anything into a club normally goes straight to the latrine (restroom) so that they can retrieve the weapon, drugs, knives or whatever it is they smuggled into the venue. That's just what he did.

I'm at the door doing my job, but also working my side hustle. The club has a no-free reentry policy. If you left for any reason, you had to pay the full fee to re-enter. I think it was like $20 dollars and the price would go up as the evening progressed. This discouraged people from going to their trucks and cars to consume alcohol and forced them to pay the overpriced rates at the bar.

Many patrons would come to the door asking me if I knew where the nearest ATM machine was at. I would make them an offer they couldn't refuse. I'd say, "Let me help you and save you the trip."

I would sell them 85 singles one-dollar bills for $100 dollars.

*But what about the other $15 dollars?!?*

Well, you're gonna pay more than that to get back in the club, plus you gonna have to wait in that long-ass line, and you might not get back in.

*OK Big Man.*

I did this so much, that I would withdraw singles from the bank in stacks of 1,000 single one-dollar bills wrapped in a brick. I made a few dollars on the side, but I saved the patrons from leaving the club and becoming prey to the unsavory types patrolling the parking lot looking for victims.

Anyway, they throw this other guy out the club on this particular night and as he hits the ground he's reaching in his waistband. When he pulls out the gun, he's mad.

The other bouncers are still inside and I'm outside, by myself. He's too far away from me, for me to close the distance, disarm him, and ground & pound some sense into him.

But I also know that I cannot outrun bullets.

He points the pistol at me as he's backing up, pulls the trigger and it does not fire.

I maneuver around the nearest car and he's on the other side, attempting to correct his pistol malfunction.

He pulls the slide back, pulled the trigger again, and again it didn't fire!

*He hasn't reset the trigger.*

He's attempting to pull the slide back, but since he hasn't allowed the trigger to reset, whenever he points the gun at me, and releases the trigger and pulls it again, it doesn't fire.

Every time he attempts to shoot me, he throws the pistol forward a little bit, as if that will make the bullets come out faster or something. Straight Big Pookie and Ray-Ray style.

196

His third or fourth attempt and he's talking smack to me, asking me very stupid questions. *"Why you ducking big man, why you – ducking!?!"* As he says the word "ducking" that's when he pulls the trigger.

I say to myself, *"Because you're trying to kill me fool", but you keep backing up away from me.*

By this time, many people are outside the club now, and a crowd is gathered, all crouching behind other parked cars. He keeps attempting to correct his malfunction, and talking as he almost running backwards towards his car. *Is he going to retrieve a bigger weapon?*

Because everybody in the dirty-south knows what happens when someone says, they're gonna pop the trunk of their car.

Just then someone around me did pop their trunk. *\*I didn't get a good look at him, at all.*

I think that guy took out a AR-15 that was a 5.56mm, magazine fed, gas operated, air cooled, semi-automatic (not fully automatic) rifle, with an EOTech holographic weapon sight & forward handgrip with the bipod legs inside, modeled after the military's current modern M-4 carbine. *\*But, I'm just guessing because like I said, I really didn't get a good look at him.*

I think that guy feared for his life, and the lives of others around the venue, when he "returned" fire back at the shooter, and tore up the shooters car. *\*But again, it was so long ago, and like I said I really didn't get a good look at him.*

I just saw the muzzle flash that came from his weapon at night, every time he fired. For many of the civilians it probably looked like flames were coming out of that weapon, plus I bet it sounded loud too! *\*But like I said, I really didn't get a good look at the guy that was returning fire at the shooter, plus it was a long long time ago.*

I just remember that night, they were shooting.

# 13

# KILL EVERYBODY

Another night, another club, more guns, more drama.

This time there was an entertainment venue located on Hay Street in the downtown business district of Fayetteville, North Carolina – very close to where the current headquarters office of Shadow Protective Services, LLC (SPS500) is located at now. The club is no longer active, it shut down after several name changes, but the building still remains standing. There is a completely different establishment there now.

Anyway, I was performing armed security outside of the club and the bouncers inside the venue were unarmed. There were almost a thousand patrons there on this particular night.

At that time, NC State law prevented people from bringing concealed handguns into an establishment that sells alcohol, like a bar or a club. I'm outside at the door and there is a commotion inside, and the security needs my presence. I secured my handgun in the trunk of my POV (parked near the entrance) before I went inside the club, so I wouldn't get caught inside the venue with my weapon (even though I worked there). But this means that when I come back outside I am initially unarmed, until I retrieve my weapon, from my trunk.

I know that an armed security officer working at a night club, not being allowed to go inside with his weapon may seem silly, but there were all sorts of rules that didn't make sense to me. For example; I'm outside on another night when a local Law Enforcement Official (LEO) wants to speak with me. I ask him if I can help, and he replies that I need to go get the club manager, so he can issue them a ticket or citation for a noise complaint. I look at the LEO in a very confused manner and ask him to repeat himself. He again states that he can hear the music coming from inside the venue, and he was issuing a noise complaint to the manager. I go get the manager, and he tells me to get the owner. The owner tells me to get the manager. Whatever happened, anyway if the venue which had an alcohol license and permit to operate as a "night club" with thousands of patrons could be issued a ticket/citation for loud noise, than I know how far someone could take it when firearms are concerned.

Anyway, on this particular night during the short period of time that I was inside the venue, the owner of the club and the promoter of the event that night got into a heated argument on the outside, directly in front of the club.

The promoter had about four armed guards wearing business suits with him. The owner of the club wasn't intimidated; however, you can tell the moment I step outside the venue he escalated the argument instead of de-escalating it.

He reached into his pocket and pulled out a handgun and pointed it at the ground. Then in a loud voice he states, *"You ain't the only one with a gun. We got guns too!"*

The promoter steps back and all four of his guys draw their handguns out in the parking lot and attempt to surround (and protect their boss the promoter), the club owner (my boss) and me.

I'm thinking of my best verbal judo to de-escalate this situation: when it gets worse.

The club owner was known to many people in town as a person you did not want to mess with.

A local gangster that frequented the club comes up the street, carrying his weapon at waist level and yells to me these words (that I will never forget), as he pulls back the charging handle of his AK-47.

200

"*Move out da way Brother Muhammad, I'm finna kill all these bitches! Dat motherfucker feeds me!*" (meaning when he's incarcerated, the club owner puts spending money on his books) "*I just got out* [the penitentiary], *I'll kill all these bitches and go back tonight!*"

The club owner didn't ask him to do that, I was there, I saw the whole thing transpire. He just commanded that type of respect in the streets. The event promoter and his shooters must not have known how loyal some people were to that club owner.

I walk down the street towards the guy with the AK-47 (I was familiar with him), with my palms open, fingers extended and spread out, and I tell the guy; "*I'm out here with him, you think I'm gonna let something happen to him*" "*Put that chopper away!*"

Then I walk back over to both the club owner and the promoter and I say, "*What are y'all doing? Y'all both bosses about to have your guys shoot it out, over what!?? Won't y'all both go back inside to your office and settle whatever it is like bosses?*"

Of course, the entire time I was talking verbally, my body langue was facing the club owner.

He says, "*You're right Brother Muhammad*" and I escort them both back inside the club. I tell the bouncers that are inside the club, and the club manager what happened, then I go back outside.

I talk to the event promoters' guys and a few of them are hardcore, I've seen the look before. But two of them are visibly shook, one guy lights a cigarette up, an appears to smoke the entire cigarette in one drag – pull.

I diffused a volatile situation with verbal judo, but that night, they almost started shooting!

# 14

CHAPTER FOURTEEN
# TWO-WAY RIFLE RANGE

After my 20-year retirement from U.S. Army in 2006, I briefly worked as Observer-Controller (Instructor) for the U.S. Army's Special Forces Qualification Course (SFQC) or "Q-course" teaching the SUT (Small Unit Tactics) phase of the Q-course. At that time it was called phase II (two).

It was a government contracting job where I worked as a DoD Civilian for a company that was a subsidiary of Northrup Grumman. Long story short, Northrup Grumman lost the contract that year, and many of us were not picked up by the new company that underbid and won the contact. Many government contracts are awarded to the lowest bidder. Just like many of you shop around for not necessarily the best product, but the least expensive.

I worked a few other security & bodyguard protection gigs, but eventually I deployed overseas with a Private Military Company (PMC) that supported the U.S. Department of States (DoS) in support of the United States mission in Iraq.

There were months of training and vetting involved just to get into the program and even more evaluating and vetting after we were done, awaiting deployment into theatre. I eventually, deployed into theatre at a location other than the capital of Iraq in Baghdad. The PMC's headquarters, the old U.S. Embassy (before the NEC was completed) and the military headquarters for Operation IRAQ FREEDOM in Iraq were located there. So, in military parlance, everywhere else in country is considered "away from the flag pole".

203

When I arrived, we were sent straight to the range.

I mean, you did not unpack your bags, you got off the plane, were assigned your individual weapons, issued ammunition and taken straight to the range. If you did not qualify or "meet the standard" you were sent back on that same aircraft, that same day. I have seen many of people sent back home (or someplace else), the same day they arrived.

I'm at the range, and we start with the 9mm handgun (Glock 17's or 19's) at the 50-yard line for qualification.

Yes, you read that correctly, I said handgun at the 50-yard line.

Then we progress forward to the 25-yard line, then the 15, then the 10 and so on and so forth. Once those that do NOT qualify are sent home, with the ones leaving to go on their vacation/rotation the real training for familiarization begins.

Now, I am going to preface what I am about to tell you by saying this:

**Do NOT try this at home!**

Do NOT do any of the stuff I am going to tell you, anywhere, ever. Extreme physical injury and death could occur if you do. The only reason I'm restating this is because I am telling you the reader what I've experienced in the past, and do NOT wish anyone to even think about doing, some of the things I have done.

Anyway, I developed a re-action time that was faster than normal. I mean I had become extremely fast when it came to firing and qualifying on the weapons range. If you fired your weapon before the appropriate time, whether the pro-timer clock, whistle or whatever, you were considered a negligent discharge and a safety violation, and a NO-GO. Many people received letters of "Lack of Confidence" from the US government, revocation of their security clearance and fired from this job because of that.

So, I developed a reaction time where, even if the next iteration was to engage a specific set of targets in a specific set of time, I would "wait" until others on the firing line started first, and only then when I heard them engage would I start. Then I was so fast (because I had to make up for the lost second or two)

I would be finished before many of those (men & women) who started before me were.

So, this particular day we were training and were on maybe the third or fourth iteration. We are all are firing from the 50-yard line. Then we finish that set and moved forward toward the 25-yard line. Then as I am holstering my side-arm I notice movement from my peripheral vision on my right side. It looks like one of the other shooters has stepped in front of the firing line. So, I'm about to yell, "CEASE FIRE"!!!

Now, I've spent some time doing SOF training with weapons, and a lot of time doing infantry training with weapons. So, I know one of the cardinal guidelines of firing weapons is to ensure that NOBODY is down range, or in front of the firing line. But another unwritten rule is that if you are the new guy in the unit, "shut-up" and learn before you open your mouth. So, since I'm not on the range by myself I know everyone else sees this shooter step forward of the firing line and nobody else has called, "CEASE FIRE".

Then the shooter keeps walking down range to like the 15-yard line and starts to engage his targets again. Then I notice another shooter walk forward in his firing lane and start to engage his targets again. Then another, then another.

Then it hits me.

I realize that I'm also supposed to walk forward to my next designated position (while everyone else is still shooting) and re-engage my targets. On the live firing range.

I watch as a shooter finishes near the 5-yard line and then changes his targets with fresh new ones. Then he does an about face, and start to walk towards us (while staying in his lane) to start over again.

I go through my complete iteration of ammunition like I was trained to do, I am not thinking, I am on auto-pilot, completely.

When I get down range to the target stands, I can see the impact of the bullets hitting the targets and the dirt berms behind the targets on my immediate left and right. I have 100% faith (and then some) that those shooters are shooting into their targets "on their lanes". However, when I change my Izzy target and turn around, I now see the firing line from a completely different view point.

I am walking towards my new starting position (not all the way back at the 50-yard line this time) but I can see everyone else shooting at their targets from the targets perspective.

Although everyone on the range was "friendly" that is a sight I would never hope anyone would actually see and experience in their lifetime. But there was no terror or fear in me, it was just pure training and instinct.

It was at that moment I now understood the term, "Big Boy Rules".

I mean once I get on the road and start running missions with these guys: and the shooting starts. I can't just tell everyone, *"Ok everybody, all the good guys get on the ground. I need to differentiate between the good and the bad guys so I'll know who to shoot"*.

If fact I can't have all the good guys get behind me, or abreast and alongside me like we normally do at firing ranges. There will be good and bad people mixed up together, and I'll have to insure I shoot who I intend to shoot and not the people we're protecting, any innocent civilians that have nothing to do with it, or any of my teammates.

Friendly fire ain't friendly.

We would train like this until we had our training down to perfection.

Then we would do it again.

This was in Iraq in 2007, shortly after the incident in Nisour Square in Baghdad, involving Personal Security Specialist (PSS) personnel working for the former company called Blackwater.

So, the pressure for perfection was even greater. Now, if you made a mistake, not only would you lose your billion-dollar-a-day job, not only would you risk losing your security clearance, receiving a loss of confidence letter from the U.S. Government, not only do you risk the trauma of accidently killing your friends your team mates – now the pressure for perfection included you might be going to jail, an Iraqi jail at that.

We were also assigned machineguns, so we trained constantly on the 5.56mm M-249 Squad Automatic Weapon (SAW) light machinegun and the 7.62mm

M-240 medium machinegun (there are several variants of the NATO MAG 58, called the M-240B/C/D/E/G/H/L/N). The standard for machinegun qualification was not scored numerically. It was scored as every round was a hit or miss. Imagine you're given a belt of ammunition and the standard is: EVERY ROUND MUST HIT THE TARGET, no exception, period. Then the actual physical target you qualified on is sent up to the US State Department (DoS) for record evaluation and safe keeping.

You either qualified 100% or you were a NO-GO at that station.

I remember thinking I was a Special Forces Weapons Sergeant, an Airborne Infantry Fire Team Leader, Squad Leader and Platoon Sergeant. I taught weapons to hundreds if not thousands of students and there can't be that many people like me with my skill set working on this contract.

My inquisitive mind would receive the answers I wanted on my very first mission outside the wire.

*Guess what was the first question posed to me, by guys who were already down-range?* We're on my first mission outside the wire (in the red zone) protecting diplomats, and this is what I'm asked by some of my team mates.

They didn't ask me my tactical background, like was I an Army Ranger, Navy Seal, Marine, or whatever?

They didn't ask me my preference in music or food, or any of the gazzilion other topics we would all eventually discuss over the next few years.

The first question I was asked, stung me because it was so blatant.

The first question asked of me was, "*Shadow is your wife white*"?

*WTF!?!*

I guess some people are preoccupied with race relations and its topics. It didn't faze me because I know I'm a blackman in a racist society, I've been black my whole life.

My reply to him at that time, *My answer was (is) NO, but what dafuq did that have to do with anything? Whether my wife was Latino, Asian, of european decent or Black like me, what difference should it have made at that point in time?!? "I'm black, my wife is black, my weapon is black, this truck we're in is black and if I buy the farm on this mission my bodybag is black!"* The bodybags were actually a dark greyish color, but I wasn't thinking about that at the time.

But I have always been the only black guy in several of my units, the only black guy on my team, one of the only two black guys in my scout platoons. If I wasn't the only one, there were never more than two or three others to the best of my recollection. So, I completely understand the dynamics of small unit cohesion.

I already know that there is not going to be any playing of any "black" music of any type in this vehicle. No Teddy Pendergrass, no Barry White, no Tupac, no Biggie, not even James Brown. I've come to understand the isolation that occurs when you're not only a minority of the group, but the only one.

So, when asked, *"If I liked Van Halen?"* There is an awkward silence in the vehicle.

My reply is, ***"As long it's David Lee Roth; Jump, Panama or Hot for Teacher, type of Van Halen and not that Sammy Hagar; I Can't Drive 55 Van Halen!"***

Laughter ensues, and everyone is comfortable before our mission.

Now, right before we left, we took a group photo near our vehicle. Each team has several vehicles, but each particular vehicle crew took a photo called a "Herndon Photo."

The PMC company headquarters was in the city of Herndon, Virginia back in the United States and we all knew (because we've all been there) that the hallway wall was full of photos of guys who had been killed in combat. But since we're civilian contractors now, and not active duty military the world will probably never know about all those who gave their lives, protecting others.

As I was looking through my archives to research this book for historical accuracy, I noticed that I have hundreds of possible "Herndon Photos" from the hundreds of missions I have done over the years.

But this first mission is one that gave me further confirmation that I was with the big dogs now, playing by "Big Boy Rules".

As, as I'm riding in the vehicle watching my sector, the guy on the other passenger side is back to back with me, the entire way. During the small talk, it is discovered that he was regular Army before this lifestyle. Since many of the higher-ranking members of the PMC were in the Marine Corps, specifically Marines who had worked in a U.S. Embassy overseas someplace, it was a welcome surprise to hear that he was an Army guy.

*What unit were you in?*
He says, *"I was a company commander in the 2ⁿᵈ Ranger Battalion at Fort Lewis."*

*"Oh."* He didn't say he was a Ranger at Fort Lewis, or even a Noncommissioned Officer (NCO) like I was. He just said, he was a freaking company commander and here he is licking windows like me, WTF?!?

I look at the driver.

*"Hey, what unit were you in?"*
He says, *"I wasn't in the military."*

*"Oh, what's your background?"*
He says, *"I come from law enforcement."*

I think to myself, oh that's great, there are several guys here that were on SWAT Teams back at their major metropolitan city police departments, and for whatever reasons they all wind-up driving. Maybe it's because of all that time driving patrol cars back CONUS.

But he interrupts my train of thought when he says, *"I was the Chief of Police of my Police Department back CONUS."*

The guy sitting in the trunk money seat where the machine gunner would normally be at, was a medic. He tells me that, *"I'm is from Colorado and was one of the first medics to respond and treat the kids who got shot up at the high school in Columbine during that massacre in 1999."*

Then the vehicle commander.

209

He was also a regular Army guy. But the story goes that he was also a former U.S. Army Infantry Company Commander, and he was killed, twice, during combat in support of Operation IRAQI FREEDOM.

Once he died for a few moments, but the doctors were able to revive him, and another time he reportedly died on the operating table, but was brought back to life.

So, I understood that I was amongst great men and women who were in this unit from all walks of life, who were the best of the best and really put it all on the line when the explosions started and the shooting happened.

I received a written commendation from the leadership of the PMC company I worked for, and eventually worked my way up to becoming a member of the United States Ambassador to Iraq's personal Protective Detail (APD) before leaving that company.

There were three companies that I was intimately aware of, and keep in touch with alumni up to this very day; (1) DynCorp International, (2) Triple Canopy & (3) Blackwater USA.

It was common knowledge as a security contractor, that if there was ever any issue while you were operating in country, you just told them, whoever them was (whether it was the U.S. Military, Iraqi Military, Iraqi Police, Iraqi National Guard, civilians, whoever) many team just yelled Blackwater, Blackwater as they bypassed the drama.

So, Blackwater really got a bad reputation from members of some of the other companies that operated in Iraq at the same time.

Some of the other companies that I heard were hiring personnel for various jobs in Iraq back during those day were: *AD Consultancy, Aegis Defense Services, AirScan, AKE limited, American International Security, Applied Marine Technology Inc, ArmorGroup, BH Defense, Blackheart International, LLC, BritAm Defense Ltd, CACI, Camelian International Risks, CastleForce Consultancy LTD, Centurion Risk Assessment Services, Cochise Consultancy Inc, Combat Support Associates, Control Risks Group, Critical Intervention Services, Custer Battles, Decision Strategies, Diligence Middle East, D S Vance Iraq, DTS Security LLC, EOD Technology, Erinys International, Genric, Global Risk Strategies Ltd, Global Security Source, Group 4 Falck A/S, Halo Group, HartGroup, Henderson Risk Ltd, Hill and Associates, Lld,*

*ICP Group Ltd, ISI, Janusian Security Risk Management Ltd, Kroll Security International Ltd, ManTech International Corp, Meteoric Tactical Solutions, Meyer & Associates, MPRI, MZM, Inc, Neareast Security, New Korea Total Service, Olive Security (UK) Limited, Optimal Solution Services, Overseas Security & Strategic Information, Inc/Safenet – Iraq, Pilgrims Group, RamOPS Risk Management Group, Ronco Consulting Corporation, Rubicon International Services, Saladin Security, Security Applications Systems International LLC, SOC-SMG (Special Operations Consulting – Security Management Group), Steele Foundation, Sumer International Security, Titan Corp, Unity Resources, USA Environmental, Vance International, Vinnell Corporation, Wade-Boyd and Associates LLC, and Worldwide Language Resources, INC*

It doesn't matter which company was operating in Iraq on whatever day.

On any given day between 2004 and 2007, 2008, 2009, 2010, 2011, 2012 and 2013 while I was in serving in Iraq, somebody, somewhere, was Shooting!

# 15

CHAPTER FIFTEEN
# SIZE THIRTEEN

My current business partner at Shadow Protective Services and I both worked various security jobs in the Fayetteville, North Carolina area. From club bouncer to armed security officers, he even worked fugitive recovery for a bail bondsman for some time. I was a U.S. Army soldier before I retired, and he had served, honorably, in the U.S. Marine Corps. We both had worked as Armed Security Contractors for a Private Military Company (PMC) in Iraq, that was contracted by the U.S. Department of State (DoS) to protect U.S. diplomats, amongst other things, and other designated personnel in support of Operation IRAQI FREEDOM and Operation NEW DAWN.

One particular morning we were over there, working in the Security Contractor capacity and resided somewhere on the massive United States Embassy Compound. Since it was the "new" U.S. Embassy in Iraq that was built after the old one was closed down, it was referred to as the NEC (New Embassy Compound).

So, both he and I linked-up outside to go conduct our morning PT (physical training) session, specifically the heavy weight lifting at the NEC gym. It was about 04:30 hours (4:30am) in the morning, still quiet and a little dark. We both started walking towards the gym, and because of my previous knee repair surgeries (from jumping out of airplanes as a U.S. Army paratrooper for over 20 years) I am just a little slower than what I used to be.

*Example: If I had too, I could probably run per the U.S. Army physical fitness standards, a 2-mile course in a 15:30 time (that is an average of 7 minutes & 45 seconds per mile) that would equal a barely passing score of 66% in the 17-21 age group category, and a 94% score in the 52-56 age group category. However, way back in the day, when I was a young thunder cat, my best 2-mile run time was 10:15 (that's 5 minutes & 8 seconds per mile) or about a 127% score in the 17-21 year old age group category, and a 144% score in the 52-56 year old age group category.*

This particular morning it was so quiet that he and I both heard it.

The distinct sound of, SWOOCH!!! SWOOCH!!! SWOOCH!!!

Whatever it was, we heard the sound of the rockets or mortars leaving their launch tubes. So, either insurgents are inside the green zone launching mortars from their mortar tubes over the walls into the NEC, or rockets were launched over our head towards something.

Neither he nor I waited for the impact.

We both ran as fast as we could for protection inside the nearest concrete bunker (called a duck and cover bunker). Those bunkers were everywhere. Funny thing, when he reached the bunker, and he was running for his life as fast as he could, I was already inside.

Whenever I heard the sound of incoming mortars or rockets, I was always the first person inside the duck and cover, or as the TCN's would always say,

*"Da big guy is always da first pa-son inside da bunker".*

We hear the explosions impact someplace outside the immediate vicinity, so we were right next to whoever launched the rockets that morning, but not the intended targets.

We finished our workout and proceed with the rest of our duty day.

Seven days a week, the same thing. There are no weekends, or weekdays in the combat environment. Every single day is the same danger. If there is no "planned" mission that day, we still must be ready within a moment's notice.

For whatever reason, we had some down time that afternoon, and another teammate joined us. The 3 of us were leaving the NEC and walking inside the green zone to another American military base called, FOB Union III.

We would periodically go there because that FOB had another AAFES (Army & Air Force Exchange Service) PX, and some other local vendors call "haji shops". The haji shops sold everything from fake name brand military boots to jewelry boxes, from incense & hookah pipes to bootleg movies. Many service members and other persons in Iraq would bring some of these items with them back home CONUS as gifts.

I was specifically looking for a pair of shower shoes or flip flops, that only cost one dollar, but the PX on the NEC didn't have my size, a 13.

So, it's me, my business partner and another brother shopping on our time off.

I distinctly remember it wasn't a Friday, but several of the "haji shops" were closed. They are normally closed or open late on Fridays, because over there Friday's is the religious day of the week equivalent to our Sundays in the United States.

> Many Muslims go to the Mosque on Friday's.
> Many Jews go to the Temple on Saturday's.
> Many Christians go to the Church on Sunday's.

But to many of us working over in Iraq it was just another day, and it wasn't Friday.

So why were so many shops closed?

Many of the shops were co-located together inside the "Wall of Babylon, near the Big Blue Dome" on FOB Union III. We were leaving the area, after shopping for a few minutes and a Local National (LN) woman runs past us to open her shop for business. She must be late, missing out on all the service members spending money, or at least that's what I thought.

We leave the blue dome area and stop at the LN tailor. Remember we were all on the APD detail, and wore suits and ties (slacks and collared shirts at a minimum) whenever we were working. We were also wearing body armor

215

and all the rest of the gear. Eventually you will need to see a tailor or seamstress.

So, we leave the tailor and head inside the AAFEE's PX trailer. It's like four single wide trailers put together to form a big square store. About three or four TCN cashiers (from like Bangladesh or Sri Lanka) work inside. They have lots of items that we're accustom too but take for granted back in the United States, like; toothpaste, soap, rubbing alcohol, toe nail clippers, baby wipes, magazines, etc. It looks nice and colorful inside, but the wall was still corrugated tin and the building wasn't even reinforced yet.

I find a pair of size 13 flip-flop shower shoes and some deodorant. I'm happy and laughing. I show my business partner and glance at the other guy on our team.

Then the explosion happened, BOOM!

Then another explosion, BOOM!!!

Then several more explosions, BOOM!!! BOOM!!! BOOM!!! BOOM!!! BOOM!!! BOOM!!!

The ground is shaking and we realize this is a sustained attack!

Instinct and training hits, and we all dive for cover. But there is no cover, so we hit the dirt (lay on the ground as fast as you can) and listen, feel and taste these explosions.

Right after the first explosion, all the TCN's and whoever else was in the PX disappeared out the door into the nearest duck & cover bunker.

But the three of us cannot make it there. If we try to run to the bunker, we will definitely get blown up my one of the rockets or mortars impacting around us. At the least were gonna catch enough shrapnel to kill us all. I mean, the ground was actually shaking violently, with enough force to lift us up off the floor. This attack, it was like laying down in an impact area, because the rounds are landing danger close. This is the loudest sound I've ever heard. Not because the explosions are loud, they were. But because I knew this was the sound of my impending inevitable doom, and I could do nothing to prevent it from happening.

More explosions, BOOM!!!

BOOM!!!

BOOM!!!

So now we realize this is it. This is not a harassment mortar attack, where the insurgent launch two or three rockets and run. This is a sustained attack, where almost 20 rockets are impacting all around us.

I see my business partner and look him dead in the eye, without saying a word I convey the final look of; *"Damn homie, this is how it ends huh?!?"*

There is no way we are going to survive this one.

BOOM!!!

BOOM!!!

He looks back at me and we both know that we are both going to die.

BOOM-BOOM-BOOM-BOOM!!! BOOM-BOOM!!!

BOOM!!! BOOM!!! BOOM!!!

Then it stops.

So now I'm waiting for one of two things to happen. Either the ground attack is coming, and we'll know because we will start to hear automatic machine gun fire or some other type of small arms fire. Or were gonna hear a bunch of shouting and a big explosion from a suicide bomber or a Vehicle-Bourne Improvised Explosive Devise (VBIED).

Just then the AAFES front door opens and one of the TCN's who works in this little PX bursts inside. The big cloud of dust comes into the door with him, and the rocks and shrapnel are still falling outside.

This little TCN actually says to us, *"Put the merchandise down and come with me"*!

*"Are you serious?!?"*

*"Did this little motherfucker just say what I think he said?"*

It's just then that I realize that the three of us are all black or what many people call "African-American's". My business partner is from Chicago; the other guy is from California and I'm from New York. You don't get much more "American" than that.

This little TCN was racially profiling us, and his skin complexion was darker than mine. He actually thought we were gonna "steal" the merchandise. He risked his life, not to come guide us to safety, but to tell us to "drop the merchandise" and come with him.

Some one-dollar flip-flops.

*"FUCK YOU, YOU LITTLE FUCKING WEASLE LOOKING RAT-FACE GOAT-MOUTH MOTHERFUCKER!!! I AIN'T FUCKING GOING NOWHERE!!! GET THE FUCK OUTTA MY FACE!!! BEFORE I FUCKING KILL YOU!!!"* Or words to that effect is what I remember saying to him, yelling at the top of my lungs.

Just then the sirens and the alarms goes off on the base. The emergency responders are activated. There is no ground attack coming, we now know this because the base (FOB Union III) loudspeaker system comes on.

STAY AWAY FROM THE PX!

STAY AWAY FROM THE PX!

UNEXPLODED ORDINACE (UXO) IN THE AREA!!!

STAY AWAY FROM THE PX!

We got to get the hell outta here y'all. We all rush out of the area, and respond to all the activity of our radios. Accountability is priority now, and there is an attempt to locate causalities.

As we leave the PX I look over to my right side and I see the TCN who is now back inside the duck & cover bunker. He is peeking his little head out from inside of it, looking at me, and I wanna go kill him for that racist bullshit he just pulled. But I gotta get back to my ready room.

As we leave the PX area, we look to the left and what do we see? The UXO is partially imbedded in the ground, right next to the PX on the other side of the corrugated tin that the PX trailer was made out of.

The three of us were lucky to survive that day, because they sure were shooting!

# 16

# TRIGGER PULLERS!

I have posted the following [or a variation of this] on my social media pages several times.

*If you are a friend of mine, and wish to exercise your Second Amendment Rights to the United States Constitution, "the right of the people to keep and bear arms shall not be infringed" contact me if you need help, we can talk (If you're a friend of mine, you already have my personal cellphone number and/or personal e-mail address). I don't charge my friends money to help them defend themselves and their families.*

*Plus, I have just a little bit of experience with firearms that you may find useful.*

*I was once an Airborne Infantry Fire Team Leader as a Specialist (E-4), in the U.S. Army's 6th Infantry Division (Artic) at Fort Richardson with the 1/501.*

*I was once an Airborne Infantry Rifle Squad Leader as a Sergeant (E-5), in the U.S. Army's 82nd Airborne Division at Fort Bragg with the 4/325.*

*I was once an Air Assault Infantry Rifle Squad Leader as a Staff Sergeant (E-6), in the U.S. Army's 2nd Infantry Division at Camp Greaves, South Korea with the 1/506.*

*I was once an Airborne Infantry Platoon Sergeant as a young Sergeant First Class (E-7), in the U.S. Army's 173rd Airborne Brigade at Caserma Ederle, Italy with the 2/503.*

*I was an Expert Infantryman in Alaska, 6th Infantry Division (2/17)*

*I was a Combat Infantryman in Iraq, 1ˢᵗ Cavalry Division (2/5) Sadr City, Baghdad*

*I was a U.S. Army Special Forces Weapons Sergeant (18B) Green Beret*

*I was an Infantry Doctrine writer at the U.S. Army Infantry Center & School, and the Primary Weapons Instructor while assigned to the Combined Arms & Training Directorate (CAT-D); Officer Candidate School (OCS), Infantry Officers Basic Course (IOBC), Infantry Captains Career Course (ICCC) & the Tactics Certification Course (TCC).*

*I was a Special Forces "Observer/Controller" (Instructor) for Phase II Small Unit Tactics (SUT) teaching weapons instruction, infantry tactics & small unit leadership to future generations of our country's "Green Berets".*

*I have served as an Armed Security Contractor, Diplomatic Personal Security Specialist (PSS), Counter Assault Team (CAT) Leader and member of the United States Ambassador to Iraq's Protection Detail (APD) in Iraq (Operation IRAQI FREEDOM & Operation NEW DAWN) for almost 7 years; 2007, 2008, 2009, 2010, 2011, 2012 & 2013.*

*I am the founder of Shadow Protective Services, LLC (a Private Investigation and Executive, Celebrity & VIP Protection Company) with operational offices in the Fayetteville/Fort Bragg, North Carolina area and the Maryland & Washington – District of Columbia area.*

*AND*

*I was born in the South Bronx and raised in Harlem, New York.*

*I have said this many times and I'll say it again.*

*I have no ill will towards anybody, nothing but love and affection, but to anyone wishing to do me harm and forcing me to defend myself... in the words of the 26ᵗʰ U.S. Secretary of Defense James Norman "Jim" Mattis former USMC General who's quoted in the Armed Forces Journal (August 2006) as saying, "I come in peace. I didn't bring artillery. But I'm pleading with you with tears in my eyes. If you fuck with me, I'll kill you all".*

There are key words I'll hear in a conversation that will indicate the proficiency level of a firearms enthusiast to me. If you use terms like "a gat", "the toolie" or "the roscoe" to refer to your handgun, I don't doubt that you have used one before, it just calls your level of training into question to me. Especially when a person doesn't use commonly recognized terms like; handgun, firearm or sidearm - to refer to their pistol.

When using semi-automatic weapons, you load bullets (or the ammunition) into magazines, and then insert the magazines into the weapons, to load and fire them. Whenever I hear the term "load a clip" or "the clip was empty", it just screams to me that somebody needs some training. Yes, there is a such thing as a clip of ammunition. However, that's talking about something like the method used when firing a M-1 Rifle, which holds an eight round "clip" of .30-06 ammunition. When the last cartridge of ammunition is fired, the M-1 Rifle bolt locks in the open position and the clip is ejected.

But when talking about handguns; whether revolver, semi-automatic or fully automatic there are some things that are just basic. If we're discussing firearms and someone tells me that there EDC (everyday carry) weapon is a .380 or a .45 caliber weapon, I immediately cringe with apprehension in preparation of the eventual disappointment.

The most popular misconception about firearms when talking to many women is: they will say that their friend told them it's best for them to get a .380, and they have never had any training.

The most popular misconception about firearms when talking to many men is: they will say that they prefer a .45 caliber because it has "more knock down power" than that of many of the smaller caliber ammunitions. I normally ask them, *"How many men have you knocked down (killed)?"*

Because of the mass media perception of what firearms do, and don't do, this has led many people astray.

Starting with the bullet traveling in a straight line that many movies portray, in slow motion. People forget the effects of gravity that play on everything, and that it will have the bullet start to drop in its trajectory "immediately" after leaving the barrel of whatever weapon is firing it. Hence the barrel of most weapons is canted upwards slightly to compensate for this effect.

I always say, the novice individual handling firearms will almost **NEVER** have **THREE** things.

223

**First, they never seem to have spare magazines of ammunition.**
Because you almost never see your favorite Hollywood action movie star re-load his/her ammunition in the action scene. He or she will have a semi-automatic weapon that fires one round or bullet, for each one time their trigger is pulled (you must release or re-set the trigger again to fire another round of ammunition). But on television and in movies they just hold the trigger to the rear, or they keep pulling the trigger and never re-load the weapon, causing military veterans to cringe at the movie or television show because of that one grossly inaccurate scene. The hero shoots 50 people with one handgun that only holds 12, or 15 rounds. In turn, many people don't carry spare magazines when they do carry a weapon (legally or illegally).

**Second, they never have a decent handgun holster.**
It's like a great stereo system, that has cheap crappy speakers. It's like a great automobile, with cheap tires. It's like a great gourmet meal, served on cheap paper plates. Except the consequences are not just bad sounding music, poor automobile road handling or the overall dining experience. The consequences of having a cheap carry holster (or none at all) could be deadly, and normally result in self-inflicted wounds. If you tuck a loaded weapon (without a holster) in the waist band of your pants, you risk shooting yourself in the buttocks, the hips or in the genitals depending on where you carry it. I once heard a story of a famous NFL football player who was in a crowded night club in NYC with a loaded handgun tucked into the waistband of his pants, you know like they do in the movies. Story goes that he had on baggy jeans, you know like they do on television. The story I heard was that he was walking down some stairs inside a club and both of his hands were holding something; a bottle of bubbly champagne, a beautiful woman, I don't know I wasn't there (I am just telling you what the word on the street was to illustrate my point). Anyway, the story goes that as he was walking down the stairs, the gun stars to slide down the inside of his pants leg. I heard he let go of whatever was in one of his hands in an attempt to grab the weapon bulge from the outside of his pants, in an attempt to catch the weapon. Well, when he grabbed it, he grabbed the trigger, of his loaded weapon, and since it was already sliding down his leg it didn't take much pressure or trigger pull to discharge his own weapon, accidently shooting himself, in the leg. Although he had an expired concealed carry license from Florida, he didn't have a New York license. So, he turned himself into the police to face charges of criminal possession of a handgun. He was arrested, indicted and convicted of two counts of criminal possession of a

weapon in the second degree, and a single count of reckless endangerment in the second degree (all felonies).

He was imprisoned for nearly two years (20 months), for accidently shooting - himself.

If you carry a loaded weapon in your purse, handbag or backpack <u>without</u> a sturdy holster, you too can cause the weapon to get caught on something else inside of the bag, and cause a negligent or accidental discharge. Again, you could wind up hurting yourself, or more likely shooting some innocent person.

**Third and finally, the novice almost never has a tight shot group.**
Since they almost never train, or many have never received any formal instruction on how to shoot, they don't have the fundamentals or basic rules of firearms handling down to muscle memory.

I have a simple training drill that I'll share with you right now, just because you purchased this book. Go test yourself and see where your level of proficiency is at.

Let's start with the back story.

*How close do you think the distance will be for the average gun fight?*

Close proximity means the distance you will be from an attacker or perpetrator of a crime against you; like an armed robbery, carjacking or a home invasion. The FBI statistics show that the average distance of a lethal encounter or gun fight is around ten (10) feet. Several reputable departments, companies and agencies states that distance is more like twenty (20) feet. But just for the sake of this chapter: I'll do one even better.

I'll give you a scenario that is more realistic and something the majority of you readers can relate too.

*What do you think the distance is across the street, in the average residential neighborhood?*

If you use an average of 10 feet as the distance for the width of the average traffic lane, and a two-way street would be 20 feet in width, and parking on either side would be 40 feet total, give or take 4 feet (10%). That would make that distance thirty-six (36) feet.

Well a survey conducted by the *Institute of Urban and Regional Planning on Residential Street Standards & Neighborhood Traffic Control* states that the average distance in a typical subdivision is thirty-six (36) feet across.

Now imagine a scenario where you have to use self-defense measures, with lethal results.

In other words, if someone was shooting at you, trying to kill you from across the street, in the average neighborhood, that distance would be about 36 feet.

So, take a standard man size target, and send it down range anywhere between 30 and 40 feet in distance, since many gun ranges are in ten-foot increments. I prefer to use the "Izzy" target that is preferred by the U.S. Department of State (DoS) because it doesn't brainwash me into shooting a "dark" or "black" silhouette on a white background. Although the "Izzy" target was based upon a real-life DoS Firearms Instructor named Izzy (from like 20 years ago), I found it to be the most neutral and realistic based upon the state of the world today.

*Anyway, with no rush, but still using a little sense of urgency (in other words take your time but hurry up), engage your target at that gun range, at that distance, with ten (10) shots at your own pace.*

First thing you will learn, especially if you have a revolver, is that you have to stop and reload your weapon when you run out of ammunition. Take that loud silence and dedicate it to your memory banks. So that you will never forget, what it sounded like, when you attempted to engage a stationary target(s) at a distance of 30 to 40 feet, with 10 rounds with a revolver, when you ran out of ammunition after 6 bullets, and had to reload.

If that don't teach you about the difference between a revolver and a semi-automatic, just wait until you're at a two-way range, where people are shooting back at you.

Next, even if you have a semi-automatic *(I hope you're not using a fully automatic handgun, they do exist, like the Glock 18: but I hope a novice doesn't have one)* you will learn from this drill.

226

Now engage the target with a total of 10 rounds.

Many people fail this test before they even start, because they don't count nor keep a track of the rounds they shoot.

They get so caught up in the adrenalin, and the rush at a standard gun range, that they forget how many rounds they fired. Now image when you're standing in a court of law, attempting to defend yourself (even if you're within your rights) having to account for every round you shot.

**Every single person will get 10 out of 10 hits,
if they fired 10 rounds, guarantee!**

However, the average person will NOT get 10 out of 10 hits, on their *"intended target"*, but every bullet will hit - something.

They normally get between 3 – 6 hits on their intended target. But every now and then I get friend who is a novice, and they get 8 hits on their intended target. They feel they have accomplished something with their 80% passing score.

But I always inform them of a few scenarios.

*Would they jump from an airplane with a parachute that is guaranteed to work 80% of the time?*

*Would they want to eat some food that has an 80% guarantee chance of it not having any poison in it.*

*Or how about the big one that really gets people's attention?*

*Would you be satisfied on your job, on payday, if you only got 80% of your paycheck, that you earned.*

No!

The standard is 100%; and as in the last part, of the third stanza, of the U.S. Army's Ranger Creed "And Then Some!"

I tell people that every round they fired, hit something. Even if it didn't hit their intended target, from a distance that is equal to standing across the street in almost any major American city, or suburban neighborhood in this country. I illustrate that maybe one of their rounds that did NOT hit it's intended target, maybe it hit an innocent little kid that was just playing inside their home. Or maybe it hit a woman, just sitting on her front porch. Or any of the hundreds of other possibilities, to highlight the fact that you as a responsible firearms owner, user and/or holder, are responsible for every round that leaves that weapon.

And that's BEFORE we even get to the basic rules of firearms handling, or the fundamentals of marksmanship, or any of the other 30 plus years of firearms tactics, techniques & procedures I have amassed (close/mid/long range engagements, trigger discipline, trigger slack and trigger reset, magazine change drills, what to look and listen for if you witness a shooting, active shooter scenarios, and how not to become a victim of friendly fire "after" you have successfully defended yourself).

The National Rifle Association (NRA), has three basic rules for firearms safety.

1.  **Always keep the gun pointed in a safe direction.**
2.  **Always keep your finger off the trigger until ready to shoot.**
3.  **Always keep the gun unloaded until ready to use.**

There are many variations of the basic gun safety rules, but I have often used the ones attributed to Jeff Cooper the influential modern firearms figure.

- **All Guns are always loaded.**
- **Never let the muzzle cover anything you are not willing to destroy.**
- **Keep your finger off the trigger until your sights are on the target.**
- **Be sure of your target and what is beyond it.**

After I get the reality check across to the individual, and reinforce the responsibility they have I will go over drills and training exercises I have used within the various units and companies I have deployed with.

I highly encourage all of you readers to get with a local highly qualified firearms instructor, preferably one with NRA endorsements and learn. Even if you don't like firearms, or are "afraid" of guns. What happens when you are attacked by someone with a gun, when the "fight or flight" mode kicks in, if you have no choice you will probably fight for your life.

Now just imagine if you somehow wind up holding the firearm because you wrestled the gun away from the person that was intent on killing you.

But because you were "afraid or uncomfortable" with firearms and guns in the past, you never learned the basics, not even how to properly operate or employ a basic handgun.

You don't even know where the safety is located and if it's on or not.

There are an estimated 300 million firearms in the United States, and somebody somewhere is shooting.

# 17

CHAPTER SEVENTEEN
# NO PLACE LIKE HOME

*One of the first things a good leader must know is his or her weakness. Whatever you wish to accomplish in life, you must not only know your strengths, but you must also know what your vulnerabilities and your weaknesses are. Then when you identify them, many successful people turn their weakness into their greatest strengths.*

*But first, one of the hardest things you must learn is;
you don't know - what you don't know.*

*During our training in either the Special Forces Assessment & Selection (SFAS) course or the Special Forces Qualification Course (SFQC), we were faced with an obstacle that identified one of those weaknesses for me. As I stated before, my best friend and I both attended both of those two schools together. He and I faced an obstacle during training one day that required us to be with several other students in a very dark and confined space. When I say dark, I mean complete pitch-black darkness, where you cannot see your hand held up in front of your face.*

*This scenario happened where there were several students in a controlled environment, but we didn't know it at the time. Timothy Garnes was in front of me and for whatever reason he could not move forward. The student in front of him could not move forward, and the student behind me prevented us from going backwards. So, whatever this event was, there were dozens of us in the dark trying to negotiate whatever obstacle we were dealing with. We could not stand up or lay down because there was not enough room to do so.*

*My best friend Tim Garnes, was claustrophobic. He may still be. He was trying to prevent his body from touching the walls, in an attempt to trick himself into believing that he was not in a confined space. As long as he didn't touch the walls or the top, he was ok.*

*I did not like the dark. I had my eyes closed, and when I opened them it was completely pitch-black dark, so I closed them again. I kept my eyes closed in an attempt to convince myself that it was only dark because my eyes were closed. Not because it was pitch black dark.*

*Then the screaming started.*

*Other students were dealing with whatever issues they were dealing with, but the fear and negative energy was contagious. You couldn't move forward, you couldn't move backward, you couldn't stand up, you couldn't lay down, it was pitch black and now people are screaming, WTF?!?*

*Weeks later during another training event, I would have to deal with my dislike of the darkness.*

*I would be willing to bet that many people have never been alone in the woods, by themselves at night either. I know I hadn't.*

*Born and raised in New York City, it is impossible to be alone. You may find yourself on a secluded street or dark alley, but you are not alone. Even if you wind up in an abandoned warehouse in the Hunts Point section of the South Bronx, or the old Brooklyn Navy Ship Yard, you are still not alone. Somebody is around somewhere.*

*You are not in the dark in a major metropolitan city. There is plenty of ambient light from the street lights, advertising signs, passing cars or reflections off some surface of some type of light. In JUL 1977, smack dab in the middle of a NYC summer there was a complete blackout of power all over the city. I remember the violence, the looting, the fires all over the Bronx. I don't know the extent of it, but I do know this. We lived across the street from the Bronx Zoo, which is the largest metropolitan zoo of its kind in the United States, somehow some way – some – of the animals got free. I remember people*

232

chasing the peacock birds running loose down Bryant Avenue and 181st Street, trying to get the pretty peacock feathers from them.

Anyway, my point is that you are probably never alone in the dark in a major metropolitan city or urban environment.

Scouting and camping in the woods as a child, well there were still other Boy Scouts around.

Most members of the military, unless they are undergoing some type of survival training; are not going to be alone in the woods. When an entire unit deploys, or goes to conduct Field Training Exercises (FTX), everyone goes. Hundreds and thousands of other military members, even if you wonder off, someone is around you somewhere.

Now drive down a dark country road at night, I'm talking when it's completely dark. You know the kind of darkness, when you have tunnel vision from the vehicles headlights because there is complete darkness on both sides of the road?

Now stop the vehicle in the middle of nowhere, and get out and walk about 10 miles.

No, not on the road.

But through the woods. To an objective that you must find. With no other persons' assistance, and did I say – it's a timed event.

No, I'm not gonna tell you how much time you have.

Maybe one hour, maybe five hours, maybe ten hours, I'm not gonna tell you and neither are the instructors. But what they will tell you is something like, "If you're still moving at 12 noon tomorrow, still looking for your objective, you obviously have failed. So just stop what you're doing and move to the nearest road intersection and wait for us to come pick you up" (and take you to the shack of shame).

I'm very good at land navigation, terrain association, dead reckoning and I just have a natural internal sort of "sixth sense" when it comes to finding home, or where I'm supposed to be.

233

*In the early 1990's the Special Forces Qualification Course was divided up into three phases. I understand that it has completely evolved in numerical phases now, but essentially the training goal is the same. Create and produce the best warriors this country has, to fight and win this countries wars, period.*

*Back then Phase 1 was a lot of Individual Training and Small Unit Tactics. Phase 2 was the Individual MOS Training. Phase 3 was very long and a culmination of the previous two training phases.*

*Many people who failed or did not complete the entire training course would pass Phase 1, but fail the MOS Phase 2 portion. I would bet that out of 50 soldiers who were training to become 18D Special Forces Medics who went down to Phase 2 at Fort Sam Houston, Texas only 10 or 15 of them would make it back and graduate from Phase 2 to even "start" the Phase 3 portion.*

*So, the U.S. Army re-arranged the 3 phases of training back then. A soldier would attend the MOS portion first, Phase 2, and then attend & complete Phases 1 and 3 sequentially. At that time Phase 1 and 3 were unofficially called Phase Thirteen (13).*

*So, having already completed and graduated the 18B Special Forces Weapons Sergeant MOS porting of training (Phase 2), I began along with my peers' Phase 1 & 3, or Phase 13 as we use to call it.*

*During Phase 1 when we conducted Land Navigation Training, I would get dropped off at a starting point and do my work. Then I would proceed into the woods about 50 meters, or less, and watch the instructor. I would not move from that location. I guess hindsight looking back I was paralyzed by fear of the dark. I would not move from the vicinity of the starting point, and I would watch the instructor for hours.*

*Sometimes I would see another student approach that objective (point), who had been previously dropped off hours earlier at another site. I would watch him receive new directives from that cadre instructor, and then proceed to his presumably third or fourth objective.*

*I still would not move from my first.*

234

*Then when sunlight first cracks the skyline, it's not sunrise yet, but it's no longer completely dark – only then would I would start.*

*The military calls that time: Before Morning Nautical Twilight (BMNT).*

*I would run to my first objective. With full field uniform, weapon and heavy ruck sack I would run through the woods as fast as I possibly could.*

*Whenever I got to my first objective there would already be students there, possibly done with all of their objectives. They don't tell you how many you must find or how far you must travel, and neither will I. But I never got to my first objective without some students already finishing all of theirs, because they had like a four, five or six-hour head start in the darkness ahead of me.*

*Because I didn't move at night, because of my fear of the darkness back then. That first instructor would always look at me puzzled, but his nonverbal communication to me would be saying, "Where the hell have you been? This can't be your first point! Why don't you just stop and quit, VW right now (so, I can take you to the shack of shame)!"*

*But because I was so good at land navigation, I would plot the next objective they gave me and run through the woods to that one! Then again, like a freaking Forrest Gump character whenever the other SFQC students saw me, I was running!*

*No matter how good I was, I wasn't that good.*

*I failed the land navigation portion.*

*All the students who passed Phase 1 left Camp Mackall for like two or three days, enroute to the main post on Fort Bragg. I remained behind with the other students who had received NO-GO's in any of the events, in order to retake those events again. If we failed any re-test, we were going to be sent home, back to our parent units or to the needs of the U.S. Army, on the very same trucks our classmates would be returning from their "two or three-day liberty pass" on.*

*When I took the re-test for the land navigation it was nothing like the initial test: it was worse.*

*Because now I knew that not only would I have to move at night, not only would I be alone, but there wasn't even a chance of me seeing another student because the majority of them were back at Fort Bragg on liberty pass, while I was in these woods again.*

*When they took me to my first point it was dark, completely freaking dark.*

*Even the illumination from the moon was gone.*

*You know how bright it is in the sky at night when it's a full moon? I mean it's still dark on the ground, but there is some illumination from above?*

*Well, this must have been a new moon, which is the opposite of a full moon because there was zero illumination in the sky.*

*When I plotted my first objective from my starting point it must have been 15 kilometers straight south to the bottom of the map sheet. That's like 10 miles away, and when I get there I have plotted this objective is supposed to be on the other side of a freaking swamp.*

*I do my normal routine and go about 50 meters into the woods. Then I stop and turn around and face the instructor. Then I hear a voice. The voice was female, and I later presume it to be one of my ancestors. It sounded like she was inside my head and the voice said, "turn around".*

*I turn around and face the darkness, and I hear her say, "run".*

*She didn't yell, it wasn't loud, it was just clear as day, she said, "run".*

*So, I ran the entire 10 miles straight south. I do not remember even taking my compass out to plot an azimuth. I just remember running, straight through the woods at night, in complete darkness, tree branches were tearing my face up. I'd run into a tree go around the left side, next time I ran into a tree, go around the right side. I get tired, slow down and jog, but keep moving, keep running. When I get to the swap at the bottom of the map, I remember the water getting up to my arm pits at times, but the voice said, "keep going."*

*Now I have visions of other people following me, and I know I'm not going crazy. But these visions are of black people, I can't make out their faces and I now think we are running away from slave-catchers.*

236

*Dogs are barking now. I can't tell if they are in my head, or are they really barking in the distance. But I keep running. I'm using my running pace count and I assume I'm in the vicinity of where I'm supposed to be, and guess what happened.*

*I freaking ran right into the instructor at the point.*

*How?*

*I don't know, but I'm really having an out of body experience and it feels good. Most people call it the zone, some runners high, whatever. You know the feeling when you swing a baseball bat and hear the perfect sound, Crack! You know it's a homerun, before it even gets towards the outfield.*

*You know the feeling you get when you shoot a basketball and you know it's not only going in the basket, but it's not going to even touch the rim, all net!*

*I was in the zone, dialed in and switched on.*

*When he gave me my next objective, after plotting it I started running again. Then the next objective, I ran. Then the next, I ran. Every decision seemed like it was coming from inside my head, the voice never said go left or right: it always said go 'dis away or 'dat away.*

*When that exam was over it looked like I had drawn a line from the top of the map sheet, to the bottom left corner, back up to the top right side, straight across the map to the other side, then back down to the lower right side, then back up to the top of the top map sheet.*

*A good guess would be maybe 50 kilometers for that one day. Probably a whole lot more, or a whole lot less. I'm not saying. But it did look like I drew a giant star on a standard 1:50,000 military scale map. Maybe that's why the unofficial name of the SFQC's Land Navigation Course is called, the Star Exam.*

*Or maybe because your navigating all day and all night and you will have to navigate by the stars in the sky, depending upon when you attend the training.*

*Or maybe it has to do with after walking (or running) for so long until your feet start bleeding you will start seeing stars as you get dizzy before you pass out from exhaustion.*

*Or maybe it has nothing to do with any of that at all.*

*I'm just glad that I overcame a weakness and now it's one of my strongest leadership points. I can teach land navigation, especially at night. I have physically held masonic classes for my lodge outside at night, under a real starry canopy.*

*And most importantly, I have learned to listen to that female voice of my ancestor, whoever she is because that would not be the last time she spoke to me and guided me safely home.*

***

I was very good at Land Navigation. Part of it may have come from my many times camping & scouting with the Boy Scouts of America as a youth; at the Scout Camp in Alpine, New Jersey or upstate New York at Ten Mile River Scout Camps (Aquehonga, Kunatah, and Keowa) in Narrowsburg, NY. I still remember the fight song, almost 50 years later;

> *Our camp Keowa hats off to thee,*
> *To our colors true we will always be,*
> *Firm and strong united are we,*
> *Rah, Rah, Rah — Shish Boom Bah,*
> *The best darn camp in TMR,*
> *Onward to victory!*
>
> *And then its - boom shicka boom, hey!*
> *Boom shicka boom, hey!*
> *Boom shicka boom, hey!*
> *Boom, Boom*
>
> *Rah-Ooh-Rah*
> *Rah-Ooh-Rah*
> *Keowa, Keowa, Yeah - Keowa!*

Or part of my land navigation skills may have come from living in New York City which is laid out in a grid format with Boulevards and Avenues running in the North & South direction, and the Streets running in the East to West direction in sequential numerical order.

I wasn't much better than many other NCO's because it (land navigation) was a common skill set for all soldiers to perform. However, I just developed a teaching style and skill ability that allowed me to do this one thing, much better than almost anyone else I knew.

When I was an 18th Airborne Corps NCO Academy instructor, I've never had a student fail the Land Navigation exam during my tenure there at the XVIII Airborne Corps & Fort Bragg Noncommissioned Officers Academy.

Never.

I taught 11B Basic Noncommissioned Officers Course (BNCOC) as a Small Group Leader (SGL) at Fort Bragg, North Carolina. This was way back when 11B Infantry BNCOC was taught at major U.S. Army installations around the world, it is now consolidated and only taught at the U.S. Army Infantry Center and School at Fort Benning, Georgia. I also taught the Primary Leadership Development Course (PLDC) as a SGL and as a Senior Small Group Leader (SSGL).

---

**The U.S. Army's Primary Leadership Development Course (PLDC) eventually became known as the Warrior Leaders Course (WLC).**

**The WLC is now known as the Basic Leader Course (BLC).**

---

Since the PLDC course was designed to teach Specialist and Corporals in the pay grade of E-4 the basic skills required to lead small groups of soldiers, regardless of their MOS, and was a mandatory requirement of all U.S. Army soldiers before they could be promoted to the rank & pay grade of Sergeant (E-5), we saw soldiers from every facet of the U.S. Army.

## Combat Arms (CA)

Infantry, Armor, Field Artillery, Air Defense Artillery, Corps of Engineers, Army Aviation, Armored Cavalry, Light Cavalry, Air Cavalry and Special Forces (at the time SF students had to already be graduates of PLDC)

## Combat Support (CS)

Chemical Corps, Military Intelligence Corps, Military Police Corps, Signal Corps, Civil Affairs Corps and the Psychological Operations Corps

## Combat Service Support (CSS)

Acquisition Corps, Adjutant General (AG) Corps, Finance Corps, Logistical Corps, Ordnance Corps, Quartermaster Corps, Transportation Corps, Chaplain Corps, Judge Advocate General's (JAG) Corps, and the Army Medical Department (AMEDD) to include the Dental Corps, Medical Corps, Medical Services Corps, Medical Specialist Corps, Nurse Corps and the Veterinary Corps

The course was taught for 30 consecutive days and the various students (soldiers) were divided into squads of 8 soldiers each, each squad lead by a SGL.

Two squads were grouped together to form a "Teaching Squad" of 16 students (soldiers) and the two SGL's for each squad were considered teaching partners. The teaching partners (SGL's) would alternate teaching 2 days on and then 2 days off, for 30 consecutive days (including Saturdays and Sundays). Additionally, there were mandatory events and days (like field training) where all SGL's had to teach or work, so an SGL could expect to work 20-22 days out of the month.

*The same amount of days as anyone else working Monday through Friday (or 5 work days out of the 7-day week). Four weeks a month is; 20 days out of 28.*

My teaching partner was a female soldier who was a SSG *(What's up teaching partner TP!?!)* She not only taught me about working with female soldiers, but about working with soldiers from all facets of the Army to create the; "One-Team One-Fight" mentality. In turn, I taught her so much about the infantry and land navigation that many students thought she was the first female 11-Bravo in the U.S. Army *(several years later, after I retired there would be female infantry soldiers in the U.S. Army)*.

You see, before I was paired with her as my teaching partner, I was under the tutelage of another female soldier who was a SGT who was so proficient, that she eventually went to work for the White House Communications Agency in Washington, DC.

Next in my Chain of Command and NCO Support System was my Platoon Sergeant, the Senior Small Group Leader (SSGL), a SSG and a female soldier. She was a great professional soldier who at one time toured with the U.S. Army's Soldiers Show.

Next in my Chain of Command was our First Sergeant, who also was a female. She was an awesome First Sergeant who always led from the front, including Physical Training (PT). I would bet my career that she could have easily performed in the top 10% of all the Infantry Unit First Sergeants I've ever served with, and I've seen some of the best. That 1SG was so feared & respected that many other SGL's *(including me)*, that we affectionately called her, *"Xena the Warrior Princess."* Bottom line up front, she was one of the best First Sergeants I've ever had.

My Commandant at the time was a Command Sergeant Major who was a squared away soldier, and like all the other soldiers in my chain of command a woman. If you asked me, *"She should have been the first female Sergeant Major of the Army"* – because she was that good!

Together they all gave me, *"the worst NCOER Rating (NCO report card)"* that I have ever received.

> Rater (SSGL)
> Senior Rater (First Sergeant)
> Reviewer (Commandant)

Not because I was a bad NCO.

But because, I didn't know anything about the U.S. Army but: Infantry "Kill-Kill-Kill!!!", What makes the grass grown? "Blood-Blood-Blood!!!", Kick down the door and shoot 'em in the face! Every cadence I knew was profanity laced and about killing. I didn't know how to talk to soldiers, I was accustomed to yelling and screaming at Infantryman, and Infantrymen cuss. We sprinkle profanity on our sentences like people in the ghetto sprinkle salt on their food, before they even taste it. Abundantly!

Yes, there is a need, a place and a time for warriors in an Army!

But there is so much more to the military apparatus than just the tip of the spear. Everyone must work together in order to succeed.

The tip of the spear may be the pointy killing end of it, but who sharpens that point?

Who polishes and maintains the pointy end, and what's the tip made of?

Iron, steel, bronze or flint?

What about the long shaft? The tip of the spear is much more effective when it is attached to a sturdy shaft.

And what is it attached to the shaft with?

In fact, who is gonna produced more spears when they break in combat? And how are they gonna get to the battlefield?

Before the Second World War (WWII) I believe the ratio of Infantrymen to Combat Support and Combat Service Support personnel was 9:1, but in today's technological advanced military its 1:9.

*There are probably about nine CS & CSS personnel for every one Infantryman on active duty.*

So, I had to learn the hard way. If I did not learn to navigate the military system beyond the small unit level, I would have become one of those good NCO's that continued to get passed over for promotion, but people would refer to as a "Good Field Soldier". Eventually I would have been forced out of the U.S. Army before reaching retirement eligibility, whereas the U.S. Army has a "Up or Out" policy called **Retention Control Points** or RCP's.

These soldiers listed below in the following ranks/pay grades can NOT remain on active duty beyond their RCP's.

| | |
|---|---|
| 5 years | Private (PVT/E-1) |
| 5 years | Private (PV2/E-2) |
| 5 years | Private First Class (PFC/E-3) |
| 8 years | Specialist (SPC/E-4) |
| 8 years | Corporal (CPL/E-4) |
| 10 years | Specialist *promotable* (SPC/E-4P) |
| 10 years | Corporal *promotable* (CPL/E-4P) |
| 14 years | Sergeant (SGT/E-5) |
| 15 years | Sergeant *promotable* (SGT/E-5P) |

The RCP's change from time to time, but as of this date only the following soldiers, in these ranks/pay grades listed below CAN remain on active duty up to 20 years and beyond, to reach a normal military retirement at 20 years:

| | |
|---|---|
| 20 years | Staff Sergeant (SSG/E-6) |
| 24 years | Sergeant First Class (SFC/E-7) |
| 26 years | Master Sergeant (MSG/E-8) |
| 26 years | First Sergeant (1SG/E-8) |
| 30 years | Master Sergeant *promotable* (MSG/E-8P) |
| 30 years | First Sergeant *promotable* (1SG/E-8P) |
| 30 years | Sergeant Major (SGM/E-9) |
| 30 years | Command Sergeant Major (CSM/E-9) |

In the U.S. Army, once a soldier has completed all the training and requirements to be advanced to the next higher pay grade, they are considered in a *promotable* status. Thus, they carry the (P) after their rank and are given many of the duties and responsibilities of the next higher rank, *"but not the pay of the next higher pay grade."*

So, if a soldier doesn't get promoted to the next higher rank/grade before they reach their RCP they are administratively separated from active duty.

Anyway, I was so good at land navigation, that eventually each and every soldier who had previously failed to pass the Land Navigation portion of the PLDC course was assigned to my teaching squad when they returned to the XVIII Airborne Corps & Fort Bragg NCO Academy as a recycle student, or they were attached by other SGL's for that period of training.

The first thing I told my former students was that they should feel at home with me.

That I understood they belong to their parent unit, and that they were having difficulties with map reading and land navigation, but that they should relax with me as if they were home. I explained that I never lost a student (to failure in land navigation) and I didn't plan on starting with them.

A map is a geographical representation of a portion of the earth's surface, drawn to scale, as seen from above. It's kind of hard to visualize this concept when today just about every vehicle has a GPS navigation system. But there was a time, when GPS was fairly new to the regular Army. Plus, everyone must still know how to navigate without GPS, with just a compass and a map, for the time when the GPS goes out.

Most U.S. Military maps are based upon an agreed NATO standard that all NATO countries use, just like our standard NATO 5.56mm & 7.62mm ammunition. The maps all have a system of grid lines superimposed on them creating little squares. This system of lines is called the Military Grid Reference System (MGRS). So even today if a person has a high-speed digital watch capable of determining GPS coordinates; many military members will prefer to use the MGRS system verse the civilian latitude and longitude (lat/long) coordinates.

The MGRS works by taking the round earth and making it into a flat map. Then starting at the north pole, drawing a line straight down to the opposite side at the south pole somewhere. Go all the way around the earth and make 60 lines, or sixty slices of the earth.

If each slice was 6 degrees wide, six times sixty (6 x 60) would equal 360 degrees, a complete circle.

Now number those slices from left to right, starting just west of Alaska.

Most of the western coast of the United States to include Washington, Oregon and California would be in the 10th or 11th slice or Universal Transverse Mercator (UTM) Zone.

Most of the east coast to include New York, Washington DC, Fort Bragg, North Carolina and Florida would be in the 17th and 18th UTM Zone.

Most of Europe would be in the 30<sup>th</sup> through the 34<sup>th</sup> UTM Zone.

The continent of Africa starts in the 28<sup>th</sup> UTM Zone and goes all the way across through the 39<sup>th</sup> UTM Zone.

The country of Iraq is in the 38<sup>th</sup> UTM Zone, trust me I know that one by memory and so does every other soldier who has ever served in Iraq in support of Operation IRAQI FREEDOM.

Parts of Russia end in the 60<sup>th</sup> UTM Zone when it starts all over again.

Now take anyone of those 60 UTM Zones (slices) and further divide that into parts starting at the bottom all the way up to the top near the north pole. Let's start with UTM Zone 1 (or the 1<sup>st</sup> slice). So now you have a 1C, 1D, 1E, 1F, 1G, 1H, 1J all the way up to 1W and 1X within UTM Zone 1.

You repeat this process for the second UTM Zone as 2C, 2D, 2E, 2F, 2G, 2H, 2J all the way up to 2W and 2X.

Then the third slice UTM Zone, the fourth, the fifth, all the way until you get to the fifty-ninth and then the sixtieth UTM Zone.

Now the equator is somewhere around the letter N so all the letters on the northern hemisphere are above that. For example; all the 48 contiguous or connected United States (excluding Alaska & Hawaii) are in R, S, T and U of their respective UTM zones.

Southern Iraq is 38R and northern Iraq is 38S parts of western Iraq are 37R and 37S.

The letters "A & B" are reserved for the area in the northern artic region (North Pole), and the letters "Y & Z" are reserved for the southern artic region of the continent of Antarctica.

Additionally, to avoid confusion the military has determined on maps that we will not use the letter "O" as in Oscar because it could get confused with the number "0" as in Zero.

The same goes for the letter "I" as in India because it could be confused with the number "1" as in One.

Next take that any one square and further divide that into smaller squares of 100,000 meters, or 100 kilometers (km) each. For example, inside the 37R UTM zone is a smaller area we will designate as row A and column A.

So, that 100,000-meter area we be called 37R AA, and the one 100,000 meters next to it will be called 37R AB, and the one 100,000 meters next to that will be called 37R AC, and then 37R AD all the way across the entire big square of 37R.

Then you also label them going north in the 37R column as well. So, the 100,000 meters above the 37R AA grid zone will be called 37 BA, and above that the next 100,000-meter grid zone will be called 37R CA, then DA, the EA, then FA and so on, and so on.

Now that we have identified what a UTM Zone is, and how it is broken down into smaller groups, and that is broken down into 100,000-meter grid zones I'll explain how we identify a point within that zone on a map.

Use a simple mathematical 1-10 system for every 10 kilometer (km) starting from the left edge to the right, as in "read to the right."

Then do the same going up every 10,000 meters or 10 km starting at the bottom going up to the top.

Resulting in a technique of map reading called "read right, then up".

So, if you're reading a map and looking for a location at grid coordinates 37R AA 1 5.

We know that location will be on the left edge of the map because of the 1, and it will be half way up the map because of the 5.
**That location will be accurate to 10 kilometers (6.2 mile) radius.**

If you want to get a more precise location, you must use more information or more digits within the grid coordinates you are using. For example, if I sent a letter to John Doe in Dallas, Texas it is a strong possibility that the U.S. Postal Service (USPS) would have a better chance of locating him if I also gave them a street address.

So, John Doe in Dallas, Texas on Main Street is a little bit more accurate than just John Doe in Dallas, Texas.

So, we're reading a map and looking for a location at grid coordinates 37R AA 15 50. We know that location will still be on the left edge of the map because of the 15 (out of 100 going across), and it will be half way up the map because of the 50 (out of 100 going up).
**That location will be accurate to 1 kilometer (1 km or 1 click).**

Using the 4 digits is more accurate than just 2 digits.

**The location 37R AA 157 505 is accurate to within 100 meters, because of the two groups of three numerals, or the six digit coordinates..**

**If anyone uses 8 digits to describe a location "37R AA 1575 5050", that location would be accurate to within a 10-meter radius.**

8 digits is the military standard that NATO member militaries use when communicating. Imagine calling for transportation to pick you up from a location; trucks, helicopters or whatever mode of transportation you are requesting should be able to find you, if you give them an 8-digit grid coordinate.

**The requirement to any location on a map to get within 1-meter accuracy radius is a 12-digit grid coordinate.**
37R AA 15755 50505 is the one meter.

This is a copy of the After Action Report (AAR) that LTC Hal Moore wrote for his units battle at LZ X-Ray in Vietnam in 1965.

Notice he did not use the UTM Grid Zone designator for Vietnam 48 & 49 nor the P or Q band because the entire operation was inside Vietnam, within the same UTM grid zone.

> *On 10 November, the battalion moved from the base camp at An Khe, coordinates BR476476, by CV--2 to a forward airstrip and assembly area south of Pleiku, coordinates ZA198340. From there, all companies were shuttled the same day by UH-1D into a search and destroy operation in an area to the east of Plei Me, vicinity coordinates ZA2007 to ZA7606.*

However, he did use the two letter 100,000-meter grid zone identifier for whatever maps he was referring to at the time. His unit was being transported across the country of Vietnam by helicopter and operated on several different map sheets.

The Great Pyramid Complex on the Giza Plateau on the outskirts of Cairo, Egypt with the massive sculpture known as the Great Sphinx, near the Nile River Valley on the African Continent is located at military grid coordinates 36R UU 28873 26476.
**I know because I've been there.**

An event occurred on 16 SEP 2007 in the country of Iraq during Operation IRAQI FREEDOM involving security contractors in support of the United States DoS mission in the vicinity of military grid coordinates 38S MB 40080 84973,.commonly referred to as the Nisour Square incident.

I wasn't there at the time, but two months later I was.

In fact, I was on the exact same spot and called it my home for several years.

That location is directly outside the former "Green Zone" in central Baghdad, in the country of Iraq.

While in country before I was assigned to a movement team on the WPPS contract, I worked on the static security side of Security Contracting. I was responsible for direct supervision of a platoon size group of 30–40 Ugandan TCN's who were performing base defense security functions.

I know from living in the New York metropolitan area that when bullets go up, they also come back down and many times they kill innocent people. So, because of the numerous celebratory gun firing that goes off in NYC during New Year's Eve, if you don't have to go outside or be near a window of a major metropolitan city on New Year's Eve, don't.

It was rumored that a female soldier in Iraq, presumably an officer, was sitting down at a table just eating chow in one of the DFAC's and was stuck in the head by a bullet that came down from the sky thru the soft covering or tent that was over the DFAC. She supposedly she died as a result of being struck in the head from the falling random bullet. *Whether that story was true or not I don't know, but I do know what I am about to tell you is true.*

I had several Ugandan TCN's up inside several guard towers that surrounded the FOB, the base camp we worked on. We lived someplace else on another FOB that is no longer there. In addition to their regular surveillance duties and other responsibilities, they were required to report every single incident of Small Arms Fire (SAF), machine gun fire, explosions or whatever they saw or heard from their various guard towers.

CLACK-BOOM!!!

The entire FOB would shake, the ground and all the buildings, everyone on the FOB would see a large plum of white, grey or black smoke rising from somewhere else in the city.

My radio would ring from the closest Ugandan TCN guard tower, calling me to report the incident.

*Shadow, Shadow - Tower 99, OVER.*
**Tower 99 send it for Shadow, OVER.**

*Roger, Shadow Tower 99 reports – explosion 90 degrees, 2,000 meters OVER.*
**Copy Tower 99; 90 degrees 2,000 meters.**

Then I would continue with my security rounds and other responsibilities. Because this was going on all night and I had to turn in my report to my superiors when I'm relieved.

Serious incidents or incidents that effected our location were reported immediately.

A bunch of people dying 2,000 meters away was not that serious, because I was trying to prevent people from dying who were sleeping just 200 meters away. Remember this was an active war zone during operation IRAQI FREEDOM.

Twenty minutes later another explosion, followed by SAF.

CLACK-BOOM, blam blam blam blam, dedededededede-dow, deeeeeee-dow, blam, blam

*Shadow, Shadow - Tower 88, OVER.*
**Tower 88 go for Shadow, OVER.**

*Roger, Shadow Tower 88 reports – explosion 280 degrees, 1,500 meters followed by SAF, OVER.*
**Copy Tower 88, explosion 280, a click (1 kilometer) and a half followed by SAF.**

This would happen all night every night, sometimes up to 50 incidents a night.

The next morning during the intel brief I would hear all the activity reports from the previous nights and I could put two and two together. Intelligence Report says 14 people were killed by a VBIED during a large car bomb explosion last night at 01:30 hours.

*Yeah, I remember that explosion.*

Iraqi Security forces engaged insurgents at this part of town or that part of town.

*Yeah, I remember that explosion and fire fight.*

Well, I can still hear this following report I'm about to tell you in my head like it was yesterday.

Because the concrete T-walls were over 20-feet high surrounding around the FOB, so we would never hear this gunfire, but the report was always the same.

*Shadow, Shadow - Tower 33, OVER.*
**Tower 33, go for Shadow, OVER.**

*Roger, Shadow Tower 33 reports – Small Arms Fire 360 degrees, 50 meters, OVER.*
**Tower 33, say again meters, OVER.**
*Roger, Five Zero meters, over.*

**I'm thinking to myself why is he reporting a single gunshot outside the perimeter, and 50 meters is right in front of his position, WTF?!? He must mean 500 meters. Let me go up in that tower and check for myself.**

What I saw was unbelievable and I could not get my mind to believe what my eyes were seeing.

There was an Iraqi Policeman (IP) standing inside the traffic circle with an AK-47 and there was traffic entering and exiting the traffic circle in all directions. In a distance, there would be a very important vehicle approaching at a high rate of speed, that needed to navigate the traffic circle like; an Iraq ambulance (they didn't have Red Crosses on them, they had Red Crescent Moons), or an Iraqi Army (IA) or Iraqi National Guard (ING) military vehicle.

So, this Iraqi Traffic Cop would put his AK-47 on his shoulder, and fire off several rounds straight up into the air, and all cars coming into the traffic circle would understand that was the signal to stop.

*WTH?!?*

Then after the VIP, military or EMS vehicle would pass through, the IP Traffic Cop would fire off, just one single round into the air, with his AK-47 and all the traffic would resume moving again.

*WTF?!?*

I reported this and was told a simple explanation.

*Shadow, do you see any traffic signals out there?*
**No Sir.**

*Even if you did, does the electricity work in this country 24 hours a day.*
**No Sir.**

*Ok, that's the way it's done here in their country, that's the way they do it.*

I can only imagine what would happen if an American Military Convoy, or a U.S. Diplomatic Motorcade was entering the traffic circle under duress at high rate of speed.

***Imagine they had taken causalities and had wounded personnel and they were trying to get to the Medical Aid Station inside on the FOB or the Hospital inside the Green Zone?***

251

*Imagine them seeing automatic gun fire in a distance and believing they were just fired upon?*

*What would happen if they returned fire?*

*Well the IP's would probably fire on them.*

*Then the convoy or the motorcade would fire on them.*

*Then we would have a scenario where Blue Forces (US friendly) would be firing on other Blue Forces (US friendly). Or as the military calls it Blue on Green or Green on Blue (US friendly) on (HCN friendly).*

Positive ID in the fog of war is required otherwise a person could shoot his buddies.

However, it's easy to understand how it could happen. Especially when I'm looking right at this IP directing traffic by starting and stopping cars with his AK-47 by firing bullets into the air!

I talked with my Ugandan TCN's about it, and found out that one of them was actually in the tower a month or so ago, when the infamous shooting incident at Nisour Square happened on 16 SEP 2007. He stated that he had been interviewed by the federal authorities several times and was hoping to travel to the United States one day for a personal visit, not in an official capacity.

That day his comrades gave that Ugandan TCN the call sign of "F.B.I.".

But enough about grid coordinates hopefully you get the point, let's talk about reading those grid coordinates on an actual map.

Now there is a basic tool that can be used to assist and aid you when reading a map. However, that devise called a protractor must not be used as a crutch. Especially, when small units of soldiers are operating in a smaller portion of the map and traveling on foot. Every NCO should be able to read and plot information onto and from a military map using the MGRS system.

The most common size for military maps is 1:50,000 because anything smaller than that will cause you to lose important details, and anything larger than that will be too big. Example, if you zoom out of a GPS map in your car, you will not be able to see important details, like roads and intersections. If you zoom in too close you will not be able to see the surrounding areas.

Now once you have learned how to read a map, with or without a protractor, you have to navigate with it on the ground.

This is accomplished by using a standard military M-1950 Lensatic Compass.

All compass's point to an agreed upon point called the North, but there are several different types of North.

For military land navigation purposes, there is:

- **Magnetic North**
- **Grid North**
- **True North**

**Magnetic North** is the location that all compasses point towards, period. Don't believe me, go buy one. It will always magnetically point to a location we can agree is called magnetic north, and we can navigate from our orientation to is. Go in the opposite direction of the compass, you're traveling 180 degrees or directly south. If you travel with the north towards your right, you are headed 270 degrees or straight west (like from Virginia to California). If you're traveling with the arrow of the compass point towards your left, you are traveling on an azimuth of 90 degrees and your traveling to the east (like from Oregon towards Chicago).

But the magnetic north doesn't line up accurately with the grid line on a map, because the map is a flat square piece of paper, and the earth is round.

Almost everyone agrees that the earth is round. However, some people say the earth is round and flat. With a large dome above it called a firmament, like a snow globe. Some people say it is round and spherical like a ball. But either way we can all agree, that the earth is round.

**Grid North:** If you try to line up a round earth with a square flat map there will be some distortion. That distortion is accounted for by the map makers when they drew the grid lines, so all maps point to a location called "Grid North". We just must take into account the angular deviation or difference when converting from Grid to Magnetic, or from converting from Magnetic to Grid.

We teach younger soldiers another acronym that Grid stands for General and Magnetic stands for Major. So, you subtract when converting from Grid to Magnetic (like a General getting demoted to Major) and we add when we convert from Magnetic to Grid (like a Major getting promoted to General). Now this formula doesn't apply in all areas of the earth's surface, but for most map reading purposes in North America this will work.

**True North**: Now that we understand what Magnetic North is, and what Grid North is, the final north we can discuss is called True North. I used to tell all my young soldiers, that true north is where the fictional Santa Claus lives and that usually clears up any confusion.

**Next you have a pace count.**

If you can read and plot points on a map, you now can determine where you are and where you want to go.

The azimuth you receive from a compass will tell you what direction you need to travel, and the conversion to grid north on your map to magnetic north on your compass has already been explained (or from magnetic to grid depending on your task).

Now you just have to determine how far (distance) you have traveled.

Imagine you were in a large metropolitan city after a major disaster, like a hurricane, tornado or in the event of a war. Imagine there were no street signs anymore and there was no electricity.

*How would you now navigate and determine how far you have traveled, without the obvious landmarks like street signs?*

Since I'm originally from New York City which many people believe is the capital of the world, we'll use that location for this example. Besides many people say if you can make it there, you can make it anywhere, New York, NEW YORK (*in my Frank Sinatra voice*)!

So, in New York City approximately every 10 city blocks (that are *avenues*) equal 1 mile.

Most of the avenues run from north to south, straight up and down the borough of Manhattan like a grid system. Most of them are in numerical order; 1st Avenue, 2nd Avenue, 3rd Avenue, 4th Avenue, 5th Avenue, etc.

Also, in New York City approximately every 20 city blocks (that are *streets*) equal 1 mile.

Most of the streets run from east to west, left and right across the borough of Manhattan, again – just like a grid system. Most of them are also in numerical order; 125th Street, 126th Street, 127th Street, 128th Street, etc.

There are five boroughs in New York City (NYC); (1) the Bronx, (2) Manhattan, (3) Brooklyn, (4) Queens and (5) Staten Island. All the other surrounding areas make up the New York City Metropolitan area, but just those five boroughs make up the actual NYC.

Most of the other boroughs have a similar system of grid for the streets and avenues, but for simplicity I'm just using the island that is the borough of Manhattan for this example.

Now if you walked up or down an avenue and crossed city streets you would notice a pattern.

You can count your foot steps and notice it would take about 120 steps to get to the next block before you cross the street. Take another 120 steps and you will cross the next street.

If you take another 120 steps, guess what?

You will probably be crossing another street.

Since all the block are approximately the same length and width, it would be easy to navigate (your distance) in the city just by counting your foot-steps. Since you can get bored counting all the way up to 120 over and over (plus the chances of error), why not just count every time your left foot hits the ground, or your right foot.

That way you know 60 left foot paces is the same as, 120 total steps using both feet.

Now if I had a bunch of small pebbles or rocks in my pocket, I could use them to assist me in my counting.

I need to go 10 city blocks. So, start with 10 pebbles or rocks and every time you count to your 60 paces, discard a rock. When you're out of rocks, you are probably at your predetermined distance.

Now notice I did not say, throw the rocks away. Don't want somebody trying to sue me because they read in a book that *"Shadow said throw rocks!"*

Anyway, if I had 40 small pebbles or rocks in my pocket, every 60 paces I could drop one of them on the ground, leaving a trail. When I ran out of all 40 pebbles I would know that I walked approximately 40 increments of street blocks or about 2 miles.

I've seen people at the novice level write tick-marks on their arm to signify every increment. However, they start to sweat and get all discombobulated and lose track of their accurate pace count.

Every person's pace count will differ, depending upon your gait, stride length and physical composition.

Plus, if your carrying heavy packs and equipment it will take you even more steps to get from one point to another. I remember as a Light Infantryman weighting 165 pounds when I carried an over 80-pound rucksack (backpack) and another 40 pounds of weapons, equipment and ammunition. So, carrying a total of 120 pounds of weight, on my 165-pound body frame there were times when my pace count for 100 meters was over 85 paces (or 170 steps).

However, if you are running you will probably take longer strides, hops or steps and have a much shorter pace count. I used to teach my student to have a running pace count, just for emergencies.

So, simple mathematics say if you worked in downtown Manhattan on 14th Street and you lived up in Bronx, you could enjoy the 7 to 8-mile subway or bus ride to work every day.

But say there was a natural disaster, and for some reason you had to walk the 8 miles to the Bronx. Now add the fact that the street signs are not readable because its dark (or they are missing) because of whatever reason (vandalism, anarchy, lack of timely maintenance by the city) this is what could happen.

You could leave wherever you were at on 14th Street and start walking straight up 8th Avenue going north until you got to 145th Street. Then turn right and go east for 2 blocks and go across the 145th Street Bridge from Manhattan into the Bronx.

You could start by walking up 8th Avenue and count your paces.

If your pace count was 60 (for every city block), then when you would just count 120 total steps (or 60 paces) and you would be on 8th Avenue and 15th Street.

Go another 60 paces up 8th Avenue and you would cross 16th Street.

Go another 60 paces up 8th Avenue and you would cross 17th Street.

Go another 60 paces up 8th Avenue and you would start to enter the Chelsea neighborhood of lower Manhattan. If you continue this act of counting your 60 paces to continue traversing one city block, you would pass the New York Fashion Institute of Technology around 8th Avenue and 25th Street. You will continue to see it on your left on 8th Avenue all the way up to 8th Avenue and 28th Street.

Go another 60 paces and you cross 29th Street. When you go another 60 paces up 8th Avenue you would reach 30th Street and then you would see the world-famous Madison Square Garden on your right-side. You would also be at the world-famous Penn Station where all the Amtrak and other railroad trains enter into New York City at, but you would not see them from the street level, because Penn Station is underneath Madison Square Garden.

Going up 8th Avenue you would see Madison Square Garden on your right side, and the Main General Post Office (GPO) Building for New York City on your left-side. The main GPO is zip code 10001, and it was the only post office in New York City that was open to the general public 24-hours a day, 7-days a week. I know a lot about the U.S. Post Office because my dad was a letter carrier for over 32 years before he retired. But enough about the post office, let's get back to the pace count exercise *"See I told you that you could get distracted and might need to keep track of your pace by counting rocks or pebbles or something."*

Keep going up north on 8th Avenue and when you get to 40th Street the tall skyscraper on your left would be the New York Times headquarters building. This would continue into the big building on your left that goes all the way up to 41st Street until you get to 42nd Street. That's the world-famous New York City Port Authority Bus Terminal. That building is where almost all the Greyhound, Trailways and other buses arriving/departing New York City come and go from. *Just don't get caught slipping like the guy from Mississippi who gets off the bus in Stevie Wonder's song "Living for The City" (1973) when someone says to you, "Hey brother you look hip – wanna make yourself $5 bucks?"* I've spent many days there departing for Boy Scout camps in my younger days growing up. I'd travel to the local Boy Scout camping grounds with my troop to Alpine, New Jersey. Or to the main Boy Scout camp grounds upstate in Narrowsburg, New York, called Ten Mile River Scout Camps.

*"Again, off track on a tangent and you need them rocks or beads to keep focused."*

As you cross 42nd Street it will be hard to remain focused because it is known as one of the busiest streets in the world. Millions of people gather there every year to celebrate the New Year's Eve festivities. But if you stay focused and continue on this exercise up 8th Avenue you will pass 43rd Street, then 44th Street, then 45th Street. As you cross 45th Street look to the east, just one block on your right and you will see the famous toy store that has been shown in several major movie & film productions. Looking west just one block on your left, you will see the 9th Avenue area known as Hell's Kitchen.

Another city block, another 60 paces.

Now you're around 8th Avenue and 49th Street, you will see another skyscraper called One Worldwide Plaza. This is the headquarters of the CBS Network. Did I tell you that I really, really, really like the CBS network? Some of my favorite shows are running on that network, and my favorite shows of all time is called HUNTED on CBS (the UK version of Hunted is pretty good too). The first season of HUNTED on CBS has already aired, and if you missed it I suggest you put this book down and go watch it on demand now.

*Especially, the first Season - Episodes One and Two. The entire season of HUNTED on CBS is awesome! But for some reason I can't get that first episode out of my mind. I'll probably remember that episode of HUNTED on CBS for the rest of my life!*

Walk another 60 paces north on 8th Avenue and you're now at 50th Street. Look just one city block to the east on your right-side, and you will see the famous Broadway Avenue running parallel to 8th Avenue. You're also at the beginning of the famous theatre district. Shows and performances that are considered On-Broadway are physically in an area called the theatre district in New York City that is actually "on Broadway". These group of select theatres have a seating capacity of more than 500 people each and annually gross millions of dollars in revenue (probably a billion dollars).

Then there are shows that are considered Off-Broadway. They are held in theatres with seating capacity of 100-499 people and the theatre locations are normally, you guessed it, right off of Broadway (hence the name) near where you are right now.

Then you have Off-Off-Broadway productions and shows in theatres that have a seating capacity of less than 100, or they may employ union actors, but the theatre is physically located someplace else in the New York City area.

So now you see how easily you can become distracted, and how you must incorporate trick of the trade, and additional tools to assist you in maintaining your pace count, because were not done yet. In fact, where not even half-way to the Bronx. So back to the repetitions of another 60 paces and another "one" city block. Now you're at 51st Street.

Another 60 paces, and another city block – 52nd Street.

Repeat again and it's 53rd Street.

Then 60 more paces and its 54th Street.

You will continue this and even if you closed your eyes (and someone else was walking with you to guide you on your azimuth and direction), you could still maintain your pace and distance. Keep doing this until you get to 8th Avenue and 59th Street. At this location, you are entering a very important traffic circle in New York City called "Columbus Circle".

If you took an analog clock and placed it on the ground, with yourself in the center: your direction of travel in front of you, will always be at your 12 o'clock position, and behind you would always be your 6 o'clock position. To your right would be your 3 o'clock position and to your left would be your 9 o'clock position *(if someone was going to hit you from outside of your peripheral vision to your far left, and a soldier yelled at you, "On your nine" – you now know which way the threat was coming from).*

Anyway, at Columbus circle traveling up north on 8th avenue you would enter the traffic circle at the 6 o'clock position and continue around in a counter clockwise manner and exit at the 12 o'clock position (commonly referred to as in at 6 out at 12). Broadway would enter the same traffic circle from the 5'oclock position. The skyscrapers around the traffic circle include the Time Warner headquarters building, the Lincoln Center, the New York headquarters of CNN and the Trump International Hotel & Tower. But with all the additional law enforcement personnel in the area you're advised to, how do they say it in the movies? *Keep it moving, nothing to see hear, keep moving.*

Continue north on 8th avenue but be advised that the name of the street has now changed to Central Park West (the entire western boundary of Central Park). But remember we are not using the street signs to navigate so it doesn't matter anyway.

Continue up Central Park West and 61st Street, then 62nd Street, then 63rd Street.

If you research, you will find that many celebrities and entertainers who reside in New York City live on the West side of Central Park. While many of the very wealthy and affluent folks reside on the East side of Central Park. I am not a celebrity and I am not financially wealthy, so I don't know for a fact. But I was born and raised in New York City and it is either urban myth or common knowledge that many famous people live along Central Park West.

As you continue up Central Park West counting every 60 paces as you cross yet another street numerically numbered you will eventually reach the infamous Dakota Building on 72nd street, where John Lennon of the Beatles was murdered.

Another 60 paces, and another city block – 73rd Street.

Repeat again and it's 74th Street. Then 75th Street, then 76th Street. Then 77th Street.

At this location, I would suggest you stop and observe the building on your left. You are now looking at the American Museum of Natural History and the Hayden Planetarium. I have spent many field trips here as a child (as many native New Yorkers have) and I must tell you this is one of the most fascinating museums I have ever had the pleasure of visiting. The dinosaur exhibits alone are worth the price of admission. This museum is one of my three favorite museums in the entire world that I have ever visited. Right after the African-American History Museum in Washington, DC and the Ancient Egyptian Museum in Cairo, Egypt on the African continent.

But you can't stay there long because we should complete this land navigation exercise about pace count and distance.

Continue up 8th Avenue (I mean Central Park West), and cross 80th Street, then 81st, the 82nd, the 83rd and so on, and so forth. Each time counting your pace count of 120 steps of 60 paces to traverse one city block.

Eventually you will reach 96th Street. This used to be the most important stop for me growing up. You see in my youth whenever I traveled back up to the Bronx from downtown on the underground subway, I used to travel on the express number 2 train to the Tremont Avenue Station in the West Farms area of the Bronx. It didn't matter how crowded the subway train was, when it got to 96th street the demographics changed like 99% immediately. It seemed like all the Black, Brown, Hispanic, impoverished and people on the lower end of the social economic structure remained on the subway train. But the all the middle class and upper-class citizens who would appear to be of european decent would exit the subway train at that 96th Street subway stop.

No matter what.

Maybe they were transferring to the local number 1 train, that continued underground in Manhattan. Whereas the IRT number 2 subway train would continue for the next three or four stops in Harlem and then enter into the South Bronx.

I grew up on the late 60's, 70's and early 80's and the subway route was underground until it entered the Bronx at 149th Street and Grand Concourse.

It remained underground at the next stop 149th Street and 3rd Avenue (in the Bronx) and then the track would emerge from underground and become an elevated line (the El).

As it would pass every stop in the Bronx it was worse than any urban blight you could ever imagine. Jackson Avenue, Prospect Avenue, Intervale Avenue, Simpson Street, Freeman Street, 174th Street, West Farms Square (East Tremont Avenue) and then East 180th Street *(although I lived on 180th Street, the East Tremont subway station stop was actually closer to the housing development where I lived. Technically is wasn't public housings so they didn't call it the "projects", but the Government cheese truck used to drop of them big blocks of cheese, and I knew what color each denomination of the food stamp were)*. The train stops at Intervale, Simpson, Freeman and 174th Streets were gone.

I mean the stations were there but nobody lived there from my point of view.

I'm talking about destruction to the point where after the landlords who owned the tenement buildings in the South Bronx burned them up for the insurance money, and the fire department put the fires out and saved the people, the gutless building structures remained. I mean there was like one occupied building for every 5 to 10 vacant buildings. Total devastation and completely destroyed structures on every street, in every direction. In one of the most crowded cities in the United States of America there was death and destruction to the point where it looked like the photographs of Hiroshima or Nagasaki during WWII after an atomic bomb was dropped on them.

During my youth, this was the poorest and most crime ridden congressional district in all of the United States, and when the crack epidemic hit in the 1980's it got even worse.

But let me get back to the 96th Street subway station. The unofficial boundary line for Harlem actually starts at the norther boundary of Central Park, which is 110th Street. So, if you did not want to go to into Harlem (or further into the Bronx) you had better get off the subway train at 96th Street.

There was a movie and a hit song in 1972 called, *"Across 110th Street"* and in the song, it vividly describes what you would see when you entered into Harlem.

So, stay on 8th Avenue, I mean Central Park West and continue to travel up north past 96th Street. Then another 60 paces to 97th Street, then another 60 paces to 98th Street, then 99th Street, then 100th, then 101st Street, then 102nd and continue until you get to 109th Street.

You will see another traffic circle like the one at the bottom of Central Park at 59th Street. This one is a lot less prominent and has a statue of Frederick Douglass in the center of it. So, guess what they named 8th Avenue?

That's right Frederick Douglass Boulevard. It's the same Street or Avenue, but it's going through historic Harlem past the Frederick Douglass statue and its now called Frederick Douglas Boulevard.

*But where is the urban blight and the crime ridden neighborhoods, the pimps and prostitutes and the drug dealers you heard so much about?*

**Well welcome to gentrification.**

Where the property values of a particular neighbor drop so low and the services rendered to that community is so bad that the citizens just leave, or die. Then the upper-class or "gentry" folks come in and buy the property for pennies on a dollar and revitalize everything.

Add in government subsidies, grants & contracts and it looks like them poor folks didn't know what they were doing, look what we the upper-class folks did with the same community.

According to the federal census, before the year 2000 the Harlem area of New York city was over 87.6% black.

By 2010 it was down to 54.4% black.

Where there was once urban blight, there is now Starbucks and a policeman on every corner. I distinctly remember growing up in the 1970's and 80's where the City of New York was practically giving away Brownstone tenements building for just $1 dollar. That's right one dollar. Today those same structures sell for $5 and $10 million dollars in value.

Talk about gentrification!

*"I told you that you were gonna need to keep track of the distance we traveled on this journey."*

Stay on Frederick Douglas Boulevard and head north past 111th Street. Then 112th Street, then 113th Street and every 60 paces you will cross another city block in numerical order until you cross 116th Street.

Go north on Frederick Douglas Boulevard for 9 more city blocks and you're at 125th Street.

Keep going north on Frederick Douglas for 10 more city blocks and you're at 135th Street.

Keep going on Frederick Douglas for 10 more city blocks and you're finally at 145th Street (Frederick Douglas Boulevard continues up to 155th Street), since we are traveling to the Bronx – we can just make a right turn (headed east) and go over two city blocks, until we prepare to cross the 145th Street bridge and into the notorious borough called, "the Bronx", "the Boogie Down Bronx", or simply "da B.X.".

Just remember those two blocks your traveling from 8th Avenue (I mean Frederick Douglas Boulevard) to 7th Avenue, and then from 7th Avenue to Lenox Avenue where the bridge is at, will seem twice as long as a normal city block. Because as I stated earlier from city Avenue to Avenue is twice as long, as the distance from city Street to Street.

Just some of the rules I learned on the streets of New York City that I can apply to any area in the world.

Now imagine navigating in the desert, or the jungle, or the woods. There are no city landmarks or major intersections. But if you know your pace count for a specific distance, say 100 meters: you can continue counting in 100-meter increments just like you did city blocks during this exercise.

As stated in earlier chapters, I enlisted in the U.S. Army at the age of 17 with my parents' permission at Fort Hamilton, New York at the southern tip of the NYC borough of Brooklyn. That's where the Military Entrance Processing Station (MEPS) is for all military members regardless of their branch of service. I enlisted under the U.S. Army's Delayed Entry Program (DEP) in SEP 1982 and remained an "inactive" enlistee my entire Senior year of High School until

I departed for actual basic training in JUL 1983, after graduation from Theodore Roosevelt High School in the South Bronx.

Basic training was at Fort McClellan, Alabama for a few months and then I departed for Advanced Individual Training (AIT) at Fort Gordon, Georgia.

There I became an Avionic Mechanic, Military Occupation Specialty (MOS) 35K.

Upon graduation, I reported to my first duty station at Fort Hood, Texas in early 1984. Initially assigned to the 1st Cavalry Division, I was diverted to the newly re-activated 6th Cavalry Brigade (Air Combat), and reported for duty at Alpha Troop, 7th Squadron, 17th Cavalry of the 6th Cavalry Brigade in the spring of 1984. *The 1st Cavalry Division was my first unit of assignment and several years later it would be my last unit when I was attached during OIF2 before I retired.*

The next year, I volunteered for training at airborne school and hoped to join my AIT classmates at Fort Bragg, NC who were assigned to the 82nd Aviation Brigade of the 82nd Airborne Division. However, after graduating airborne school at Fort Benning, Georgia I was Permanent Change of Station (PCS) to Fort Lewis, WA.

I remember my time at the replacement/holding center for Fort Lewis, WA where they were attempting to re-assign me to an aviation unit on the main post because of the needs of the military at that base. In contradiction to those orders, I reported to the 1st Special Forces Group (Airborne) In Accordance With (IAW) my original orders sending me to Fort Lewis, WA.

While assigned to the 1st Special Forces Group (Airborne) – 1st SFG(A) I was initially assigned to the internal support company called Service Company with other mechanics, cooks, clerks and non-Special Forces qualified personnel. *This is where I harnessed the desire to eventually go attend, graduate and complete the Special Forces training pipeline later in my career.*

The first day I reported to the 1SFG(A) headquarters element called the S-1 section I met a soldier with the exact same name as me. We favored in appearance somewhat, but he was obviously a little more mature, bigger and older than I. His name was also Muhammad Bilal and he was a Sergeant/E-5. So, as I am explaining to him my situation; how the main post was trying to keep me there and reassigned me to another unit on that side of post, he smiled and said with confidence that I was staying right here in the 1st SFG(A) IAW my original orders.

During my tenure with the 1st SFG(A) I would constantly get my mail and another documents mixed up with his, especially once I got promoted and became a Sergeant too. I was SGT Bilal, Muhammad T. (for Timothy) and he was SGT Bilal, Muhammad A. (for Abdul).

During my time with the 1st SFG(A) as an Avionic Mechanic, just like almost every other MOS in the U.S. Army on active duty, there is off or down time. Usually the duty day consists of training around 05:30 or 06:30 in the morning until 17:00 hours (5pm) local time. After that and on the weekends Saturday & Sunday, soldiers are usually off-duty unless they have additional duties or training they must complete. It is during this "off duty" time that soldiers complete their civilian college courses, enjoy their hobbies, relax, socialize and/or fellowship with their family and friends. Married soldiers usually go off-base (unless they live in on-base housing) and single soldiers normally find some type of trouble to get into.

*Trouble is so easy to find that all branches of the U.S. Armed Forces currently award a "Good Conduct Medal" to any active duty enlisted member who completes three consecutive years of "honorable and faithful service". Meaning they receive the award if they don't get into trouble, but if they get some negative disciplinary infraction or nonjudicial punishment (NJP) or court martialed, the three-year time period resets to the beginning.*

Whereas Fort Lewis, Washington was my second duty station, because Fort Hood was my first, I was not a "rookie" soldier in the ways of the military.

However, I will admit that I was a rookie in this thing called life, because I was not even 21 years old yet.

I knew if I wanted to meet pretty women, laugh, dance, party, and have a good time then; I should go to the Main NCO Club on that base. There were several smaller clubs and pubs on base (almost every base) back in those days. I distinctly remember that the soldier who was the manager of the club on base was actually a former U.S. Army MOS.

266

Remember this was the early 1980's and soldiers could still have a beer for lunch, illegal drug use was still rampant in the military and there were female strippers dancing in the clubs "on-base" during those days.

During basic at Fort McClellan, Alabama and AIT at Fort Gordon, Georgia soldiers didn't have much of a choice in whatever they wanted to do, or not do. This even included chow, you got what they gave you, ate it in a hurry and tasted it later when you burped it back up. Many soldiers would consider it the "jackpot" if they got to eat chow in the mess hall (before it was called a dining facility or DFAC) with me in their vicinity. Either one or two soldiers before me or after me. I was still that "Little Timmy" who did not eat anything that didn't please my desire.

Plain food was all that I wanted, nothing else.

Scrambled eggs too runny, I didn't want it. Bacon, sausage or ham, I didn't want it. The U.S. Army had this thing called Cream of Wheat they would serve you as they poured it over a biscuit. Soldiers called it, *"SOS or Shit on a Shingle"* I didn't want it. So, sticking to the hash brown or grits, the other soldiers would just devour whatever else was on my plate, as I looked at them in disgust like, *"how could y'all eat that?!?"*

This translated over to illegal drug use. Without exaggerating I would say well over 50% of the enlisted soldiers used illegal drugs, prescription drugs or some other illegal substance back in the early 1980's. Urinalysis exams were random, but someone always knew when they were going to be performed. The unit would designate everyone whose last number of their Social Security Number (SSN) was a 6 to take the exam, the next day it would be everyone whose first number of their last four digits of their SSN was a 2, or whatever the system was.

Anyway, the older Specialist would say, "Oh look at him or him, he's gonna get popped and caught because his piss is so hot that it will burn a hole in that cup". Meaning they thought a particular soldier was going to have a positive test for marijuana, or something else.

Of all the illegal drug use that I saw in the U.S. Army back in those days I think marijuana use was about 75% of it. Anyway, they said the same to me (that I was gonna get popped) and I replied, *"That I have never used an illegal drug in my life, in fact I have never even smoked a cigarette."*

267

*That was a true statement then, and it is still true to this day.*

Well, when I said that you would have thought I had just said that I'm an alien and I come from another planet.

I proceeded to complete my urinalysis exam and weeks later, several other soldiers tested positive and were counseled for drug use, admitted to the military substance abuse treatment program, or Chaptered out of the military with an, Other-Than-Honorable Discharge.

I had a very scary noncommissioned officer (NCO) at Fort Hood in the early 1980's, that was in my NCO support channel, which mirrors a soldier's chain of command. You will never believe what he had me do; I was told to provide some of my "clean" urine for other soldiers, so they could pass the urinalysis test also. You would be amazed at what uninformed and impressionable young privates would do.

I was one of them.

Anyway, by the time I was PCS'ed to Fort Lewis, WA I was no longer a fresh private, I had progressed and advanced to my very own "sham" shield.

I enlisted as a Private (E-1) and was promoted through the ranks of Private (E-2) and Private First Class (E-3). At Fort Hood, TX I had learned the system, with its many rules and regulations of the U.S. Army and knew that everything had to be done by the book. They proverbial original "Blue Book" that Barron Von Stuben taught the original Continental Soldiers from in the Revolutionary War.

If the regulations said do something, even if it appeared wrong soldiers did it. If the regulations prevented something, even if it was the right thing to do, again soldiers would not do it because it was against "regs".

So, I attended a Basic Leadership School at Fort Hood, Texas before I left as a PFC and was promoted to Specialist 4th class (E-4).

Soldiers wearing the newly issued Battle Dress Uniform (BDU) at the time are instinctively taught to look at another soldiers' rank to determine hierarchy and other military customs and courtesies.

Immediately after that, since the rank of a soldier (both officer & enlisted) is sewed into the collar, their eye's drop down to the soldiers left breast pocket to see what the additional skillset identification badges and awards are.

Then immediately to the left shoulder to see if he (and now she) is wearing a Ranger Tab, or some other additional skill identifier, then look at the right shoulder to see if they are wearing a combat patch. The right shoulder sleeve insignia or a particular unit patch, is worn by soldiers who have served overseas in combat with that unit.

Then finally, look at a person overall physically physique to determine the perceived level of physical fitness, and then finally at their face; "Oh hey soldiers, I didn't know that was you".

But it all starts with the rank.

Rank insignia on dress uniforms are bright yellow chevrons and rockers for enlisted soldiers, and silver or gold bars, cluster, eagles and stars for "commissioned" officers. But in a subdued BDU or duty uniform, the silver is black and the gold is a brown color.

For enlisted soldiers the bright yellow of the stripes, rockers or specialist shields is all drawn and sewn in black.

One of the tricks I was taught in leadership school is the date of your rank. When you see a Senior NCO, you have no idea how long ago he or she had been promoted to that rank, unless you judge them by the way they act. You can tell new power in almost any profession, just like you can tell someone who has acquired *"new money"* because they lack the confidence and professional acumen of those with *"old money"*.

So, I was taught that whenever I got promoted to a new rank, do not sew on brand new and defined subdued rank insignia. To go find someone who was recently promoted up out of the rank you were just promoted into, and get all of their old rank insignia, many times they will gladly give it all away to you.

So, as a PFC when I got promoted to Specialist (E-4) I just found someone who was recently promoted to the rank of Sergeant (E-5), normally a young buck affectionally called a buck-sergeant and asked him for his old Specialist rank insignia patches.

269

So, as a newly promoted Specialist (E-4) I wore the worn and old insignia of an old and season Specialist (E-4) and that's how I arrived at my next duty station at Fort Lewis, WA. Shortly after arrival and assignment to the Aviation Detachment of the Service Company I was approached by my senior leadership to see if I was ready to go appear before the promotion board for Noncommissioned Officers. I successfully appeared before the board and was promoted to the rank of sergeant.

However, this was at that particular unit level, and not the entire U.S. Army level.

So, my pay grade was still Enlisted 4 or (E-4).

Yes, you read that correctly I was a Sergeant (E-4) and that's what appeared on my military ID card SGT/E-4.

Soldiers in that rank capacity are considered "Acting Jacks" although they wear that rank of a Sergeant, because they were promoted to it – it is not permanent. Normally you would have to get promoted in pay grade, in addition to promotion in rank, before you PCS'ed to another unit. If that did not happen, many times an Acting Sergeant who was still in the pay grade of an E-4, would be changed to the rank of Corporal (E-4) before he PCS'ed to another unit or to another base.

*I do NOT know if the correct administrative term would be promoted (Specialist to Corporal), or demoted (Sergeant to Corporal), or elevated (Sergeant to Specialist to Corporal), or transferred. You would have to talk to a seasoned administrative military clerk.*

As you can see I was not new to the ways of the military, but I was definitely new to the ways of life. What do you really know about life at 18 and 19 years old?

I couldn't wait to take my new ID card and get inside the base's NCO Club system. The main NCO club near I-5, is where I would prefer to party at, but I was closer on North Fort Lewis to a military club called the *"Tre Club"*. It had two levels, the main dance floor and bars downstairs, with an open second floor where you could see down into the main floor while walking around the perimeter of the second floor full of tables and chairs for socializing.

Separate from the main post of Fort Lewis, north post or North Fort Lewis housed the *1ˢᵗ Special Forces Group (Airborne)*, the *I Corps & Fort Lewis NCO Academy*, the *Ranger Indoctrination Program (RIP)* for the *2ⁿᵈ Ranger Battalion* and the military *Community Correctional Facility (CCF)*.

All the units there were housed in old "World War II" era barracks.

The 1ˢᵗ SFG(A) I was in, did NOT have dividers between the stalls in the latrine (or bathroom). In fact, there were no stalls at all, just rows of commodes. So, camaraderie and friendship was at an entirely nother level back then, when you just asked the man sitting just six inches away from you; to please hand you some toilet paper.

Showers were communal and the plywood walls between individual barracks rooms was psychological, because you could hear every sound coming from the next room, and I mean every sound.

So, North Fort Lewis had a bad reputation that you just did not go there unless you were a tough individual during duty hours, and after duty hours it was viewed as a definite invitation for trouble.

It was there at the in 1986 that I met a very beautiful woman.

Shortly after we started dating she told me she was pregnant, and I was going to be a father. I was a very young impressionable soldier, and we continued the relationship of a very young G.I. with an older pregnant girlfriend. We had some really good times and a few bad times, but I can honestly look back on those days and say, I was transitioning from a young boy to a grown man.

*I had enlisted at the age of 17, and completed my first four-year enlistment. I was an honorably discharged military veteran before the age of 21.*

I was given doubts about the paternity of our child to be, mainly from two people.

The first was her closest friend at the time, who told me exactly these words, *"Tim you are not the father, Mike is"*. But at that time, I didn't believe her, you see I thought that she just wanted me to distance myself from her best friend, so they could spend more time together.

271

I cannot remember the woman's name, but she was a very attractive chocolate completion woman with a very shapely physique.

The second person that told me I was not the future child's father was one my girlfriends relatives. She said, *"Tim you know you're not the baby's father right."* Or words to that effect.

When I confronted my girlfriend about that, she told me that her relative and her entire family wanted her to be with another guy.

That she was entitled to some type of inheritance from her father who had passed away, and they (her family) thought I just wanted her money. As our creator is our witness, I truly loved that woman (at that time) and money was the furthest thing from my mind.

Our relationship went back and forth until FEB 1987.

That was the time when she went into labor and I was told that she was at a particular hospital in Seattle. I did not own a car back then, like most New Yorkers who grow up in the city we just don't own automobiles, because mass transportation is so prevalent. I didn't know at the time, but both at Fort Hood, Texas and at Fort Lewis, Washington my not owning a car actually meant that I had a larger amount of disposable income than many other soldiers. I didn't have the obligation of a car note, insurance, taxes, registration, gas, oil changes, tires and other maintenance related issues.

So, I had a friend at the time, I think his name was Foster, who was also stationed down at Fort Lewis in the 1st SFG (A) with me. He drove me up to Seattle to see my girlfriend and my newborn child.

Upon our arrival at the hospital, I was NOT allowed immediately to proceed upstairs to the delivery or labor room. After waiting for what seemed like hours, we could finally go upstairs and visit. I immediately asked my girlfriend at the time what was that long delay about and she said, *"She didn't want any drama between me and her family, so I had to wait until they left"*, or words to that effect.

That was the moment that I finally got to hold the baby, and was told that she was a little girl.

She told me the baby girls name, and I asked her where did she get that name from?

If I had anything to do with naming her, she would have carried a variation of either my paternal or maternal grandmothers' names. But the name my girlfriend told me at the time sounded beautiful and I agreed that it did. However, I thought that it sounded asexual because, I knew men and women who had the same name; but who am I to complain because my maternal grandmothers name is Richardeen and my paternal grandad used to call her Richard.

Anyway, for the next four or five months I would commute from the military base down on Fort Lewis up to Seattle on I-5 just about every day.

We lived in downtown Seattle, in Federal Way, and in Renton if I'm not mistaken. I would not be honest if I said that everything was her fault, because I wasn't the best boyfriend at the time, and we constantly argued and fought.

I do not mean physically fight, but there were tension and arguments about almost everything, and I can honestly say that the bad days were starting to outnumber the good ones.

One day that I wish I could erase from my memory is when I came home early from the military base down at Fort Lewis. I noticed a white military sedan *(the kind the military recruiters use)* with a military duty uniform on a hangar in the rear window. I said to myself, *"Hey there is another Soldier or Marine living in the neighborhood"*. I approached the front door to the house we were renting and stuck my key inside to open it.

As it opened partially, she slammed the door back shut from the inside!

I swear I was so young and gullible back then, because I thought that she must have been preparing to surprise me. So, then I remember thinking what I just saw during that brief glimpse when the door was open.

*"Did I just see another man running towards the back of the house?"*

*WTF?!?*

273

I remember her running outside the front with the baby and the man running out the back. I ran after the man with half effort, because my initial desire was to run after my girlfriend. Yelling, screaming, and crying what the hell has just happened?!?

*"Give me my daughter, I'm outta here and you can go to hell!"* I'm quite sure that I used much more profane words than that, but there is no need to disrespect anyone through words retelling a story from over 30 years ago, the truth hurts bad enough.

*"She's not yours anyway"*, are the last words I remember her telling me.

In a trance, I remember driving back down to Fort Lewis from Seattle, and a few months later I was supposed to complete my initial four-year active duty commitment (JUL 1983 – JUL 1987).

The military had a program back then, that if you were going to Expiration Term of Service (ETS) anyway, you could opt out 60 days early.

Because of that news from her, I opted out and ETS'ed from active duty on the early out program, two months early than I was supposed to, in MAY 1987.

I remember driving across country from the Seattle area to New York City in my burgundy Ford Topaz, with the black leather bra on the front of the headlights, to camouflage the front-end damage I had sustained. I remember listening to Jessie Johnson's; *"Can You Help Me"*, *"I Want To Be Your Man"*, Ready For The World's; *"Oh Sheila"*, *"Baby (Let Me Love You)"*, *"Long Time Coming"*, *"Do You Get Enough"*, and *"Mary Goes 'Round"* on the car stereo cassette player over and over and over for days!

All soldiers back then had an initial commitment of six years.

So, although I elected to serve four years on active duty, I still had another two years to serve in an "Inactive Duty Status" called the Individual Ready Reserves (IRR).

My plan was simple, go back home to New York City and enroll in college at Saint John's University in Queens, majoring in Political Science. While in the ROTC program, I planned on going back into the U.S. Army as a "Commissioned Officer", instead of being in the IRR.

Simultaneously I was in the New York National Guard/U.S. Army Reserve's (NY-NGAR) 101st Long Range Surveillance Detachment (LRSD) out on Staten Island, New York.

The G.I. Bill could sustain me, and I would eat "Ramen Noodles" if I had too as I worked my way through college. I've slept in fighting positions (called foxholes) in the dirt, I could certainly sleep on a relative's couch until I graduated college.

Although I was studying in school and working a part time job, I still could not get the thought of what was happening to "my daughter" out of my mind. I know my ex-girlfriend back in Seattle just had to be lying to me, like everyone else.

*"That really was my daughter,"* I told myself, *"she had to be!"*

Her momma just didn't want me in her life, I thought.

So, after communication with her on the phone for weeks, and months you know what happened. You already know how this story goes, but I'll continue to tell it to you anyway.

The baby got sick and had to go to the doctor or something like that, but she wasn't listed as my military dependent specifically, and since her mother and I weren't married she wasn't listed into the military DEERS system automatically at birth. *Heck, I wasn't even in the delivery room when she was born, so my name ain't even on her birth certificate.*

My parents didn't raise me like this, I have to do right by her, have to do right by my daughter so guess what? I told her to come to New York and we'll work it out, even get married and somehow live happily ever after.

She arrived with our daughter and I couldn't have been any happier in life if I tried to be.

By JUN 1988 we had taken a trip upstate to Niagara Falls, New York and gotten married. Although, we were married, she stayed at home "with my mother" while I went to school and work every day.

*That didn't work out.*

275

I would come home from college or work, and both my mother and my wife were not speaking to each other.

The tension in the house was unbearable and I could only hope and pray that it wasn't physical altercations between the both of them when I wasn't there.

What man on earth wants to have to make this choice?

In fact, this wasn't no choice at all.

*Choose between your wife & daughter, or your own mother.*

*Damn!*

Part of the origin of the friction between my wife and my mother was monetary.

I didn't have a lot of money, if any at all. I enlisted in the U.S. military because I wanted too, not for the money. So, I used to send the majority of whatever money I did receive back home to my mother in the form of a military allotment, from my monthly paycheck, to help raise my younger brother.

My parents had recently gotten a divorced and my father was a different person at the time. The street life of New York City in the late 1980's was the closest thing to hell on earth that I could describe. I could write a whole entire book just about that, and maybe I will one day. But basically, my time, resources and money could not be divided between two people who physically could not co-exist.

So, my mom's put us out on the street.

She knew things I did not, and had a mothers' intuition. I could not understand it at the time, but I do now. Tough love is what she showed me, and I love her for it now more than ever. But at the time I was floored.

*Get your stuff and get out: now!*

About 10 p.m. one night, moms said, *"Get y'all shit and get out of my house."*

*"Mom, it's 10 p.m. at night, are you serious?!?"*

We packed up our belongings and I remember standing on the curb of 180th Street and Bryant Avenue wondering where are we all gonna go, what am "I" gonna do?

*Wife, daughter and all these bags, WTF?!?*

At the time, I went to the only place I knew for refuge, the only place I felt unconditional love existed on this planet; my Paternal Grandma Velma's house.

My maternal grandmother **Richardeen** had been murdered 15-years earlier in the South Bronx when I was about 9-years old. Rumor has it that her best friend stabbed her to death over $5 dollars' worth of food stamps, and she bled to death right in front of her apartment building on Southern Boulevard and Third Avenue.

The building is no longer there. But I remember seeing the blood-stained sidewalk and I can still remember my Maternal Grandmother when I think about her. She never ever raised her voice and she was one of the happiest persons you'll ever meet. She used to drink wine all the time, so her lips stayed moist and she would kiss me with these big sloppy wet grandma kisses. She was the type of person when they got drunk would tell everyone how much they loved them and cry tears of joy.

Man, how I love and miss that woman.

When we got put out by my moms, my first though was to go there, but since that grandmother was with the ancient ancestors now, my attention diverted to my other grandmother.

There is only one reason that my paternal grandmother **Velma** was not my default choice, and that is because she loved - everyone.

I don't think my paternal grandmother had a lock on her door, or if she did I don't think it ever worked. Her door was always open.

At that time, in 1988 she lived in the Soundview Section of the Bronx, over on Rosedale Avenue in a complex called "Academy Gardens" in a one-bedroom apartment on the first floor.

When we (my wife, daughter & I) showed up, my grandmother already had maybe five people living there in that one-bedroom apartment.

Pick a spot, if you could find a place to sleep you were welcome in her house (apartment).

We stayed with her, until eventually I got a "second job" working as an Unarmed Uniformed Security Officer in Academy Gardens complex where my grandmother lived.

Since I had the job working security there, my grandmother pulled some strings with some people in management and my wife, daughter & I got our own one-bed room apartment, in the same building, up on the 5th floor I believe.

Times were good, but life was extremely hard for me.

I would leave the Bronx early in the mornings and go to P.T. with the ROTC program in Queens at Saint John's University. Then depending on the day of the week, I would attend whatever class I had scheduled while I tried to remain active on campus at the same time.

I had to be back in the Bronx to work from 12 noon until 8 p.m., or the late shift from 4 p.m. until midnight, depending on whatever shift I was doing.

Then I was going back to Queens to my other job at a Major Car Rental company at LaGuardia Airport, parking and cleaning cars. It didn't matter what time I came home, it was always after 2 a.m. one way or another, and then I had another dilemma.

You see, going away to a residential University has a unique set of problems for many students. However, attending a College or School "inside" of a major metropolitan city, while maintaining an apartment and trying to raise a family is a whole entire different story!

I would pass the fellas is "the hood" and at the time 1987 – 88, the hip hop culture of the inner city had succumbed to "gangsta rap". When approached by the brothers in the neighborhood to consume alcohol or to have a drink with them, you were actually facing a civilian version of what the military calls a "Challenge & Password".

278

*Oh, you into them books, you too good to drink with the homies?!?*

*I could say naw I'll pass, I could hold my own, but at the time I'm thinking I have family members, a wife and a daughter that have to survive off of my reputation in this "hood".*

*If, I'm not perceived as "Down by Law" (hood-law), anyone in my family could get touched.*

That's street language for mugged, robbed, beaten, raped or killed.

Or worse.

Yes, there is pain worse than death – I've seen it.

So anyway, the 21-year old version of me, Sarge is what they called me at the time, would drink 40oz's of Malt Liquor with the fellas.

> *Hood Rules: On another note, if someone in the circle passes you a 40oz bottle of malt liquor, and you wiped off the bottle before you put your lips on it to take a drink: you just told that man who handed you the bottle, that you didn't trust him – and people have been shot for that.*

So, the same 40oz bottle that everyone else drank from, I drank, and drank, and drank.

Now I would finally get in the house about 4 a.m. and here it comes from the wife. *"Where the fuck have you been all day?!? You work but you don't come home! I've been dealing with this baby all day! You spend some time with her!"* Constant barrages or arguments whether I was right or wrong, no excuses, but remember I was already a military veteran at 21 years of age.

Then the cycle would repeat itself, every day, until I couldn't take it no more.

I just want the weekend to get here, so I can get some rest.

Guess what?

This weekend just so happens to be the military drill weekend for the NYARNG unit I belong to over on Staten Island *(the 101ˢᵗ Long Range Surveillance Detachment (LRSD) of the 42ⁿᵈ Infantry Division)*. The good news was that being a member of the New York National Guard allowed me to receive physical passes for the toll bridges, between the individual boroughs within New York City. So, I didn't have to pay tolls on the bridges & tunnels inside the State of New York, going back and forth to drill.

But the bad news was that, I was running on fumes, mentally, physically, spiritually, financially, emotionally and whatever else way you could think of.

By this time my wife was working and I was dealing with more perceived infidelity (whether it was true or not). My first wife was a very beautiful woman, so maybe it was just youthful insecurity and jealousy. I don't know. But for whatever reason, there is a name or number of some guy and I argue and fight with her about it. It's some guy whom she knew from the military base back near Seattle, Washington who lives in the New York area. I tell her I don't want her seeing the guy.

Her reply was, I already have.

*WTF?!?*

How could you be so bold?

She replies, *"That I'm always gonna have me somebody waiting for me if you don't work out."*

Another big fight.

Hindsight being 20-20, I realized she would call friends or relatives on the phone, then pick a fight with me like I just explained, and then have them listen to me damn near have a nervous breakdown, yelling and screaming to the top of my lungs. I would yell, and scream and make a whole lot of noise, but I have never hit that woman in my life.

**Never, and I put that on both my dead grandmothers!**

*But in my mind shaking the hell out of her, wasn't the same as hitting her (which I never did hit her, nor would ever do).*

280

I "now" know that I should never have put my hands on her in "any fashion", or on any woman for that matter, under any circumstances. Even if she hits me. There are other ways to defend myself. Hell, leaving some women will hurt them more than raising your hand ever would. I now understand that **emotional abuse** can be just as bad as **physical abuse**.

But over 30 years ago, a younger version of me at 21 & 22 years old, I erroneously thought that screaming and shaking her, for cheating on me, in my house, and she admitted it, was not the same as physically striking her.

**Which I say again, I have never done, ever.**

We are having this fight and she grabs our daughter and holds her up in front of me.

I don't know if she is handing her to me, using her as a perceived shield or what, but she physically dropped our daughter.

*I'm thinking what the hell did you just do?*

I grab my daughter and race to my car, I drive with the emergency flashers on to the local hospital's emergency room. Because she is a baby, that set off a chain of events when the child protective services are involved. I'm trying to explain my version of the events, but it is obvious that this is growing out of control.

She doesn't leave, she makes a proposal to me.

She says, *"Tim this isn't working out. Let's move back to Seattle where it was better. Every time we have a fight or an argument here, you have everyone here on your side. Your mom, dad, sister, brother, uncles, aunts, cousins, grandparents and friends and I have nobody here in NYC for me."*

What do I know?

*OK, I agree to move back to Seattle.*

I tell my mom and she replies, *"Don't you go out to Seattle with that woman."*

No less than about ten family members, friends or whoever all tell me the same thing, *"Don't you go out to Seattle with that woman."*

281

*What the fuck is wrong with y'all?!?*

*Why can't all of y'all see that, that woman y'all keep talking about -is my wife!*

*And my daughter!*

*Fuck all of y'all, I'm Audi 5000!*

So basically, I have to "disown" my entire family so I can be with my wife and daughter. We move back to Seattle, and rent a house from an elderly Asian couple. I don't know the address, but I know its location, directly around the corner from a very popular night club we used to frequent back in the early 1980's.

I don't know how long our perceived happiness and bliss lasted, but we are still having fights and arguments, **and now they are getting worse**.

The last fight we have, she tells me, *"That my daughter really ain't my biological daughter and she knows who the real biological dad is."* She says, *"She's has known it all along, and tells me his name (confidential)."*

That was the worse fight we ever had!

I swear I don't remember putting my hands on her, but when I returned from the police station, I remember being in a very lonely house.

In my mind, I can hear everyone in New York City telling me, *"I told you so!"*

The Asian man we rented the home from, he knocks on the door and tells me we have to leave.

*"Where am I gonna go?"*

*I don't care, you must go now, or I call police!*

*"But I'm not doing anything?"*

I was actually sitting in the house alone, and he says you have to go, now!

I had just returned from the police station, and I didn't want no more trouble, so I left. I remember taking a series of busses from Seattle down towards the SEA-TAC airport, and then a bus to Tacoma. Because I had recently ETS (separated) from military service at that same base, I still had a few friends who were still stationed there.

One of them actually let me stay, *"in his barracks room."*

Then when that welcome was worn out, I stayed in another friend's barracks room. Then I had another friend who stayed with a female soldier who resided in on-base housing. She was eligible for on-base housing because she had children, but the children didn't physically live with her (they were in Florida), so her place was known as the party house. I stayed there for a short period of time and eventually that welcome was worn out too.

Your welcome is worn out pretty quickly, when you don't have any money.

My final stop was with a military woman I met in Tacoma. I remember that last day with her like it was yesterday. She said to me, *"Tim this ain't working out, so you don't have to leave but I have a new nigga"* or words to that effect. I remember the look he gave me, as he walked past me in the living room, while they were enroute back to her bedroom. The sounds of them having sex was more than enough to let me know that it was over between her and I, and that I should just leave.

It was late at night, and I walked for miles, aimlessly not knowing where to go or what to do.

The homeless shelter was nothing but Gladiator School.

I couldn't stay there because I wasn't originally from the area, and everybody was divided up into informal cliques and gangs.

So, I was actually sleeping on the park benches for a short period of time. But then the atmospheric conditions of the Pacific Northwest decided to do their thing.

Rain.

*Do you know what it feels like to sleep on a park bench in the rain?!?*

This is not working out to good for me.

So, I still have a storage unit at a location in Seattle. So, for a few nights I sleep in the storage shed. But I remember it was extremely cold in there. Eventually, the storage place got some kind of electronic locks, that recorded when you entered and left. So, I couldn't sleep in the storage shed any more.

My pride wouldn't let me call any of my family members back in New York City for any help, I figured I'll figure it out on my own.

I eventually get a manual day labor job working for a road-construction company. To this day, when I see the man/woman holding the STOP Sign at a construction site, turning it from STOP to SLOW – *I wonder what his or her story is?*

Because I sure had one.

It rained all the time in Seattle, I was getting soaked in the rain during the day and trying to save money to get back to New York at night, so I can figure this all out.

Eventually I get a bright idea.

**Well it's not so bright, but it sounded great in my mind, at the time.**

After working all day, at day labor jobs, road construction sites, constructing apartment building, you name it I would do it. As long as I got paid at the end of the day. There were times when I would eat every other day, because I was trying to save up some money to get back "home", and have some money when I got back there.

So here is my bright idea. I would walk down the street in the rain, and pull on the door handles of the cars as I passed by. If I found a car door that was unlocked, I would jump into the back seat and go to sleep. Safe and dry from the elements. But I really didn't sleep, I just got a little rest.

I would make sure that I awoke before the sun came back up, and that I was gone before the POV owner found me sleeping in the back-seat of their car, and maybe shoot me.

Because I wasn't stealing anything, I just wanted to get out of the rain.

This routine went on for a while, until I finally contacted one of my old high school friends **B.L.** who left New York City and had moved to down south.

I still have the Western Union receipt where B.L., sent me some money for a bus ticket to return back home to NYC. I purchased a one-way ticket and rode a greyhound bus from Seattle to New York City, with no money in my pocket. It took me maybe four days of travel. 24 hours a day, we stopped in every little town along the way, as we traveled from state to state.

I remember someplace around Wyoming or Montana or Minnesota, an older gentleman approached me and said, *"I noticed that at every stop you don't get off the bus to use the restroom or to eat, or stretch your legs or anything, are you ok?"*

My pride (the same pride that had me too proud to ask for help and homeless in the first place) said, *"yeah, I'm good."*

When he got back on the bus after that rest stop, he approached me again and said, *"here"* as he handed me a folded up $20-dollar bill. I remember him looking just like my 5th grade school teacher Mr. Gellis (P.S. 6 Bronx, NY) and he wore blue topaz jewelry and lots of silver. I remember his grey moustache and goatee and the feather he wore.

As the bus pulled off I couldn't wait until we arrived in the next station, in the next town. I think I de-bussed faster than we did at boot camp when the drill sergeants said, *"We had 10 seconds to get off the bus, and 8 of them are already gone."*

Up until this day, because of my past being homeless I have never denied anyone who asked me for, shoes or food.

As I was trying to figure this thing called life out, I received divorce papers from my first wife in the mail. They came from her family attorney in Seattle and I still have a copy of them too, all scanned as electronic files.

The most noticeable words in that document to me were, *"you have no children, and none were produced during this marriage."*

I remember signing those papers, but I never told my Paternal Grandmother. As far as she knew, until the day she died – her first born grandchild was a father, and she was a great-grandmother.

Once I'm in back in New York City, I run across a U.S. Army Recruiter who tells me I can join the Army. I tell him that I can't, because I was already in before, and I was a Veteran.

He says, *"So what? I can put you back in the U.S. Army, get you your stripes back and send you to Germany."*

**I didn't know I could do that?**

Where do I sign? I Re-Enlist in the U.S. Army, but when I get back down to Fort Hamilton, in Brooklyn at the MEPS station, that Recruiter there has this computer screen that only he can see. Hindsight, I felt like he was a used car salesman.

The first military marching cadence many people learn is,
**"My Recruiter lied to me!"**

So, I get told that the MOS I used to have is now closed. I'll have to take another one if I want to re-enlist, 2EZ.

Then I'm told that because I am re-classifying to another MOS, I'll have to re-enlist at a lower rank, like a SPC/E-4. You may have been a SGT/E-5 when you got out, but you can't re-enlist as a SGT/E-5 into another MOS. Or something like that is what I'm told.

Then he says, you've been out of the U.S. Army for too long, so you'll lose another stripe. You'll have to come in as a PFC/E-3 if you want to re-enlist. But if you go "Combat Arms" I can get you back in as an SPC/E-4.

**Sign me up, Airborne Infantry, Ranger, I don't care what it is, as long as I'm headed to Fort Benning, GA tomorrow, I'll sign.**

Problem is; I can leave until about 30 days from now.

Long ass 30 days. Every day my mom would say to me, *"what you gonna do with your life?"*

Mom, *"I re-enlisted in the military. I leave in about three or four weeks."*

The very next day, my mom would say, *"What are you gonna do with your life?"*

She did this, every day - until I left.

I get to Fort Benning, Georgia home of the Infantry. I'm told that I can leave the "Reception AG Battalion" and go down to my unit to train, but Fort Benning doesn't have any more size 12 or 13 boots to issue me, at that time.

So, I remain in the Reception Battalion, and miss my intended 11B Infantry AIT, which would be to join a One Station Unit Training (OSUT) Class, after they finish the Basic Training (BT) portion, and start the Advance Infantry training (AIT) portion.

I miss my intended class, so by the time Fort Benning gets boots in my size, I get sent down to *Echo Company, 1st Battalion, 19th Infantry (Training)* and join them in their 2nd week of "Basic Training".

My duty station is changed from Germany to Alaska, and I'm going to be Airborne Infantry in Alaska instead. OK, needs of the Army I guess.

It's 1989, and Patti LaBelle has a hit song on the radio called *"Yo Mister [How's Your Daughter]."* After everything I've been through I am still thinking about that little girl. I've experienced jail, homelessness, physical, mental and spiritual pain I never hope to experience again. But I can't get that little girl out of my mind.

So, guess what I did?

Because you can't fly to Anchorage, Alaska from Atlanta, Georgia without a stopover in Seattle, Washington (at least back then). I get in touch with her mother (my ex-wife).

Although we can't stand each other and have both moved on with our lives, I rationalize that there was once a time, when we did love each other. So maybe we can be friends, is what I think.

I get up to Alaska, and we begin to converse; with her in Seattle, Washington and me in Anchorage, Alaska.

I'm back in the military, getting back on track with my life, stationed in Alaska and she & I have been friends for a few months now. Life is going good when out of nowhere, she blindsides me.

*"Where's my money?"*

**"Huh, what are you talking about woman?"**

She repeats herself, *"Where's my money? Don't you get paid extra money for being married in the military?"*

I tell her, **"Yeah if we were still married I'd be entitled to some additional allowance called a BAQ (Basic Allowance for Quarters). But since we're divorced, I don't get paid that. I signed them divorce paper you sent to me last year!"**

*"Yeah, you signed them, but I never filed them."*

She says, *"Were still married, and I want my money. Or I'll contact your Commanding Officer."*

**WHAT THE FUCK?!?**

I eventually wind up sending her $314.40 a month, that I didn't get. The amount equal to what I would have gotten, had I got the additional allowance. I eventually apply for and get the allowance and continue to send her the money. One day I ask her, how's "the daughter" was doing? *I am deliberately not saying her name, she was still a minor at the time.*

She tells me don't worry about that, just continue to send her, her money, so she can buy her boyfriend a sweater. I wanted to jump through that phone. I stopped sending her the money "one month" because I didn't think it was fair. My military Chain of Command, threatened to "Chapter me out of the military" with an "Other Than Honorable Discharge" if I didn't get my personal affairs in order.

Eventfully, I got a divorce and she had the nerve to ask me, *"Well what about your daughter?"*

Fast-forward 15-20 years, later.

I get a call from her, telling me that "my daughter" wants to see her dad?

>*"Well, what are you telling me for? Isn't (confidential) her dad?"*

>*"That's what you told me!"*

>*"Yeah, we had a DNA test done, and he's not the father Tim, you are."*

Home is where the heart is.

# 18

# THE BLACK JELLYBEAN

*I have served on active duty with the United States Military for over 20 years. Four (4) years on active duty with the U.S. Army, then two (2) years in the National Guard, and then seventeen (17) more years on active duty, again with the U.S. Army. I can say without a doubt, based upon my personal experience, that the United States Army Special Forces are the LEAST racist of ANY units that I have ever encountered over the course of my career.*

*At the same time, although it may NOT have been initially developed that way as an institution, it is also the MOST DIFFUCULT unit for ANY service member or person who is NOT of the same racial demographics of the dominate society or a person of european decent, especially for a strong "Black Man" to exist in.*

*To make myself perfectly clear so there are no misunderstandings, from my personal point of view, I am stating that, "it is the <u>least</u> and the <u>most</u> difficult unit in regard to race, for a blackman to operate in, at the same time."*

291

*There is a saying in the U.S. Army, that there is no color.*

*Everyone is green, U.S. Army green for that matter, just like them little green army men. There are no black soldiers, or white soldiers, or asian soldiers, or latino soldiers, it's just soldiers, period.*

*And you're all freakin green.*

*But you dark green soldiers better learn how to swim!*

*The U.S. Army's Special Forces "Green Berets" are members of the U.S. Army's Special Operation Forces (SOF) with several other types of SOF units (Rangers, Special Ops Aviation, Psychological Operations, etc). Again, I'm not stating anything other than what can be found on the SOF unit's websites and social media presences, or a quick search using the average open source on-line search engine.*

*The U.S. Army's Special Forces "Green Berets" five primary missions are Unconventional Warfare (UW), Direct Action (DA), Counter-Terrorism (CT), Special Reconnaissance (SR) and Foreign Internal Defense (FID).*

*Although there are other units that conduct these same missions, just like the U.S. Army's Special Forces (UW, DA, CT & SR). NONE of the entire United States "other" military branches in general (Air Force, Navy, Marines or Coast Guard), and other units in the big U.S. Army specifically, are designed, trained and equipped to conduct Foreign Internal Defense (FID) like the U.S. Army's "Green Beret's" – period.*

There is a U.S. military publication called; Joint Publication (JP) 3-22 dated July 2010 that explains what FID is. The first sentence of that overview states:

Foreign Internal Defense (FID) is the participation by civilian and military agencies of a government in any of the action programs taken by another government or other designated organization, to free and protect its society from subversion, lawlessness, insurgency, terrorism, and other threats to their security.

*But to break it down to Barney level, or as many who preach from the pulpit say, "to put it down where the goats can get it".*

*Foreign Internal Defense (FID) at its basic level is one of two options.*

1. *If a "friendly" foreign government was experiencing an "insurgency", and a foreign enemy country was helping the rebels to overthrow that friendly country, members of the U.S. Army's Special Forces "could" deploy to that region to help the friendly government suppress the uprising, and defeat the illegal rebels.*

2. *On the other side of the coin, if there was an oppressive government that was slaughtering its people, or the government became bad and was getting help from another bad government, and they were performing some type of ethnic cleansing, killing and exterminating its population, and the citizens (the good guys) needed help, members of the U.S. Army's Special Forces "could" deploy to that region to help the friendly citizens of that country.*

\*\*\*

*Either way it goes, which do you think the American people would prefer?*

(A) *The United States goes to war and helps a good government suppress an illegal insurgency, or the U.S. goes to war to help another country's people from being slaughtered; either way many American Service Members (men & women) will die on foreign soil over there.*

*OR*

(B) *We send a small group of "military advisors" to another region to help the people there solve their own problems, for themselves. A 12-man Operational Detachment Alpha (ODA) of "Green Beret's" is designed to recruit, equip, train and advise a battalion of up to 500-men on the idiosyncrasies of warfare.*

*In order to do that, they must speak the language of the people they are trying to help (you can't rely on interpreters for everything). As I've stated in earlier chapters, every single member of the U.S. Army's Special Forces units who are "Green Beret" qualified, speaks at least English and one other language. Many men speak multiple languages, and all of us (SF qualified men) are all bilingual or we are not "green berets."*

*The maturity required to pass the foreign language school, cultural understanding and training to teach foreign troops (or civilians) in their native language alone is enough to weed out the rookies, and those who practice a racist dogma. It's just not possible. When conducting FID, the U.S. Army Special Forces "Green Berets" are not designed to live on a big American base someplace, they live with the foreign troops they lead in combat, I mean foreign troop they teach. There may not even be an American military presence over there yet, or ever. They eat what the foreign troops eat. They sleep where the foreign troops sleep. They speak the same language and dialect as the foreign troops (or civilians) that they are there to help speak.*

*Since I believe that NOBODY in this world is born a racist, they must learn that behavior. I believe that they can also "un-learn" racism also.*

*I'm not talking about systemic institutionalized racism, I'm talking about individual prejudices, bigotry and racism.*

*It is almost impossible for a member of the U.S. Army's Special Forces "Green Berets" to go through years and years of training, and maintain an ideology of racism and hate (without someone knowing about it).*

*The motto of the U.S. Army's Special Forces "Green Beret" is:*
*"De Oppresso Liber" which means: To Free the Oppressed.*

294

*Many people believe that it actually means; "To Free from Oppression" or "To Liberate the Oppressed".*

*Some people believe the translation from the Latin language means "From (Being) An Oppressed Man, (To Being) A Free One". Either way, if the actual green beret motto is about freeing oppressed people, it's kinda hard to be racist against the LBG's you're actually trying to help.*

*Everywhere across the globe I've heard the term for most people "other than Americans" as LBG's which stands for "Little Brown Guys". I didn't create the term, I'm explaining a phrase in common usage around the world. Many countries around the world call us, "Big Ugly Americans", so it goes both ways.*

*Many military units' safety briefings for U.S. military members traveling or training OCONUS includes, "Don't be the Big Ugly American".*

*As I stated before, by design the United States Army Special Forces is the LEAST RACIST unit I have ever encountered in over 20 years of active duty service.*

*However, one of my first days of training this is what happened to me and a few others melinated SF candidates. A senior ranking instructor out at Camp Mackall (let's just call him MSG Smith) called a few of us "brothers" over towards him. He looked at us and said in all seriousness, "My name is Master Sergeant Smith – but you can call me Massa. Now ain't but 3 of y'all gonna graduate this here training, so y'all go figure it out amongst yourself", and then he walked off.*

*Not believing what we just heard him say, we all looked at each other in disbelief. But I was not in total disbelief, because this was not my first time experiencing racist behavior in the military.*

*As I've said before, many men have died going through Special Forces training; either in SFAS, SFQC or one of the many other dangerous training courses & programs. As I'm writing this chapter (SEP 2017), I just heard yesterday on the news that there was an incident within the Special Forces Qualification "Q" Course where several soldiers were injured and one student "was killed" during the dangerous demolition portion of training.*

Without disclosing the actual size of an SFAS (SF try-outs) class, I will say that in the late 1980's and early 1990's some soldiers died during training, in an attempt to earn the coveted "green beret". So, the SFAS class that I attended had about three times as many service members as normal, due to the lack of classes being held during the summer months (with the high heat index that year). So, my class started with about 500 men, of which I could only count about 8 black soldiers. Of the 500 that started, only 101 of us made it to the end, on the last day. Of the 101 that made it to the end, only 63 of us got selected, graduated SFAS and were ordered to return back to start SFQC training, after clearing our original parent units.

Of that 63 men who graduated, there were only 3 of us black soldiers.

So maybe that was just a coincidence, and that MSG Smith made a lucky guess.

Because there is no feedback from the cadre during SFAS (SF try-outs), no one is able to determine their actual status. Candidates were even prohibited from wearing a wrist watch. You are just told, "Candidate this is a timed event, do the best you can do!"

So, I'm quite sure that I will be summoned by someone of authority at the Department of the Army real soon, or someone of higher rank and authority within the SF community who will have access to my class records, to correct me with the "exact numbers".

But as of this writing (and I've been retired from the U.S. Army for over 10 years now), I have never seen the exact figures.

I can only tell you what I know from memory – because I was there.

There is a lot of training that goes into making a Special Forces soldier. Some of it deliberate repetitions of basic movements, tactics, techniques & procedures that make him an "expert" at the simple stuff. Some of it open source that involved training with "other units" on Fort Bragg to participate in their role-playing maneuvers. Some of it extremely dangerous and so realistic that SF candidates & students have been killed during training (like I have repeatedly said). Some of it classified at a much higher level than I'm authorized to discuss in an open source forum such as this book.

But the bottom line is this, it is "Special" and that's why they called it the "Special Forces" and not the "Regular Forces."

The 2010 US Census states that there are approximately 323 million people who live in the United States (323,127,513) of which 46.8 million are considered "black folks", so that's like 14% of the population. With all things being equal, statically speaking, that means about 14% of the people in all professions would be black, unless there is a specific reason for it.

Fourteen percent of all the doctors would be black, 14% of all the teachers, 14% of all the firemen, 14% of all the truck drivers, 14% of all the construction workers, 14% of the unemployed, 14% of the military service members, etc.

But we all know that statistic doesn't stand up to truth across the board.

Take the National Basketball Association (NBA) for example. There are a total of 30 individual professional basketball teams in the NBA (29 in the United States and 1 in Canada). Each team can have a maximum of 15 players (of which 12 can "dress" and only 5 actually play at a time). That makes the total number of 450 professional basketball players in the entire NBA. The NBA currently has a ratio of; about 74% black players and 23% white players. There is a reason for this.

When you look at the 30 owners of the actual teams, Robert Johnson was the first black majority team owner in the NBA (2004-2005), and he was succeeded by Michael Jordan. In 2013-2014 another team was owned by a man of Indian decent, that meant for the first time in the history of the major league professional sports in the United States, when there were two majority owners, in any league: that were NOT rich white men.

If just one NBA team owner out of 10 were black that would be 10%, and still lower than the statistical average of the population.

If just one NBA team owner out of 20 were black, that would be 5%, and an even lower number/percentage wise of the statistical average of the population.

But there is just one majority owner out of all 30 teams.

There is a reason for this too.

*What is that reason?*

*I don't know.*

*You'll have to go get a book about the racial disparity in professional sports. This ain't that type of book. I am just using those statistics to illustrate my point.*

*That point being, that whenever there is NOT an equitable representation across the board of all racial demographics, there is reason for it.*

*Good or bad, there is always a rhyme and reason to everything, even if we don't agree or understand it.*

*Well in the U.S. military the demographics are overwhelming in favor of black Americans serving our country, whether for patriotic or other reasons. This is true even before the founding of this country (way before the American Revolutionary War, up until this present day).*

*A free black man named Prince Hall, along with fourteen (14) other free melinated men of color, petitioned to become Masons and members of the masonic order prior to the American Revolution. They were denied acceptance, because although they were "Free Men", they were still "Black Men", and some people couldn't get over racism & white supremacy.*

*Some people still can't.*

*Prince Hall and these other men continued their pursuit of more light in Masonry, and were initiated into the Masonic Order through Lodge #441 of the Grand Lodge of Ireland in 1775. The lodge was attached to the 38th Foot (renamed the 1st Staffordshire Regiment) and was attached to the British forces stationed in Boston, Massachusetts. Because back then, and now still, Masonry was and is a worldwide brotherhood that transcends all races, religions, creeds and colors.*

*I know, because I have been tried and accepted by those who are.*

*I have fellowshipped with other masons from all over the world in lodges, cities and countries other than my own. We have "secret signs, symbols, handshakes, passwords and codes" that are recognizable by other masons all across the planet (even when two brothers meet that do not speak the same language). Any current member, of any masonic lodge, can go travel and visit any other lodge, in any other city, state or country; except "Black Men" in "some" lodges in the southern portion of our United States of America.*

*Don't believe me, don't believe nothing I say, do your own research.*

*Look it up in your own local phone book or a quick online research. The organization may be full of secrets, but the organization itself is not secret.*

*Why are there two Grand Lodges for Masonry in many states and jurisdiction in the United States?*

*One reason is because many of them, are still segregated.*

*Many states still have a Grand Masonic Lodge for white masons, and a Grand Masonic Lodge for black masons. Or should I say, a Grand Masonic lodge for "regular" masons and a Grand Masonic Lodge for Prince Hall Affiliated masons (PHA).*

*Shouldn't be a big surprise, because many of you right now go to;*
*a segregated mosque on Fridays,*
*or a segregated synagogue on Saturdays,*
*or a segregated church on Sundays,*
*or whatever your religious belief system is.*

*Every Prince Hall (PHA) lodge I've ever visited was "integrated" and men of all races, religions and creeds were welcome, as long as they were dully tried, true and tested (and have a current dues card). But that is not the same in "many" of the other lodges in the deep south.*

*Here's the reason why (then I'll get back to my Special Forces story).*

*Because for any man, to join any masonic lodge, besides all the other administrative and jurisdictional requirements there is a vote by the lodge members. The vote is always two ways to insure peace and harmony within that specific blue lodge. It (the vote) is held by the members of that lodge; unanimously and anonymously, period.*

Every member present must "vote for or vote against" any new person who petitions to join that particular masonic lodge. Each voting member must choose "a large white ball or a large black ball". Lodges that do not have that level of affluence may use "a small white marble or a small black marble", or some other method. When all the balls are collected, and the vote is tallied one ball at a time, if all the balls aren't "white" meaning if there is just "one black ball", the person is denied entry into the lodge and acceptance into the brotherhood fraternity, period. Remember I said unanimous and it must be anonymously.

Let me just "make up" an example to use for clarity purposes (but not violate my obligation to the masonic order).

If each lodge member walked up to the voting box with a bag over it, and selected a white ball or a black ball from the tray, and placed it farther inside the bag. No one could tell who selected what color balls.

Then in a lodge of 100 members, it doesn't matter if there are 99 white balls, if there is just one "black ball" in the bag, the person is denied admission into the lodge, and no one knows who voted against that candidate, or why.

That candidate is now: BLACK BALLED.

Now the reason could be valid.

The lodge is about brotherhood, friendship, fellowship, peace & unity. But if you're already a member and a new candidate is petitioning to join your lodge, who maybe tried you steal your woman, or take your girl, or whatever. Chances are you're not gonna vote in favor of that person joining your brotherhood, or at least not joining your particular lodge; to preserve the peace and harmony.

Now imagine the same thing happening in a racist society. I know because I have friends who are masonic brothers from some of them "other lodges", who tell me "exactly" what goes on behind closed doors. They, like me and many of you are patiently awaiting the day when those old racist people change their ways, or just simply die off from old age.

Hopefully, they take their racism and hatred with them to the grave.

So, I went all the way around Robin Hoods Barn to say this about the U.S. Army's Special Forces program (I know I used an idiomatic expression, but I also know what it means; because Robin Hood had no barn).

According to the Statistic Brain Research Institute, the entire U.S. military apparatus is 74.6% white (including hispanics), 17.8% black and 7.6% other. So, black people serve in the US military in a <u>higher percentage</u> to our overall population percentage, which we already established is 14%.

But some people will still perpetuate the incorrect negative stereotype; that black folks ain't patriotic.

U.S.A. Motherfucker, U.S.A.!!!

According to that same research, statically speaking black folks make up:

> 21.5% of the U.S. Army
> 19.3% of the U.S. Navy
> 15.6% of the U.S. Air Force
> 11.1% of the U.S. Marine Corps
> 6.1% of the U.S. Coast Guard

So again, black folks are higher represented in the U.S. Army, statically speaking than any other branch, and more than our percentage of the population.

So, although black people make up:

> 14% of the United States population.
> 17.8% of the U.S. Military (all branches combined)
> 21.5% of the U.S. Army

Within the Special Operations community in general, and the U.S. Army Special Forces community specifically, they are less than 5% of the operators (I say they because I have been retired for over 10 years now and those numbers were significantly less than 1% for black men when I graduated SFAS & SFQC back in the late 1980's and early 1990's).

I was there and I'm telling you the truth.

*Out of 330 million people that live in this country, less than 2 million are on Active Duty in the "entire" U.S. military, so I understand the nature of the numbers. Black men where represented in the U.S. Army Special Forces less than "a percentage" of 1% when I served. But don't believe me, research for yourself. Don't have the time to research the official reports, don't worry I have some of them right here, this one from the RAND Institute:*

The nonprofit RAND institute sponsored by the U.S. Special Operations Command (USSOCOM), conducted a research report in RAND's National Defense Research Institute, a federally funded research and development center supported by the Office of the Secretary of Defense, the Joint Staff, the unified commands and the defense agencies.

**BARRIERS TO MINORITY PARTICIPATION IN SPECIAL OPERATIONS FORCES (1999)**

Because RAND was asked by USSOCOM to undertake a study of minority representation in Special Operation Forces (SOF) as a result of concerns expressed by the [U.S.] House of Representatives regarding the "significant underrepresentation of minorities in certain areas of the SOF [community]". *That report is approximately 140 pages long, you can read it open source on-line (that's what I did), but let me save you the trouble, and I'll tell you what they found out.*

They noted that approximately only 40% of all black soldiers were eligible to apply for Special Forces, and when the requirement for a GT score [100] or higher is applied, it significantly reduced the number of eligible minority applicants from 40% down to 26.7% for black soldiers.

*(Remember although this is an all-volunteer military, everyone who volunteers to serve, is not "eligible" to serve. Then, of the small number of soldiers who actually do serve in the U.S. Army, all of them are not eligible to apply for Special Forces. Some are too old, some are too young, some don't have enough rank, this was before SF babies, some have too much rank).*

Then the report goes on to quote another study (Books and Zazanis, 1997) that states that although the U.S. Army swim test for SOF forces in general, and U.S. Army Special Forces in particular, was considerably less demanding than that of other services, black soldiers were still "six-times more likely to fail the swim test" than white soldiers.

*Here is another report from the U.S. Army Research Institute for Behavioral and Social Sciences:*

The U.S. Army Research Institute for the Behavioral and Social Sciences, wrote a Research Report #1629

**MINORITY REPRESENTATION IN THE ENLISTED SPECIAL FORCES (1992)**

It was directed by the Office of the Deputy Chief of Staff for Personnel to examine reasons for the low proportion of minorities in Special Forces (SF). It determined that the minimum General Technical (GT) score [then 110, now 100] required in SF markedly reduced the proportion of eligible minorities [soldiers] from 40% to 28%. It also stated that the required swim test also eliminated a disproportionate number of minorities (blacks, in particular) from Special Forces Assessment and Selection (SFAS) [the SF try-outs].

*Here is another report:*

The Daily Caller, posted an article.

**OFFICIALS SAY U.S. SPECIAL FORCES ARE TOO WHITE AND TOO MALE (2015)**

In it, it states that they are hoping for a major demographic shift because of the current disparities in units like the Navy SEAL's and U.S. Army's Green Berets. They state that blacks comprise 17% of the U.S. Army which is slightly higher than [black folks] representation in the overall population. However, blacks account for only 9.4% of the officers in the military. They site just 5.6% of the U.S. Army's Green Berets are black, 2% of the U.S. Navy's SEAL's, and about a half of 1% of the US Air Force para-rescuers [PJ's] were black.

*I'm willing to bet that amongst all the reasons that these reports cite as barriers to minority participation; two reasons will always be said.*

   *(1) Black soldiers don't score high enough on the GT portion of the ASVAB test (IMPLYING THAT BLACK FOLKS AIN'T SMART).*

   *(2) Black soldiers can't pass the swim test (IMPLYING THAT BLACK FOLKS CAN'T SWIM).*

Both of those negative stereotypes are *INCORRECT, FALSE* and *MALICIOUS: and I'll explain why in a moment.*

*Here is another report:*

---

Another article:

**RACISM IN SPECIAL OPS? BETTER TELL BECK (2010)**

Which reprinted a portion of their article from "Media Matters", which sites and quotes several other articles states the following:

13% of the Pentagon's highly trained Special Operations Forces (SOF) personnel are racial minorities, including blacks.

15% of the U.S. Army's [SOF which included] Special Forces and Rangers [and other units] are persons of color (which included black soldiers), compared to about 40% of the entire U.S. Army.

11% of the U.S. Navy SEAL's are minorities.

8% of the U.S. Air Force's Special Tactics and Pararescue Groups are minority members.

---

*Within the U.S. Army's Special Forces units (which are a part of the larger U.S. Army's SOF community), there are less than 250 black men serving [who are SFQC graduates and qualified to wear the highly coveted "Green Beret"] in the entire U.S. Army's Special Forces!*

*Now, I'm NOT going to cite their numbers about how many total SOF personnel there are, or how many total SF "Green Berets" there are. That's why I use the statistics and percentages. Even though you can put this book down, and do the research for yourself. I just don't feel that our countries adversaries should have access to that type of information, even if someone else wrote those reports.*

*The article goes on to quote a black Special Forces General named Remo Butler who stated that [while working out at the post gym] he was frequently mistaken for being a First Sergeant rather than a General.*

*He stated in the article that when he would attempt to recruit young black soldiers for Special Forces he would consistently hear these comments like: "That there are no blacks in Special Forces", obviously not knowing he is [was] a General Officer in Special Forces at the time. Or he would hear, "Sir, Special Forces is full of rednecks and klansmen".*

*I wasn't there when these comments were made, but perception is reality, and I did have a roommate while I was in Special Forces training who was in the klan, because he told me so. I did everything I could to try to break the stereotypes that he was taught about melinated people of color in general, and black folks in particular.*

*BLACK FOLKS CAN'T SEE AT NIGHT.*
*Well I tried to walk point every chance I got while on patrol, just to show him that not only can we see at night, but that I'm now the freaking best at this.*

*BLACK GUYS CAN'T SWIM.*
*Well I was an open water lifeguard, so that stereotype didn't work too well around me.*

*BLACK PEOPLE AREN'T SMART.*
*Not tooting my own horn and claiming that I'm smart. But, I used to beat so many people playing chess, that they would bring guys from other units to play me, and I would beat them as well. I would demoralize them by playing "New York City guy just got out the penitentiary street style – like I learned" on them. I'd talk shit, predict moves like Muhammad Ali predicted the round he would knock out his opponent. I'd snatch their pieces off the board and throw them across the barracks. "DON'T YOU TOUCH THAT BISHOP, I KNOW YOU WANNA MOVE THAT BISHOP" is what I'd say! Two moves later I'd physically throw their Bishop across the barracks as I captured their piece, saying "I TOLD YO ASS – NOT TO TOUCH THAT DAMN BISHOP! GIVE ME THIS PAWN, CHECK! THIS ONE TOO, CHECK!!" The game would continue, and I would obliterate anyone even thinking about playing next. "CHECK!!! GIVE ME THAT FUNKY BITCH (as I snatched their queen off of the board) YOU DON'T KNOW WHAT TO DO WITH HER. I'LL SHOW YOU HOW TO TREAT HER RIGHT!" I would consistently beat stronger rated players, because I got into their heads and caused them to doubt themselves. I'd play some people without even looking at the board. I'd tell them what pieces to move for me, I was that good.*

*I once solved a Rubik's Cube in less than 30 seconds before.*

*I was an avid reader at the time. I mean I read now, but back then it was books all day every day! I was given the moniker "Ruffneck Nerd" by the woman who would later become my wife.*

*Here is another report:*

---

There is another article from, VIEW FROM THE RIGHT, The passing scene and what it's about from the traditionalist politicly incorrect Right

**NOTWITHSTANDING THE EXTREMELY LOW NUMBER OF BLACKS IN SPECIAL FORCES, THERE ARE AS YET NO QUOTAS (2012)**

It repeats the same facts that every other study states. It quotes the San Diego Union-Tribune and the Military Times.

*It quotes the number of Navy SEAL's, and the number of Army Rangers, and that the Air Force only had 8 blacks out of almost 500 men in their Special Tactics Groups, and the low number of Army Special Forces "Green Beret's" and everyone is looking at the facts, the end results, and the outcome.*

---

*BUT WHEN IS SOMEONE GONNA REALIZE THAT YOU MUST UNDERSTAND THE NATURE, THE ROOT CAUSE OF THE PROBLEM, BEFORE YOU CAN FIX IT?!?*

*Because you may find out in the end, that the system is NOT broken, it may have been intentionally designed that way, and it doesn't need fixing at all.*

*Or you may be able to find a simple solution to a really complex problem.*

*Example: Your child comes up to you with a cut on their arm and they want a bandage. You patch them up and tell them to go back outside and play. The next day they come to you again, with another cut, and you give them another bandage. By the third day when they come to you with another cut, you may stop what you're doing and say, "let me go outside and see what this child is cutting themselves on." What is the cause of the problem? Because I'm either gonna run out of bandages, they're gonna bleed to death, or I need to stop treating the "SYMPTOMS" of the problem, and I can go find the root "CAUSE" of the problem, and eliminate that.*

306

*Eliminate the cause, NOT treat the symptom.*

*Many people say that 70% of black people can't swim. If that is a true statement and a fact, that is a SYMPTOM; not the CAUSE of the problem. Investigate and find out why, and then eliminate the cause.*

*One of the United States of America's greatest sins has been the institution of chattel slavery and the racism that allowed it to exist for hundreds of years.*

*When it was over is 1865, and slavery was abolished with the U.S. Congressional Amendments after the conclusion of the American Civil War, black folks as a whole were not given anything to start a new life after building this country for free, for almost 400 years.*

*No land grants, no funds, no knowledge, nothing. The small gains that black folks as a whole did make, were intimidating to many people who subscribe to racism white supremacy.*

*So, they destroyed the Black Wall streets.*

*There is a popular hit song called, "You Dropped A Bomb on Me (1982)" by the Gap Band. Many people say that song pays homage to that time when racist domestic terrorist used airplanes and dropped dynamite bombs on the black residents of the affluent Greenwood district of Tulsa, Oklahoma. During the race attacks of 1921 (erroneously labeled as some type of "race riots"), that area of segregated Tulsa was targeted by jealous, insecure, racist people.*

*Since the black folks were "prohibited" from shopping elsewhere, and they were forced to shop with each other, that area became affluent because of community "Group Economics."*

*Black folks created their own businesses and services including but not limited to: several grocery stores, two independent newspapers, two movie theaters, nightclubs, churches, black doctors, black dentist, black lawyers and clergy members.*

*Then a 19-year old black man (who was an elevator operator), allegedly touched a 17-year old white woman. That touch was considered an assault by the jealous, insecure, racist authorities of the dominate society. So, the* majority dominant population of european decent started "a riot" that torched 35 square blocks of homes and businesses. They killed hundreds of people, and left an estimated 10,000 more people homeless, destroyed all 191 businesses, the junior high school, churches and the only hospital. 1,256 houses were burned and another 215 were looted (but not burned). The City of Tulsa conspired with the jealous, insecure, racist white mob and arrested more than 6,000 black residents.

Racist LEO's secured six bi-wing airplanes trainers left over from WWI with other privately-owned aircraft, and dropped firebombs on buildings, homes and fleeing families, stating they were protecting against a "Negro uprising". The Tulsa, Oklahoma massacre of black folks and the destruction of that "black wall street" was omitted from state and local records, and rarely mentioned in history books, classrooms or even spoken about in private.

The Gap Band as a musical group, stands for (G.A.P.) Greenwood, Archer and Pine Streets. The neighborhood that use to make up the area of the former black wall street in the historic Greenwood section of Tulsa, Oklahoma where the group originated.

Every time black folks were forced to practice group economics with themselves, because of racism that prevented them from participating in the larger society as a whole; that progress was eventually destroyed or taken away by members of the dominate society. The Freedmen's Bureau, undermined the black Congressmen, black Senators and installed a system of Second Class Citizenship, Jim Crow laws, segregation, beatings, rape, lynching's and outright murder against black folks.

This existed in our country for another 100 years, from 1865 until the civil rights era in 1965.

There are older people still living today, who knew their "immediate" relatives who were enslaved here in America.

My paternal granddad was born in 1917, he would be 100 years old this year if he was still alive. I can only imagine the stories he would have been able to tell about his granddad.

I know an elder here in Fayetteville, North Carolina named Mr. Woods who is 100 years old. I wish I had permission to publish his photo in this book, *because he walks fully upright with no walking cane. He tells me stories about how Fayetteville was way back in the days, I'm talking about the 1920's when he was a young child. How he would ride across the Cape Fear River in a horse buggy, the roads weren't paved and how proud black folks weren't even allowed to be on the Hay Street side of the Slave Market House. Yes, the building that has several other historical events linked to it, but was once used to sell "black folks" as slaves right here.*

*Can you just imagine the stories he can tell you about his grandparents?*

*There are many people still living today, who are old enough to be those same young white kids who can be seen smiling with their parents in the photos and post cards taken "back in the day" when black people were shot, burned, castrated, lynched and murdered for fun, or for sport. For reading books, for acting uppity, or for laughing in public.*

*Did you know it was illegal for black folks to laugh in public in certain places in the south? If something was funny to them, they had to go to a barrel in the corner of "Massa's Big House" and put their head in a barrel, and laugh inside the barrel. Now you know where the term "A Barrel of Laughs" comes from. Some racist people were so insecure, that they thought that if a slave was laughing: they must be laughing at them.*

*There are people still living today, who can ask their grandparents, about "their" grandparents, and they will tell you they were actually former slaves.*

*There are older people living today, who if you asked them, if they had any pictures of "their" grandparents – they would tell you that, "they didn't take pictures of slaves or unimportant people back then.*

*There are people today who can tell you stories that will make your soul hurt and make you physically sick to your stomach.*

*So, after hundreds of years of slavery, there was another hundred years of Jim Crow segregation laws.*

*It doesn't take a rocket scientist to figure out that during that period of segregation, when it was legal in this country to separate people by race, (Separate but Equal was a farce). Not only was it wrong, but it definitely wasn't equal.*

309

Public funds from tax payer monies from everyone, went to pay for all public schools. But how much money was spent on the traditionally white schools, and how much was spent on the traditionally black schools?

The ignorant say, "Well black people ain't smart, they all come from the inner-city, gang banging killing each other, selling crack to each other and making babies." That's not true, but many people will continue to perpetuate that negative narrative, without putting it into context. Or discussing the root cause of the problem.

Give them guns, give them drugs, don't give them no jobs, no hope, then sit back and say; "look at them!"

WHO BUILT THE INNER-CITY GHETTO'S, AND WHY?

Crabs in a barrel, always pulling each other down. Never letting anyone succeed in getting out of the barrel to pull the rest of them out. They always trying to keep each other down.

That may be true, but the barrels are not the "natural habitat" of the crabs. They function extremely well, when they are in their own native environment.

THE QUESTION IS, WHO BUILT THE BARRELS, AND WHO PUT THE CRABS IN THEM?

See, I'm a critical thinker. You can't tell me about the man in South Carolina who went inside the black church killing all them black folks, because he supposedly was a white supremacist. Unless, you can tell me who took all the photos of him, that he was posing in, that was all over the news.

Who took the photos, and who were his co-conspirators?
Oh, we not gonna talk about that, huh?

Who built the inner-city ghettos and why?

Look up the practice of "Red-Lining", where black, brown and other poor melinated people of color where deliberately "red lined "on a map into these communities in the 1930's, 40's and 50's. After serving our country in a segregated U.S. Military during World War II, both of my grandfathers were "red lined" into the newly built "projects".

310

They wanted to live in the nice new homes out on Long Island, but were "denied" the use of their G.I. Bill for that. They were given preferential treatment to move into the "new housing developments" in New York City. That's how my mother's-father, and my father's-father got to live in the urban areas that would later become the ghettos of New York City.

So, if entire communities were separate but equal, and we all know that separate means that the old raggedy run-down version went to one community, while the better services and supplies went to the other community.

## WHAT DO YOU THINK THE COMMUNITY POOLS IN "THE GHETTO" LOOKED LIKE BACK THEN?

If you don't have access to a pool, you probably couldn't swim. If you couldn't swim, you probably didn't teach your children to swim. If you're reading this book, and you do know how to swim, I'm willing to bet that your parents taught you how, or at least they afforded you the "opportunity" and they themselves knew how to swim.

It ain't hard to swim, considering the fact that 60% of the average human body today is made of water!

Every human that is born, was carried inside their mother's womb, inside a sack filled with water (a clear colorless liquid amniotic fluid) that protected you from the outside world until about 9 months later, when you were born.

Everyone can swim, it's just a matter of freaking opportunities to perfect the art of swimming.

"If" the powers that be wanted too, they could make swimming mandatory in the entire U.S. Military and teach every Service Member how to swim, period.

You fail Physical Training (PT) your unit doesn't lower the standard for PT, or at least I hope they don't. You just do more PT, you do remedial PT, you do extra PT, you do PT on the weekends and your days off. If your only physical activity consists of Army PT you're already in the hurt locker. But if you're an avid runner, weightlifter, bodybuilder, crossfitter, or whatever; if your already into physical fitness, then Army PT won't be a problem for you.

*There was an issue with sexual harassment and sexual assault in the U.S. military, so they came up with a way to raise awareness and prevent that.*

*There are alcohol and drug abuse, prevention and awareness classes and counselors.*

*There are Equal Opportunity NCO's on every base in the military.*

*If you do NOT go to the military dentist at least once every year, they will place you on a list called Dental Readiness Category (DRC) 4: rendering you Non-Deployable. That system insures you will go seek the dentist for your annual exam, on your own, to prevent tooth and gum disease.*

(1) *DRC 1 is assigned to personnel who have a current examination and do not require dental treatment or evaluation.*
   *\*Cat 1 dental patients are deployable.*

(2) *DRC 2 is assigned to personnel who have a current examination and require non-urgent dental treatment or evaluation that is unlikely to result in a dental emergency within 1 year.*
   *\*Cat 2 dental patients are considered deployable.*

(3) *DRC 3 is assigned to personnel who require urgent dental treatment.*
   *\*Cat 3 dental patients are NOT "NORMALLY" considered deployable*

(4) *DRC 4 is assigned to patients who require a periodic dental examination or have an unknown dental readiness classification.*
   *\*Cat 4 dental patients are NOT considered worldwide deployable.*

*Why such an extensive military dental readiness program?*

*Why all this focus on your teeth and gums?*

*Because I don't care how badass you think you are, a tooth ache can put you down hard. There may not be time or the ability to access a dentist when you get "downrange". So, the military wants you to be ready to deploy. It was a problem, and they wanted to "fix it" so it's now Standard Operating Procedure (SOP), mess around and get put on a Dental Cat 4 list if you want too!*

*Every time you try to do something "good" in the military, your name will pop-up on that damn Category 4 dental list.*

*You get put in for an achievement award, sorry you can't get it because you're considered a Cat 4.*
*You earned a three-day pass, sorry you're a Cat 4.*
*You want to get promoted, I'm sorry you're Cat 4.*
*You want to eat, sorry you're a Cat 4.*
*You want to sleep, sorry you're a dental Cat 4!*

*I'm exaggerating, but you get my point.*

*The U.S. military "can" fix the things they want to fix.*

*But I personally believe that if the big emphasis on swimming is what keeps minority soldiers (especially black soldiers) from participating in Special Forces training, then that's the way its gonna stay.*

*You don't need no affirmative action training, or to lower the standards.*

*In fact, I say "raise" the standards if you ask me.*

*Just teach everybody to swim as a culture and I'm sure you will see a difference in a few years.*

*In fact, since desegregation occurred (AFTER I was born), you can still find the public swimming pool in many cities is still in a certain part of town, but not the other. Unless a new pool was built in your city within the last 40-50 years.*

**Well Shadow, since you know so much:** *What about all the people that grew up in rural areas, and on the coastal cities of America. How do you explain the disparities of black people not being able to swim there?*

*As many as 70% of black folks can't swim. It must be all that heavy muscle mass, the dense bones, the quick twitch fibers, the melanin, the hair, the sun, the moon, the stars. It has to be some genetic fault, right?*

*Nope.*

*It's racism white supremacy, period.*

313

*I don't live in South Carolina, but I have visited the coastline there several times. There is a beautiful community and area called Myrtle Beach, SC. It has been a vacation destination for Soldiers leaving Fort Bragg and Marines leaving Camp Lejeune both in North Carolina for several years. There was even a U.S. Air Force base in Myrtle Beach, SC, and service members (including myself) would stay there for pennies on the dollar, in the base's lodging facilities verses the expensive tourist prices of the beach front. But here is an ugly historical fact.*

*Back in the day, Myrtle Beach was also segregated.*

*It's a multicultural destination now and I love going there. "Except, I will NEVER EVER plan on going there during black bike week!!! You wanna talk about black-on-black crime!"*

*But during segregation many black folks were regulated to the rough parts of the coast line and not the nice beaches, which were reserved for others. Many black people drowned or were seriously injured, in the rough rivers, lakes and parts of some beaches of our country. That just added to the decrease in the numbers of black folk swimming and perceived stereotype that black people "can't" swim.*

*I've heard that even black performers who played and performed for all-white audiences in Myrtle Beach, SC stayed in nearby Atlantic Beach, SC. Whether it was because of choice or segregation I don't know. I've heard stories of famous or rich black folks performing at an all-white establishment and swimming in the pool after hours, or one story has it that a famous black entertainer put her foot in the pool, and they drained and cleaned the entire pool because of it.*

*I don't know if any of those stories are true or urban myths or legends, but what I do know, and you can see for yourself is that in 1964 (during segregation) a hotel manager poured acid in the water (while people were in it) because black people and white integrationist were swimming together in the motel pool. That's how deep racial hatred was (still is) for some people against melinated people of color (black folks).*

*Don't believe me look it up for yourself.*

During that Jim Crow era in America, black people were segregated at many beaches in our country. Along the Eastern Coast near where I-95 runs North through South, from Florida up into Virginia many black folks would travel to Atlantic Beach, SC when they weren't allowed access at the segregated places. Atlantic Beach, or "the Back Pearl" as it was nicknamed around 1934 was formed by mostly Gullah/Geechee people, descendants of slaves who lived for 300 years on the Seas Islands from Wilmington, North Carolina through Jacksonville, Florida.

Black people would travel to Atlantic Beach, South Carolina from Virginia through Florida because it was the vacation spot for Black folks. The hotels, night clubs, restaurants, shops and the pavilion were packed with people every May through September. After integration, many black folks forgot about "the Black Pearl" which welcomed melinated families of color for years when Black folks were shunned and prohibited from vacationing elsewhere. Today, Atlantic Beach remains the only black owned beach in the nation. Nestled between North Myrtle Beach and Myrtle Beach it still awaits all vacationers, but especially the black folks that it welcomed with open arms, when nobody else would accept them.

Give people a chance to learn to swim, change the culture and you won't have to change or lower the standard. In fact, you should raise the standard like I said before "if you ask me".

Back to all those Special Forces studies that said black people can't swim, and are not smart.

Just like the other candidates, I took several swim tests during my Special Forces training days.

One of those tests I remember vividly.

It was during Special Forces Assessment and Selection (SFAS). We took a PT test wearing BDU fatigue uniforms and running shoes. There was a soldier who forgot to bring his sneakers, so while all the rest of us ran in uniform and running sneakers, he ran the whole thing wearing his uniform and in his Army boots. I remember him because he was running "ahead of me" the whole time. Anyway, after the push-ups, the sit-ups and the 2-mile timed run event, we were marched straight to the pool area and only had time to put on our combat boots.

All the black soldiers were ordered to come to the front of the line (many still tired from the run), and then I saw all sorts of civilians and high-ranking members of our chain of command. They were there to observe and watch us perform the swim test portion.

I was numerically assigned to the closest lane to the pool, maybe because of my name or roster number; I don't know.

Anyway, we were instructed to enter the pool on the deep side and tread water, and I did so. Then we are told to swim using any stroke to the end of the pool, turn around and come back, without touching the sides or bottom of the pool (in complete duty uniform including boots). I remember seeing lifeguards "in the pool" and with every other student watching us, it made me feel like; what some of my ancestors must have felt like when they use to put black people in the freaking zoos with animals back in the day.

Just go research "Human Zoo's", see what you come up with. But stop at Human Zoo's, because if you keep researching you'll find the origin of the "dunk tank". Before the dunk tank, they use to throw the baseball at a hole in a curtain where a black person would have his face at (or a black baby would be at). Patrons at carnivals, fairs and circus all across our country would throw these baseballs and try to hit the "nigger baby" or the "African in the face" with a baseball, so the game was called "African Dodger Ball", or just Dodger ball.

So anyway, I swim down to the shallow end and I'm using like only 10% of my energy, because remember I said I was an open water life guard. My high school didn't have an athletic field, but we did have a pool.

I swim back towards the deep end and notice there are three people walking along the side of the pool with me, step for step, while I'm swimming, WTF?!?

I get down to the deep end and remember that I'm not supposed to touch the finish line until the instructor says so. He turns away, making as if he's momentarily distracted talking to someone behind him. So, I stop just short of getting out and submerge myself about an inch below the surface, with my eyes open watching the instructor. When he turns around and tells me to get out of the pool, I spit water up in the air, like a dolphin, as I'm treading water on my back. He tells me to get my "smart ass" out of the water, and I proceed to the next station in the pool.

316

*Then you have the fact that they implied that black people are not as smart as white people, by saying that they have to lower the GT score requirement to get more black soldiers into Special Forces.*

*That's complete Bullshit!*

*As of this writing, I am a high school graduate with about three and one-half years of college. You need 60 college credits to get an Associate's Degree (AA), and about 120 credits to get a Bachelor's of Science (BS) or Bachelors of Arts (BA) degree.*

*I currently have about 106 credit hours.*

*I stated in an earlier chapter that I graduated from a New York inner city public high school called, Theodore Roosevelt High School (TRHS) in the Bronx borough of New York City. It was located directly across the street from Fordham University. From the 1930's to 1960's several people who would later become celebrities attended Theodore Roosevelt High School. Rocky Colavito, who played professional Major League Baseball with the Cleveland Indians. Ace Frehley, founding member of the rock band KISS and former lead guitarist. Chazz Palminteri, an academy award nominated actor; The Last Dragon (1985), A Bronx Tale (1993), The Usual Suspects (1995), and Comedian Jimmie Walker, Let's Do It Again (1975), Airplane! (1980) and the television show Good Times (1974-79).*

*However, in the 1970's "The Bronx was Burning" and TRHS did not escape its devastation and destruction. Children like me, living in New York City's most criminal and violent area, policed by some of the city's most corrupt and violent officers, were zoned to Theodore Roosevelt High School, which had the city's highest dropout rate in 1984. Improvements were negligible until a new principal was hired in 1992. She led the high school to an astonishing turn around until 1999, when she was promoted to superintendent of schools in Central Harlem. TRHS deteriorated rapidly upon her departure, and in 2002 Theodore Roosevelt High School accepted its final freshman class, which graduated at 3%. That's right I said 3%, which means 97% of all freshmen that year would NOT graduate TRHS within 4 years, if at all, and many students would succumb to inner-city violence.*

*The physical building of the former TRHS is still there; but the city board of education closed the high school.*

*Although I was fortunate enough to be receptive to books and learning (1979-83), many of my peers did not make it. I graduated and received a letter of recommendation from my U.S. Congressman to attend the United States Military Academy at West Point (I didn't go because there was no mentor to guide me at that time). Still I was one of the lucky ones.*

*As large as TRHS was, it was once considered the worst and most violent high school in America. There was no football field, no baseball field, no student parking lot, in fact from the outside it resembled a prison.*

*So, I think that would constitute as passing the initial ASVAB test in High School, as taken under adverse conditions, don't you?*

*Anyway, I enlisted in the U.S. Army and my GT score was a 97. That was good, but not good enough for Special Forces training.*

*So, the military did NOT lower the standards to let my black-ass in, they just allowed me (and other soldiers both black and white) the opportunity to "raise" our scores.*

*There used to be a program in the U.S. Army called Basic Skills Education Program (BSEP).*

*It was basically a 2-week program, where they teach you how to take a test. It ain't gonna make you no smarter, but you learn how to take tests. Example, you learn that on one particular portion of a test, you're penalized for incorrect answers, so don't guess if you don't know the answer. On another portion they only count the correct answers, so answer all the easy questions first, then the hard ones, then guess the rest.*

*I finished that 2-week U.S. Army training program, re-took the ASVAB test, and received a new GT score of 126. I was no smarter or dumber within those two weeks, I just was afforded the opportunity to train.*

I'm 6'3" tall, weigh 270 pounds, and my name is Muhammad.

As the preverbal "big blackman" I can tell you a thing or two about racism in America. I still get random hate mail and messages in my inbox.

I was one of the "only" people of color in one of my "specialized" training schools after retirement from the military. It was held in the mountains of West Virginia, in a County where the racial demographics are; 94.99% white, 2.62% black and 1.70% Hispanic.

The composition of the training class was roughly the same.

After retirement of the U.S. military I wasn't making a lot of money, so when I reported for training at this school I did NOT have the disposable income that many of the other class members had. Since I had no "extra" money, I couldn't go drinking and partying with my peers after training, which caused me to be ostracized somewhat, and that lasted up until graduation day.

Now, there were some members of that class that were real stand-ups guys. I'd go to war with those men any day. Most notable good guys were *Soup*, *Nomad, Jonesy* and *Coach (of course that's not their real names).*

But then there were several others who constantly rode me, and exposed any mistake I made in training, in an attempt to make themselves look better. Last day of training, the instructor says, *"Let's get together for a class group photo".* *"Get your shit together, because were only gonna do this once".*

A long time ago, I was informed to never stand on the outside of any group photo.

*"Why"*, I asked, as a young Djedi.

*"Because they will crop your big black ass out the photo"*, I was told.

So, I always attempt to now stand in the middle back, or kneel in the middle front, especially if I'm the only melinated person of color or black guy in the group. Anyway, I'm standing in the middle back of this graduating photo with the rest of the tall guys. I'm just a little taller than most. Then I hear this bullshit, *"Let's all stand up on our tippy toes, so we can block Bilal out from the picture!"* I had not been bestowed the call-sign "Shadow" yet.

He said it jokingly, but he was dead serious *(cracking and fact'n)*, I know because he was one of the guys who rode me during training. So now I'm standing on "my" freaking tippy-toes in an attempt to NOT get blocked out of our group photo, by a bunch of guys who all joined in by standing on their tippy toes in the photo.

✳✳✳

Another time, another place, Security Clearance background investigation.

Investigator asks me, *"Have you ever used drugs in the last seven years?"*

My answer is, **"NO."**

Investigator then asks me, *"Have you ever used drugs in your entire life?"*

My answer is, **"NO! I've never used a drug in my entire life, I don't even know what it feels like to be high. I've never even smoked a cigarette."**

*"But you're black, and you're from the Bronx"*, is what he says to me.

*My mind thinks, "I was raised as a black-moose lamb and I was taught that you [the white man] thought that about me, before I ever met you. No, I never drank alcohol (growing up), never did drugs, never even smoked a cigarette in my life. I ate clean my entire life. As a youth in my teens after the Nation of Islam (NOI), I was briefly involved with a group called "the five percenters", an urban off-shoot of the NOI.*

*I used to believe that men like you were part of the wicked 10% of the population that tries to manipulate and control the 85% of the masses of people, and that the 5% of the people like us knew the truth. I had to read the labels of everything I ever ate. If I couldn't pronounce something, I couldn't eat it. In high school, I distinctly remember some of the other brothers surrounding me in a cypher (an intimidating circle, for knowledge or violence, you never know) where I was instructed to recite todays mathematics.*

*The Black Man Is God!*
*The Original Asiatic Blackman Of the Planet Earth!*
*The Earth Is 93 Million Miles from The Sun!*

*It Weighs 6 Sextillion Tons!*

*WHAT YOU GOT IN YA HAND SUN?*
*"A Twinkie", I reply.*

*MANIFEST YOURSELF (meaning read the ingredients)!*
*I read out loud: Enriched Bleached Wheat Flour [Reduced Iron, "B" Vitamins (Thiamine Mononitrate (B1), Riboflavin (B2), Folic Acid], Water, Sugar, Corn Syrup, High Fructose Corn Syrup, Partially Hydrogenated Vegetable And/Or Animal Shortening... POW, BAM, POW, SLAP, PUNCH, KICK, KICK, SLAP, KICK, PUNCH... as soon as I got to the words ANIMAL SHORTENING all the brothers in the circle jumped me.*

*They started beating my ass, punching me, kicking me, teaching me, YOU OUT HERE EATING THAT FUCKING SWINE! YOU'RE EATING THAT PIG! YOU EATING THAT PORK!!! THAT'S WHAT THE WHITEMAN WANTS YOU TO DO! HE WANTS YOU TO KILL YOURSELF! EAT THAT BULLSHIT!!! DRINK HIS POISION!!! SMOKE CIGARETTES!!! HE WANTS YOU TO DO DRUGS!!! WE NEED WARRIORS IN THE NATION OF GODS, AND EARTHS AND YOU DOWN WITH DAT BULLSHIT!!! These are just some of the thoughts I was thinking as I repeated to him, "No Sir I have never done drugs in my life.*

✳✳✳

Another time, another place.

I'm in Iraq and it's 2008. Barrack Obama has just been elected the 44th President of the United States of America, and you would think that someone personally slapped their momma. We're in the ready room about to receive a mission briefing, I'm there early, because one of the many stereotypes about black people is that we are always late.

Therefore, I make it a habit to NEVER be late, to nothing.

I will show up an hour before I'm supposed to and read a book while I'm waiting, but I ain't gonna be late if I have anything to do with the arrival. I teach that to employees and affiliates of my company to this day. There is no such thing as an excuse to be late. I tell them all that, I bet if I said you get your $10,000-dollar bonus tomorrow morning at 08:00 hours (8am) you'd be there.

But if you're one minute late you don't get nothing. I bet yo ass won't be late then! You'll sleep in this office if you have too, because you don't want to be late!

*If something is important to you, you will find a way. If it's not, you'll find an excuse.*

As I'm sitting in the ready room and the first one comes up to me.

*"Shadow why did y'all elect Obama?!?"*

**Huh? What da hell you talking about? It's not like all black people had a secret meeting, and we all decided to elect Obama. If they had a meeting back home, my black ass is over here with you bro?**

*"I mean, they had to all have voted for him just because he was black"*, he says to me!

*"John McCain is a freaking War Hero for Christs Sake."*

I reply, **"man even "if" every eligible black person voted for Barrack Obama, he still wouldn't have won, because black folks only make up 14% of the population."**

He storms away, mad. Not at me, but at life.

Then another one approaches me.

*"You know Stinky is going on leave, maybe he'll get rid our problem for us".*

Stinky was our Designated Defensive Marksman (DDM) or Sniper, and he was "implying" that maybe Stinky would shoot someone. He was also incorrect in assuming that I thought like him. The hatred was that real. I totally ignored that guy and he went away.

He thought, just like a lot of people incorrectly think:
THAT ALL BLACK PEOPLE WILL ALWAYS VOTE FOR THE BLACK CANIDATE, NO MATTER WHAT!

**Well just ask many of the Black Conservative or Republican Candidates and personalities what percentage of the "black vote or support" do they get?** Whether they be Tim Scott, Clarence Thomas, Herman Cain, Alan Keyes,

322

Michael Steele, Don King, Larry Elder, J.C. Watts, Armstrong Williams, Stacey Dash or whoever it is. Black folks as a whole will normally vote for the Democratic Candidate, not necessarily the "Black Candidate".

Me, I'm a Registered Independent, neither Republican nor Democrat.

I do not want to be locked into voting a straight party ticket. I'd rather research each candidate individually; whether it's for the County Dog Catcher, Water & Soil Conservationist, State Governor, or U.S. President. Then I'll vote for the candidate that best fulfills my personal needs.

My mind was currently on the upcoming mission.

Whenever we went on a mission, we were wired so tight it would take a day or so to come back down to earth. Mentally when you're on a mission, you are looking at everything and everyone as a potential threat. I felt absolutely no racial animosity from my teammates when we were on a mission, none at all.

Even when I was the only black guy on a team.

The bull shit started whenever there was down time.

✳✳✳

*"Hey Shadow, man what kind of music do you listen too?"*
**Depends on what you're playing bro.**

*"Do you listen to Rock?"*
**Yeah, I can get with some Classic Rock.**

*"What you know about Classic Rock?"*
**I can get with the Beatles, The Who, The [Rolling] Stones, Eagles, The Doors, Santana, Van Halen...**

*"What you know about Van Halen Shadow?"*
**I can get with David Lee Roth, you know, "JUMP", "PANAMA", the guitars on "HOT FOR TEACHER", man! But I'm not really into that Sammy Hagar "I CAN'T DRIVE 55", you can keep that type of Van Halen.**

(Sort of like how "some" black folks like big Luther Vandross, not little Luther. Or songs by sad depressed Mary J. Blige not happy Mary. Or the Bobby Brown version of New Edition, not the Johnny Gill version of New Edition).

*"Man, Shadow you're cool. You're not like some of the other guys."*
**I'm thinking to myself, "what other [black] guys, I'm the only one here"? So, he must be comparing me to some other "brothers" he has come across in his lifetime.**

I complete our conversation and prepare for another mission. Part of that preparation, in addition to vehicle and weapons maintenance, meant preparing my music playlist. I would run an ear bud down from my ear, down my pants leg into a portable iPod mini I used to carry and listen to that on missions. "COME ON [Mother Fucker]" by the Notorious B.I.G. and "HOLLER IF YA HEAR ME" by 2Pac Shakur were on constant repeat in my ears, over my comms, inside my Peltors!

I never had a racial incident while I was out on mission, not once, NEVER!

We joked, we talked, but our focus was so dialed in, and switched on, that we didn't have time for no racist bullshit. American lives were at risk and we were the "sheepdogs", the defenders of the sheep against the wolves out there. Whenever we went out, there were different people assigned to different missions.

There is one vehicle in a PSD or diplomatic motorcade that you don't ever want to fuck with! That's the vehicle that is designated as the "Hate Truck".

I'm not going into details about mission profiles, TTP's or which vehicle is the CAT vehicle. But I will tell you that if something goes horribly wrong, like an ambush, or a deliberate Attack on Motorcade (AOM), or even worse, an Attack on [the] Principle (AOP), the guys in the "hate truck" are designed to get the rest of the guys, who are protecting the big guy (the principal) out of danger, off the X, and out of the kill zone!

If the men protecting the big guy are considered "sheepdogs" then the guys in the "Hate Truck" are considered Silverback Gorillas! *Thanks Hammer Man for putting together such a bad ass QRF crew in the hate-truck when Raven 23 became Spartan 23.*

The only music being played in that truck is Megadeath, Metallica and Hardcore Gangsta Rap. Everyone in that truck felt like we were definitely gonna die, or are already dead. We had all done our Last Will & Testament, the Powers-of-Attorneys, and necessary paperwork back home. Some guys use to mix NO-Xplode with Red Bull's, Monsters or Rip It's energy drinks. Heck we all rode with our own body bags. We didn't have a death wish, we just resigned ourselves to that inevitable fate, and planned on saving everyone else if called upon, even at the cost of our own lives (and taking a whole lot of bad guys with us).

Those were some of the guys that I served with.

Fought and bled with, and watched some of them die serving for the greater good.

And, yes some of them were racist.

✳✳✳

Back during the days of heavy fighting during the war, there was a difference between the Department of Defense (DoD) guys, and the Department of State (DoS) guys.

One of the big differences was that all the DoD soldiers, sailors, airmen, marines, coast guardsmen, civilians and DoD contractors (whether Flour, KBR, or whoever) were all under the punitive restrictions of General Order Number 1. It forbids, amongst other things; possessing, consuming, introducing, purchasing, selling, transferring or manufacturing any alcoholic beverages. I understood that, and I understood its necessity in a combat zone.

Members under the DoS or U.S. State Department, were NOT under that rule.

They are now.

But back then we weren't. Many people don't realize that there was a U.S. Embassy and DoS presence BEFORE the war started, and there will be one long after all the Service Members are gone, and the War is over.

It wasn't like we could drink and go on a mission, that was strictly prohibited.

But many times, after returning back inside the wire, from a long mission, guys would loosen up with a cold one. Especially after a team got hit, and men died.

I had several roommates over the years, because normally we were doubled up, in whatever bunking facilities we were assigned too. One particular roommate I had was racist. I mean not like a regular part time racist, but I mean a real true believer in his cause. I knew that some of the killings that occurred in combat were authorized because the insurgents were LBG's. If the same combat engagements happened in Bosnia, instead of Haiti or Iraq, I know from experience that some of that shit would not hold up to scrutiny.

I know, I've known men who were racist skinheads, and klansmen and whatever else they professed to be. It's kind of hard to hide your beliefs when your bunking in the same room as someone.

I knew a contractor (who was my roommate), who had the nazi SS tattoo branded on his body. I've seen men who "earned" their spider web tattoos on their elbows by killing a black person before, not like these young people today, who get tattoos without knowing their true meaning or origin.

I confronted my roommate about his SS tattoo, and he tried to tell me that it stood for USMC Scout Sniper.

That's bullshit.

I was stationed in Europe with the military for three-years in my past, several times "we" U.S. military forces were stationed in former German military bases and barracks. So, I know what I'm talking about.

Over the months, he had to bunk with me in the same trailer, behind them large 20-foot-tall reinforced Alaska Barrier T-Walls (the 3-foot-tall T-walls, the small one's were called Jersey Barriers, and the original 12-foot-tall T-walls ones were called Texas Barriers, they were originally called Bremer Barriers). Every moment of our movement was monitored, outside the wire on mission and back on the base. When on missions there were a gazillion cameras and microphones recording everything in every vehicle. On the base, we keep radios on us, with everyone monitoring them 24 hours a day, the operations center was notified if you left the area, whether it was for chow, or to the PX, or to the gym.

**"Shadow enroute to the small arms repair shop"**, is what I would say over the radio whenever I was going to the gym to work-out. It was a code, because believe it or not, we couldn't work out at various times of the day.

It got so bad that the less people started dying, the more stupid rules the higher ups made. Someone even decided that we were physically "too big" and had all the "heavy dumbbells" removed from the gym. Yes, some of the people we protected when their safety wasn't as pertinent because deadly attacks may have dropped down to five or six per month, instead of 25-50 per day, thought the people protecting them were too big and strong! The dumbbell weights in the gym at mancamp use to go up to 150-pounds each. Someone in authority prohibited anything above 80-pound dumbbells from being in the gym.

Anyway, because of the guard communication channel, we always knew when someone got in trouble, because they were called to the Operational TOC in such a manner that EVERYONE on the radio would say, *"What the heck did he do?"*

You might hear over the radio, *"Bubba report to the TOC with your Shift Leader."* You knew right then, that Bubba did something and he was going to be sent home.

Well, like I said guys would drink and party in our own compound after duty hours, and I heard my roommates name called over the commo-net. I knew that he had made a mistake, but I didn't know what it was yet.

Rumor got back to me, that he got into it with a high-ranking DoS official, who happened to be a black man, and called him a nigger. When asked to clarify himself, he repeated the derogatory slur.

I can't think of a faster way to get fired, then to call your black boss "a nigger", with the "a" or the "er".

When he comes back to pack his bags, and explain to me what happened, he says, *"Shadow man I don't know what happened, you know I'm not a racist, right?"*

I looked straight in his eyes and told him this to his face.

*I said brother you don't have a race problem, you have a drinking problem, and if you don't get your alcoholism under wraps, you're gonna get yourself killed.*

I know how he got to be the way he was, because he was taught hatred.

I was taught it too.

Although I wasn't taught hatred to the level that I would want to kill someone just because of the color of their skin. Both of my parents taught me to be happy and to be proud to be black. To not succumb to the pressures of society that teach everything black is bad, and everything white is good. Remember in earlier chapters I explained that my father was born down in Birmingham, Alabama in the deep south. That he was sent up north to live; because the kkk was gonna hang him, back in the 1940's and 50's. Let that sink in for a moment.

The klan was gonna lynch my dad, why do you think he became so radical, and what do you think he taught me?

My mother always told me and my siblings about the time in the 1950's that she and one of her brothers had to go down south to live for a few years with family in Bamberg, South Carolina. About how she went from being an innocent little city girl in New York with friends who were Asian, Caucasian, Hispanic, Black, whatever; to picking cotton until her hands bled in the cotton fields of the south.

On the same farm (former plantation) where our ancestors where enslaved and some are buried. She explained about the deep racism that she experienced, personally. About how Mr. Charlie rode around the plantation, I mean farm, on a big white horse. How as a young girl, she met her grandmothers-grandmother who was still alive at the time, who had been a formerly enslaved person. What do you think she taught me about race relationships between black and white people?

So, I knew exactly how my roommate got to feel the way he did, because he was taught that way. He was surrounded by other people who felt the same way he did, so they reinforced that idea. He survived in a system that demonized melinated people of color and it was easy to become the way he did.

*I told him that there were people over here that hated, short people.*

*That there were people over here that hated, left handed people.*

We had a guy on our team that was half Korean and half Irish. Visualize that one.

*I told him, that most people have prejudices which is actually; to "pre-judge" someone. But you have to but find out for yourself, if what you were taught was actually true.*

*I told him that most people can keep their personal bigotry, prejudices or nontraditional beliefs in check, just enough to survive in the world with other people of different races, religions, creeds, languages and colors.*

*However, I told him that once that alcohol got in his system, he was no longer in control, and whatever hatred was in his heart, was gonna come to the surface.*

*I told him to please go seek some help for his alcoholism, and to please stay in touch with me.*

I didn't want him to be another of the almost 22 veterans a day that commit suicide because of the horrors that many veterans carry in their minds from some of the things they have seen. Or from the perceived lack of treatment programs or assistance from the U.S. Veterans Administration. No matter how he felt, he was still a military veteran, and this was just a civilian job. He could find another one, but he had to get his alcoholism in check.

*I even helped him write a resume to find a new job.*

He stayed in touch and months later he called me.

*He said that I was right, and that he was in trouble. He said that he got really drunk and the last thing he remember he was traveling. He was now in another state; all his money was gone and he didn't really know where he was.*

*He got religion right there, and gave his life mission over to God.*

*He became a born again Christian and hasn't touched alcohol since.*

He now travels all over the world, helping reform people who use to think like he did.

He is a much better person and has renounced his ways of the past. I am so proud of him, and glad that I was used by our ancestors to be an instrument in his redemption. I am so glad for him, for his spirituality, whatever you believe, just believe in something and love your fellow man.

I know Hindus, and Buddhist, and Christians, and Jews, and Muslims, and people from all other faiths and walks of life. When I go, if every one of my friends, and people who knew me where able to show up for the services around the Fort Bragg, North Carolina area, it would probably look like the freaking United Nations.

There are some former contractors I have served with that I speak too all the time.

Then there are some that wouldn't give me the time of day.

A very famous national preacher once gave a sermon, maybe you've seen it on social media like I have. He explains in detail the differences between the 3 types of friends a person has; (1) Confidants, (2) Constituents and (3) Comrades. Without explaining his video, he can do it better than I can, and you can go look it up for yourself, he highlights the fact that friends of yours who are in the Comrade category; are people who are AGAINST what you are against.

So, since there is a common enemy in many countries in the middle east that we must come together to defeat, many security contractors are close as brothers overseas, where our lives are literally in each other's hands. But once we return back to the world, some of them do NOT have a multicultural point of view.

One of them even told another brother who served overseas with me, *"Hey listen what we had over there was over there, don't call me no more"*.

I've talked about the SOF community and the Security Contractor community in this chapter. I've highlighted race relationship issues, which were a constant but small part of the overall big picture. If that time were to exist, I would gladly go over there again and serve with the same men & women who put it all on the line, for the greater good of saving American lives, and the lives of our fellow coalition, allied and "friendly" host nation forces (whether they were friendly Iraqi or another government).

But when you talk about the military as a whole, and the U.S. Army specifically I have a quick experiment I'd like you to look at.

✳✳✳

The U.S. Army like the rest of the military operates with a Chain of Command. That is the succession of leaders, who are in legally authorized positions of command from a soldiers first-line supervisor, all the way up to the Commander-In-Chief of our Armed Forces (the President of the United States). So, a Private can say, that he follows the lawful orders of his Team Leader who may be a Corporal. That Corporal would follow the lawful orders of a Squad Leader, who may be a Staff Sergeant.

The Staff Sergeant as a SQUAD LEADER would have two immediate superior leaders; his PLATOON LEADER (PL), normally a Second Lieutenant who can give and issue DIRECT ORDERS because his commissioning authority comes straight from the President of the United States, via the Uniform Code of Military Justice (UCMJ). He would also have a PLATOON SERGEANT (PSG), normally a Sergeant First Class who can give LAWFUL ORDERS. The PSG is a member of the NCO support channel that compliments the Chain of Command at almost every level. Sort of like a mother and father (parent team).

The Second Lieutenant who is the Platoon Leader would have an immediate superior leader; his Company Commander, normally a Captain, again who can give DIRECT ORDERS because his commissioning authority comes straight from the President of the United States via the UCMJ and a Company First Sergeant who can give LAWFUL ORDERS, who is a member of the NCO Support Channel.

The Captain who is the Company Commander would have an immediate superior leader; his Battalion Commander, normally a Lieutenant Colonel, again who can give DIRECT ORDERS because his commissioning authority comes straight from the President of the United States via the UCMJ and a Battalion Command Sergeant Major who can give LAWFUL ORDERS, who is a member of the NCO Support Channel. This will repeat all the way up to the

President of the United States, who is the Commander in Chief of all of our Armed Forces. Or more specifically, this Chain of Command flows downhill (not up). So, Typically the Chain of Command will look something like this:

*Sample Chain of Command*

| CHAIN OF COMMAND | NCO SUPPORT CHANNEL |
|---|---|
| **President of the United States** <br> Civilian | |
| **Secretary of the Defense** <br> Civilian | |
| **Secretary of the Army** <br> Civilian | |
| **Chief of Staff of the Army** <br> GEN/O-10 | **Sergeant Major of the Army** <br> SMA/E-9 |
| **FORSCOM Commander** <br> GEN/O-10 | **FORSCOM Command Sergeant Major** <br> CSM/E-9 |
| **Corps Commander** <br> LTG/O-9 | **Corps Command Sergeant Major** <br> CSM/E-9 |
| **Division Commander** <br> MG/O-8 | **Division Command Sergeant Major** <br> CSM/E-9 |
| **Brigade Commander** <br> COL/O-6 | **Brigade Command Sergeant Major** <br> CSM/E-9 |
| **Battalion Commander** <br> LTC/O-5 | **Battalion Command Sergeant Major** <br> CSM/E-9 |
| | |
| **Company Commander** <br> CPT/O-3 | **Company First Sergeant** <br> 1SG/E-8 |
| **Platoon Leader** <br> 2LT/O-1 | **Platoon Sergeant** <br> SFC/E-7 |
| **Squad Leader** <br> SSG/E-6 | Squad Leader <br> SSG/E-6 |
| | **Team Leader** <br> SGT/E-5 |
| **Private John Q. Citizen** <br> PFC/E-3 | |

*Notice: Private First Class Citizen's Squad Leader is a member of both PFC Citizen's Chain of Command and PFC Citizen's NCO Support Channel*

I noticed very early in my military career, there was a Chain of Command board inside every unit I've ever served in.

They posted all the photos, of all the members of every units Command Team (Chain of Command & NCO Support Channel) starting with the Company Commander and the First Sergeant, all the way up to the current President of the United States. Or more accurately; starting with the President, all the way down to their units Commander & First Sergeant.

Ask any Soldier who his/her Chain of Command is, and he/she should be able to name them all in sequential order. Because, their names and photos are on the wall of their unit. Now I cannot say that every single unit in the entire U.S. Army does this, but I have never seen a unit "without" this chain of command board in my 20-years of active duty.

Melinated service members who not members of the dominate society, have held command positions in each and every level I've seen. Whether they were Hispanic, Asian, Black, or whatever. I've seen black Colonels, Generals, heck the former President of the United States was a black man.

However, by overwhelming numbers I've notice a similar trend, based upon the racial composition and demographics of the leaders on that board.

Almost all the Commanders in the Chain of Command were men of european decent, and almost all the members of the NCO Support Channel were melinated people of color in general, and black or latino people specifically.

Again, there have been exceptions in every position. We as a people (all people) have made great strides and progress, almost to the point where we are almost NOT talking about the first black person to do this, or the first black person to do that.

But I cannot deny the truth as I saw it.

Now, I retired from the U.S. military over 10 years ago. I'm sure that someone will contact me after the release of this book, and show me that the overwhelming majority of commissioned officers in the military are NOT members of european decent, but melinated people of color.

They will show me that minority members of the military (I despise using that term "minority" because melinated people of color are not the minority population on this earth), but they will be glad to prove me wrong, and show that my view of the racial composition and demographics of many unit's chain of command is not only equal to the minority representation of the country (14% black folks), but even better representation in the commissioned officer ranks

I'll wait.

✳✳✳

I don't believe that the military has a race issue. At least not like it was in the past.

The military that I know and loved is probably the leading institution in America when it comes to leading the way in progress and positive strides in regard to race. There is one very important reason for that.

That's because no matter how much of a social experiment the civilian community will try to make the military, it is designed to defend our nation in times of war.

Bottom line, that means killing the enemy and destroying things.

At the end of the day, any Commander worth his weight is only gonna ask for one thing from his subordinates. That is to go do your job or mission, period.

The enemy don't care what your personal differences are!

There are people who hate American citizens and our way of life with every fiber of their being. During the mission called Operation IRAQI FREEDOM there was a woman who worked on an American military base as a barber. You know what those insurgents did to her?

They cut her fucking arms off, because she touched American service members.

Hatred is taught, in every language, culture and way of life.

Some soldiers who have not been taught to be professional, cannot do their job without hatred. They must demonize their adversary and make the enemy less than human in their eyes In Order To (IOT) kill. They must call the enemy gooks, and rag heads, and japs, and niggers, and other vile dehumanizing terms IOT justify the removal of them in their minds, because to them, they have reduced them to something less than human.

You ever see a real professional fighter?

Whether they are in a cage, ring or whatever they don't hate their opponents. They will do whatever it takes to defeat their opponents, but as soon as the fight is over they may embrace, because they understood what hatred (or the dark side) would do to a human.

You don't ever want to go to that dark place, because I have known men who have and some have never come back.

Yes, I know that evil has manifested itself in some humans. Heck, I know that everyone walking around ain't even human. There is a difference between "man and mankind". But someone must deal with the evil that exist in this world, and there was a time when I was fully capable of doing just that.

There was a time when I wasn't only a sheepdog, protecting the sheep from the wolf. I was a damn silverback gorilla who was happier "outside the wire" in so-called enemy territory than I was inside the fence.

**Sometimes you have to communicate with people in a language they understand.**

- **You can't negotiate with bullies.**
- **You can't bargain with them.**

**Sometimes, some people just need killing!**

*Now, put this into proper context. Shadow did NOT say to kill all bullies. I am saying in an environment like I operated in for several years, where people have killed innocent people, and are determined to do it again. They will even make a propaganda video of themselves "sawing your head off" while you beg and pled for your life. Well to stop some people like that, you just have to kill them, period.*

***

But this chapter is about more than just black or white. So, let me lighten this up a bit, and talk about another subject.

Let's talk about sex.

There was an incident that happened at the NCO Academy when I was an instructor (SGL) there. Well, I had several incidents.

To illustrate the safety requirements and mandatory precautions you should take, even in a training environment. I took an artillery simulator and switched it with an inert M18A1 Claymore mine we used for training. When the soldier clacked the M-57 firing device, I'm sure he crapped his pants. As this loud BOOM!!! echoed throughout the training environment.

***

Another time, another teaching lesson.

We're in the field and my teaching squad of 16 students (bigger than a normal squad, smaller than a platoon) is organized in a Patrol Base (PB) covering a perimeter of 360 degrees. I tell them if someone trips a warning flare to fire one magazine of blank ammo in their sector, fire from left to right, then right to left, and then change magazines and prepare to follow their Patrol Leader's instructions. Since each fighting position had overlapping fields of fire with the adjacent, the entire perimeter should have been covered.

That night I low crawled into their Patrol Base (PB) around 03:00, and everyone is asleep. I have some soft skill students CS and CSS (band, admin, cooks) mixed in with the combat arms CA (infantry, engineers, artillery). But none of them are pulling security, some of them are even sleeping in the field with no boots on.

So, what did I do?

I low-crawled to each position and secured their individual weapon from their vicinity (since it was laying on the ground unsecure) and crawled back to the center of the PB. Then I did it again with the next student, and again, and again

336

until I had everyone's weapon. Some soldiers slept with the sling wrapped around their hand, but I had removed the weapon from the sling.

Then I had time, so I collected combat boots.

I took all of the boots if they slept without them and put them in a pile as well.

Then I awoke the entire patrol by blowing-up their PB with pyrotechnics and explosive simulators and scared the heck of them. I made them run to their alternate PB which was their alternate plan.

Then I asked them, *"What happened to your weapons? Why didn't anyone return fire when the PB was attacked. Why did it take so long to get to this alternate PB in the dark?"*

When they would get back to the original PB for the AAR, I would shine a light on the pile of captured weapons, I would explain that somebody better be up & awoke, no matter what!

Even in garrison there is a Fire Guard, a Charge of Quarters (CQ) or a Staff Duty NCO (SDNCO) on duty.

I explained that this was an open post (back then it was, Fort Bragg is now a closed post) and any hunter or wanderer could stumble upon this patrol base. Ex-soldiers who have been kicked out of the military due to drugs, and Bad Conduct would rob other soldiers in the field at gun point because they knew we were training with blank ammunition.

I explained how many of our countries adversaries in what we call Third World Countries, only need two things to be combat effective; that's a weapon in their hands and some flip flops on their feet. I explained how they could not run barefoot across the battlefield with any level of effectiveness without their damn boots on.

Back at the headquarters, I have to see the Commandant again. Sergeant Bilal, *"Why are student running around the field with no shoes on? Where is that at in the P.O.I.?"*

But the most memorable one occurred before a parachute jump.

In addition to being one of the largest NCO Academies in the U.S. Army, Fort Bragg was also home of the bulk of the U.S. Army's Airborne Forces. Units like; the XVIII Airborne Corps, the 82nd Airborne Division, the 3rd Special Forces Group (back then 7th Special Forces Group) and all the other Airborne units on post (that are no longer airborne). So, all the students in the NCO Academy went to the field by aircraft into Hurtz Drop Zone on the other side of Simmons Army Airfield, near the intersection of McArthur and Johnson Farm Roads.

All the airborne qualified soldiers would conduct a CH-47 parachute jump into the PLDC FTX on Hurtz DZ, and all the non-airborne soldiers would conduct an air assault and air-land by CH-47 Chinook and UH-60 Blackhawk Helicopters onto Hurtz LZ.

As one of the jumpmasters on the jumpmaster team, it was my duty to inspect the soldiers who were rigged up with all their gear to insure they were safely ready to jump.

I was inspecting a soldier who happened to be extremely short, I'm talking maybe 4'11" or something like that. I remember that another student, a Corporal was watching me like a hawk.

When I got to the point when I had to inspect the soldiers adjustable leg straps, to see if they were twisted, cut, frayed or incorrectly routed around their left & right thigh, I could see where they were attached on the rear of the parachute harness just by looking, because, like I said the soldier was extremely small. I looked at both leg straps from a few inches away, continued my inspection and the soldier had a satisfactory jump.

I get called to see the Commandant, again.

*"Sergeant Bilal, did you not place two fingers inside the space between the leg and the adjustable leg strap of the parachutist and trace them up to the adjusting buckle, and then do the same with the other leg?!?"*

**Sergeant Major, NO - I did not, because I could see with my own eyes, there was no reason to stick or jam my two-fingers in there when I'm looking right at the entire strap.**

*"Well Sergeant, did the fact that, that parachutist was a female soldier have anything to do with it?"*

**Huh? Sergeant Major what-what did you say?**

*"You heard me. Where you intimidated because she was a female soldier. Would you have done it any different if it was a short male soldier?"*

**Sergeant Major, Yes. If it was a male soldier, I wouldn't have even thought about what I was doing, I would have just did it.**

*"Well that female soldier deserves the same treatment, no more no less! Her safety, and her life is just as valuable!"*

**I am thinking out loud (to myself), I just don't understand what difference jamming my fingers between the legs of this female soldier to see and feel the adjustable legs straps would have been?**

*"Well for starters, if her leg strap became undone, she could have fell to her death. So, I have a corrective training for you."*

**The Command Sergeant Major is reading my mind now, because I know I didn't say anything out loud!**

So next weekend I report for my extra duty corrective training.

Airborne qualified soldiers "on jump status" must perform at least one satisfactory parachute jump from an aircraft, while in-flight at least once every three months, in order to remain "current on jump status" and receive the "extra jump pay". Sometime through no fault of the soldier, their parent unit will not have a scheduled parachute jump before they become a "pay hurt" or "pay loss" status. But because Fort Bragg is the home of the Airborne, there is always another unit conducting a "Fun Jump" on the weekend, at least once a month.

That's right show up, and jump out of an airplane for fun, on your day off.

My corrective training.

As a Jumpmaster (JM), I am qualified to assist "this current JM team" with the JMPI inspections of all the parachutist before they board their aircraft.

However, I am instructed to stand at this station and "every female parachutist on Fort Bragg is directed to go to my station until I get over my fear of inspecting female soldiers".

*WTF?!?*

Many of them ate it up, *"Oh he scared of women?!?"*

*"Do me next?!?"*

Especially the final jumpmaster seal of approval, where the JM smacks the parachutist on his/her fourth point of contact. You can believe that I never had a problem with a jumper during JMPI ever again, male or female. In fact, I became so thorough, that when I went to my next duty station after the NCO Academy, I eventually became that Airborne Brigade's "Master Jumpmaster" I was that good.

✱✱✱

**Speaking of females, since this is the time, the place and I am discussing my memoirs, my semi-autobiography. Let me tell you my position on abortion. Regardless of the current laws in this country, I have a position. Just because something is "legal" doesn't make it right.**

Segregation of people by race was "legal" in this country at one time before, where black people couldn't eat here, or sleep there, or even use the bathroom in some places without having to go to the side of the road someplace.

Prohibition was "legal" in this country at one time, where you couldn't manufacture, transport or sell intoxicating liquors (alcohol) within the United States. No beer, no wine, no liquor, no spirits. Now, I do agree that there is a problem with alcoholism in our country, but I don't think the government should make a law preventing people from consuming beer, wine, liquor or whatever it is they choose to consume. *The U.S. Congress also agreed, so they repealed that constitutional amendment with another one called the 18th amendment.*

Even slavery was "legal" at one point in this country, where advertisements for the sale of human beings was advertised in the local newspapers, and black folks were auctioned off like cattle in this country.

So just because something is currently legal, don't make it right.

**I am for Pro-life.**

I am not Pro-Choice, although I do understand why some people are that way.

If you will bear with me and let me explain my position, you may not totally agree with me, but you may begin to understand why I feel this way. Here are my three of my reasons.

FIRST, I have been personally affected by abortion, twice. Let me start out by saying that, I have children and I love them with everything I have. They know that, and if they ever forget I'll remind them that I use to change their shitty diapers when they were just babies and couldn't even do for themselves. But for whatever reason, I don't have any biological children. That is the one regret that I have in this world. I know several friends and even family members who are paying extreme amounts of "child support" to their ex-wives and baby mommas. Some of them wish they could trade places with me. Wish they had the freedom of disposable income, the ability to make a decent living without child support garnishments. Heck, I have family members who were "imprisoned for months" because they lacked the financial means to pay child support. *So how much money do you think they were making in jail?* Zero, nothing! And while they were incarcerated for nonpayment of child support, the amount they did owe was growing because the amount of arrears was gaining compounding interest penalties every day. Many of them constantly tell me, "Yo B (Shadow) you don't know what it's like, I wish I had [been dealt] your hand, I'd throw mines in!" But little do they know, I would give everything I have away just to produce a child. To be there when the baby is born. To have another me created in this world.

If you have children, you may not know it: but you're the luckiest person that ever lived. Because self-preservation is the key element in this world. Every plant, every animal, every person wants to live. But everything also wants to keep on living, and we do that through our offspring. I don't have that, so maybe that's one of the reasons I am so driven to write this story.

No matter what religion you subscribe to, or if you are a spiritual person rather than a religious person, and don't subscribe to any particular religious doctrine at all; there are three basic elements we are all inherently taught to survive on this planet.

341

1. Don't kill each other.
2. Treat each other the way you would want to be treated.
3. Go forth, be fruitful and multiply.

Well, it doesn't matter what people tell me, **that all the killing I was involved in was in defense of my country**. That I killed bad people, in defense of good people. The bottom line is that "I", have to meet our maker one day, when this is all over. I must answer to our creator for what I have done, period.

As far as the second one goes, well. I have known some pretty freaky people in my time here on this planet. I have been a professional bodyguard and witnessed things you would not believe, even if I had the pictures to show you (I don't). I have known people who were into sadomasochism where they get sexual pleasure from receiving pain inflicted upon themselves.

I have known rich people, High Net Worth (HNW) individuals and very rich people Very High Net Worth (VHNW) individuals, who received sexual pleasure from the humiliation they "pay" other people to do to them. Vile disgusting acts, some involving urine and consumption of other people's human defecation. Some of them really, really get off on that.

So, I don't necessarily subscribe to the *"treat others the way you want to be treated"* mantra. I don't even like to tell a lot of people, to do what makes you happy. Because I have known people who were *"happy killing"*, period.

If there was not a position where they could go and kill, like a combat zone or some other profession, guess what they do? They take a vacation and go into the mountains and hunt bears and other wild animals, not for their meat to eat, not to reduce the population that is endangering other wildlife (like wolves attacking deer or sheep).

No, they go out and hunt and kill wild animals because they really, really get a thrill out of killing, period. So, I really don't want them to "do what makes them happy" in an everyday normal life setting. So again, I'll have to ask the big guy upstairs, the grand architect of the universe about that one too.

Then finally, the go be fruitful and multiply part.

These are the two instances where it has affected me more than you'll ever know. The first time was in the early 1980's when I was stationed out in the

342

Pacific Northwest, way before I met my first wife. I was dating a girl and didn't know she became pregnant.

My military unit went on a mission to Korea, it was in connection with Exercise BALIKATAN or Exercise COBRA GOLD, or some other training exercise in the Orient. We deployed to the region called "the far east" for training, and we returned back to the Seattle area in a month or two.

Everyone who is familiar with the way the U.S. Army works, knows that U.S. Army soldiers, when they get transferred to OCONUS to South Korea, they will be there for at least 1-year unaccompanied tour of duty. The other military branches of service many have another method or policy, but this is how the U.S. Army, did it back in the day.

We also didn't have cellphones and technology like we have now.

So, without being able to communicate with me, she only knew when she went to visit me at the military base I was stationed at, and was told that I *"went to Korea."*

Mistakenly thinking that I left her (because that's what a lot of soldiers did, get a girl pregnant and then run away from their responsibilities), with her thinking that I was gone for a year, and probably moving on to another military base after Korea, and never coming back to her: she went and got an abortion.

To her surprise I returned in a month or two (maybe 45 days), and she was sad.

She was always crying, and I couldn't understand what was happening. When she told me about the abortion, I was devastated. I didn't know what to feel.

I just knew that I never wanted to feel the way I did at that time, ever again in my life. I often wonder what a 35-year old version of me would look like today, if it was a boy or girl.

Guess I'll never know.

The second time was years later when I was with "another woman" who I don't like to talk about, because the pain of reliving those memories hurts so much. We were together for years and she had a miscarriage.

I went through all the pains and emotions of any couple that has a miscarriage when they are really both planning on starting a happy life together and making a family. Well, I later found out that she did NOT have a miscarriage. I found out from her "best friend" at the time, that she had an abortion.

That she used her best friends "medical identification" to get it done. That she had an affair while we were together with another man, and didn't know if the baby was his or mine, so she aborted the child: without telling me.

Those two instances cemented in my mind that the institution of abortion is wrong, and I would never support it.

I understand that if a woman is raped, that she shouldn't have to be forced to have that child, that was conceived against her will. But I'm not talking about that, I'm talking about the times legal abortion affected me.

The SECOND reason I am a Pro-life advocate, and not a Pro-choice person is because I have seen enough death and destruction on this planet.

To "add race" to the equation, I was always told and taught that since the early 1930's and 1940's the Most Honorable Elijah Muhammad used to teach black folks to have large families of many children. I was told that he taught black families to have at least 7 children, because of the overt racist society of that time would kill many black people. Remember black folks back then were still being incarcerated for long periods of time, for minor offenses or set-up on fabricated charges. The attitudes and life styles were so racist that many black folks left what little homes or land they had in the south and fled north. Then there was a law created that allowed LEO's back then, to arrest black folks standing around at bus depots and train stations (because they wanted to escape the overt racism of the south).

*How else are you supposed to get on a bus or train to head up north?*

*You'd have to wait at the station or depot, right.*

I know this to be true, because they recently built a new transportation hub in a nearby city here in North Carolina. It's for all the city's local buses, the "Greyhound" buses, and the "Mega-Bus. There is a large homeless population in the area and vagrancy is a problem. They "the powers that be" found an "old law" that would allow LEO's to arrest the vagrants and homeless people, just hanging around the new gazillion dollar transit hub.

*Now what old law do you think that they found?*

Don't believe me, look it up, it was published in the local newspaper.

Then back in the day, black folks were still being lynched, shot and/or murdered for offenses such as acting uppity, reading books or looking at a person of eurpoean decent in a manner they didn't approve of.

The Kaiser Family Foundation has a study (available on their website) that cites the life expectancy in years, of all Americans in our country by race;

- 86.6 Asian
- 82.8 Latino
- 78.9 White
- 76.9 Native American
- 74.6 Black

So, for whatever the reason is, black folks statistically do not live as long as other races of Americans in this same country, and I think that is wrong. I think since we all live in the same country, the life expectancy rates should be the same for all races of people, but obviously that is not the case.

To "take race out" of the equation, it is a very dangerous time we all live in. The odds of living for a long period of time, is not the best in our country (the United States) for anyone according to the World Factbook produced by the Central Intelligence Agency (CIA).

The United States does NOT rank in the top 10 of life expectancy at birth by measuring overall quality of life in a specific country. We do not rank in the top 20, 25 nor the top 40.

We are ranked at 42nd of all countries in the world at (79.8 years of age, average of all races in our country).

345

*Singapore, Japan, Iceland, Italy, Sweden* are just some of the countries that rank ahead of the United States in life expectancy at birth.

Monaco is ranked first with an overall life expectancy of 89.5 years of age.

But regardless of the life expectancy rates, most people who are in the professions that I choose are pro-life because they have seen so much death and destruction. Soldiers, Sailors, Airmen, Marines and Coast Guard members who've seen combat, who have seen their friends, comrades and other service members killed understand the value of human life. When you witness what one human being could do to another, regardless of the reason, you'll begin to appreciate life just a little more, if you don't already.

When you operate in the executive protection and bodyguard professional and you see just how easy a human life can be taken, you begin to understand the value of it.

In most urban neighborhood and ghettos of America, human life cost less than $5,000 dollars. That's the average cost *"I've heard"* that it would take for someone to voluntary murder someone else in *"the hood."*

If you would ask many convicted murderers (after they have been incarcerated) would they do it again; if they knew then, what they know now, about the value of human life. 9 times out of 10 you will probably get an answer saying, NO, they wouldn't have done what they did. Human life is precious and should be protected.

It takes 9 months to create a child in the womb of a woman, and decisions to destroy that life happen without much thought about the consequences many time.

*Finally, when does human life begin?*

At conception, while the child is forming in the womb, or after the child is born?

*If you say a human fetus is not really "a life" yet, because a child has not been born. Then how come if a drunk driver kills a pregnant woman, they charge the driver with the deaths of the pregnant woman, and the unborn child?*

346

We supposedly found one ameba cell, in one molecule of water on Mars, so some people say that proves that life exist in other places. But a woman can have not just one cell, but an entire late term abortion, because it is legal in this country. Is that not life too?

It takes nine months to carry a baby full term (for weeks per month, nine months, that's like 36/37 weeks). There are women who have abortions at 13, 14, 17, even 21 weeks.

A baby that is actually "born" between 24 and 36 weeks is considered a preemie baby, born prematurely before the full nine months (36/37 week).

Then we have on the other side of the coin, men who haven't stepped up to the plate. I don't care how many wives' you can have in your culture. In the United States, whether you are married to the mother of your child or not, as a man; your supposed to take care of your offspring.

**The only excuse is if you never knew the woman was pregnant, or never knew she had a child.**

It used to be "shameful" in this country to have a child out of wedlock. To have a child without being married, used to bring shame on your family. If you lived in the south, they would send a pregnant woman "up north" to live with relatives, rather than bring shame on the family. If you lived up north, they would send an unmarried pregnant woman "down south", to not bring shame upon the family. Children born out of wedlock (meaning the parents were not married at a wedding) used to be called "bastard children".

There was a time, when if you as a man got a young girl pregnant, the father of that woman would "make" you marry that young girl under threat of the barrel of his shotgun.

*Where do you think the term shotgun wedding came from?*

Studies have shown that in 1965, the unmarried single mother rate in the United States was around; 24% for black mothers and 3.1% for white mothers.

By 1990 those rates had risen up to 64% for black mothers and 18% for white mothers.

347

The year 1990 was well over 25 years ago, so I'm sure that those number have risen higher.

Just look at our current culture, look at the daytime reality shows that applaud the degradation of the moral values in America. YOU ARE "NOT" THE FATHER! Then men (black & white) get up and dance like they just won the lottery, because they have avoided the unjust child support system. It's a sad state and it's getting worse.

Let me ask all the men reading this a personal rhetorical question.

*"Of all the girls and women that you have EVER dated or had sex with, how many of their fathers have you asked permission to court, or date their daughter?"*

Don't tell me, just check your own dating history and see if you're part of the solution, or part of the problem.

Finally, my THIRD reason that I am pro-life and against pro-choice, is because of its origins. If you as a woman choose to have an abortion, who the hell am I to judge you, with all the killing and sin'in I have done in my lifetime.

You live your life and I'll live mine. But in this book, I am explaining my position, and hopefully even if you don't agree with me, you'll understand.

Margaret Sanger (1879-1966) was a eugenicist who popularized the term "birth control" and founded the American Birth Control League that evolved into the Planned Parenthood of America. Whether she disagreed with other eugenics who wanted to "exterminate" members of the populations whom they considered "inferior" or whether she only wanted to ensure that the poor & down trodden women who couldn't afford families where afforded the opportunity to have abortions (without regards to race), I don't know.

But I do know that results of what she and people like her started in the early 1900's, in regard to abortions in this country, are still being felt in communities across the United States today. Especially, in urban communities of color.

According to statistics from Abort73 which received nationwide abortion statistics from the Guttmacher Institute (AGI) and the Centers for Disease

Control (CDC) there are approximately 1 million abortions (908,000 in 2015) performed in our country each and every year.

One Million.

There are about 195 individual countries on this planet, and only 9 of them have a higher reported abortion rate than the United States; (1) Bulgaria, (2) Cuba, (3) Estonia, (4) Georgia, (5) Kazakhstan, (6) Romania, (7) Russia, (8) Sweden and (9) Ukraine.

*We in the United States have an abortion rate that is "higher than 186 other countries", and there are only 195 countries, WTF?!?*

Also, according to the CDC (2013), in New York City 37.4% (that's almost 40%), of all pregnancies ended in abortion.

Unmarried women account for 85.2% of all abortions.

Black women were 3.75 times more likely to have an abortion than white women. Even though the population of white people out number black people in this country by five to one.

One million per year means approximately 2,614 babies are murdered, I mean aborted, every day in our country! Of that number 967 White, 941 Black, and 497 Hispanic.

*Black people make up 14% of the US population according to the US census, but black women make up 36% of all the abortion in this country. This has got to stop. We have to do something about the culture of abortion in this country, especially in the black community.*

The culture of abortion is not getting better it's getting worse. The CDC reports that these are the percentages of abortions performed on black women in the US by decade, remember black folks only make up 14% of the overall population:

- **24% of all abortions in the 1970's**
- **30% of all abortions in the 1980's**
- **34% of all abortions in the 1990's**
- **36% of all abortions in the 2000's**

We have to do something about this culture. CBS News reported in 2009, that Hispanics have surpassed Blacks as the largest minority group. Here is one of the reasons that was possible, no its not immigration (legal or illegal). But, because Hispanic people tend to NOT murder their babies, I mean have abortions, at the same rate of black folks.

Hispanic women account for 19% of all abortions, and Black women account for 36%.

## THIRTY SIX PERCENT

Martin Luther King, Jr. once said, *"The Negro cannot win as long as he is willing to sacrifice the lives of his children for comfort and safety."*

How can the "Dream" survive if we murder the children?

We have to remove the language of "baby-daddy" and "baby-momma" from our vernacular. We have to start holding people accountable for their actions. We have to turn down the over sexual nature of every commercial, every magazine, every song on the radio; *"baby baby won't you just let me lick-it, stick-if, flip it"*.

So, that's just some of the reasons why I am an advocate of pro-life and not pro-choice, because Bottom Line Up Front (BLUF) Pro-Choice negatively effects black folks disproportionally almost up to the point of almost being called: genocide.

There are guys who instead of practicing safe sex or abstaining from creating babies, will just include the cost of an abortion in with the cost of dating. Some guys brag about "shooting up her club" (ejaculating inside of a woman). There are women who will trick some men into thinking they are pregnant, just so they can get the "abortion money" from them to go buy sneakers, designer handbag purses or to get their "hair and nails did".

*There are women that have had 5, 6, 7 or even 8 abortions, What The Fuck?!?*

We have got to do better people.

✳✳✳

I'm about the end this chapter on black & white race relations and other "touchy" subjects. But before I conclude, I'd like to touch on a few topics that I always seem get a question about my position on.

*Shadow, what is your position on Black Lives Matter (BLM)*

I believe that the phrase "Black Lives Matter" no matter who created it, is both **spoken** incorrectly and **heard** incorrectly.

*I'm NOT talking about the BLM organization, I'm talking about the phrase!*

- I personally believe that the people who are advocating and saying Black Lives Matter, are really trying to say; Black Lives Matter "ALSO".

- I believe that the people who are protesting the phrase are hearing; Black Lives Matter "ONLY".

*Now the actual BLM organization and movement, I have "nothing" to say about, because I am not a part of that movement.*

But the phrase; I can and will talk about.

I would hope and pray, that everyone believes, that black lives matter "also".

Formed under the media spotlight and the highlight that several members of our society who are melinated people of color have been killed, by other members of our society who are of european decent (whether LEO or not). It seemed like no matter how many other murders, deaths and atrocities that have occurred in our country, only the ones that have a racial element to it are being highlighted in the media.

Talk about social engineering.

So instead of focusing on carrying the phrase black lives matter "also", the members who have taken to the streets to demand justice have allowed that organizations [BLM] antics to over shadow the original good intentions of the group.

It's kind of like, years ago, I purchased a rainbow-colored air-freshener for my car.

I was told that I could not display that in my vehicle unless I wanted people to think I was homosexual. Well, I'm not a homosexual, I don't practice an alternative lifestyle, I just like the colors of that air-freshener. Well, I was told it doesn't matter what I think. If the majority of people "think" the rainbow represents the homosexual segment of society, that's what everyone who sees my rainbow-colored air-freshener will believe.

I just wanted an air-freshener for my POV, but it doesn't matter what I want, it's what people will perceive.

So now I just use "black ice" air-freshener.

So, no matter how good the original intentions of the BLM movement may have been in the beginning, it has been associated with so much violence and negative press that the "majority" of the people in this country will view it in a negative light, and completely miss the message.

Then on the other side of the discussion, there are people who hear the phrase, "Black Lives Matter" with their ears, but will actually hear the words; "Black Lives Matter - ONLY" in their minds.

So, they will create a counter-rally cry that; Blue Lives Matter, Green Lives Matter, All Lives Matter.

Well, of course All Lives Matter!

But that's not the discussion that was being had. If a disproportionate number of unarmed "little people" were being killed in this country. I mean if every night when you turned on the news, you saw that a person under 5 feet tall was killed. Then the statistics started showing you that unarmed "little people" were killed by other members of society (civilian, LEO or whatever) and those members for whatever reason were not convicted of any wrong crime, because legally they didn't break a law. Then if "little people" got together and started a campaign called; "Little People Lives Matter" to bring awareness to their plight. But we as a country started a counter movement to the little people and said, well "ALL" Lives Matter.

We would be correct, but that is not what the little people were talking about.

If you have an event with everyone wearing pink ribbons to highlight the plight of the deadly disease of breast cancer, and you were showing the solidarity with members of our society who have survived cancer. I or anybody else would appear cold, callous, and heartless to holla out, *"Well, sickle cell anemia is a disease too!"*

That may be true, but that's not what the discussion is about at this time.

✳✳✳

*Well Shadow, what about black-on-black crime?*

**If you have <u>never</u> used the phrase white-on-white crime, then you should never use the phrase black-on-black crime.**

Crime is crime, period.

Criminals should be isolated from the rest of society, and there was a time when communities would "police after themselves".

Some communities still do. When was the last time you heard on the news or social media about a mugging or a robbery of a citizen down in "the China Town part" of your community?

Or better yet, when was the last time you saw a homeless person of Asian descent in your community?

Take your time to think about that, I'll wait.

The Black community used to police itself. We used to have respect for our elders. The concept of it takes a village to raise a child was everywhere. Everyone knew who the bad children were, and they normally grew up to prove everyone right, bad.

But for whatever the hell reason, we in the black community have adopted the criminal's code of no snitching on each other.

If it were up to me, when the LEO's came into the community to look for a rapist, or a murder, or someone who molested children and mugged the elderly, they wouldn't need to break the no snitching code. They would just find their body laid out in the street, period.

*But it aint up to me, and I'm not the law.*
*And I'm not advocating that you take the law into your own hands either.*

Criminals created the "no snitching" code amongst and for; **themselves**. A group of six criminals robbed a bank, **THEY** believed that just because one of them got caught, that one shouldn't "snitch" on the other five.

BUT THAT'S THE CRIMINALS CODE!

✻✻✻

Another unwritten code of the street by LEO's if you're apprehended for a crime is, "If you tell on three, they set you free."

I don't know if that's true, I'm just telling you the code of the street. I do know that almost 90% of all criminal court cases - never go to a trial by jury.

You do the math.

If I talked about the criminal justice system, I'd have to right a whole nother book. Just look at the film called 13th by Ava DuVernay which compares the American prison system to modern day slavery. Or research the year in which the version of the Department of Corrections was created in your State or jurisdiction.

Yes, racism exist.

I have been talking trying to combat it about it all throughout this book. I have been discriminated against, just because of the color of my skin. Heavens only knows the amount of times I have been discriminated against. I have been discriminated against just because of my name. How many times has my application been denied for whatever I was applying for, just because of my name.

How many business contracts did I not get just because of my name.

In the hyper xenophobic society, we live in today I still get hate messages via social media, and thru the mail just because of my name. For over 30 years my name Muhammad would conjure up images of the world's greatest boxer and humanitarian Muhammad Ali.

But after 9-11, just the whisper of my name was tantamount to yelling bomb on an aircraft. In my last few years in the U.S. Army as an Infantry Doctrine Writer and Military Instructor, I would fly all over the country to teach, validate and update U.S. Army National Guard and Army Reserve units in our country. The contingent I served with included an Australian Sergeant Major, really good guy, he was a great leader. Anyway, on several cross-country flights, he would have a few drinks to many and yell across the plane, *"Hey Muhammad, tell 'em ya name. Tell 'em ya name MOE-HAM-MAD!"*

***You can only imagine the treatment I would receive from the airline attendants.***

Showing up at the airport, everything would always be great and happy, until the ticket agent would see my name. Then either I am "randomly selected" for additional screening, again. Or they would ask for "additional" identification. Passport, driver's license, military ID, social security card, library card, WTF?!? Armed LEO's or military personnel with their M-4 carbines would stand behind me, the K-9 officer would be there with the dog, not because of anything I did. But because of my name.

Years later, I sent some money via Western Union to a friend who needed some help. After I left the location I contacted him and gave him the Money Transfer Control (MTC) number over the phone that he would need to secure the funds on his end. It was just a few hundred dollars, but that's not the point.

Minutes later, after I had left the location I get a call on my cellphone, from someone says that they are Western Union, asking me to verify my name and social before they transfer the funds. I reply, that I am not going to give out my social security number over the phone to anyone, and that I have never heard of Western Union calling someone, after the transaction, to verify if they "sent money". I knew that was a scam, so I hung up the phone.

A few hours later, my friend calls me and says, you must call them back and give them some information before they release the funds to him. WTF?!?

**\*\*\***

Another time I am going to purchase another firearm.

I have several already, and since I'm a Register Armed Private Investigator and a Professional Bodyguard who is Licensed and Bonded by profession, it only seems natural that I would have firearms.

Anyway, I'm at a local gun store to purchase another firearm and the dealer tell me this, after I have paid for the weapon. He says, *"Listen man when I run a name through the system to see if you're cleared to receive a firearm, I get a YES you are good to go, or a NO do not sell the weapon. But your name came up with a HOLD. So, I can't release the weapon to you at this time. I'll call you when I receive word."*

OK, not understanding the system, because I have at least two firearms on me at all times, my personal sidearm and my back-up. But I'll comply and see how this plays out. A few moments later, he calls me and says, *"Hey man, come on back to the store and pick up your weapon, you're cleared, and good to go."* When I get back to the gun store, I ask him, **"What that was all about?"**

He replies, *"I don't know. But were you in the military, and maybe a Sniper or Special Forces or something?"*

I reply with, **"Yeah, I was in the military, but I was in the band. No, I was a cook, yeah, a cook."** That's what I say.

Well, he laughs and says, *"They be tracking the purchases of some of you "special people" and I don't know what you used to do, but here's your weapon."*

I do a little investigating, like I said, I am a Private Investigator. I already know that I have the most widely used name "on the planet". There are about 7 billion people that live on this planet, and it's estimated that at least 1 billion of them have the name "Muhammad" in some variation or another. There is a guy with my "same first name and my same last name" who is on the international terrorist watch list. But of course, his middle name is different.

That explains why I had to validate my identity so much. Then you have some people who always assume that "all black people look alike", so I deal with that B.S. too.

✳✳✳

**I was stopped for DWB (Driving While Black).**

A few years ago, I was asleep as a passenger in the front right seat of our SUV, when an officer pulls us over. I awaken when the smooth ride of the road becomes extremely bumpy, when she gets on the shoulder with the gravel and dirt.

*What's wrong I ask?*

*What happened?*

She replies, *"I don't know I was doing 70 and the posted speed limit is 70"*.

The LEO arrives on my passenger side of the SUV and says, *"Do you know why I pulled y'all over?"* I reply, the way the current laws of my state mandates me to reply, when pulled over by a LEO since I am a Concealed Carry Weapon (CCW) holder.

I state, **"Officer, before we go any further, I must inform you that I am a CCW holder and I am currently in possession of my sidearm. How would you like to proceed?"**

He asks me, *"Where is your weapon?"*

I reply, **"My personal sidearm is inside my waist band on my right hip, my spare magazines are on my left hip."**

Before I get to say anything else, and normally, at this point the LEO and I would get into a discussion about what type of duty weapon do I carry, and what do I prefer verses another weapon. Did I serve in the military? You know, that type of talk.

But not this guy.

*"Well, would you mind giving it to me until our interaction is over,"* he says.

**"Yes, officer you can secure my weapon until this transaction is over, but I'm not reaching for it. You can get it if you want it."**

I'm thinking that this will be the last we talk about weapons, and he will get on with the reason for the traffic stop in the first place. But no.

So, this officer repeats himself, *"where is your sidearm?"*

I repeat, **"Right here on my right hip"**, as I lean over, away from him, towards her in the driver's seat. He then, reaches inside the vehicle and removes the weapon from my IWB holster. Then he removes the magazine of ammunition from inside the weapon, and is trying to remove the round that is inside the chamber.

I tell him, **"Officer, she is a CCW holder also, and is in possession of her firearm as well."**

Now he has this very confused look on his face. My weapon is tucked under his arm pit, with the upper slide racked to the rear. My magazine full of bullets is in his hand, and the round that was in the chamber is in his hand as well. I can see that he is trying to figure out a way to disarm her as well, but that is not going to happen, and I know this.

At this point he just doesn't know this.

So, I say to him. **"In addition to her being a CCW holder, my backup is in the arm rest, my shotgun is behind the seat, and my AK-47 is in the back of this vehicle. Do you plan on securing all of my weapons, before you tell us what you stopped us for?"**

He does not answer my question.

Instead he asks a question of his own. *"Why do y'all have so many weapons?"*

*Well officer, I normally only carry my personal duty sidearm and my back-up on me. But when I'm traveling with my family, for their protection, I bring as much as I feel is necessary just in case we happen across a road construction detour, that takes us through some backwoods town, or if we come across a racist individual who has ill intentions towards us. I'm gonna protect my family, and it ain't gonna go like he thinks.*

At that point, he hands me back my weapon, my magazine and the round he took out of it.

Then he says, *"Well the reason I pulled y'all over was because I clocked ya doing 71 mph in a 70 zone. This is a holiday weekend and we have a "zero tolerance" policy this weekend. Do me a favor and please don't load that weapon until you're back on the road. Y'all be safe now, ya hear."*

Maybe I wasn't pulled over for DWB. Maybe that LEO was really concerned about our safety that day, and out of all the vehicles on that crowded road that day, he just was really concerned about "us."

***Have you ever been pulled over for doing 1 mile over the posted speed limit?***

I mean I have seen that on a military installation, where the MP's are enforcing the Post Commanders wishes. But on an Interstate Highway?!?

Maybe our speed odometer hasn't been calibrated, and we thought we were doing 70mph, when he clocked us 1 mph over the posted speed limit at 71mph?!?

✸✸✸

There have been other incidents like this, and there have been times where I will play the game, knowing all the time that I was right and did nothing wrong.

But I teach young men all the time, during an encounter with LEO is not the time to assert your rights, and you shouldn't be belligerent with an officer.

In fact, you shouldn't be belligerent with anybody who has a position of authority over you, or if they have something you want. Like a teacher who makes your grade (the difference between rounding a 69.5% up to a 70% D passing or down to a 69% F failing grade), the waiter who brings you your food (no salt fries on my fries = black folk being difficult/do something to ya food, ranch dressing = black folks, extra hot sauce = black folks, extra well done = black folks, no mayonnaise = black folks they give you that real special sauce), my friends who are LEO know this rule, they never order food from new restaurants in uniforms, it ain't about what you think, it's always about surviving the encounter.

You only have one job and that's to "Survive the Encounter."

*Do you have to blast your "Fuck the police" rap music loud during your traffic stop?*

*No.*

*Do you have to shuck and jive and play the "I be good nigga massa" game?*

*No.*

Your job in all manners of social interaction with other people is to "Survive the Encounter."

To anyone reading this who thinks, "well if you're not doing anything wrong you have nothing to worry about." Then I would say to you, you don't know what it's like to experience the types of racism that some people face in this society today.

✳✳✳

But I've been black my whole life, and in every "hood" in America the rules are the same. Learn them or your gonna pay the price.

Wear the wrong color hat, shirt or even shoe laces in the wrong neighborhood, and you can be shot. You from up North, come down South and think *"these country bumpkin's"* try to run game, go home up North in a pine box.

You from down South, come up North and say *"hello"* to the wrong person, **"what nigga you know me or something?"** *"No, I was just saying…"* **"I don't give a fuck what you was saying, you trying to set me up or something?"** *"No, I was just…"* **"Nigga hold this BLAM!! BLAM!!"** you're going back down south in a pine box.

There is an unwritten code in the streets. If the cops gotta run after you to catch you, for any reason, you're gonna get your ass beat when they finally catch you.

**\*\*\***

Another day in the South Bronx.

I am outside enjoying the sunlight when a little kid no older than 13 or 14 says to me, *"You can't stand here!"*

**"What did you say to me shorty?"**

He repeats himself, *"I said you can't stand here, dis my corner."*

**"Shorty, I don't know if you know who I am, but I was living here in this building before you were born."**

Listen man he says, *"I'm gonna go up the block, and when I get back you betta not be standing here, or we gonna have a problem."*

When he leaves my manhood and machismo says, **"Fuck that little kid. I'll whip his little ass when he gets back."**

But the City of New York has some very strict gun control laws, so only the LEO's and the bad guys have guns (because the criminals/bad guys don't care about the law anyway), so the only people who become preyed upon are the unarmed citizens who are obeying the law.

There is a memorial with about twenty of them lit *"Jesus Candles"* in front of the building right now, from the last guy who was murdered in front of this building. The buildings front façades are all riddled with bullet holes.

So, common sense says, go upstairs and tell my "little brother" who still lives in the hood what just happen. I come back down stairs with my little brother, and he sees the kid. *"Hey little nigga"*, is what my brother says.

The little kid says, *"Oh, that's your peoples"*, my bad bro. *"I was gonna smoke him!"*

I didn't know that in the years since I was gone, my old neighborhood had gone from being the bad South Bronx, to being a "Bloods & Crips gang infested again" bad South Bronx.

*Since when did we start gang-banging in the B.X., again?*

*I thought that went out with the 1970's?*

As I said before, black or white, cop or crook, violence is violence. I guess that young kid has never heard the phrase "Black Lives Matter (Also)".

✳✳✳

*What about the famous NFL football player who refuses to stand for the national anthem?*

I have served on active duty with the U.S. military for over 20 years and I'm a Combat Veteran. I have held men take their last breath. When I die, if my wishes are fulfilled, before they put me in the dirt with the rest of the American Paratroopers (black & white) out in the Sandhill's Veterans Cemetery in Spring Lake, North Carolina adjacent to Fort Bragg, North Carolina. There will be an American Flag over my coffin.

I take my old tattered American flags to the Special Operations Museum in Fayetteville, North Carolina. They have a box in front of the museum, that resembles a nice mail box. It is a receiving receptacle for old tattered American Flags, built by Boy Scouts doing their Eagle Scout Project – so flags could be properly disposed of.

I will NOT support nor condone the physical desecration of the American flag in any way, shape or form, period.

Mainly because I don't believe that all black folks came over here on no damn slave ships from Africa.

Yes, the slave trade did happen.

**But the majority of the "black folks" here in America were already here!**

The majority of the black folks here in this country look more like the Negrito's of the ethnic groups that inhabit parts of Southeast Asia, the Pacific Islands, and the original inhabitants of North and South America. If you do an image search and look at images of the **Negrito's**, you may think you were looking at images of people black people in the South Bronx.

If you do an image search and look at images of the **Aeta** people, the melinated group of indigenous people who live in parts of the Philippines, you may think you were looking at black people on the South side of Chicago.

If you go do an image search and look for the **Maniq** people, they are a melinated group of indigenous people who live in Thailand, you may think you were looking at black folks in South central Los Angeles.

If you go do an image search and look at the **Semang** people of Malaysia, you may think you were looking at black people in Detroit or Cincinnati.

Do an image search for the **Fijians**, the people who live in the country of Fiji. You can't tell them apart from the melinated people of color, the black folks in any major metropolitan city in America.

If I showed you a picture of the last Queen of Hawaii, Queen Liliuokalani when she was young, you couldn't tell her apart from any beautiful "sister" in any black beauty salon in America.

Now, if I started to talk about the 17 Olmec Head Statues that were found right here on this "North American continent", somebody would really would have some serious explaining to do. Those statues were from a culture of melinated people of color with big black people noses, and big black folks' lips, with cornrow braids in their hair (that the so-called African-American people still wear to this day) that flourished in North America from 1500 B.C. to 400 B.C. Just in case you didn't do the math, that was 3,517 years ago, and the statues are still here. Don't believe me go look for yourself. A full-size replica of the Olmec head statue called "San Lorenzo Head #4" is on display in Washington, DC near the Constitution Avenue entrance of the Smithsonian National Museum of Natural History.

Then to further clarify my belief that many of the black folks, that live in our country called the United States of America today, are descendants of melinated people of color who **were already here**, I refer to mathematics.

Because men lie, women lie, number don't lie.

The Trans-Atlantic Slave Trade Database states that between 1525 and 1866, at least 12.5 million people who were enslaved were shipped to North and South America, with only 388,000 going directly to the United States.

However, we know because our history teaches us that the first "Africans" who were enslaved did not arrive on the North America continent in the country we now call the United States until August 1619.

They arrived on an English ship called the *White Lion,* and it's 20 enslaved captives were from the African country we now call Angola. So, mathematics says, there were a full 94 years (1525 – 1619) of slavery in what is now called America BEFORE the first captured Africans arrived, and common sense asks where did *"those people"* who were enslaved come from, if they did not come from Africa?

*That's almost 100 years of slavery BEFORE the first captured Africans arrived in North America.*

Then we have the historical fact that the United States of America as a country stated that Africans captured on the African continent, and then enslaved could not be brought into the United States after 1808 because of the Congressional Act Prohibiting [the] importation of Slaves (1807). So mathematically that's 58 more years (1808 – 1866) when no new slaves could be imported, so where did *"those people"* who were enslaved come from, if they didn't come from Africa?

So, although there was 441 years of slavery in our country (341 years of actual slavery, plus another 100 years of Jim Crow, segregation and second-class citizenship), there were only 189 years of actual importation of people captured on the African continent, enslaved, and then shipped to the United States of America.

*But for those "other 152" years of chattel slavery (1525 – 1619) and (1808 – 1866) where did "those people" come from?*

*I propose that, "we were already here.*

Let's take emotion out of the equation and stick with mathematics, like the number 146,000.

We are taught in our history books, that 400 captured Africans were chained together on a ship for 6 weeks (45 days) during the voyage to North and South America. If one slave ship left the African coast "every day" with 400 captured

364

people and there was a ship that set sail "every day" for an entire year (365 days), that would only equal 146,000 people.

So, if 146,000 people per year were transported, and that's with the **impossible** task of sailing one ship "every day" for a year, how many continuous years of sailing would it take to bring 12.5 million captured people to the new world?

*None of them fought to the death?*

Every single ship sailed and reached its destination full, with 400 captured Africans. This is the literal meaning of the phrase *"frustrated cargo"*. Then when you get whatever number you got, double that, because after the ships dropped off their human cargo, we are taught that the ships loaded up with spices, sugar, rum & cotton from the new world and sailed with that cargo to europe.

But wait a minute, the ships then had to sail from europe to the African coast to get more enslaved people, so you now have to triple that number because each leg of the voyage of this "slave triangle" takes time.

Now whatever that number is, hundreds, thousands or millions, I want to ask you one question.

*Have you ever in your entire life seen a slave ship?*

I'm not talking about the pieces of the one ship, that they "maybe" have found, that might be a former slave ship, off of the coast of Africa that sunk a gabillion years ago.

*I'm asking where are the ships?*

We have seen Viking ships, and Colonial ships and Ironclad ships from the American Civil War. They have even recovered the ancient solar ship of the African King Pharaoh Khufu that was sealed in a pit at the foot of the Great Pyramid in Giza, Egypt. That ship was built 2500 B.C. (that's 4,517 years ago, if you didn't do the math).

*But not one slave ship.*

Of the gazillions of slave ships that there were supposed to have been, they can't produce one.

In 1963 Martin Luther King, Jr. gave a speech in Washington, DC which many people have heard called the "I have a dream Speech". In it he starts by saying he is was happy to join in [what at that time was] the greatest demonstration for freedom in the history of our nation. But he also stated, if you were listening, that "the Negro (what black people were called back then) was in the corners of American society and finds himself in exile **"in his own land!"**

In 1964 Malcolm X gave a speech to the Organization of Afro-American Unity in which he stated, "We didn't land on Plymouth Rock. Plymouth Rock **landed on us!"**

Every country, on every continent, in every part of our planet has an indigenous population of melinated peoples who are indigenous to the land; except the United States?

Ninja please!

So, in addition to my Indigenous American claims, I have several of my ancestors on both my mothers and fathers side of my family who have direct "Native American" ancestry. So, when I claim to be an American, I'm talking about being more American than you can ever imagine. There are people here in this country whose grandparents weren't even born here, talking about, "Go back to Africa" with their racist mentality.

*I'm more American than you. My grandfather's grandfather was born here, and I can prove it, your grandfather was an immigrant!*

Plus, because I know that the Red, White & Blue of our country was taken as it alludes to the Ancient Egyptian Mystery system. You can believe that Betsy Ross sewed the flag for George Washington if you want to. Just remember I was a Master Mason, and KOSA of the year for all of Western Europe back in the day. So maybe I just know a little something-something.

So, I said all of that to lay the foundation for my feelings about the professional football player Colin Kaepernick, and his position of protest against the America Flag while the countries National Anthem "the Star-Spangled Banner" is played before NFL football games.

366

*It hurts me deeply down to my soul to know that more people are concerned that he is protesting, the way he is protesting, versus the "reasons" for the protest.*

When he first started his protest, he chose to sit down, rather than stand up as a show of respect for the national anthem. Although he did not physically desecrate the flag, I can see how that can be seen as a sign of disrespect.

*But many of the overweight couch potatoes who complain that he is disrespecting the flag by sitting down, are sitting on their fourth point of contact at home, and they themselves are NOT standing for the national anthem.*

I personally stand, and sometimes I cry, because of all my friends, the fellow service members that have died defending this country. Men & women who have given their lives for people like him (and those supporting or criticizing him), to have the "right" to choose.

The freedom to stand, rather than compulsory like in many countries.

So, his sitting down was taken as a disrespectful gesture against military veterans and active duty SM who are currently serving our great nation. I understand that a veteran spoke with him. I understand that he was a professional football player in the NFL also. He is a military combat veteran of Iraq and Afghanistan, who is a U.S. Army Special Forces qualified soldier, entitled to the moniker of being called a "Green Beret". I wasn't there so I can only report what I read, researched and saw in the news like many of you readers. I watched the interview that he did in August 2016 with the NFL.

I have read the *"Nate Boyer writes open letter to Colin Kaepernick"* in the *ArmyTimes* magazine on-line and I was moved. I was especially moved by the phrase in the letter where Nate Boyer, a man of european decent, and thus a member of the dominate class in our society says, "he has never had to deal with prejudice because of the color of his skin."

Were he also says, that for him to say that he can relate to what [Colin Kaepernick] is going through is as ignorant as someone who has never been in a combat zone telling him what it's like going to war.

367

But the most important part to me is after their meeting, and the discussion the two of them had, Colin Kaepernick's protest method changed.

He began kneeling, **rather than sitting** for the National Anthem.

*To me that was powerful!*

Just about anybody can sit on their ass and do nothing, can sit on their ass and protest, can sit on their ass and arm chair quarterback every situation.

But to take a knee, that's powerful, that's symbolic. For anyone who has ever pledged in any college fraternity, sorority or any other organization; that's deep.

*To me taking a knee is way more "respectful" than sitting on your ass.*

In 1969 when Tommy Smith and John Carlos won their Olympic medals, they protested the conditions of melinated people of color and the way black folks in our country were treated by raising their fist in the air while the countries National Anthem is played. Legal slavery was abolished in the United States in 1865 at the end of the Civil War. But black folks weren't legally protected with the right to vote in the United States until 1965 when the Voting Rights Act was signed. It suspended poll taxes (that prevented people of color from voting) and it suspended literacy test (that disproportionately prevent poor and people of color from voting). In 1966 a Sheriff in Alabama was still using cattle prods against people who were marching for their civil rights. Not equal rights, to be taken from one person's ill-gotten gains to level the playing field, but "civil rights", to be treated in a civil manner. There were riots in 1966 & '67 in the cities and enclaves of Watts in South Central Los Angeles, New York City (in Harlem, Brooklyn and the Bronx), Atlanta, San Francisco, Oakland, Baltimore, Seattle, Tacoma, Cleveland, Cincinnati, Columbus, Newark, Chicago and Detroit. MLK was assassinated in 1968, because he felt that all people in our country should be treated fair and have equal protection under the law. So, when Tommy Smith and John Carlos protested, many of the people of that era, who were members of the dominant class of society didn't understand because it didn't affect them personally.

Today many people (who are not melinated people of color, or poor black & brown people) who are not affected by the unwritten policies, condition and activities in neighborhoods outside of their own, can no longer turn a blind eye to the racism that exist in our country, or the entire world for that matter, anymore. Because of the technological advancements of smart phones, video cameras and 24-hour news cycles, events are sometimes streamed live as they happen.

In a democratic society, the majority wins. So, if the majority of the people don't see a problem with something, many times things will never change.

**MLK Jr. was able to organize peaceful protest and let the racist people attack them with water hoses, beat them with billy clubs, attack them with vicious dogs, just so these atrocities could be captured on film and the masses of society could not ignore the problem any more.**

A famous anti-racism activist & educator named Jane Elliot who is a white person, gave a speech to a large group of other white people. During her presentation, she posed this question to them. She said, *"If any of you white people (like her) want to be treated the way black people are treated in this society – please stand."*

Nobody stood up.

She then said, *"That means you know what's happening, you don't want it for you, I want to know why you are so willing to accept it or allow it to happen for others".*

✱✱✱

I once heard the phrase that racism will continue to exist as long as we wear black to funerals and white to weddings. Implying that black is bad and sad, and white is good and happy.

Sometimes people say to me, *"Shadow why you always talk about that black stuff?"*

*Because I'm black, duh?!?*

*If I was Asian, Id' probably talk about Asian stuff.*

*If I was Latino, I'd probably talk about Latino stuff. WTF?!?*

If people are receptive to change, I sometimes enlighten them with this. Nothing is by accident. Everything that is done, is done for a reason, even if you don't know the reason why you're doing it. They have people that specialize in social engineering. So, try this exercise out.

Ask a bunch of people to answer this question, *"What is the nastiest tasting jelly bean?"*

Many people answer, *"the black one."*

*Why?*

*Because somebody planned it that way, that's why.*

Pull up Shadow, you're in too deep. They gonna give you a tin foil hat with all that conspiracy stuff.

*"When they make the jellybeans, what color are they?"*

They don't have a color.

They're all the same. Then somebody has to separate the jellybeans and make the different batches of jellybeans, different colors. These they make red, these will be yellow, these will be green, these will be orange, these will be white, these will be black and so on.

*"Now, what do they taste like?"*

It don't matter, they all taste the same.

Because nobody has added any **flavor** to them yet.

Someone has to deliberately make a decision to say, were gonna put a cherry flavor to the red jellybeans so they'll taste like cherries, a banana flavor to the yellow ones so they'll taste like bananas, an apple flavor to these green one so they'll taste like apples, an orange flavor to the orange ones (so they'll taste like oranges), a vanilla flavor to the white ones so they'll taste like vanilla, and were gonna scrape the bottom of our shoes for the flavor of these black one so they'll taste like shit.

I'm making light of the situation, but hopefully you get my point.

✳✳✳

I understand the concentric rings with the ascending or descending numbers on the targets at the gun range. I can even comprehend the red ring in the center. *But why the black silhouette on a white background?*

*Shadow No!*

*Where not gonna go there. It's not racist, it's a freaking paper target.*

But do you think it may have just a little bit of influence in the training and muscle memory of people who eventually wind up shooting unarmed people of color? But to be politically correct, don't use the white targets with the black silhouettes, just shoot at the paper targets with the zombies on them (to prepare for the zombie apocalypse).
*Remember, zombies don't swim (well at least 70% of them don't).*

✳✳✳

This is too deep Shadow, let's lighten it up with a friendly game of chess?
*OK, but why the white chess pieces gotta move first?*

✳✳✳

No more games, let's just go eat a piece of cake, everybody loves cake, right?
*Yeah, but why the Angel food cake is White vanilla, and the Devil food cake is Dark chocolate.*

371

Merriam-Webster dictionary (since 1828)

Black: having dark skin hair and eyes, relating to any of the various population groups having dark pigmentation of the skin, of or relating to the African-American people or their culture, dirty soiled, sinister or evil *black deed*, indicative of condemnation or discredit *black mark*, connected with or invoking the supernatural and especially the devil *black magic black arts*, very sad gloomy or calamitous, marked by occurrence of disaster *black Friday*, grim, distorted or grotesque satire *black humor*, covert intelligence operations *black government programs*

White: free from color, lustrous pale gray, being a member of a group or race characterized by light pigmentation of the skin, relating to the characteristic or consisting of white people or their culture. The stereotypical association of good character with northern european descent, *that's mighty white of you*, not intended to cause harm, *a white lie, white magic*

These are my suggestions for methods and ways to end racism. First, we have to stop believing lies, and living in our own comfort zones. Read books you wouldn't normally read. Watch movies you wouldn't normally watch, and study.

The number one piece of advice I have: is to travel.

When you travel, you are bound to learn something "that you did not know, that you did not know." Once you get outside of your own "Circle of Circumference of Knowledge" as **Dr. Ray Hagins**, the Founder, Chief Elder & Spiritual Leader of The Afrikan Village & Cultural Center says during his lectures.

Go order the DVD called *"Hidden Colors"* by **Tariq "Elite" Nasheed**. He has a series of them, but I highly recommend the first one (Hidden Colors 1) to anyone reading this book. That is probably the most eye opening educational video ever produced when it comes to breaking down to elementary level the reasons why the history of color has been hidden. Don't get a "bootleg copy" of the DVD. If you don't purchase an authentic copy of the DVD, how is he gonna make more of the series?

372

One of the most eye-opening books I have ever read, that was written about race relationships is called *"The Isis Papers"* by **Dr. Frances Cress Welsing**. Whether you agree with her theory or not, some parts of her book make for a very compelling argument. Like when she describes how the game of pool (pocket billiards) may seem innocent, but could have been created and designed as racist (intentional or not). How the game is played on a flat green surface, representing the planet. How the (only) white cue ball is used to knock all the colored balls off of the table (surface of the earth) into one of the six pockets in the corners or the side. How the white ball is placed back on the table, in any location, if it accidently goes off the board. But you win the game after you knock all the colored billiards off the board, and save the last one, the black until last.

Find a lecture by someone who knows what they are talking about when it pertains to "black folks" because they are qualified either through academia, or they have traveled extensively throughout the world and have "evidence" of what they are teaching; **Dr. Umar Abdullah Johnson** the Prince of Pan-Afrikanism, based in Philadelphia, Pennsylvania or **Dr. Kaba Kamene (Booker T. Coleman)** who teaches about the history, life and existence of black folks as written on the Shabaka Stone.

I highly recommend you research Master Teacher **Ashra Kwesi** of *Kemet Nu* productions. Their mission is to promote African historical consciousness by means of visually documented, inspirational and educational lectures, tours, videos and audios. Their information is based upon over three decades (that's 30 years) of travel in Africa. I have an extensive list of my recommended reading material in the back of this book. Don't believe nothing I say, do your own research and check for yourself.

Please check out and support these Spoken-Word Artist that have really enlighten me; Sunni Patterson, D-Black, and 13 of Nazareth.

- **D-Black** does a piece called, *"I Apologize"* that has got to be the most inspiring spoken word that I have ever hear.
- **Sunni Patterson** did a piece called *"We Made It"* that is a timeless classic, that had stood the test of time.
- **13 of Nazareth** made a CD called *"Stained Glass"* with a track called "Hittin Ms" that is constantly played on my workout mix.

If you find any other these authors, scholars or teachers to be at fault; contact them. I'm sure they will be more than happy to answer any questions you may have for them.

The most important piece of information I wish to convey to anyone who reads these words, is that "NO ONE" that I know, knows the final answer to this thing called life. We may have heard what someone told us, or we may have read what someone wrote, but since none of us remember what happened BEFORE we came into this plane of existence, and since none of us know what happen AFTER we leave this plane of existence. Let's try to be peaceful to each other and leave this world a better place than the way we found it.

Help someone who can never repay you.

**It's not about the color of your skin. When the drama starts, and you need a blood transfusion to stay alive, it doesn't matter if their Asian, Latino, Black or White. As long as the blood is red and the type of blood that you need, it's all good.**

Like the U.S. Army says, you're all green.

Ain't no black, white, asian, latino - you're all just green.

Just like them little green toy army soldiers.

*But you dark green soldiers better learn how to swim.*

# 19

# EVERYBODY WANT A JOB, NOBODY WANNA WORK

*It started with the black beret.*

*When the U.S. Army made the decision to "take" the coveted Black Beret from the U.S. Army Rangers, and issue the Black Beret to "every soldier" like some sort of participation trophy; it was all downhill from there.*

*Sure, the Rangers looked sharp, professional and motivated. But the Black Beret did not make the Rangers look sharp. Just the opposite, the Rangers made the Beret look sharp, there is a difference.*

*Napoleon is reported to have one said, "If I had enough ribbon I could rule the world." Alluding to the fact that some people are motivated by ribbons, and medals and trophy's.*

*Where does this stop?*

*When does it stop?*

*Since the military can ONLY recruit its soldiers from the population, I can only guess that's what society has come too.*

*Everybody want a job, but nobody wanna work.*

*So yeah, I have heard the rumblings of the community. That the U.S. Army is creating a "new" unit, just "like" the U.S. Army Special Forces that will have a "special headgear" very similar in color of the actual "Green Beret."*

*One of the very first questions asked of us, during training at "the Q course" back in the early 1990's was: "If it wasn't for the Green Beret and the Special Forces Tab, would you still be here?!?*

*The real warriors don't care about no damn headgear, or patches and badges. But we still want to honor and protect the lineage and history of the units we served in, and the men who have gone before us. Some who have made the ultimate sacrifice.*

I've been retired from the US Army for well over ten years now. I make my living as a Private Investigator and an Executive Protection Specialist (Professional Bodyguard) now. But most fans now, do NOT even want an autograph with their favorite artist. They don't even want to spend time with their favorite artist, everyone wants a "selfie" with the artist.

1.  If you offered the average millennial a choice of spending one hour with their favorite artist. Discussing the background to their music, and really fellowshipping with them, but no photographs.

OR

2.  One half a minute with their favorite artist (and a photo).

Many of them would choose the 30 second interaction. Because it's not even for them anymore. They can't even enjoy the talents or music of the people that they like. They have to get a photo, as some sort of "proof" or validation from their friends that, yeah you did meet so and so!

Participation trophies for everybody is the standard now.

The championship team gets the big trophy, and everyone on the winning team gets a small gold replica of that, along with the first-place medals. The second-place and third place would normally get; the silver and bronze medals. Everybody else would get a Certificate of Appreciation, and a invitation to work harder next time. Sometimes you work as hard as you can, and it's still just not your day.

*But, many parents have resorted to spending their own money, to "buy" and purchase their child a trophy, so they don't "feel bad".*

You are not setting your child up for success, nor the realities of life. You especially, are not setting them up for the rigors of combat. What are you gonna tell the enemy, wait I wasn't ready yet?!?

Life ain't fair, and don't nobody owe you nuffin!

Do the right thing, just because it's the right thing to do, period!

I can't talk about the network television show that I am on, because of the Confidentiality Agreement and the iron clad Nondisclosure Agreements (NDA) I've entered. All I can say is, wait for Season 2.

**Get right with your Creator, whatever you believe!**

Hope, Pray and Work for a better future. Stay Positive. Learn to Swim. Go get your passport and travel the world. Learn to speak a foreign language.

Thank You to the following radio stations for having me on as a guest in the past WIDU (1600 AM), WFNC (640 AM), WUKS (107.7 FM), WZFX (Foxy 99 FM) and WMGU (106.9 FM).

Again, I want to thank all of those who have contributed to the HOPE project - Humanitarian Operations Protecting Elephants. I will post the photos from that trip on the website (www.BrotherShadow.com) upon my return.

I have saved the most import for last, and I mean this. If I was to hit the lottery with an astronomical amount of money, say $100 million dollars "after" taxes. I would give MOST of it away. I would insure that my wife got $50 million dollars (half) to do as she pleases.

Then I would take $8 million and give it to my family.

- I would give $2 million to my relatives in the **Jamison** family. One million to my mother to do as she pleases. The other million to be placed in a trust fund of some type where only the "interest" is available to the members of the "Jamison" family. Members would have to solicit the approval of at least four of the seven family elders in charge of the fund.

- I would give $2 million to the **Cooper** family. One million to my father to do as she pleases. The other million would be placed in a trust fund where only the "interest" is available to the members of the "Cooper" family. Members would have to solicit the approval of at least four of the seven family elders in charge of the fund. Alabama stand up!

- I would give $2 million to the **Blue** and **Jones** families in Fayetteville, North Carolina. One million to my mother-in-law to do as she pleases. The other million would be placed in a trust fund of some type where only the "interest" is available to the members of the "Jones or Blue" family. Members would have to solicit the approval of at least four of the seven family elders in charge of the fund.

- I would give $2 million to the **Williams** family. One million to my father-in-law to do as she pleases. The other million would be placed in a trust fund of some type where only the "interest" is available to the members of the "Williams" family. Members would have to solicit the approval of at least four of the seven family elders in charge of the fund.

**Then I would personally give $10 million dollars to go to the coffers of a beautiful institution called:** *Simon Temple AME Zion Church*, **in Fayetteville, North Carolina. To pay off the building fund and other projects**

- I would earmark $8 million of that $10 million to the actual church, its officers and the Fayetteville/Fort Bragg community to which it serves.

- I would earmark $1 million dollars of the $10 million to be divided **"equally"** between each, and every, registered member in good standing of Simon Temple.

378

- The final $1 million dollars I would earmark, and just personally give it to **Reverend Brian R. Thompson** who I have witnessed to be a righteous man. I've seen him in the jails visiting our troubled members of society. I've seen him in the hospitals, visiting the sick and shut-in. I see the Simon Temple van at the homeless shelter, putting in work in the community. If I could I would tell him to take one million dollars and do something nice for his family - that has done so much for me and mine, in the spiritual realm, you wouldn't even understand!

The most important thing y'all can do is get some Life Insurance for the next generation, so they don't start off in the hole. More importantly, so they don't have to set up an on-line account to raise funds to bury you behind. Y'all better go get the book: "The Memo: Five Rules For Your Economic Liberation" from author John Hope Bryant. He said, "It's not a Civil Right movement, it's a Silver Right movement!"

Thank you - **Angel** the smartest money management advisor that I know!

Thank you – **Rahsaan** the best DJ in New York City!

Thank you - **Patricia**, the E.E. Smith Homecoming Queen Class of '85. I know it's not easy living with a man who suffers from PTSD. You have witnessed more behind the scenes action in the last 25 years than anyone. Thank you for understanding and for your support, and for your love. Promise you, I did the best I could with them two; **Tavy Wavy** and **A.J.**, they were just 2 years old, and 2 months old when we met. But look at them now, they are in their twenties and we've been together for over 25 years.

Wow!

Be on the lookout for Brother Shadow's next books:

**IT AIN'T NO FUN:**
**WHEN THE RABBIT GETS THE GUN**
**(The Adventures of Brother Shadow)**

and

**SHADOW'S SELF DEFENSE MANUAL FOR WOMEN**

# GLOSSARY OF TERMS, ACRONYMS AND POPULAR SLANG

**AAFES**: Army and Air Force Exchange Service

**AAR**: After Action Review Report

**ABN**: Airborne

**ACAP**: Army Career and Alumni Program

**ACS**: Army Community Service (Family Programs)

**ACU**: Army Combat Uniform

**A.E.A.O.N.M.S.**: Ancient Egyptian Arabic Order, Noble Mystic Shrine

**AER**: Army Emergency Relief

**AIT**: Advanced Individual Training

**AIR**: Airborne Infantry Regiment, A.I.R.

**AKO**: Army Knowledge Online

**Alphabet**: Name used whenever someone has a very long or foreign spelling name

**ANCOC**: Advanced Noncommissioned Officers Course (mandatory US Army educational development course for SSG/E-6 to get promoted to SFC/E-7)

**APFT**: Army Physical Fitness Test

**Army Brat**: Son or Daughter of a career military person who does not grow up in a stable environment because of the constant moving of duty locations. *slang*

**ASAP**: As Soon As Possible

**ASVAB**: Armed Services Vocational Aptitude Battery test

**AWOL**: Absent Without Leave

**AWR**: Alpha Whiskey Romeo (Allah's Waiting Room). After being fired upon, SM's in combat tend to force the enemy to retreat, and they normally retreat to the same building, where SM's call in air strikes on said position.

**The "B's"**: Military barracks or dorm type rooms for single soldiers

**BAQ**: Basic Allowance for Quarters (pay SM receive verses living on-base in housing or barracks)

**BAS**: Basic Allowance for Subsistence (pay SM receives verses eating in a DFAC, chow hall or mess hall)

**Barracks Lawyer**: SM who has knowledge of the Rules, Regulation, Policies and law of the UCMJ when it comes to working the system. Similar to "jailhouse lawyer" or "shithouse lawyer". *Slang*

**Barracks Rat**: SM who stays in the barracks and never goes out or off-base while in garrison. *slang*

**Battle Rattle**: All the extra combat gear (minus weapon that a SM must wear). Helmet, hearing protection, eye protection, gloves, etc.

**Beat Your Face**: Do push-ups

**BCT**: Basic Combat Training, Boot Camp

**BCD**: Birth Control Devises, standard military issued eyeglasses that are so repulsive to servicemembers that they assume to render the wearer, un-dateable.

**BCG**: Birth Control Glasses, see BCD

**BDU**: Battle Dress Uniform

**Big Chicken Dinner**: Bad Conduct Discharge

**Bird**: Helicopter

**Black Hat:** Airborne School Instructor, referred to as Sergeant Airborne!

**Blanket Party:** The act of several unit members throwing a blanket over someone's head while they sleep and beating them so they cannot identify the perpetrators. Usually used in units where mass punishment" is issued (like Basic Training) and one SM is causing the others extra work or painful duty.

**Blast:** A Parachute Jump. The first jump after airborne school (number 6) is the "Cherry Blast". A Jumpmaster or Master Rated Parachutist is a "Master Blaster". An administrative Nontactical Jump for Pay purposes is called a "Hollywood Blast". *Slang*

**Blood Wings:** Forcing the two pin prongs of the Airborne Wings into the chest of the proud graduate of the US Army Airborne School, rather than pinning the grommets on the back.

**Blowed Up:** Hit an IED

**Blue Falcon:** Buddy Fucker *derogatory*, Bravo Foxtrot *slang*

**BNCOC:** Basic Noncommissioned Officers Course (mandatory US Army educational development course for SGT/E-5 to get promoted to SSG/E-6)

**BOB:** Big Orange Ball, stands for Sun in the sky. Many infantrymen believe that if you say the word "S" word during austere and adverse weather condition, it won't come out and will continue to rain or whatever.

**BOHICA:** Bend Over Here IT Comes Again

**BOLO:** to fail an exam, test or qualification *slang*, Be On the Look Out for *military*

**Brain Bucket:** Military helmet, also called the "dome of obedience"

**Brass:** Any commissioned officer whose insignia of rank is gold and silver brass bars, oak leaf's, birds and stars

**Broke Dick:** SM who is always on Sick Call, is accident prone or has a medical limiting profile on what he/she can and can not do. *derogatory slang*

**Buck Sergeant:** US Army Sergeant, SGT/E-5 with three stripes, *"buck'* to distinguish it from the higher-ranking Sergeants like; Staff Sergeant, Section Sergeant, Sergeant First Class, Platoon Sergeant, Master Sergeant, First Sergeant, Sergeant Major and the Command Sergeant Major.

**Bullwinkle Badge:** US Army Air Assault Badge

**Burn Bag:** Bag holding shredded and torn documents to be burned in a burn pit

**Butter Bar:** US Army Second Lieutenant 2LT/O-1 as distinguished by the gold bar of rank worn

**CAB:** Combat Action Badge. US Army award for soldiers in combat who are <u>NOT</u> eligible for a *"Combat Infantryman Badge"* (CIB) which is only awarded to Infantrymen & Special Forces in combat. *Military*

**CAB Chaser:** A FOBBITT who only leaves the confines of the FOB to earn their CAB, then never leave the wire again if possible for the remainder of their deployment. *derogatory*

**CAC:** Common Access Card

**Cadidiot:** Combination of a ROTC cadet and an Idiot. *derogatory slang*

**Cannon Cocker:** Artillerymen *military*, Gun Bunny *slang*

**Cannon Fodder:** Infantrymen *slang*

**CCP:** Casualty Collection Point

**Charlie Foxtrot:** Cluster Fuck

**Chemlight Battery:** Nonexistence Item

**Cherry:** A new service member. Signifies first as in: cherry mission, cherry jump

**Chicken Plates:** Small Arms Protective Inserts worn inside body armor

**Chief:** Unofficial form of addressing any Warrant Officer *slang*

**Chocolate Chip BDU's**: The five-color version of the DCU's worn by US forces during Operation DESERT SHEILD and Operation DESERT STORM.

**CHU**: Container Housing Unit (singlewide trailer reinforced or not)

**CIB**: Combat Infantryman Badge

**CID**: Criminal Investigation Division

**CG**: Commanding General

**Class A's**: Military Dress Uniform to include medals and decorations. Normally worn by SM's for inspection on the last day of the month in garrison. Then they are released to go pay bills and other monthly obligations and the NCO of the battalion from each company get together and conduct NCOPD (or at least that's how we used to do it).

**Class 1 offload**: To urinate, to go do number 1 *slang*

**Class 2 download**: To defecate, to go do number 2 *slang*

**Class 6 store**: Liquor store *military*

**Command Specialist Major**: Nonexistent rank, used to denote the title of the leader of the infamous "E-4 mafia". Corporal and Specialist are both paygrade E-4, but Corporals are NCO's and Specialist are not. So, Corporals "out rank" Specialist and are many times unofficially be referred to as the Command Specialist Major.

**CONUS**: Continental United States (48 of the 50 states) Alaska & Hawaii for military purposes are considered OCONUS

**CoC**: Chain of Command

**Cunt Cap**: US Army Garrison Cap *derogatory* term

**DA**: Department of the Army

**Dash Ten**: The US Army's operator's manual for every piece of equipment at the operator's level ends with -10.

**DCU**: Desert Camouflage Uniform version of the BDU

**Dear John**: Referring to a break-up letter sent to a SM

**Dee Dee Mao**: Retreat, run away, leave *Vietnam era*

**Desert Dime**: a female SM of any branch who is considered so attractive that she rates a 10 (dime) on a scale of 1-10 because "downrange" in the desert, there are not many members of the opposite sex, but upon return to CONUS she would rate a 1, 2 or a 3 on a scale of 1-10. *slang* also Desert Fox *slang*

**DFAC**: Dining Facility

**Dickskinners**: Hands *slang*, also Dickbeaters *slang*

**Dirt Dart**: USAF term for US Army paratroopers, *derogatory*

**Dirty Bird**: SM's with personal hygiene problems, don't shower after PT, wear dirty uniforms, and have dirty messy barracks areas. *slang*

**Digit Midget**: Referring to a countdown timer, as in, *"I'm a single digit midget, I can rappel off the side of a dime"*. Meaning he has about 9 days, or less, remaining at this duty station or before starting leave or whatever he/she is counting down days for.

**DILLIGAFF**: Do I look Like I Give A Flying Fuck?

**DNA**: Deoxyribonucleic Acid

**DMZ**: Demilitarized Zone

**Doc**: Any member of the medical profession, especially to an Infantryman, from the X-ray Technician to the Veterinarian

**DoD**: Department of Defense

**DoE**: Department of Energy

**DoJ**: Department of Justice

**DoS**: Department of State, US State Department

**Down Range**: Refers to any location in front of the firing line on a live fire weapons range *military*, physically in a combat zone *slang*

**DSS**: Diplomatic Security Service of the DoS

**Donkey Dick**: Flexible metal hose that fits a 5-gallon fuel or water can, *slang*.

**DUI**: Driving Under the Influence

**DWI**: Driving While Intoxicated

**DZ**: Drop Zone

**EIB**: Expert Infantryman Badge

**EOD**: Explosive Ordnance Personnel

**EEO**: Equal Employment Opportunity

**E-Fuzzy**: US Army enlisted soldiers wear their rank insignia on Velcro portions of many uniforms. Since there is no rank insignia for the basic private or PVT/E-1 the "fuzzy Velcro" patch is open to the elements, sometimes referred to informally as "E-nothing".

**Eleven Up, Three Down**: Arithmetic for "Eight Up" or "Ate Up"

**Embed**: Journalist or Reporter assigned to (embedded with) a particular military unit

**EUSA**: Eighth Army

**Expectant**: Military casualty who is expected to pass away

**Fart Sack**: Sleeping Bag or military bunk

**Fast Mover**: Military aircraft (jets, not helicopters), Civilian POV's driving fast around military or diplomatic convoys

**Fast Tracker**: Term used for SM who move up in rank and/or position much faster than normal.

**FDC**: Fire Direction Controller

**Fifty**: M-2 .50 caliber machinegun

**FM**: Military Field Manual

**FNG**: Fucking New Guy. New guy into the unit that no one want to know or get close to so when you get killed they don't have to feel too attached.

**FOB**: Forward Operating Base

**FOBBIT**: Person who never leaves the FOB for direct combat action, ever.

**FOI**: Fruit of Islam, NOI Security Force

**FOIA**: Freedom of Information Act

**Football Bat**: Useless Item

**FORSCOM**: US Army Forces Command

**Fort Living Room**: The civilian life "after" separation from service

**FOUO**: For Official Use Only

**Fourth Point of Contact**: Buttocks. Referring to a Parachute Landing Fall (PLF) conducted by 5 points of the body contacting the ground to dissipate the energy of the landing; (1) balls of the feet, (2) side of the calf, (3) side of the thigh, (4) side of the buttocks, and (5) side of the back (push-up muscle), then rolling over and contacting the other side in reverse order, (5) other side of the back (other push-up muscle), (4) other side of the buttocks, (3) other side of other thigh, (2) other side of the other calf, and finally the other side of the other foot.

**Front Leaning Rest**: The push-up position

**FTA**: Fuck The Army *derogatory* term

**FUBAR**: Fucked Up Beyond All Recognition

**FUGAZI**: Fucked Up, Got Ambushed, Zipped In (as in a body bag) *Vietnam era military*, or Fake and a really bad imitation, Not real *civilian*

**Full Bird Colonel**: US Army COL/O-6 normally a Brigade Commander (from the eagle insignia of rank that is worn), as to differentiate from the LTC/O-5 Lieutenant (or light) Colonel normally a Battalion Commander which rank insignia is that of a silver oak leaf.

**FY**: Fiscal Year

**G**: Grenadier

**Gay Pride Ribbon**: Army Service Ribbon (ASR) awarded by the Army, Army Reserve and Army National Guard to all SM's who successfully complete their; basic training and advanced individual training (AIT) called initial entry training. It has sequential vertical stripes of red, orange, yellow, green, blue, green, yellow, orange and red colors. *slang*

**GI**: Government Issue

**GI Party**: A really great time

**GEARDO**: US Army soldier who spends enormous amounts of his/her personal money on extra military gear (knives, brass knuckles, binoculars, etc) that they will never use.

**Getting A Range Named After You**: Sarcastic comment used in combat to remind someone to be safe, as in; "Don't go trying to be no hero, and get a rifle-range named after you"

**Go Fasters**: Running Shoes verses Combat Boots *slang*

**Green Beret**: Distinctive head gear worn by members of the US Army Special Forces, after they earn the right to wear it upon successful completion of the Special Forces Assessment & Selection (SFAS), Special Forces Qualification "Q" Course (SFQC) & Foreign Language School *military*

**Ground Pounder**: see Grunt

**Grunt**: Infantryman, associated with the sound an Infantryman makes when putting on the heavy ruck sack pack.

**Gut truck**: Civilian food vendor truck usually owned by AAFES and driven by a former salty Senior NCO. As in "I used to be Top Sergeant around this place"!

**Hajji**: A title given to a muslim person who believes in the religion of Islam and has successfully completed "the Hajj to Mecca" *historical*, A racist term for Iraqis, Arabs, Afghans, Middle Easterners, North Africans and South Asian people in general. Comparable to the term "gook" used by military personnel during the Vietnam War *slang*. Synonymous with civilian as in; Afghan house = Hajji house, Iraqi car = Hajji car, bootleg black-market dvd movie = Hajji movie

**Hardball**: Hard surfaced road, verses dirt or unimproved road

**Hard Stripes**: US Army Enlisted pay grade E-4, E-5, E-6, E-7 and E-8 used to have to separate ranks for each pay grade, one for the NCO and one for the Specialist depending on the SM's MOS and duty description. The Hard Stripe referred to the NCO, example find me a E-4 hard stripe, meaning a Corporal not a Specialist.

**HCN**: Host Country National

**Helicopters**: AH-1, AH-64 (Attack Helicopter), CH-47, (Cargo Helicopter), UH-1, UH-60 (Utility Helicopter), OH-6, OH-58 (Observation Helicopter)

**HHC**: Headquarters & Headquarters Company

**High Speed**: Individual who is extremely motivated and proficient

**Hooch**: SM's living quarters while in-country

**Humping**: Long distance walking or marching with heavy rucksack backpacks

**IAW**: In Accordance With

**IED**: Improvised explosive Devise

**In Country**: Physically In a combat zone

**I.S.**: Intermediate School (Middle School or Junior High School)

**Jesus Cruisers**: Shower Shoes for walking on the dirt water in the shower stall

**Jody**: A no good shady individual who sleeps with soldier's wives and girlfriends while they are deployed or away for training.

**Joe**: U.S. Army soldier (as in G.I. Joe)

**John Wayne**: Wearing your ballistic helmet with the chin strap unfastened *slang*, shooting from the hip *slang*

**JMTC**: Joint Multinational Training Center

**JOTC**: Jungle Operations Training Center

**JRTC**: Joint Readiness Training Center

**Jump Boots**: Combat boots with lacing up to the calf, a capped toe and flat sole developed for Paratroopers during WWII. Designed by General William P. Yarborough in 1941 *(who also designed the US Army's airborne wings & years later received authorization from President John F. Kennedy, the 35th President of the United States of America, in 1961 to have the US Army Special Forces wear the distinctive "green beret)* for use in the 501st Parachute Test Battalion, they are still worn today by all US Army Airborne personnel "on jump status" in lieu of the low-quarter dress shoe in Class-A uniform.

**K-Pot**: Kevlar Helmet

**KIA**: Killed in Action

**Kill Zone**: the area that is designated for the ambush or killing *military*, the "X" location of an ambush *contractor*, an area where lower enlisted must not ever walk like a highly wax portion of a unit's floor *slang*, or the area where the unit emblem is embalmed on the ground, or the grass in front of the CSM's office.

**Kinetic**: Violent

**KJV**: King James Version

**Klicks**: Kilometer (1,000 meters increments) a little more than 1/6th of a mile

**KP**: Kitchen Patrol

**Land of the Big PX**: The United States of America, primary motivating factor of some foreign-national women marrying US service members, once in the US or the land of the "big PX" they remain with the SM until they receive their "Green Card" from Immigration, then divorce the husband and take half his stuff. *slang*

**Left Handed Monkey Wrench**: Nonexistence item

**Leg**: So Dirty, So Nasty *derogatory slang* All non-airborne personnel.

**LES**: Leave & Earning Statement (military paystub)

**Lifer**: SM who is a career person and follows the rules to the letter *slang*

**LPC's**: Leather Personnel Carriers or Combat Boots.

**LZ**: Landing Zone

**Ma Deuce**: M-2 Browning .50 caliber machinegun

**Mad Minute**: A moment of tremendous firepower, where everyone in the unit fires everything at an intended target *Vietnam era*

**MARINE**: Muscles Required Intelligence Not Expected, *derogatory* term

**Meat Gazer**: The NCO appointed duties as Unit Urinalysis who observes as the SM's urinate into the specimen bottle. *derogatory*

**MEPS**: Military Entrance Processing Station

**Mickey Mouse Boots**: Inflatable black or white rubber boots designed for extremely cold weather operations. Used in Alaska, Korea, Germany, Fort Drum, Fort Carson and other cold weather environments.

**Mikes**: Minutes

**MilSpec**: Military Specification

**MOLLE**: Modular Lightweight Load Carrying Equipment, M.O.L.L.E.

**MOS**: Military Occupational Specialty

**Mosquito Wings**: US Army rank insignia of a Private or PV2/E-2, one stripe.

**Mouth Breather**: Derogatory term for a SM who is ignorant or constantly has his mouth open

**MRE**: Meals Ready to Eat, also Meal Refusing to Exit *slang*

**MRE Bomb**: Placing the chemical heating pouch from the MRE ration into a plastic bottle, inserting a Chemlight glow stick and inserting water. Then quickly closing the cap causing the chemical reaction to expand and eventually explode as a prank.

**Mustang**: Commissioned Officer who used to be an Enlisted Soldier

**MP**: Military Police

**MTC**: Movement to Contact

**MtDNA**: Mitochondrial Deoxyribonucleic Acid

**Mud Puppy**: Military Policemen *slang*

**MWR**: Morale, Welfare & Recreation

**NATO**: North Atlantic Treaty Organization – Alliance between 3 permanent members (United States, France and the United Kingdom) and 26 other independent countries across North America and Europe. Headquartered in Brussels, Belgium signed in 1949.

**NBA**: National Basketball Association

**NCO**: Noncommissioned Officer, *derogatory term* - No Chance Outside (referring to NCO's who remain committed to active duty because they lack the survival & people skills for civilian employment.

**NCOPD**: Noncommissioned Officers Professional development

**NCPPSB**: North Carolina Private Protective Services Board

**NDA**: nondisclosure Agreement

**NFL**: National Football League

**NOI**: Nation of Islam

**NTC**: National Training Center

**Nut to Butt**: Soldiers lined up, one behind the other in extremely close proximity where ones nuts are in extremely close proximity to another's butt.

**OBJ**: Military Objective, O.B.J.

**OCONUS**: Outside the Continental United States (overseas, to include the US states of Alaska and Hawaii)

**OCS**: Officers Candidate School

**OEF**: Operation ENDURING FREEDOM

**OIF**: Operation IRAQI FREEDOM

**OJT**: On-The-Job Training

**OP**: Observation Post

**OPFOR**: Opposing Force

**PAO**: Public Affairs Officer

**PCS**: Military Permanent Change of Station (move)

**PHA**: Prince Hall Affiliated (Masons)

**Pig**: M-60 7.62mm Medium Machinegun *Vietnam era*, replaced by the M-240 7.62mm family of Medium Machineguns

**PIR**: Parachute Infantry regiment

**PL**: Patrol Leader, Platoon Leader

**PLDC**: Primary Leadership Development Course (mandatory US Army educational development course for SPC/E-4 and CPL/E-4 to get promoted to SGT/E-5)

**Platoon Daddy**: Unofficial term for Platoon Sergeant. Platoon Leaders are normally new Second Lieutenants with 15 days of active duty experience and the Platoon Sergeant (Second In Command) normally has about 15 years of active duty experience. So, the Platoon Leader is sometime referred to as the Momma and the Platoon Sergeant is normally referred to as the Platoon Daddy.

**PMC**: Private Military Company (Blackwater, Triple Canopy, Olive Group, Dyncorp, etc)

**Pogue**: Any SM who never participates in Field Training Exercises or Maneuvers, all non-combat arms soldiers and to Infantrymen – anyone who is not an Infantryman (except Doc) *slang*

**Pogey Bait**: A Pogue is a SM who does not serve in the front lines (or outside the wire, see Fobbitt) and the Pogey Bait (candy or goods) is used to receive expedited service from them. Now used to mean all nonstandard candy and comfort foods.

**POW**: Prisoner Of War

**Power Point Bitch**: Military IT Specialist who are forced to make Power Point slides for high ranking officers who think the IT Specialist is their secretary. *derogatory slang*

**P.S.**: Public School. The New York City Department of Education (NYCDOE) manages the New York City Public School System which is the largest school system in the United States, with over 1.1 million students, more than 1,800 separate schools over all five boroughs of NYC (the Bronx, Brooklyn, Manhattan, Queens & Staten Island) and has an annual budget of nearly 25 billion dollars. The elementary schools are numerically labeled, *example* I attended P.S.6 in the Bronx, another student may say they attended P.S. 861 on Staten Island.

**PSG**: Platoon Sergeant/E-7

**PT** Physical Training

**PTSD**: Post Traumatic Stress Disorder

**Pull A Jody**: Have sex with another SM's wife or girlfriend.

**Pussy Pad**: Foam bed roll used as a sleeping mat in the ground. Named because macho soldiers deemed its use unnecessary. *slang*

**PX**: Post Exchange, Army department store (also BX)

**PX Ranger**: Civilian or SM who purchases badges, rank or patches from the Post Exchange and attempts to claim they earned them.

**Q**: Q-Course, Special Forces Qualification Course

**Quarters**: Military living quarters

**Queen for a Year**: See Desert Dime *slang*

**QMP**: Qualitative Management Program

**R**: Rifleman

**RCP**: Retention Control Point

**Real World**: Civilian Life

**REMF**: Rear Echelon Mother Fucker *Vietnam era military*, see FOBBITT

**RE-UP**: ReEnlist

**RHIP**: Rank Has Its Privileges

**Ring Knockers**: Officers who are West Point graduates, because of their big class ring they wear. Distinguishable from Commissioned Officers who were commissioned via "other" commissioning sources; ROTC, OCS, Direct Appointment *slang*

**RIF**: Reduction in Force

**RIP**: Rest in Peace

**RnR**: Rest and Relaxation (R&R)

**ROAD**: retired On Active Duty, meaning someone very close to their retirement date who is not motivated to work up until the last date.

**Rubber Duck**: An inert nonfunctioning rubber and metal replica rifle used for training, M-16 or M-4 version.

**The Sand Box**: Deploying anywhere near the area considered the "Middle East" or to any desert environment. *slang*

**Sergeant Major**: Whenever a SM is NOT referring to the military rank of the Command Sergeant Major as in; the Battalion Command Sergeant Major, the Brigade Command Sergeant Major, the Division Command Sergeant Major, the Corps Command Sergeant Major or whatever, he or she is referring to the spouse at home. As in, *"let me check with my Sergeant Major before I buy this new car"*.

**Self-Propelled Sandbag**: *derogatory* term for US Marine

**SF**: Special Forces, or Standard Form (as in SF88 Form)

**SFAS**: Special Forces Assessment & Selection program

**SFQC**: Special Forces Qualification Course

**SGL**: Small Group Leader

**SSGL**: Senior Small Group Leader

**Shallow Grave**: Term used for "Hasty Fighting Position" when time for a deliberate fighting position is not available. A natural hole in the ground or man-made crater can work as long as it provides 2 to 3 feet of cover when a SM is lying prone inside of it, keeps the silhouette of the body low and has basic protection from small arms fire. *Slang*

**Shammerai Warrior**: See E-4 Mafia

**Sham Shield**: US Army rank insignia of a Specialist/E-4 which resembles a shield. Specialist are not Privates and they are not NCO's

**Shit Bird**: completely worthless Soldier, *derogatory slang*

**Short Timer**: SM with less than 90 days before release from service, not to be confused with retirement from service. *Slang*

**Side Straddle Hop**: Jumping Jacks *military*

**Single Mans Paradise**: Any establishment filled with the wives and girlfriends of deployed SM's

**SL**: Squad Leader *military*, Shift Leader *contractor*

**Slicky Boy**: A male civilian who steals US military equipment from SM's while they are deployed in the field, then attempts to sell the items back to the SM's off-base or at a pawn shop

**SM**: Service Member (Army, Navy, Air Force, Marine, Coast Guard, Active, Guard, Reserve or Retired).

**Smag**: Acronym for CSM or SGM or Sergeant Major, as in *"You know you done fucked up so bad that the Smag wanna see you!?!"*

**SMOKE**: Senior NCO in Artillery units (ranks above Section Sergeants but below First Sergeant), also to conduct rigorous corrective physical training (PT) until the steam or smoke rises up off the back of the subordinate SM's body.

**SMP**: Simultaneous Membership Program

**SNAFU**: Situation Normal: All Fucked Up

**Snake Eater**: Member of US Army Special Forces (Green Beret)

**Snow Bird**: SM who arrives at a training assignment or school way too early for training to begin (sometime through no fault of their own) and must wait like a snowbird doing menial task until training starts. Sometimes weeks or months. *slang*

**SOF**: Special operations Forces

**SOP**: Standard Operating Procedures

**SOS**: Distress signal used in Morse code, three letters "S" 3 quick dots, "O" 3 long dashes, and another "S" 3 quick dots, (...---...), Creamed beef on a biscuit at the DFAC called Shit on a Shingle.

**Soup Sandwich**: An object, SM, situation, mission or condition that is useless and extremely messy, like a proverbial sandwich made out of two pieces of bread and some soup.

**Spoon**: A Cook, *derogatory*

**Spotlight Ranger**: SM who seeks attention and does more than what is required whenever higher ranking personnel are around, but will shriek his/her responsibility whenever the higher ups are not around. Similar to a Brown-Noser.

**Spec-4-ever**: SM's in this rank complain about the TIG they have or will spend in that rank, as in *"I'm gonna be a Spec Four Ever"*

**Spec 4 Mafia**: Unofficial group of Specialist (the most numerous rank in the US Army) that make the difference between success and failure in many units. E-4 Mafia

**Squared Away**: Organized to the strictest of military standards

**Steel Pot**: Military Helmet *Vietnam era*, replaced by the K-Pot, replaced by the latest military Helmet

**SWAG**: Scientific Wild Ass Guess

**TA-50**: Military Issued Field Gear

**Tanker Boots**: Military Combat Boots with straps and a buckle instead of laces

**TAMFR**: This Saint My First Rodeo

**TBI**: Traumatic Brain Injury

**TCN**: Third Country National (not an American nor a HCN) like Kenya's in Iraq, or Ugandans in Afghanistan

**TDY**: Temporary Duty

**Three Men in a Boat**: A STOP Sign written in Arabic, referring to the illusion of 3 men sitting in a canoe. *slang*

**TIG**: Time in Grade

**TIS**: Time in Service

**TL**: Team Leader

**TOP**: Unofficial term for the rank of US Army First Sergeant 1SG/E-8. As in the top ranking NCO in the unit.

**TRADOC**: US Army Training & Doctrine Command

**Troop**: Term used instead of Soldier in Airborne and Cavalry units. *slang* A company sized unit in a Cavalry Squadron or Regiment, and those other units that officially don't exist. *military*

**TSP**: Thrift Savings Plan

**Turtle Farm**: Processing center at the 2nd Infantry Division in South Korea, because it takes a complete one-year tour of duty to In-Process and arrive through the In-door and Out-Process and depart through the Out-door, which are both next to each other. *slang*

**UAE**: United Arab Emirates

**UAV**: Unmanned Aerial Vehicle

**UCMJ**: Uniformed Code of Military Justice

**USA**: United States of America

**USAR**: United States Army Reserve

**US ARMY**: Uncle Sam Aint Released Me Yet.

**USMC**: Uncle Sam's Misguided Children *slang*

**UTM**: Universal Transverse Mercator

**UXO**: Unexploded Ammunition

**VBC**: Victory Base Complex

**VBIED**: Vehicle-Borne Improvised Explosive Devise

**VolunTold**: Voluntary assignment that is actually mandatory where you weren't actually "told" to do something, but it was strongly implied.

**VW**: Voluntary Withdraw (Quit)

**Wall To Wall Counseling**: To physically beat a subordinate SM to instill the seriousness of the mistake they made, by slamming them from one wall to the next wall. It is against regulations and illegal (but almost everybody seems to know about it) *slang*

**WARSAW**: Alliance Treaty between Albania, Bulgaria, Czechoslovakia, East Germany, Hungary, Poland, Romania and the former Soviet Union, signed in Warsaw, Poland in 1955.

**Weekend Warrior**: National Guardsmen and Reservist *slang*

**WIA**: Wounded In Action

**The Wire**: The perimeter of any military compound in a combat environment, COP, FOB, Camp or Base

**Woodline Counseling**: Conducted in the field verses garrison, see Wall To Wall Counseling

**The Word**: Authorization from higher up to do something. Example: "We were supposed to get off work hours ago, *but where still waiting on the word*".

**WPS**: Worldwide Protective Services

**WPPS**: Worldwide Personal Protective Services

**WTF**: What The Fuck?

**Wubbie**: Military Camouflage Poncho Liner, greatest piece of military equipment ever made (besides weapons).

**XO**: Executive Officer

**YMRASU**: Yes, My Retarded Ass Signed Up (US Army spelled backwards)

**Zero Dark Thirty**: Military time for extremely early, like 03:30 hours (03:30am) when it is still dark outside.

**Z**: Zulu Time

**5 Jump Chump**: Graduate of US Army Airborne school, who completed the required five jumps and then never assigned to an airborne unit, billet or slot. Many officers used the school as a "ticket punch" enroute to higher positions of authority.

**BA-1100 N**: Military batteries begin with the acronym "BA" but there is no BA-1100 N, so a new SM is told to just write it down so he/she doesn't forget and to go find one. Not realizing they wrote down the word "BALLOON" they show the note to the Supply Sergeant, Admin Sergeant and everyone else until they realize it. Prank pulled on new SM's to get them on a wild goose chase, where everyone else in in n the joke: except them.

**DA Form ID-10T**: "IDIOT", see BA-1100 N.

**ST-1 devise**: ST-1 or ST-ONE is "STONE", see BA-1100 N.

**PRC E-7**: "Prick E-7", see BA-1100 N.

**11 Bang-Bang**: US Army Infantryman (MOS 11B), also 11 Bullet Catcher, 11 Body Bag, 11 Boom Boom, 11 Bang Bang

**12 Bang-Bang**: US Army Combat Engineer (MOS 12B) without medium or heavy earth moving equipment, when attached to light infantry units an moving as an integral part, like Sappers.

**40 Mike-Mike**: 40mm (millimeter) ammunition

**Fort Benning, GA**: <u>Fort Beginning</u> because of the long wait trainees sometimes endure at the AG Reception Battalion BEFORE they start Basic training *slang*, and because of the beginning initial entry training for many infantry soldiers BEFORE they ever see their first duty assignment; Basic Training & Advance Infantry Training (MOS 11B & 11C), Airborne School, and a host of "other" training courses. *slang*

**Fort Bliss, TX**: <u>Fort Blister</u> because of the intense heat *slang*

**Fort Bragg, NC**: <u>Camp Bragg</u> - nickname for Camp Anaconda (Ballad, Iraq) during Operation IRAQI FREEDOM 3 (OIF 3) because of the many Fort Bragg units deployed there at the time. *military* <u>Fayettenam</u> – nickname for Fayetteville just outside of Fort Bragg *Vietnam Era, slang*. <u>Fort Drag</u> *slang* <u>Back at Bragg, Back at Bragg</u> Like a parakeet bird, many SM will start every sentence off with "Back at Bragg" referring to the way SM's on Fort Bragg do things. *slang*

**Fort Drum, NY**: <u>Fort Drunk</u> because of the many alcohol related incidents in the past

**Defense Language Institute (DLI), CA**: <u>Defense Love Institute</u> *slang*

**Fort Eustis, VA**: <u>Fort Useless</u> *slang*, <u>Fort Even Uncle Sam Thinks It Sucks</u> *slang*

**Fort Huachuca, AZ**: <u>Fort Hoochy-Koochy</u> *slang* <u>Fort We Gotcha</u> *slang*

**Fort Knox, KY**: <u>Fort Knocks</u> *slang*

**Fort Lee, VA**: Home of the Quartermaster where cooks, supply, petroleum and water specialist are trained *military* <u>Fort Leisure</u> because of the perceived easy training standards for recruits and the close proximity of VA Beach *slang*

**Fort Leonard Wood, MO**: It has been called <u>Fort Lost in the Woods, Misery</u> due to its remote location in Missouri *slang*

**Fort Ord, CA**: One side was beautiful coastal beaches and the military side (for training) looked like "another planet" it's been called <u>Planet Ord</u> *slang*

**Fort Sam Houston, TX**: Fort Sham *slang*

# PHONETIC ALPHABET

| WWII Era Military | | Standard NATO | | Law Enforcement |
|---|---|---|---|---|
| ABLE | A | ALPHA | A | ADAM |
| BAKER | B | BRAVO | B | BOY |
| CHARLIE | C | CHARLIE | C | CHARLES |
| DOG | D | DELTA | D | DAVID |
| EASY | E | ECHO | E | EDWARD |
| FOX | F | FOXTROT | F | FRANK |
| GEORGE | G | GOLF | G | GEORGE |
| HOW | H | HOTEL | H | HENRY |
| ITEM | I | INDIA | I | IDA |
| JIG | J | JULIETT | J | JOHN |
| KING | K | KILO | K | KING |
| LOVE | L | LIMA | L | LINCOLN |
| MIKE | M | MIKE | M | MARY |
| NAN | N | NOVEMBER | N | NORA |
| OBOE | O | OSCAR | O | OCEAN |
| PETER | P | PAPA | P | PAUL |
| QUEEN | Q | QUEBEC | Q | QUEEN |
| ROGER | R | ROMEO | R | ROBERT |
| SAIL/SUGAR | S | SIERRA | S | SAM |
| TARE | T | TANGO | T | TOM |
| UNCLE | U | UNIFORM | U | UNION |
| VICTOR | V | VICTOR | V | VICTOR |
| WILLIAM | W | WHISKEY | W | WILLIAM |
| X-RAY | X | X-RAY | X | X-RAY |
| YOKE | Y | YANKEE | Y | YOUNG |
| ZEBRA | Z | ZULU | Z | ZEBRA |

Several military documents omit the two letters (O) & (I), whereas OSCAR (O) and INDIA (I) can be confused with the numbers ZERO (0) and ONE (1).

# MILITARY TIME

| Civilian Time | Military Time | | Civilian Time | Military Time |
|---|---|---|---|---|
| 1am | 01:00 | | 1pm | 13:00 |
| 2am | 02:00 | | 2pm | 14:00 |
| 3am | 03:00 | | 3pm | 15:00 |
| 4am | 04:00 | | 4pm | 16:00 |
| 5am | 05:00 | | 5pm | 17:00 |
| 6am | 06:00 | | 6pm | 18:00 |
| 7am | 07:00 | | 7pm | 19:00 |
| 8am | 08:00 | | 8pm | 20:00 |
| 9am | 09:00 | | 9pm | 21:00 |
| 10am | 10:00 | | 10pm | 22:00 |
| 11am | 11:00 | | 11pm | 23:00 |
| 12pm 12 noon | 12:00 | | 12am Midnight | 24:00 |

# MILITARY CLASSES OF SUPPLY

**Class I**: RATIONS; Subsistence (food and drinking water), health and comfort items.

**Class II**: CLOTHING & EQUIPMENT; individual equipment, tools, maps and administrative supplies.

**Class III**: PETROLEUM, OIL & LUBRICANTS (POL); Petroleum, fuels, lubricants, oils, coolants, antifreeze and coal.

**Class IV**: CONSTRUCTION MATERIAL; all fortification and barrier materials.

**Class V**: AMMUNITION; bombs, explosives, mines, pyrotechnics, missiles and rockets

**Class VI**: PERSONAL ITEMS; (such as health and hygiene products, soaps and toothpaste, snack food, beverages, cigarettes, alcohol and other nonmilitary sales items).

**Class VII**: MAJOR END ITEMS; tanks, mobile machine shops, and vehicles.

**Class VIII**: MEDICAL MATERIAL; repair parts peculiar to medical equipment.

**Class VIIIa** – Medical consumable supplies not including blood & blood products

**Class VIIIb** – Blood & blood components (whole blood, platelets, plasma, packed red cells, etc.)

**Class IX**: REPAIR PARTS; kits, assemblies, and subassemblies required for maintenance support of all equipment.

**Class X**: MATERIAL TO SUPPORT NONMILITARY PROGRAMS

# COLOR CODES

## CIVILIAN COLOR CODE CONDITION
- **White** – Unprepared Potential Victim
- **Yellow** – Situational Alertness (Head on a Swivel)
- **Orange** – Potential Threat Recognized
- **Red** – Armed Encounter Ready to Fight
- **Black** – Lethal Engagement (In the Fight)

## MILITARY EQUIPMENT STATUS CLASSIFICATION
- **Green** – Mission Capable
- **Amber** (Yellow) – Damaged Equipment
- **Red** – Serious Damage (INOP)
- **Black** – Missing equipment or Totally Destroyed

## MILITARY ROAD CONDITIONS
- **Green** – Safe to Travel, Normal driving conditions
- **Amber** (Yellow) – Caution (wet roads, icy roads, etc)
- **Red** – Dangerous, NO Unnecessary Travel Authorized
- **Black** – DO NOT TRAVEL, Unless Authorized Emergency Service Vehicles

## TATICAL LOCATION COLOR CODE
- **White – Front face**
- **Black – Back side**
- **Red – Right side**
- **Green – Left side**

## US DEPARTMENT OF HOMELAND SECURITY ADVISORY SYSTEM
- **Green – Low Risk of Terrorist Attacks**
- **Blue – Guarded Risk of Terrorist Attacks**
- **Yellow – Significant Risk of Terrorist Attacks**
- **Orange – High Risk of Terrorist Attacks**
- **Red – Severe Risk of Terrorist Attacks**

# U.S. ARMY RANKS (Pay Grades)

| | | |
|---|---|---|
| SMA | Sergeant Major of the US Army | (E-9) |
| | | |
| CSM | Command Sergeant Major | (E-9) |
| SGM | Sergeant Major | (E-9) |
| 1SG | First Sergeant | (E-8) |
| MSG | Master Sergeant | (E-8) |
| SFC | Sergeant First Class | (E-7) |
| PSG | *Platoon Sergeant* | (E-7) |
| | | |
| SSG | Staff Sergeant | (E-6) |
| SGT | Sergeant | (E-5) |
| CPL | Corporal | (E-4) |
| | | |
| SP7 | *Specialist Seventh Class* | (E-7) |
| SP6 | *Specialist Sixth Class* | (E-6) |
| SP5 | *Specialist Fifth Class* | (E-5) |
| SP4 | *Specialist Fourth Class* | (E-4) |
| SPC | Specialist | (E-4) |
| | | |
| PFC | Private First Class | (E-3) |
| PV2 | Private | (E-2) |
| PVT | Private (Recruit) | (E-1) |

*Obsolete

# MOS   TITLE

| | |
|---|---|
| **02B** | US Army Cornet or Trumpet Player |
| **09R** | Simultaneous Membership Program College ROTC & USAR/NG |
| | |
| **11B** | Infantryman |
| **11C** | Indirect (Mortar) Fire Infantryman |
| **11H** | Heavy Anti-Armor Infantryman |
| **11M** | Fighting Vehicle Infantryman |
| | |
| **18A** | Special Forces Officer |
| **180A** | Special Forces Warrant Officer |
| **18B** | Special Forces Weapons Sergeant |
| **18C** | Special Forces Engineer Sergeant |
| **18D** | Special Forces Medical Sergeant |
| **18E** | Special Forces Commo Sergeant |
| **18F** | Special Forces Assistant Operations and Intelligent Sergeant |
| **18Z** | Special Forces Senior Sergeant |
| **18X** | Special Forces Enlistment Option (Basic SF Recruit) |

**35K**   Avionic Mechanic / 35K is now the numerical designation for Unmanned Aerial Vehicle (UAV) Operator

# RECOMMENDED READING LIST

The following is considered Brother Shadow's recommended reading list. It is an extensive list of just "some" of the books that I own and have read over the almost past 50 years that have help shape my mindset, my beliefs and my value system.

Some were awesome, and I highly recommend you read them. For others, my thinking and mental thought process has matured, and I may no longer subscribe to that mentality, however it is important information for any reader to begin to understand "who I used to be" and how I became the man I am today.

There are many more books that I have read that are NOT on this list, so please do not think this is an all-inclusive list – it is long and extensive, but not inclusive. Additionally, I encourage everyone to support local and independent writers by buying a physical copy of a book. Go buy two copies and give one to a friend.

I'd like to thank the New York City Public Library System for being my avenue of escape during my younger years, especially the branch on Honeywell Avenue & 180th Street in the South Bronx where I grew up. I highly recommend to anyone who wishes to avoid the mistakes and pitfalls that I've made in life, read some of the books on this list, in addition to seeking the advice and counsel of a good mentor or another successful person in the field you wish to ascend in.

> You wanna be rich, socialize with rich people.
> You wanna be smart, socialize with smart people.
> You wanna be famous, socialize with famous people.
> You wanna be a criminal, socialize with criminals.

Or an even better question to ask yourself is this; if someone gave you $100 dollars for the name, title & author of each of the last 10 books you read – *"How much money would you have?"*

# Historical Military & Fiction

***Don Ericson & John L. Rotundo, *Charlie Rangers* (1989)

***Benjamin F. Schemmer, *The Raid: The Son Tay Prison Rescue Mission* (1976)

Steven Pressfield, *Gates of Fire* (1998)

Terry Wallace, *Bloods: An Oral History of the Vietnam War by Black Veterans* (1985)

Rowe, James N., *Five Years to Freedom* (1971)

Roy P. Benavidez & John R. Craig, *Medal of Honor: A Vietnam Warrior's Story* (1995)

Colin Powell & Joseph E. Persico, *My American Journey: Colin Powell* (1995)

Howard Means, *Colin Powell: A Biography* (1992)

Harold G. Moore & Joseph L. Galloway, *We Were Soldiers Once... and Young* (1992)

Tom Clancy & John Gresham, *Special Forces* (2001)

Tom Clancy, *Airborne: A Guided Tour of an Airborne Task Force* (1997)

Tom Clancy, *The Hunt for Red October* (1984)

Tom Clancy, *Patriot Games* (1987)

Tom Clancy, *Clear and Present Danger* (1988)

Tom Clancy, *The Sum of All Fears* (1990)

Steve Fainaru, *Big Boy Rules* (2008)

Leonard B. Scott, *Charlie Mike* (1985)

Leonard B. Scott, *The Expendables* (1985)

Leonard B. Scott, *The Last Run* (1987)

Leonard B. Scott, *The Hill* (1989)

H. John Poole, *Dragon Days* (2007)

William W. Johnstone, *The Last Of The Dog Team* (1981)

Robert W. Black, *Rangers In Korea* (1989)

Shelby Stanton, *Green Berets At War* (1985)

Michael Lee Lanning, *Blood Warriors: American Military Elites* (2002)

Donald E. Zlotnik, *Fields of Honor #2: The Distinguished Service Cross* (1991)

Patrick Andrews, *The Unit: Lock And Load* (2009)

Andy McNab, *Bravo Two Zero: The Story of an SAS Patrol behind Enemy Lines in Iraq* (1993)

Mark Bowden, *Black Hawk Down: A Story of Modern War* (1999)

Sun Tzu, *The Art of War* (1972)

Chaplain J.D. Hawkins, *Spiritual Survival Guide* (2004)

✱✱✱

## Money Credit & Finances

***Angel Love, *Raise Your Credit Score in 10 Easy Steps!* (2013)

***Angel Love, *What Not to Do When You Win the Lottery!* (2016)

Alan Axelrod, *Everything I Know About Business I Learned From Monopoly* (2002)

Larry Winget, *You're Broke Because You Want To Be* (2009)

Stuart Wilde, *The Trick to Money Is Having Some!* (1989)

Robert Greene, *48 Laws of Power* (1998)

David J. Schwartz, Ph.D., *The Magic of Thinking Big* (1987)

✱✱✱

## Physical Fitness & Food

Elijah Muhammad, *How To Eat To Live* (1972)

David Zinczenko, *Eat This, Not That!* (2008)

David Zinczenko & Matt Goulding, *Eat This, Not That! (For Kids)* (2008)

David Zinczenko & Matt Goulding, *Eat This, Not That! (Supermarket Survival Guide)* (2008)

Zeek, *The Art of Shen Ku: The Ultimate Travelers Guide Of This Planet* (1999)

Kenton Robinson, *Banish Your Belly* (1997)

***

## Safety Security & Protection

***Mark "Six" James, *Inside The Bubble: Lessons Learned from a Life in Business and Protective Services* (2016)

Robert L. Oatman, *Executive Protection New Solutions for a New Era* (2006)

Benny Mares, *Executive Protection: A Professional's Guide to Bodyguarding* (1994)

Heidi Zeigler, *Bodyguard* (2003)

Connie Fletcher, *What Cops Know: Today's Police Tell The Inside Story Of Their Work On America's Streets* (1990)

***

## Hidden In Plain Sight

***Dr. Umar Johnson, *Psycho-Academic Holocaust* (2013)

William F. Pepper, *Orders To Kill: The Truth Behind The Murder Of Dr. MLK, Jr.* (1995)

Ivan Van Sertima, *They Came Before Columbus (African Presence in Ancient America)* (1976)

Sam Greenlee, *The Spook Who Sat By The Door* (1969)

Nathan McCall, *Makes Me Wanna Holla: A Young Black Man in America* (1994)

Dr. Frances Cress Welsing, *The Isis (Yssis) Papers: The Keys To The Colors* (1992)

George L. Jackson, *Blood in my Eye* (1972)

Anthony T. Browder, *Nile Valley Contributions to Civilization: Exploding the Myths* (1992)

Clayborne Carson & Spike Lee, *Malcolm X: The FBI File* (1991)

414

Cheikh Anta Diop, *The African Origin of Civilization: Myth or Reality* (1974)

Jessie Carney Smith, *Black First: Ground Breaking Events in African American History* (2003)

William H. Cosby Jr. & Alvin F. Poussaint, MD, *Come On People: From Victims to Victors* (2007)

Tony Dungy & Nathan Whitaker, *Quiet Strength: A Memoir* (2007)

Michael Eric Dyson, *Race Rules: Navigating The Color Line* (1996)

Karl Evanzz, *The Messenger: The Rise and Fall of Elijah Muhammad* (1999)

Alex Haley & Malcolm X & Betty Shabazz, *The Autobiography of Malcolm X* (1964)

C. Eric Lincoln, *The Black Muslims in America* (1961)

Lerone Bennett Jr., *Before the Mayflower: A History of Black America 1619-1962* (1962)

Robert Penn Warren, *Who Speaks For The Negro?* (1965)

Claude Brown, *Manchild In The Promised Land: the Black Experience*, (1965)

Jonathan Earle, *The Routledge Atlas of African American History* (2000)

Abraham Chapman, *Black Voices: An Anthology of Afro-American Literature* (1968)

Mattias Gardell, *In the Name of Elijah Muhammad* (1996)

Eldridge Cleaver, *Soul on Ice* (1968)

Hill Harper, *Letters to a Young Brother* (2000)

Betty Shabazz & Bruce Perry, *Malcolm X: The Last Speeches* (1989)

Anita Doreen Diggs, *The African American Resource Guide* (1994)

\*\*\*

## For Your Seventh Chakra

\*\*\*Don Serate, *The Lessons My White Father Taught Me* (2017)

\*\*\*Dr. C. P. White Ph.D., *Loving Me First: The journey to discover your inner self...* (2014)

\*\*\*Myke Cole, *Gemini Cell: For The Dead, War Never Ends* (2015)

\*\*\*Tamyra Butler, *Whispered Thoughts* (2017)

\*\*\*Nikole Morgan, *Picking Up His Pieces* (2012)

\*\*\*Ericka McKnight, *Silence The Noise* (2017)

\*\*\*Angela Smith, *Women On A Mission Leaving Our Legacy: A Powerful Anthology* (2017)

\*\*\*Coco, *Losing Yourself* (2008)

\*\*\*Kashinda Marche, *The Triumph In Me* (2016)

Dr. Kevin Leman, *The First Born Advantage: Making Your Birth Order Work For You* (2008)

Sister Souljah, *The Coldest Winter Ever* (1999)

Donald Goines, *Dopefiend* (1971)

Donald Goines, *Whoreson* (1972)

Eric Jerome Dickey, *Cheaters* (1999)

Eric Jerome Dickey, *Milk in My Coffee* (1998)

Adele Nozedar, *The Element Encyclopedia of Secret Signs and Symbols: The Ultimate A-Z Guide from Alchemy to the Zodiac* (2007)

Phyllis Vega, *What Your Birthday Reveals About You* (1999)

Judith Turner, *The Hidden World of Birthdays* (1999)

Rhonda Byrne, *The Secret* (2006)

Paul Harrington, *The Secret: to Teen Power* (2009)

T.D. Jakes, *So You Call Yourself A Man: Sixty Devotional Readings* (1997)

Drunvalo Melchizedek, *Serpent of Light (Beyond 2012)* (2007)

Douglas De Long, *Ancient Teachings for Beginners: Auras, Chakras, Astral Projection* (2000)

Hilary Wilson, *Understanding Hieroglyphs: A Complete Introductory Guide* (1993)

Susie Hodge, *Egyptian Art* (2008)

Lorna Oakes & Lucia Gahlin, *Ancient Egypt: An illustrated reference* (2002)

Nur Ankh Amen, *The Ankh: African Origin of Electromagnetism* (1997)

Robert Temple, *The Sirius Mystery: New Scientific Evidence of Alien Contact* (1998)

Barb Karg & John K. Young, Ph.D., *101 Secrets of the Freemasons: The Truth* (2009)

Mustafa El-Amin, *Freemasonry, Ancient Egypt and the Islamic Destiny* (1988)

Giles Morgan, *Freemasonry: It's History and Myths Revealed* (2008)

Christopher Knight & Robert Lomas, *The Book of Hiram: Freemasonry* (2003)

James Wasserman, *The Secrets of Masonic Washington: A Guidebook* (2008)

Michael Bradley, *Secrets of the Freemasons* (2006)

Nana Banchie Darkwah, Ph.D., *The Africans Who Wrote The Bible:* (2002)

Franjo Terhart & Janina Schulze, *World Religions: Origins Beliefs Worldview* (2008)

Tim Baker, *Why So Many Gods?* (2002)

Sid Shiff, *Ancient Egyptian Book of the Dead* (1972)

Nusach Ashkenaz, *The Rabbinical Council of America The Complete Artscroll Siddur* (1987)

James Stuart, *Holy Bible (KJV): Containing the Old and New Testaments* (1983)

Hadrat Mirza Tahir Ahmad, *The Holy Qur'an (Arabic Text with English Translation)* (2002)

Joseph Smith, *The Book of Mormon: Another Testament of Jesus Christ* (1830)

Gary Greenberg, *101 Myths of the Bible* (2000)

Jerry MacGregor & Marie Prys, *1001 Surprising Things About the Bible* (2002)

Josephus, *Josephus Thrones of Blood: A History of the Times of Jesus 37 B.C. to A.D. 70* (1988)

Rutherford Hayes Platt, *The Lost Books of the Bible and The Forgotten Books of Eden* (1926)

Dr. Wayne A. Mack, *Preparing For Marriage (God's Way)* (1986)

Jan Knappert, *African Mythology: An Encyclopedia of Myth and Legend* (1990)

Heathcote Williams, *Sacred Elephant* (1989)

***I possess an autographed copy of all the books marked with an (\*\*\*) asterisk, or they were personally autographed by the author to me, or someone I know who is mentioned in the actual book.

✳✳✳

The International Standard Book Number (ISBN) is a unique numeric commercial book identifier. An ISBN is assigned to each edition and variation (except reprintings) of a book. *For example, an e-book, a paperback and a hardcover edition of the same book would each have a different ISBN.*

The ISBN is 13 digits long if it was assigned on or after 1 JAN 2007, and 10 digits long if assigned before 2007. The method of assigning an ISBN is nation-based and varies from country to country, often depending on how large the publishing industry is within a country.

The initial ISBN configuration of recognition was generated in 1967 based upon the 9-digit Standard Book Numbering (SBN) created in 1966. The 10-digit ISBN format was developed by the International Organization for Standardization (ISO) and was published in 1970 as international standard ISO 2108 (the SBN code can be converted to a ten-digit ISBN by prefixing it with a zero).

*Sometimes a book may appear without a printed ISBN if it is printed privately or the author does not follow the usual ISBN procedure; however, this can be rectified later.*